Praise for *The Aa*

"I am struck by its sophistication ɑ _____ its beauty."

—RAM DASS, author of *Be Here Now* and *Still Here: Embracing Aging, Changing, and Dying*

"I appreciate true wisdom whatever the source. These conversations between Aaron and Q'uo offer a unique and valuable perspective—rich in wisdom and compassion—to the central issues facing everyone who wants to realize his or her potential and embody the best of what it means to be fully human."

—JAMES BARAZ, coauthor of *Awakening Joy: 10 Steps That Will Put You on the Road to Real Happiness*

"Filled with love, wisdom, practical advice, and Divine perspective ... helps demystify what the process of channeling is about, while at the same time allowing the reader to appreciate the efforts needed to channel with integrity."

—JOSIE RAVENWING, author of *The Book of Miracles: The Healing Work of Joao de Deus*

"Barbara Brodsky and Carla Rueckert are two of the most gifted channels of our time. In this magnificent book, they combine their considerable talents to create a vast treasure trove of wisdom. Whatever your questions may be, the answers are likely to be found within these pages."

—ROBERT SCHWARTZ, author of *Your Soul's Plan: Discovering the Real Meaning of the Life You Planned Before You Were Born*

"These dialogues are like being in a cozy living room with grandparents who only have your deepest interests at heart. Deeply loving, wise, respectful, and funny, what they share is not only pertinent and intimate but evolutionary."

—AJAHN THANASANTI BHIKKUNI, Buddhist nun, teacher, and founder of Awakeningtruth.org

"I absolutely love these teachings. They are a gift from Spirit filled with wisdom, love, and practical guidance for the seeker on his or her spiritual path. Every time I picked this book up, it spoke to my heart. It was a challenge to put it down."

—JOHN ORR, senior dharma teacher, founding and guiding teacher of New Hope Sangha, North Carolina

"*The Aaron/Q'uo Dialogues* is a veritable compendium of spiritual wisdom, presented in clearly understandable human explanations, which lead the reader to a greater knowing of the true human yet divine Being."

—JUDITH COATES, editor of *Jeshua: The Personal Christ*

"This book really is a gift—from voyagers of light to voyagers of light, so we may thereby heal and awaken ourselves further. I'm pleased to recommend it to all who truly love love and truly love truth. As you know, the time is now."

—SCOTT MANDELKER, PhD, author of *From Elsewhere: Being E.T. in America* and *Universal Vision: Soul Evolution and the Cosmic Plan*

"The real deal. . . . Put this book by your bed to program yourself while you sleep to be at one with the universe."

—SUZANNE TAYLOR, founder of MightyCompanions.org

THE AARON/Q'UO
DIALOGUES

Other Books by
BARBARA BRODSKY and CARLA L. RUECKERT

BARBARA BRODSKY
Presence, Kindness, and Freedom
Human
No Chain At All
Cosmic Healing: A Spiritual Journey with Aaron and John of God

CARLA L. RUECKERT
The Law of One (Books I–V—also known as *The Ra Material*)
A Wanderer's Handbook: An Owners Manual for ETs
and Other Spiritual Outsiders
A Book of Days: Channelings from the Holy Spirit
Living the Law of One 101: The Choice
A Channeling Handbook
Secrets of the UFO
The Crucifixion of Esmerelda Sweetwater

THE AARON/Q'UO DIALOGUES

An Extraordinary Conversation
between Two Spiritual Guides

BARBARA BRODSKY & CARLA L. RUECKERT

North Atlantic Books
Berkeley, California

Published by
North Atlantic Books   Cover photo by iStockphoto.com/dinn, Energy Solutions
P.O. Box 12327   Cover and book design by Suzanne Albertson
Berkeley, California 94712

Printed in the United States of America

The Aaron/Q'uo Dialogues: An Extraordinary Conversation between Two Spiritual Guides is sponsored by the Society for the Study of Native Arts and Sciences, a nonprofit educational corporation whose goals are to develop an educational and cross-cultural perspective linking various scientific, social, and artistic fields; to nurture a holistic view of arts, sciences, humanities, and healing; and to publish and distribute literature on the relationship of mind, body, and nature.

North Atlantic Books' publications are available through most bookstores. For further information, visit our website at www.northatlanticbooks.com or call 800-733-3000.

Library of Congress Cataloging-in-Publication Data

Aaron (Spirit)
    The Aaron/Q'uo dialogues : an extraordinary conversation between two spiritual guides / [channeled] by Barbara Brodsky and Carla L. Rueckert.
        p. cm.
    ISBN 978-1-55643-995-7
    I. Spirit writings. I. Q'uo (Spirit) II. Brodsky, Barbara. III. Rueckert, Carla. IV. Title.
    BF1301.A12 2011
    133.9'3—dc23   2011030520

        I 2 3 4 5 6 7 8 9 SHERIDAN I6 I5 I4 I3 I2 II

This book is dedicated to

Judy Romine
an angel in an earth-suit

and to
you, the reader,
the seeker,
the beloved

ACKNOWLEDGMENTS

Thanks to all of those men and women who participated in the nine gatherings at L/L Research and Deep Spring Center. They came with their good questions and wonderful energy to seek the truth together with Aaron and Q'uo and created this work. Every page of this book holds the impression of their concerns, hopes, and dreams.

Thanks to Judy M. Romine, whose dedication and loving care brought this material through many generations of transcription and collating of texts, for there were two taped records of these sessions, one from Barbara Brodsky's tape recorder and one from Carla Rueckert's. In addition, there was Jim McCarty's typing of what the Q'uo group said, which Barbara, who is deaf, used during the sessions, reading over Jim's shoulder. From these three sources Judy eventually created the complete version of these sessions. It was truly a labor of love!

Thanks to Steve Moffitt, whose eagle eye simplified the language of our session summaries in the Contents and the definitions in the Glossary of Terms, as well as providing for us an elegant Index. Truly, Steve, you have provided a rope and bucket for readers to use in drawing from the well.

Thanks to Ian Jaffray, whose aid in placing these sessions on the internet was invaluable.

Thanks to Dan Muir and Lalita Doke for their vital editing help with the Aaron material and introductions.

Thanks to Aaron, Q'uo, and all our brothers and sisters of Light. Without their loving presence and patient willingness to share their wisdom, none of this work could have happened.

A NOTE TO THE READER

In most books, the chapters in the Contents have titles. We reflected on adding these, but they are not authentic to the way the experience happened. We invite the reader to walk into the Unknowing with us and to allow the book to unfold just as it did for us. We raised our questions, stated our interests to Spirit, and invited whatever information might come. The chapter subtitles give a sense of the material in each chapter, as each unfolded.

CONTENTS

WEEKEND 1: Meeting for the First Time   25

   Our perceived imperfections, when they give rise to fear, inhibit
our knowing of the Creator and ourselves. By being instead of
doing, those fears are seen as illusory. We then find a deeper level
of self-acceptance and become more skillful in relating to others
and ourselves.

   In third-density experience, we have two minds, that of wisdom
and that of the womb; and four bodies, those of the physical,
the emotional, the mental, and the spiritual. These assist us in
dropping barriers to fears that limit our expression of the Divine.
Companions on the path are always near. The distortions of
anger, fear, and separation are healed with gentleness, compassion,
and patience.

WEEKEND 2   109

Contents

WEEKEND 5   221

Contents

WEEKEND 6   289

WEEKEND 7   379

Contents

WEEKEND 8   451

WEEKEND 9   515

INTRODUCTION

What Is Channeling?

Carla: I first began reading "New Age" channeled material when I was in college. As a former librarian, I know that these types of works are typically classified as "spirit communication" and placed in the same general category as myths and legends. It certainly isn't literature in the same sense as the literature coming directly from a living author. Thus unless people who explore the resources of a library are interested in religion or philosophy, mythology, or history, they might not ever come across channeled works.

Channeled material generally has been scorned by mainstream literary and cultural opinion-makers, when it has been addressed at all. Indeed, many Christian sects consider channeling evil. My own brother lectured me endlessly on this point for twenty-three years, until one day he realized that the prophets in the Bible could be considered to be channels and his heart softened.

Just as in Christianity, channeled material has a long tradition within most world religions. There are also many wonderful books written by someone acting as an instrument for the Creator, or some aspect of the Creator, that fit within no orthodox slot. Unfortunately, this discrimination against channeling as a useful source of information and inspiration has tended to keep books of channeling from reaching the mainstream reader.

When I moved from reading channeled works to actually channeling in 1974, I looked long and hard for a scientific way to describe what I was experiencing. Finding little help in external sources, I had to rely primarily on my own instincts. I think of channeling primarily in terms of how material comes into my mind so that I may pass on what I am receiving. I have two basic ways of receiving information that does not originate with me: consciously and subconsciously. But

I

sometimes, I receive subconscious information consciously when I remember a dream or a waking vision, so this distinction can blur in practice. Channeling, regardless of the route through the self, brings back to the here and now information or an experience that cannot be said to come from the world we inhabit as conscious, waking beings. Therefore, I define channeling as material from beyond the self received subconsciously and relayed consciously.

This definition is compatible with several key points about the nature of channeling. Firstly, channeling tends to be, when received lucidly, of a metaphysical or spiritual nature. Secondly, this definition does not attempt to identify the sources that come through instruments such as Barbara Brodsky or me. And lastly, the definition allows a model of relationship between this source and instrument, which includes the basic concepts of integrity and respect. I see channeled sources as being individuals unique unto themselves and not dependent in any way upon the nature of the instrument. Likewise, as instruments, we can define ourselves, independent of the channeling work that we do. I have never felt that any of my channeling sources are extensions of myself.

What is the nature of these sources? We have many hints from history. The mythology of Babylonia, Egypt, Greece, and Rome abounds with larger-than-life characters that involve humans in a soap opera, moving seamlessly between their world and ours. But there are other kinds of channeling in which the sources of the channeling do not melodramatically interact with each other. Some sources seem to offer us a picture of only the most refined and positive human qualities. Both Aaron and Q'uo are examples of this kind of channeling source.

Aaron's story is inextricably intertwined with Earth's. Five hundred and sixty years ago, according to Aaron's information about himself, he experienced his last earthly incarnation and achieved realization. After that lifetime, Aaron remained in the inner planes of Earth, acting as, among other activities, a teacher to the ongoing incarnations of the young man who saved his life and thereby offered him the opportunity for realization. Barbara Brodsky is the present incarnational name of the being that was that young man. Aaron's guidance also extends to all who request it.

Q'uo has a fairly complex and otherworldly story compared to Aaron. Q'uo is composed of three planetary populations. In addition to working together as a single entity, as the principle of Q'uo, each also works individually in service to others. The common goal of these three planetary entities is to serve in creating material that may be helpful to seekers on Planet Earth at this time of global shift. They all say that they are part of The Confederation of Angels and Planets in the Service of the One Infinite Creator.

While it is easy to see Aaron as an individual, it might seem odd to consider that Q'uo has an individual personality. Not only is the principle of Q'uo made up of three different components, but also each component is made up of many, many brothers and sisters. The capacity that they have for working in harmony and unison to offer a single, clear communication is a marvel difficult to fathom. Yet if one reads in the L/L Research archives, one can see this multidimensional personality in full flower. It is a wonderful thing to see Q'uo interact with Aaron, who has a robust and charming personality of his own.

Barbara: We all constantly channel, without awareness we are doing so. We "read" people's emotions, we feel the mood of an environment, and we even may pick up information in our dreams. None of this is conscious. When we have a conscious intention to understand something and put forth that intention, we will invite the answers. Those answers may come from a mind that is, at some level, separate from our own.

As we consider channeling an entity, it is important that we recognize that just because a being is a spirit-plane entity does not mean it is necessarily loving or intentioned to serve all beings with love. The source for such information will vary depending on our own intentions. If we are self-centered and angry, with a tightly clenched heart, we may invite a negatively polarized source. If we are deeply committed to not doing harm but seek to respond with love and for the highest good of beings, we will invite a positively polarized source. I use these terms "positively polarized" and "negatively polarized" in a precise way. Just as a battery always has two poles, so we all have both positive and negative polarity. Negative polarity intends to serve only the self without regard to how others might be harmed. Positive polarity intends to serve all beings without harming anyone or anything. The polarity of the source we invite when channeling will tend to mirror our polarity at the time of contact. We must always take personal responsibility for what we bring through.

At various times in my career as a channel, I became aware that the energy of the source felt different and the message that came through had a subtly different quality; this happened when I was angry and wanted support for my anger rather than clarity and healing. Thus, I started to see that I could call forth different beings, depending on my intention. When I was clear in my intention to learn how to deal with my pain without harm to others, the information was always resonant to that intention.

Gradually I learned always to offer an inner challenge, first to myself, to state my highest intentions, and then to ask the entity if its values were fully consistent with my own highest values. If there was any hesitation, I learned to say no, and ask again for the highest possible source. If I repeatedly invited more negatively polarized answers, it would be important to look in myself to see if my intentions to service to all, and to nonharm, were clear. Through prayer and meditation, I learned I could move my energy into a place that was most receptive to clear hearing of a positively polarized spirit.

Densities and Spiritual Evolution

Aaron and Q'uo both use the same terms and concepts[1] when referring to spiritual evolution, and it seems important to discuss this subject here. Humans are third-density beings. The word "density" refers to

---

[1] See the Glossary of Terms at the back of this book.

Introduction

the degree of light and the strength of vibration. As humans we have a lower vibration and, with our heavier emotional and physical bodies, we are denser than beings like Aaron who no longer carry a physical or emotional body. The entities we channel may be of any density. Third-density beings between human lifetimes may come through and may offer clear and loving wisdom. Higher-density beings often offer a broader perspective. I have come to think of it like the university system where we may have the teaching assistant, associate professor, and full professor. As a young student, talking with the teaching assistant may best serve my needs. The full professor may have insights that are too advanced for me to grasp.

Humans are capable of comprehending eight densities in total, encompassing the evolution of substantially all beings within the material and spirit worlds. Aaron describes the densities further, with his invaluable perspective:

> Those of you who are evolving fully through the earth plane have taken rebirth over and over, in one form or another. Your first lives on the earth plane were first density, in the form of mineral, which includes water. The lesson at that level of density is awareness. The spark moved into awareness at the moment of experiencing the illusion of separation. With this first move into personal expression, there is the beginning of the experience of a pull to the light, not yet with self-awareness, but always reaching for the light.
>
> When the lessons of first density are sufficiently mastered, the being moves into second density. The forms that density takes on earth are plant and then animal. Yes, all of you who are evolving fully through the earth plane have been mineral, plant, and animal in some of your many past lives. The main lesson of second density is growth into self-awareness. The rock begins to have awareness and then is ready to move into the simplest forms of plant life. Increasingly aware through many incarnations, the being first experiences group self-awareness and finally individual self-awareness. The ant or bee is aware on a group level. The pet

dog or cat moves into personal self-awareness. Those animals that are your pets are often in the final stages of second density.

The third density is human. Your primary lessons on this plane are faith and love. These are not the only lessons, but the primary ones.

When you move beyond the need to incarnate in human form, you are still learning. There is simply no longer any need for materialization as an aid to that learning. The karma that pulls you into the heavier vibration of materiality has been resolved. The primary fourth-density lesson is compassion, and the fifth is wisdom. Again, this does not mean you learn no wisdom and compassion as a human, but in higher densities you further develop those qualities.

There is an overlap between the lessons of wisdom and compassion. One cannot be learned entirely without the other. To aid this learning, fourth-density beings dwell in groups where sharing is at a more intimate level, and then move from there into fifth density to find deeper wisdom.

When you enter fourth density, you find yourself capable of full telepathic sharing and are beyond the dictates of the emotional body that would lead you to feel shame or pride. Thus, all sharing is honest, and you no longer need to experience something yourself to understand and learn fully. As you share in this way with your peers, your beloved companions, you enter loosely into a group energy, where beings are free to come and go as feels appropriate. You always have free will. When the time is right, a being will begin to move away from that group to better understand and find deep wisdom in its own being. When it is useful for its own learning or to teach others, the being will return to a group, moving back and forth.

The sixth density ... I find it hard to put a label on this. A friend, Ra,[2] describes it as learning of love and light. I understand what Ra means, but you may benefit by further explanation. Unfor-

---

[2] The group entity or "social memory complex" Ra, in *The Ra Material*, channeled by Don Elkins, Jim McCarty, and Carla Rueckert.

tunately, I lack the words to define it more accurately. Essentially, the end of sixth density is a movement to total knowledge and acceptance that you have never been separate, a movement back into such total unity with the One that, by the end of sixth density, you are ready to allow the dissolution of all memory and individual identity. This does not mean that you cannot put on a cloak of consciousness, cannot regrasp those memories if needed. That is what I do. In order to teach, I need personality and memory, so I resume these past attributes. The difference is that there is no attachment to them, nor any delusion that this "Aaron" is who I am.

The seventh density has been described as a gateway. It is beyond my experience. I assume the experience of the seventh-density gateway to be similar to the gateway of enlightenment experience in third density, of realization of the true self and release of self-identity with the body and ego, but in a far more profound way. To move into seventh density is to release individuation fully, not just to release self-identification and attachment to individuality, but to release individuated experience totally. Many beings hold themselves at high sixth density, not crossing that gateway, in order to continue to have access to individuated thought and expression so as to allow teaching. Please remember that seventh-density beings do not cease to exist. They only cease to maintain individuation. The energy continues and serves all beings as it enhances love and light. It is the Ground out of which all expresses. Seventh density is a gateway to the eighth density, and that I cannot describe to you at all. It is the drop of water fully returned to the sea. Let us simply label it as mystery. It is God.[3]

---

[3] Excerpted from "The Universe According to Aaron," by Aaron, channeled through Barbara Brodsky, in *Presence, Kindness, and Freedom* (Ann Arbor, MI: Deep Spring Press, 2003).

Carla's Story

Carla: I had met Don Elkins, a college professor and a researcher into the paranormal and UFOs, when I was an undergraduate English Literature major in college. In 1962, I began attending his experimental meditation group. Don's experiment had to do with creating UFO contactee messages. It was quite successful. However, I was not particularly interested in becoming a channel at that time. I obtained a master's degree in Library Science, and worked for six years as a librarian. In 1970, Don hired me as a research assistant and my path began to stray from the orthodox. We investigated everything from ghosts to UFO close encounters of the third kind. By 1974, all of the channels that the group had developed had moved away from Louisville or become disinterested in continuing the channeling experiment. Don asked me to attempt channeling in order to continue the experiment, and I agreed. I have been channeling ever since.

In 1980, Don's and my partnership became a nonprofit organization, L/L Research. We were fortunate enough to produce books that were entirely channeled. In addition, I launched a writing career, producing books by me concerning channeling and other metaphysical topics.

When I first began channeling, my contact was almost always Hatonn. Hatonn describes its group as a fourth-density entity. Fourth density, the density of love, is the next level above our own third density here on Earth. As I continued to refine my ways of tuning, I began getting a group called Latwii, which describes itself as coming from the density of wisdom or fifth density.

In 1981, shortly after I began asking for the highest and best contact through which I could carry the vibration of Jesus the Christ, I began receiving information from Ra. You may be sure that I challenged this group long and hard because I did not at all like the fact that this name was familiar to me from the pages of Egyptian mythology. However, they were able consistently to respond to my challenges, and I accepted their contact.

Because they were of the sixth density or the density of unity, their vibratory level was extremely fine-tuned and I could receive this group only when in trance. Don Elkins, Jim McCarty, and I worked with those of Ra until 1984 when Don died. I knew better than to try to access this vibration without Don in the circle, for those of Ra had specifically suggested to me that Don was integral to the contact. So I retired from channeling in trance and continued consciously channeling Hatonn, Latwii, and other Confederation sources of the fourth and fifth densities.

Two years later, I received my first communication from those of Q'uo. In good time we thought to ask Q'uo who they were, and they replied that they were a "principle" from the Confederation of Planets. They had formed the principle specifically in order to honor my request that I channel *in a conscious and stable manner* the vibration of Jesus the Christ.

Hatonn was part of the principle of Q'uo, offering the fourth-density vibration of unconditional and complete love. Latwii did the actual speaking for the group. And Ra, who is also Latwii's teacher, was the behind-the-scenes consultant. In this way, they were able to come the closest possible to responding to my request for the best possible positively oriented information I could stably receive and share with those who might find it useful.

Channeling and Polarity

You'll notice that, like Barbara, I assign great importance to tuning myself for channeling and also to the process of challenging spirits. This is because, in my understanding, we dwell in a world of strongly contrasting positive and negative polarity here in third-density Earth today. Barbara uses our positive and negative intention to describe polarity. The Confederation entities' definition of polarity is wholly compatible, but they offer a slightly different perspective. They define polarity in terms of service. They explain that this is the density of choice. There are two ways of serving the Creator and we are here to make that choice. Positive polarity consists of living, thinking, and acting in service to others, whereas negative polarity is involved with thinking of and seeing the world as that which may be of service to self. To positive-polarity thinkers, all of the creation is one thing and that one thing is love. For negative-polarity thinkers, the world is neatly divided into the self and all others. "Right" for the negatively oriented seeker consists in using all those about him as they help him. So some channeled material is very positive in orientation. Some channeled material is very negative in orientation. And a lot of channeled material is of mixed polarity.

As a channel, I have come to feel that my work preparatory to channeling has to do with tuning my own vibrational level to my highest and best. I think all of us are instruments, able to receive and transmit vibrations or frequencies, much like radios or televisions. We pick up information from the creation that is compatible in vibratory level with our tuning. In order to be a better channel for positive information, then, I tune myself with prayer, singing, chanting, and whatever else aids me in achieving my highest stable personal tuning before I open my instrument to receive a source. I then challenge whatever spirit responds to me in the name of that which I hold so dear that I would die for it if necessary. As a mystical Christian, that means that I challenge spirits in the name of Jesus the Christ.

When reading channeled material, I encourage you to look for the marks of positive channeling—fearlessness, serenity, compassion, and inclusivity. There are many channels who have begun by being very positive in their vibration and who have descended into mixed polarity in their messages. Perhaps the best advice I can give anyone who wishes to identify positive channeling is to follow your own feelings. If instead of serenity, joy, and love, a channeled source begins to invoke in you feelings of fear and doom, then you have probably encountered mixed or negatively polarized material. Please trust your discrimination as you explore channeled material. You will know what is right for you because it will resonate within you as though it were something that you already knew but had just forgotten temporarily.

Introduction

Barbara and I both grew up with a deep inner sense of our own spirituality and both of us have been able in our adult lives to live out our positive values. So we both are positively oriented channels. And we feel privileged to have become able to channel messages of love sent by Aaron and Q'uo.

Barbara's Story

In 1972, just after the birth of my first child, I unexpectedly became deaf over the course of two days. The nerves to my ears had died because the blood flow had been cut off, but my doctors could offer me no cause for the sudden failure. I struggled with deafness and the anger I felt about it for many years. By the 1980s I was still experiencing great pain around this event and the ways that loss seemed to cut me off from the world. Although I was coping well with a difficult situation, I felt stuck with anger and prayed for help. I began to experience guidance that offered clear insights to which I had no previous conscious access. Because of my strong intention to move toward healing the anger, and to live without harm, the source that came was positively polarized. I had no previous experience of channeling, nor any conscious knowledge about it. But the loving and wise answers that came supported my intention, opened my heart, and led to healing. After a period of learning, I consciously met Aaron in January 1989. It was only gradually that a more personal relationship was formed. Friends began asking to speak with him, so I began to channel him for others.

The experience of contact with a discarnate entity was bewildering. Who was he? What was I doing? I went into a local bookstore and asked for a book about channeling. They had a few channeled books, but nothing about the process. After rummaging through the shelves in vain, I returned to the front desk to ask if they knew of anything that could be ordered. There on the counter sat a brand-new copy of Carla's *A Channeling Handbook*. It had not been there ten minutes earlier. I told the store's owner that this was exactly the book I needed. He looked at it and said, "We don't carry this book; I have no idea how it got here." I accepted Spirit's gift, read the book, and wrote a fifteen-page letter to Carla. An excerpt of that first letter is below.

Dear Carla,

I've just finished reading *A Channeling Handbook* and am writing to you for two reasons. The first is to thank you for this direct and honest book. You've taken many of the issues at which I've been looking these past six months and put them into clearer focus. This clarity has been a big help to me recently as I've examined the direction my life is taking, away from my past work as a sculptor and into those areas of more direct service to others.

My second reason for writing is because I do have some questions. I find myself wishing I could sit down and talk to you for an hour or two.... [Here I describe in several pages how I met Aaron.] At first my rational mind tried to ask, "Who is Aaron?" Slowly I realized it didn't matter ... He defines himself as a "being of light," which he says we all are. I've come to know him as a being of infinite love, compassion, and wisdom. He also has a beautiful warmth and sense of humor. He is a teacher.

As my trust deepened, Aaron led me on a beautiful journey into myself, into past lives, to unearth the sources of some of the pains of this life, examining the questions of isolation and separation on which my deafness forced me to focus. Together we healed the pain of that deafness and went on to investigate the origins of these issues of separation and isolation. It has been both painful and joyous, frightening and beautiful. Always, Aaron's love has been there to help me through the rough places ...

I'd been sharing the experience with friends. A few asked me questions to ask him and I did so, listening for the answers and then summing them up for each person who'd asked. I still really knew nothing about channeling. One day a friend asked me a more complex question and for the first time I found myself fol-

Introduction

lowing Aaron's suggestion, "simply say the thought you've received." The next day a similar situation occurred, and I found myself in the middle of a long conversation, this time the first written one, as my friend was not present. I was shaken by these experiences. Below is Aaron's conversation with me from my journals about these two experiences, written out as we spoke, and therefore exact.

I am wondering about sharing this information with the friend who'd asked for it. I hadn't expected this kind of dialogue as an answer. A little shaken by what I'm doing here, I ask if I was meant to be some kind of channel?

Aaron: You are not meant to. You may choose to, if you wish.

Barbara: Is that what I should do?

A: There is no right or wrong here. You have the capacity to hear me. I have a voice and am a teacher. You must do only what feels right to you. There is no coercion. I am glad to teach anyone, but I am your guide. Others have their own guides. If they have not yet sought their own guides, and ask my understandings, I shall be glad to share through your voice if you wish to do so. In any situation, you are free to choose what feels right to you. There is never any force here. You must use this responsibility wisely.

B: I just don't feel ready to do this.

A: That's perfectly acceptable. Do what feels right to you. There is the whole question of trust that we must investigate. As you trust the process, your feelings may change. But it is not selfish to relate to me as only your personal guide. Without trust, you can do no more than that with honesty. I am your personal guide. I love you. I will not hurt you in any way. I ask only that you be as honest and responsible as possible.

If you choose to do this you must look within to be sure there is no "self" involved. The teachings must be pure. I know you understand this. Perhaps it is not distrust of me but of yourself and your motives, your ability to keep out self, that makes you hesitate.

B: I think about this and acknowledge that he is right.

A: Then do not try it further until you trust in yourself that you can recognize ego. If I see it I will tell you. You must spend much time every day without writing. These written meditations are not as deep. We cannot do some of the work this way.

And you must spend some time each day in devotional meditation, just with God. This is very important. It will keep you clear in your trust of what you learn. You must not lose track of the source and reason for all of this work.

Do not allow this to become an escape from the depth that is necessary to your learning, nor a block to the deep stillness that heals and teaches you.

Aaron and I have talked at length about the ego questions of channeling. I've gone past the concern of bringing myself into it. Here I disagree, for myself and Aaron, with Carla's statement on page 23 of *A Channeling Handbook* that "about one quarter of most good channeling is contributed by the channel." I wrote this to Carla.

Occasionally someone asks a question I know I can't answer and I lose my contact to Aaron as I attempt to search my own mind for what to say. Each time I do this, I eventually hear Aaron through the static I've created, gently reminding me, "When you're ready to move your own thoughts out of the way and let me answer, we can begin." I am learning to trust that when I open to him he will always be there.

Introduction

The ego questions that have concerned me more in recent months are those in chapter 6 of *A Channeling Handbook*—questions of power, of honestly examining my motivation to do this work, of looking at my responses to the attention it has brought me. I see that my own growth is deeply wrapped up in this, as I strive, as Aaron suggested, to examine the ego-self and transcend my attachments to this ego. The more I channel and examine and reexamine this, the more practice I get and the sooner I do recognize ego when it's there.

The important thing about channeling for others, I'm finding, is that so many people are learning so much! Many others have come to love Aaron and trust his wisdom and guidance, first my friends, then their friends, and on and on in an expanding circle. I watch it in wonder. He feels strongly about our responsibility for our own growth, and always seems to have the right questions to lead people to examine their own issues honestly. It humbles me to see myself as part of this chain of sharing, to be permitted this part in it, and to learn and watch others learning. It brings me much joy! And as I see good things coming out of this, not just for myself but for so many other people, it reinforces my trust.

Carla sent me an equally long reply on a tape. In it I learned she was living with her own severe health catalysts and pain, so she could not type easily.

Excerpts from the letter received from Carla Rueckert:

… One way to forgive yourself and your deafness is to look at it as a catalyst and to look into that catalyst for the lesson of love. That lesson, like you said, sounds like a real ordeal and I congratulate you for surviving. On the other hand I realize that you made your work harder on yourself by delaying coping with it in a deep way. But that's good. That's okay. That's human. I think we have to expect a hump of humanness, I guess I would call it. That's the way it is. We just need to accept that fact. I myself went through the same thing (with my illness).

… One thing I don't do is shut off my feelings, or go into isolation, or shut off my faith in God. It has always been there—a faith in the Lord God, and Jesus Christ, and that has helped me. When I see someone that works as hard as you do, I know I couldn't. I wonder what would happen. I really admire you for having that sense of the eternal. I get a tremendous amount of that kind of energy from your letter.

I think it's very important to appreciate that animal that carries us around and be nice to it without judging it because it got us into Gimpsville. I mean bad luck's bad luck. Life isn't fair. And do not try to be (in high voice) "No, I'm fine, there's no problem." I mean it's a bear to be deaf or lying on a couch. No need to be a Pollyanna about it or to feel sorry for ourselves. I mean that's life. The thing you're responsible for is your reaction. The deafness I think perhaps was your own higher self trying to show you that we are all one, because that probably was the trigger for it, as opposed to karma. But that's just my opinion.

I like what you said about the ego and I very much approve of Aaron's making it clear that there was no pressure to accept Aaron, and that there was no pressure to believe unless you felt it was right. These all are hallmarks of positive channeling. I think if you have a group and develop questions that are really sound that you will have a more universal message that will probably make you more pleased.

… About the process of channeling: completely, exactly, totally all you have to do is picture a concept as a baseball. Catch the concept. Put it in your words and throw it and then you're free to catch the next concept, throw it, and so forth. If you stop and say, "What?" don't fear that you've lost the channel and may not get it back … Totally suspend disbelief … Now it has never failed me … .

It's possible that you misunderstood what I meant in the book. I did not mean that a channel should contribute some of their own ideas, I meant that when one receives a concept, one must put a concept in words and so I find myself using my vocabulary, my feeling for nuance, my experience to state and conceptualize and manifest what I am hearing inside. I'm not really hearing anything; it just comes to me. It sounds like my own thoughts. So, you have to be loose as a goose and not worry about a thing. I was channeling to somebody and started hearing numbers and letters for 30 seconds so I trusted them and channeled them.

Now as to your question, "Was I meant to be some kind of channel?" and Aaron's answer, "You were not meant to; you can choose to." This brings us to a cardinal point of the spiritual cosmology. You gave yourself this assignment. You probably came to Earth and incarnated here because you had a plan. But you have free will. If you cannot say, "Not my will but thine," drop channeling. Channeling is a very serious ministry. It is rewarding, but it requests of the individual an attempt at excellence, especially morally and ethically, and basically of every aspect of life. I remain impressed by what Aaron said. He maintained that free will. Negative channels would say something like, "You have been chosen by the Galactic Command." But you really are free to choose if you want to go on or not. If that means talking to your husband until 2:00 in the morning because something is wrong, so be it. You have to allow for harmony in your life.

Let me tell you from experience—if you do good work for the light, you may come under the eye of the loyal opposition. Beware of any negative thought that comes to you. Not because it's a negative thought but because it can be intensified for you to a really scary point by psychic greeting. What you have to do in that case is love and pray for the entity and give a blessing to his sending and forgive yourself for your part in this.

When Aaron speaks about trust and doing what is right, I think that there is an implied suggestion here to challenge for the ultimate trust. When you have what feels like Aaron's vibration, no matter how many times you have had his vibration in the past, challenge that entity. You say you're a Quaker so you can challenge in the name of Jesus Christ as a disciple.

Carla's warmth and reassurance to me as I stumbled a bit on this new path were vital to my ability to continue as a channel. When I asked, "How do I know it's real?" she replied, "When you have ten thousand pages of transcripts you'll know you couldn't have made all that up." Now, ten thousand pages and more down the road, I know how right she was.

We corresponded in twenty-eight long letters each that first year, in which we explored everything from metaphysics to personal life and values to gardening. We became close friends, though we had never met in person.

How This Book Came to Be

Carla: After some of my channeling was included in *Secrets of the UFO* in 1976, I began receiving sample channelings from readers who wanted to know what I thought of their work. When *The Law of One* series, also known as *The Ra Material*, was published in 1982, many more readers were inspired to send me transcripts of their channeling. In every case I found the work either sweet but without serious content, or full of fear-based "gloom and doom" prophecy about the end times. Such fear-based channelings are mixed in polarity rather than purely positive.

Then I got a fat packet of channeling transcripts from Barbara, along with her letter asking for my guidance. I read her transcripts with increasing delight. Barbara's channeling was lucid, full of content, and entirely lacking in fear. It was also charming, witty, and fun to read. Immediately I thought of a project I had long had in mind.

For the last three decades, publications of channeled material have been spiking. There has been a mass of material available. There has also been an unfortunate tendency for channels to boast that their contact is of a higher vibration than others, or that they, as channels, were more psychic than others. Having seen this trend, I felt that it would be an excellent thing to find another positively polarized channel whose source was as different from my own as possible, and create a volume of co-channeled work. This would demonstrate three things.

Firstly, such a body of work would demonstrate that positively oriented channels check their egos at the door. They do not need to compete for "best channel." They do not feel the desire to criticize other channels. They simply offer the fruits of their channeling to those who might find it helpful. Secondly, it would demonstrate that positive sources of information such as my source, Q'uo, and Barbara's source, Aaron, have no need to compete for "best source." Thirdly, such a co-channeled book would show that positive information harmonizes.

I wrote to Barbara, sharing my thoughts about this project and inviting her to come down to Kentucky for a co-channeling weekend. She took me up on it!

Barbara: When Carla invited me to Kentucky, I accepted the invitation. On the drive down I felt a mix of joy to meet my new friend and some trepidation. Would we connect in person? How would we converse?

There need not have been concern. We knew each other instantly as old friends, and Carla's husband Jim too. What a joy to get to know each other in this lifetime. I had sent Carla a copy of the fingerspelling alphabet, which is the method I had devised for communication with friends and family. People speak slowly and spell the first letter of each word with the hand alphabet. We spent a day talking, and then decided to invite spirit in.

First we had to resolve communication issues so I could follow the ideas offered by Q'uo speaking through Carla. At first, someone tried to fingerspell and allow me to read lips, but I could only follow a part this way. Then we changed to a technique where Q'uo slowed the speech, Jim typed as fast as Q'uo talked, and words appeared magically on the computer monitor. Everything fell into place so naturally that weekend. The channeling was profound: loving, deep, and clear. I grew to love and respect Q'uo and to appreciate deeply Carla's skill as a highly positively polarized medium.

Especially beautiful to me, and to all of us who participated, was the mutual respect and real affection Q'uo and Aaron offered to each other. It was a joy to watch each entity bounce off the other's ideas and words. It made no difference that Q'uo was extraterrestrial and Aaron had evolved at least partially through the earth planes. They were both instruments of love. Clearly, they delighted to share their thoughts with us and with each other. It was evident they learned from each other too, the perfect model of teach and learn. One weekend led to the next, and increasing numbers asked to participate. One weekend Jim and Carla came to Michigan, but Carla's health made it more suitable for us to continue in Kentucky. With each gathering our circle grew in size. When we outgrew Jim and Carla's house, we assembled in the garage that Jim had dressed up for the occasion.

Carla: There came a time, after nine weekends of co-channeling over several years, when my fragile health was no longer up to the rigors of the long sessions. The reason the sessions were so long was that there were two instruments working on one question. Consequently, instead of the sessions lasting about an hour, they tended to last at least two hours and sometimes longer. And so the series ended.

The fruit of it is this volume of transcripts. *The Aaron/Q'uo Dialogues* fulfills my wishes completely. It demonstrates conclusively that positive information harmonizes and that ego does not need to enter in, either to the channels or to their sources.

Barbara and I have remained fast friends. She has moved from strength to strength as the leader of Deep Spring Center for Meditation and Spiritual Inquiry (www.deepspring.org), a meditation center with teachings especially drawn from the Buddhist tradition. I continue to be part of L/L Research (www.llresearch.org). You can investigate our work further and order our materials on these sites.

The Further Development of Barbara's Channeling

Barbara: Through the years my own channeling changed. During the time these transcripts were made, I was a conscious channel for Aaron, "catching the ball" as Carla describes above. Since I am deaf, this was unwieldy since I had to come out of the channeling space to "hear" or "see" a question, then return back into it. I also found myself increasingly exhausted by the work of listening to and finding words for Aaron's thoughts. Finally, Spirit suggested to me that it was time to release the body to Aaron and let him speak directly. I could not have done this in the early years; how do we trust another enough to offer the body fully? But by this time that trust was deep, and Spirit guided the process. I learned to tune and challenge, and when I felt ready, with the words "This body is consecrated to the Light," I simply dropped out of the body and allowed Aaron in.

This was our next method of working. Now Aaron could have my eyes open as he spoke, could get up and walk around the room, and could engage a person with direct eye contact. I no longer tried to find words; I was essentially not there. I seemed to sit in a quiet and light-filled place until he returned to get me. There was minimal work on my part, beyond resting firmly in that high-vibrational space. Aaron knew what he wanted to say and used this body as his vehicle. The only challenge for him was that he no longer had use of my vocabulary, and his command of present-day English was not as fluent as mine.

Then they taught me to remain partially present, but not to back-seat drive. This took a lot of letting go. Aaron controls the body and I fully trust him. But my mind is available for him to search for words. It still is restful. I have no sense of what is being said, but awareness is present enough for him to look into the mind when needed. So this has been the progression of channeling Aaron through the years.

How This Book Came to Be Published

Carla: While nothing is destined, there is enormous help from Spirit aiding seekers with remarkably synchronistic moments. Barbara talks about one of them when she describes how she found my work earlier in this Introduction. Another example has to do with how this book came to the attention of our publisher, North Atlantic Books.

In January 2010, I was teaching at the Earth Transformation Conference in Kona, Hawaii. After I gave my initial presentation, a marvelous woman named Suzanne Taylor asked to have a conversation with me. We spent the afternoon in my room overlooking the Pacific Ocean, listening to the surf roar and sharing our experiences and hopes. During that conversation, Suzanne discovered that I had a manuscript to offer that had recently been rejected by a publisher on the East Coast due to its length. She suggested that she might be able to show it to her nephew, Richard, who had founded the publishing house North Atlantic Books. I quickly wrote Ba—my nickname for Barbara Brodsky—with this wonderful news. Ba replied that our book was already being considered by North Atlantic Books. They were the publisher for Barbara's new book, *Cosmic Healing*. She had just passed our *Dialogues* to Richard, and he had responded that he wanted to publish it! Clearly, Aaron and Q'uo's conversation had come to the right people at the right time.

Barbara and Carla: We are absolutely delighted to offer this work of collaborative service to you. We offer it to you with all the love in our hearts and those of our contacts, Aaron and the Q'uo principle. We hope you may find it helpful on your spiritual journey.

Barbara Brodsky/Carla L. Rueckert
July 8, 2011

A NOTE ON THE TEXT

A note about the transcripts: Aaron and Q'uo always begin to speak with the statements "I am Aaron" or "I am Q'uo" or "We are those known to you as Q'uo." Those identifiers steady the contact on the vibratory frequency we are using as channels. Each identifier strengthens that frequency but means there is much repetition as each entity comes in. This is important to clear channeling but it is not important to a reader and can disturb the flow of the reading, so we have removed all such opening statements and left only the closing ones.

WEEKEND 1

Meeting for the First Time

Four of us gathered in Carla and Jim's office—Barbara, Carla, Jim, and their friend Kim who was living with Carla and Jim, assisting them in their work. During the actual channeling of weekend I, Carla reclined on a chaise lounge as she was unable to sit erect. Barbara sat in a chair. Since Barbara could not hear Q'uo, it was necessary to find a way for her to follow the channeling. During the first session, Kim fingerspelled to Barbara, while mouthing Carla's (Q'uo's) words. Fingerspelling works well when speaking to Barbara but in this situation the process effectively communicated only part of the content, so we continued to explore techniques. Barbara moved to a loveseat to sit next to Jim while he typed so that she could read Jim's transcription of Q'uo on the monitor.

Outside, winter was barely giving way to early spring. Crocuses peeked through the mud, and the air was beginning to warm. Barbara had come to visit for three days. The first day was spent getting to know each other in the body. That included partaking of Carla's delicious meals, for she is a wonderful cook and enjoys such creation. The first session took place that night, and two sessions a day followed on Saturday and Sunday.

We started every session with a process used by both Barbara and Carla called tuning. Just as we always tune a musical instrument before beginning to play, so we must tune ourselves before we open the energy field to a discarnate entity. Our high vibration calls forth the highest spirit vibration we can stably hold.

Carla and Barbara have somewhat different methods of tuning. Carla said: "Barbara's experience is entirely different from Carla's. Aaron contacted her. She patiently and with great integrity honed in on that contact and stabilized it.

"I on the other hand worked for about two months before succeeding in contacting a member of the Confederation, which I was intending and hoping to do at the request of my partner Don Elkins. So my attitude toward channeling has always been that of a dutiful worker attempting to learn her art.

"A lot of times, when Barbara is working with her own tuning, Aaron helps her. That does not happen with me unless I ask for an opinion."

We will introduce you to several of our methods as the book progresses. Here is Carla's tuning session for this session:

I begin in solitude by singing a hymn, the first lines of which are:

> *Take my life and let it be*
> *consecrated Lord to thee.*
> *Take my moments and my days,*
> *let them flow in ceaseless praise.*

I continue with prayers, praying the prayer of Saint Francis and beseeching the Holy Spirit's presence. I invoke the archangels and all those whom they represent, who come from the world of spirit in the name of Jesus Christ. I ask them to help in maintaining the purity and safety of the circle and the contact. I then go through the process of looking into and balancing my chakra system of energies. After balancing, I open up the energy system for potential channeling. Then I join the group and continue tuning with the group. Before opening to a specific contact, I challenge the perceived contact in the name of Jesus Christ and ask that it say that Jesus is Lord. I repeat this challenge three times. If all three challenges are met, I open to channel.

Then we turned our hearts to our central questions. Barbara and Carla have both found that asking the deepest questions draws forth the clearest answers and highest vibrational source.

The weekend flew past, and each of us experienced the grace of hearing these two beloved entities speak to us, and of the wonderful circle of friendship. Here is an excerpt of a letter Barbara wrote to Carla upon her return to Michigan.

Dear Carla and Jim,

Love to you both, and thank you for a wonderful visit. It was a joyous, relaxing, and fascinating few days. Carla, sister of my heart, I love you. What else can I possibly say? Jim, it's good to know you as a person and no longer just a name. Thank you both for your hospitality and love.

It was wonderful working together that way. I can't see Q'uo as I see Aaron, but can feel that presence. Perhaps this is because Aaron has lived as human while Q'uo has not, and also that Q'uo is a combination of many entities. As I mentioned, I felt another strong and loving presence, not Aaron or Q'uo but another being too. While Aaron is not telling me what to do here, I sense he feels I would be well advised to "caulk" any psychic chinks before I allow such to channel through me. I don't think he advises this because of that particular spirit but instead because I may open myself to outer plane negativity that may accompany that spirit. I trust his judgment. That's why I didn't pursue it further this weekend, although I did feel that same energy several more times.

I loved the feeling of Aaron and Q'uo both present. Through Aaron's energy/presence, Carla, I felt even closer to you. It was as if these two energies, Aaron and Q'uo, formed a bridge to connect our human energies even deeper. Could you feel that linking too? Carla, thank you for what you shared. I can rest and find comfort in your strength, trustworthiness, and the depth of your love and faith. I'm glad we've found each other and can nourish each other in such a way.

One last thing to share, what I can remember of it. In a session today Aaron said to someone that the spirit can walk on water while the human takes a few steps, says "who, me?" and falls through. We need to learn that it happens simultaneously, that we are and always have been both, and to love both the divine in ourselves and the fallible (and wet) human.

The person he was speaking to said jokingly that the human can walk on water as long as it's frozen. Aaron said it can be done without ice but you have to keep going, without letting fear stop you. We cannot keep up the pretense that the human is perfect. We can, however, accept the imperfection, stop the boat, let our everyday selves sink, and enjoy the water, while we watch our spiritual selves walk the surface and know that this perfection is also us.

With that thought I'll leave you all.

Love,
Barbara

During that first weekend, the initial focus arose from our desire to be the clearest channels it was possible for us to be. We had a concern to clear away those things that block the light. We are what Aaron calls "angels in earth-suits." We are the Divine presence and we are the heavier physical, emotional, and mental bodies. We need to allow for both. When we disallow and try to force away any part of our being, the ensuing contractions do block light.

Through the weekend, each session pointed us to the opening questions for the next session.

Session I

Weekend I, Part I of 5
(This session was preceded by a period of tuning and meditation.)

Barbara: We seek to know ourselves and the Creator but do not know how to do this, as we fear we are imperfect in ourselves and our understanding, and incapable of this knowledge. How can we proceed?

(Carla channeling)

Q'uo: Be aware that the Creator is often blocked or banished by third-density entities due to lack of awareness of the journey each came to make. However, those on Earth are never away from the heart of unity, love, and concord.

We would suggest that you again investigate yourself within this incarnational experience. Each entity is all that is lovely and all that is not. Yet each entity can make many choices, each of which orients him or her toward being a loving, giving source of love. In surrendering the life to serving, the entity becomes a miracle, a wonder. Let the self come to know, respect, and love this entity more and more. Let this entity become the great comfort, protection, and above all, companion. For when the self realizes its selfhood as a living testament to loving choices, the entity receives the greatest gift of all: true friendship, true companionship. This is not to say that an entity whose self is one's best friend will ever seem impeccable, but to say that friendship and trustful companionship must begin with the self with all of its self-perceived errors. In accepting this friendship, the pores of the spiritual skin open to drink in the elixir of felt, palpable love. When you are friends with yourself, you can relax into an aloneness that retains the comfort of true friendship.

May we speak further, my sister?

Barbara: We are eager to surrender to service, but we know how limited we are and have the fear that we cannot succeed, that we'll run out of the food of love and energy to serve. How can we address this?

Q'uo: As a spirit you need not food. As an entity in third density, respect for the incarnated self suggests an overwhelming love for that sheep that must be fed so that it may sit in perfect fullness of being and allow the voice of spirit to flow through without diminishing or exhausting the third-density, manifested self.

Is there a further question?

Barbara: How can I learn to love and accept myself fully when I see in myself so many imperfections?

Q'uo: We do not find it difficult to love your self. We gaze at your courage as you walk in spiritual darkness, making choices by faith alone. We are deeply moved by the bravery of those who choose to express manifestation when it seems risky and almost hopeless.

The solution to perceived lack of perfection is so simple that it escapes notice. This third-density experience was designed expressly so that perfection would be quite improbable. In the furnace of self-perceived fire, the fire of ever ongoing, never decreasing imperfection, the third-density spirit learns to become flexible, supple, and strong. Were an entity to express perfection in the third density, such a one would be responsible to all to whom that incarnation became known. Such a responsibility is beyond the intention of your higher self at this moment. The imperfections of which you speak are your links to those to whom you wish to offer heartfelt love.

There is one state in which perfection may be well realized, and that is the sitting in the presence of the infinite Creator, the great original Thought or Logos that is love. That perfection does you great good. When you are in tabernacle with the infinite One, there you may be fed the infinite perfection that is Love. When you open your eyes, retain that sharing of perfection. Remember at each moment this infinite perfection and allow it to make resonant, deep, wide, and spacious your perceptions of the specifically limited and often misleading events, entities, relationships, and occurrences of your relativistic time/space continuum. Perfection does not aid, except when embodied in third-density entities; that is, it does not aid the self or others. This furnace of incarnation is that which burns away the dross. Although the heart of self is always perfect, the incarnated manifestation of self is useful as the self perceives the harsh but meaningful, halting steps of will led by faith alone.

We speak to you from a density wherein we approach what you might accept as perfection; however, were we in the third density, we would have become a gambler—nothing more, nothing less. Your self gambles that, in spite of all self-perceived failures, the self will not be afraid or bow to indecision but will choose to love—again, nothing more and nothing less. Whether you perceive the self as successful or unsuccessful, perfect or imperfect, the intention will burn away the dross of which you are so aware. If you can find the courage to proceed in the hope of expressing love, then you shall be as perfect as one may hope to be within the dust-laden confusion of perceptions of your illusion. Do not be deceived by the perceptions of the senses or the intellect, both of which were designed to embrace the illusion to the exclusion of all things absolute.

May we answer further, my sister?

Barbara: Thank you very much, Q'uo. I need to wait. I think I will have further questions. Sometime tomorrow I will go over the transcript of what you said to me and then talk to you again, because I don't want to ask you to repeat. I have lost too much already by not hearing the words.

I have one very brief question. As I relaxed and stopped trying to get all of Kim's words, as she is signing what Carla is channeling, there were many times when I felt that I was getting the material without lip-reading and that it was coming in telepathically—not in words the way I channel Aaron, but picking up concepts telepathically. Is it possible that I was hearing the words, only telepathically, when I relaxed and stopped trying to lip-read?

Q'uo: You may perhaps hear our laughter. Yes, my sister, we are those known by many names, but above all, we are known as messengers of love. As social memory complexes, we may speak to any entity that is tuned to our frequency. You are indeed a sensitive instrument and we are having difficulty keeping this instrument [Carla] from grinning like a fool because we are so happy. We laugh in joy. We thank you, my sister, for the pleasure of communicating with your beloved self.

We feel that this is sufficient for this working and at this moment would leave this instrument and this group in the love and the light of the one infinite Creator. We bid you Adonai. We are known to you as the principle, Q'uo.

Carla: I've been working to learn to value *being* as opposed to *doing*. It's very important to me because my physical abilities are more and more limited. Do you have suggestions on how I can best proceed in this line of seeking?

(Barbara channeling)

Aaron: I find it a great blessing to have the privilege of being with you tonight and to speak to your questions. I might remark before we start that the light emanating from this room is brilliant and I find it very beautiful. I remarked to Barbara and Carla earlier that I am not hampered by restraints of time or space and truly can experience the light of this room at any time I choose, regardless of whether Barbara is using her senses. However, even though she perceives differently than I through her eyes and is not seeing the light but the faces, by experiencing *while* she experiences, I can perceive the effect of the energy of this room on her energy and have still deeper experience of the force of it. Thus, I can see this group without using Barbara's senses; but with her senses added, I profoundly feel the energy bursting forth.

Carla, we are looking at your question about being versus doing, and I am afraid there is something you do not quite understand here. In being, you *are* doing. This comes back to this same truth I shared above. I see you as light, just that. Each of you radiates a very beautiful and unique pattern of light. When you are being in the most pure way possible for you, you allow that universal energy to flow through you and out so that you become charged with the love of the universe, with the love of God. Then the light that channels through you is enhanced by your own inner energy so that there are truly two sources of light.

You are each a spark of God. Picture the small ember and picture the large bonfire. Yet this ember has so much power, is so unlimited, that it, itself, is its own source as well as a channel for the universal source. What more important thing can you do, what deeper way can you serve, than to magnify that love and light, simply to allow yourself to be a channel for that love and light by being? Do you imagine that you are more of a channel for that love when you are physically active than when you are physically quiet? The distinction is not so clear as you are making it, not so strong as you are making it.

It does not work the other way. In doing you are not always channeling that love and light so clearly; rather, you are using your energy, feeling that something must be done and that you in yourself are not sufficient. In a sense, this is what Q'uo was just speaking to Barbara about: beginning to understand that you are unlimited and that anything that flows through you is enhanced. As you allow this energy flow, the doing becomes simply another way of being. But as long as it is doing just for doing's sake, much of the light is lost.

Would you like further clarification of this before I go on?

Carla: What different choices can I make? Can you clarify for me what you feel I have to choose between? I feel when people write me, I want to give them something they can hold and hear.

WEEKEND 1

(Barbara channeling)

Aaron: There are two things happening here simultaneously, Carla. One is that you do find it a joy to be able to serve others in such a way, and yet at times you push yourself beyond your comfortable physical limits. There is a certain difference in giving out of joy and in feeling a very small sense of "I should do this." Can you see the judgment in that "should"? It does not negate that aspect of you that wants to serve, but both voices are speaking at the same time: the "I want to" and the "I should." Because of the historical associations within this incarnation for the "I should," there is a churning of the inner energy.

Barbara spoke to you earlier about my description last Thursday of the ways energy flows through you. In these ways you are a channel for the energy of God and of the universe. As soon as that small "I should" comes into it, it is like a twisting of the energy within your body so that it becomes a tumult within and does not flow through in the same way. What I am describing here is, very simply, the way I see the patterns of energy and light. But your experience of this blockage is as a churning in the stomach, perhaps, or some increased physical pain. There is a sense of tension. Can you begin to separate the "I want to" and the joy of that intended service from the "I should," to notice that very quiet "I should"? It is very quiet, just a whisper, but it is enough.

The more aware you become of that "I should," the more you can laugh at it and say, "Well, here comes the 'I should' again!" When you can laugh at it, you can greet it with so much less judgment, and then the energy continues to flow through you and there is no distortion of that energy. The "I should" is the doing, and the "I aspire to" is the being. Can you see that? The conflict is not in what to do, but in the way in which you do it. When the "I should" pushes you beyond your physical limits, built-up resentment can develop and, with it, some accompanying pain.

34

You are human and you are not expected to be perfect. While in a human form in this incarnation, there are emotions. To want to get rid of the emotional body is a nonacceptance of the self, because the emotional body is an essential part of the incarnate self. So what you are being given here is another opportunity to look at the emotional body and embrace it, not to hate that aspect of yourself. Each of you needs to purify yourself into that spiritual body and to move further along your spiritual path. That is easy when you are not in an incarnation. The incarnation offers the opportunity to practice when such embracing is more challenging. Do you look at the physical body and say, "I don't want it," or do you attempt to love it? It is much harder to learn to love the emotional part of the body complex.

I speak here to all of you. Can you see the ways in which you have learned to accept the physical body more completely than the emotional body? It is harder, but until you have learned to accept all of that emotional energy in yourselves, you cannot accept it in others. That is what you are feeling. I keep asking Barbara to honor the incarnation. You cannot learn unconditional love, compassion, and forgiveness as easily while as a spirit, because there is not the same force of the emotions on the spiritual plane. So here is the chance to learn.

Speaking again to you, Carla, can you see that it is not a choice of how or whether to answer these readers' letters, but how to relate to that small "I should" more lovingly so that you can begin to relate from the full being, harmonizing all its four bodies? Once you have begun to do that—not getting rid of but accepting even the "I should"—you realize there is nothing of which to be gotten rid. When it is no longer necessary it falls away. That last idea is not original to me; I quote Q'uo. And that "I should" *will* fall away! It is still necessary now because you have not learned to accept it. At that point when it falls away, you will understand that there is truly no difference between being and doing. The doing in its purest form is a way of being; and when you are being, you are always doing.

Do you have further questions?

Carla: Yes. I just don't know how best to serve. You say, "When you are being you are always doing," but I often can't *do* anything. Can you speak to this?

Aaron: I would ask one question before I answer this. Is your doubt based in not knowing in which way you would best serve then or in the physical pain that comes when you push yourself to respond, or is it in both?

Carla: The first.

Aaron: If it is acceptable to you, Carla, I will address both, as there is also a physical burden that is being put upon your body.

I ask you first to look very closely and see the places where the desire to serve another, through giving them something to hold on to, comes from a pure place of love within your heart, and where the desire to serve is to alleviate the sense of unworthiness. Both create a physical drain on your body—the sense of "I should" that I just spoke of—and feelings, that create resentment. Can you see that both exist?

I would like you to visualize your energy as I see it. When you are feeling loving and allowing your own energy to be channeled to others with as much clarity as is possible in that moment, there is still a minimal distortion. This is essential to the human form; without such fluctuation you would not be human. When you each allow that energy to be channeled within the distortion, the pattern of energy I see coming from the body looks like the concentric circles that appear when a pebble is thrown into a pond, each one of the circles radiating out. When there is any anger, greed, resentment, hate, visually what I see are sharp spikes like a child's image of the sun. When there is a mixture of love and resentment, I see both. This is why, when you are in a room with another being and feel the presence of that being's anger, that being need not be talking to you for you to know that anger. When you feel the presence of love, there need be no words. You simply walk into the room and you feel it. The anger and love are

36

tangible. Now visualize, if you will, what happens when those spikes of anger or fear hit these concentric circles of love. The sharp tips are gently softened each time they make contact, until they slowly wear down and smooth out into a circle.

When I speak of being versus doing, one of the best ways that you can serve another being is simply in sending out those concentric circles of light that will soften another being's anger or fear. You are in a position, Carla, where people are writing to you, so it is very difficult to send that love out through the mail and feel assured that they will feel it. You can send it out and know some beings are capable of feeling it. But a simple few words from you, "I love you. Thank you for your letter. Thank you," would be felt by some beings but others would misunderstand it. You are right, there.

You must ask yourself two questions here. The first comprises two parts: *To what am I responding? What is their need and what am I sending out?* When there is any feeling of resentment or pressure or even uncertainty about answering that letter, some of that is received not as a softening circle but as small spikes. I am not suggesting that your letters are not loving and skillful, but you must really look carefully for that small "I should" I just spoke of, or any physical exhaustion, so that this letter is created with a loving desire to serve.

The second question is *What is their need?* You know that you cannot learn for another, yet that is a large part of your pain because you have so much wisdom. It frustrates you that at times you share that wisdom and others cannot hear you because of their own fears.

You ask, is it unskillful to want to reach out in love to these souls that turn to you for help? First be sure that your response is purely that of love. If there is any resistance to replying, simply put it aside for later that day or for another day and then know that the response does come from that pure place of love within you— a desire to serve—and wears as minimal a distortion as you can manage. Ask yourself, *In what way am I trying to change them, to make them hear me? Am I speaking with a voice of love and reassurance? If I speak with love and they cannot hear me, is that okay?* Remind yourself that you cannot learn for them. You can open a door but you cannot push them through.

Carla, put quite simply, you have a tendency to want to solve others' problems for them. And this is one of the things you find most difficult, because you know that is not something you can do. Can you begin to relate to the source of that need to solve others' problems and to take away another's pain? Can you begin to make yourself so comfortable with your own pain, and here I do not mean physical pain, but with the pain of your own existence, that you no longer need to take away their pain? Can you see the lesson in this for you— that as you find a deeper acceptance for yourself, your response to others will become increasingly skillful, and that instead of needing to change things you will help them to find a deeper acceptance for themselves?

Do you understand and is there a further question?

Carla: Yes, but I have to think about it first.

Aaron: Is there a further question?

Carla: Yes. I have always had low physical and emotional energy. What do I need to learn and how can I work to heal that in myself and serve better? It makes me angry that I can't do everything I wish to do. Then I feel guilty because I'm angry. Help!

Aaron: I perceive a normal amount of energy within you but it is partially blocked below the heart chakra by the anger, so the energy flow is restricted. So let us talk about anger. There is the misunderstanding of assuming one has only two choices in dealing with anger, or any heavy emotion: that one express it and talk about it or that one suppress it. There is a third choice and that is just to notice it. When you quietly notice something, and touch it with your gentleness, very often it dissolves. It simply does not have the same solidity or the same hold over you. It is not necessary to practice your anger: to express it verbally or in a physical way such as throwing pillows. This practice, in a sense, enhances the anger. It does allow the being to recognize it; and for some beings who have a great deal of trouble recognizing it, it may be used as a useful first step. I prefer simply treating it as one treats the stubbed toe.

Will you try an experiment with me here? Picture yourself sitting on a mountaintop. It is a beautiful day. There is a clear view. The sun is shining with a lovely warmth, as a warm cloak on your shoulders, and a cool breeze touches your face. In the distance you see a cloud and then you turn your back to it and go back to enjoy the view. That cloud approaches, but you are totally unaware of its presence until suddenly it sweeps over the top of the mountain, enclosing you completely within it, shutting off the sun. You cannot see your hands six inches in front of your face. The air feels cold and clammy. There is a sense of panic, thinking, "How will I find the path to get down?" There is a sense of anger, of wanting this cloud to go away. Can you feel that need to push it away? Can you feel how hard it is to just sit there and let it be there? Can you feel how strong the aversion is to it?

Come back again to the sunny mountaintop and the same cloud in the distance. Enjoy the view and notice the cloud: "There's a cloud coming … it looks like it will be here in ten or fifteen minutes. Well, here it comes … another minute or two … It's a big cloud, too, and very dense looking. I think it will be here for half an hour, maybe even more. Perhaps I should put my jacket on … and here it comes." It encloses you completely again, and again you cannot see your hands in front of your face. You do miss the warm sun and the view, and it does feel cold and clammy. But you saw it coming, and you know how long it will be there. Can you see how much easier it is simply to sit with it and allow its presence, and that there is no longer a struggle with it; it is just a cloud? Can you all feel the difference?

Your anger is like that. It becomes solid when you struggle with it, when there is a sense of needing it or needing to make it go away, or to do anything special with it. When you can simply allow it as a cloud passing through and let go of your struggle with it, then there is no need to react to it. Certain conditions prompt the anger to arise; it is noticed and it dissolves, and it goes its way. It is not the anger that is a problem, it is your reaction to the anger. That is what solidifies the anger.

So how do you work with this? It is truly just a skill that may be developed, and it has two parts. One is noticing the arising of anger as quickly as you can, each time it comes, even beginning to notice the situations that may provoke anger and asking, *I wonder if anger will arise next?* And the second is noticing your reaction to the anger and asking, *Is there judgment against it? Is there hatred of it? Or can I simply hold it, holding myself in my arms as I would mentally with that stubbed toe? Can I respond to this anger the way I would respond to a child who came inside crying and saying, "A bully pushed me down"? Would I tell that child, "Well, don't be angry," or would I more skillfully hold that child in my arms and say, "I see how angry you're feeling," and reassure it that it is still loved despite the anger, that the anger has nothing to do with its lovability or with its soul's perfection?*

It is so easy for all of you to have compassion for others but not for yourselves. So I ask you, can you begin to relate to this anger in a more open and loving way? I am not suggesting here that it is skillful to walk around angry; but anger does arise, just like clouds do come over. As long as you are here in a physical body, there are going to be feelings. Even the most highly evolved being incarnate in a human body still has feelings but there is no longer attachment or aversion to those feelings. There is no longer a need to get rid of them or to struggle with them. And it is through that relaxation of the struggle that one finds a deeper peacefulness. Anger and love are not mutually exclusive. It all depends on how you relate to the anger.

In purely practical terms, I would suggest that it would be useful to play a game with yourself to help you loosen up and relate more lovingly and openly to anger. Take a notebook with you, a small notebook, and for a day or several days as seems practical to you, every time you see anger arise just jot down a line. Be a cat at a mouse-hole and think, "Aha! There's anger. I caught it. I see it this time. I'm getting faster. I can see it faster and faster." See if you can lighten up a little: "Oh my, here's anger!"

The second thing I would suggest that might be helpful is to begin to observe the pattern of how you relate to your anger; to start to note, every time you do note anger arise, that little voice that says, "I shouldn't be angry," and ask that voice, "Why shouldn't I?" There is a big difference between using your anger as a reason to act unskillfully toward another and in simply feeling anger.

Do you have further questions?

(There are no questions at this time.)

I thank you all for the opportunity to share your love and your light. Please know how much my love is with you and that the love and courage that you bring to your work is truly a light and an inspiration to all beings on all planes. That is all.

Session 2

Weekend I, Part 2 of 5

(This session was preceded by a period of tuning and meditation.)

Barbara: In yesterday's talk from Q'uo, I got just what little I was able to lip-read. I didn't want to request repetition. Would Q'uo reshare whatever they feel I missed, which they shared last night?

(Carla channeling)

Q'uo: I greet you in the love and in the light of the one infinite Creator, whose presence permeates all and is all that there is.

My sister, there is no such thing as repetition in responding to the needs of a consciousness, because each entity is at this moment a new and different person, unlike the entity of any other moment. This is why history, especially personal history, is largely irrelevant to the great work of living and loving in just this one moment.

We would speak of the saying of the one known as Jesus, that saying that he gave to his disciples: "Feed my sheep."[4] Many are the loving servants of the one Creator who are eager to feed other sheep but who do not realize that first they also need food, not the food of the earthly vehicle alone, but far more importantly, the bread and wine of spiritual companionship. There is a great companion that awaits all who heed her heart; that is, the very earth beneath your feet. This constitutes the first and second densities of your sphere and is alive and pulses with undiminished, infinite love. Each rock, each portion of grass, meadow, or pine needle beneath your feet connects a third-density entity with the heart of the Grandmother Earth. How this being loves you! The friendship of the elementals of earth, air, wind, and fire; the

---

[4] John 21:16–17 AV.

devas of plants of all kinds; the ever-rising consciousness of animal forms, all wait to embrace the one who stops to pay attention and to take comfort in the cathedral of what you call nature. When an entity allows itself to admit the entrance of these divine and loving spirits, the air is filled with cherubim, the trees with the laughter of the seraphim, and angels ascend and descend in every fire, in every storm, in every calm, in all beams of living sunlight. Here lies food indeed for the spirit.

We would move further and speak of another very true and real companion. Many are aware of this entity as Jesus the Christ. Others find it helpful to think of this sacred energy as the living Holy Spirit of the Christ, which speaks to the world yesterday, today, and forever. Imagine the spirit form of the one known as Jesus beside you, and mentally take the hand that is offered. Thus, palm to palm, heart to heart, love divine to love in manifestation—a companionship of infinite trust, infinite mercy, infinite kindness, and infinite love is born and forged anew every moment.

The need for companions along the way seems to the third-density eye impossible to be met when one is alone in the way in which it has chosen to walk the path of love and service to others. Yet every zephyr of breeze, every silent bird, and all that the senses experience are your loving companions. The fellowship of the Christ, however it is perceived, is nearer than your breathing, closer than your hands or feet, and infinitely more intimate than any third-density companion. So, in any weather of life, in storm or calm, it is the third-density entity that must call to remembrance in each present moment the very present help and companionship that those who are yet asleep do not find themselves perceiving. The love and caring is always there. It is the entity who must remember to open the door to that friendship, to reach out the hand to that love that is so palpable one could almost imagine the incarnate form of the Christed One.

Especially when outward circumstances seem murky and turgid with heavy cares, the seeker will find those cares lifted away simply by remembering to reach out the hand to the friendship of the sanctified

Christ. That sanctified presence is truly within each seeker, as is all the universe. You are the creator of your particular creation and co-creator with infinite Intelligence of that which is experienced and how it is experienced. Although you cannot be another's creation, you cannot help but be the creator of your own. So, in making the choices from moment to moment, do not let your heart flag or falter because you are alone; for there is companionship more real than the manifested forms of your density, ever waiting for your simple recognition and acceptance. How loved all entities are! Yet without the intention to reach out in trust for that love, an entity may walk forever in a fog of self-created solitude.

I am Q'uo and would ask if there is a further question at this time.

Barbara: Thank you. Q'uo, I'm aware of a desire in myself to serve that seems to come from two places. When I sense that the desire to serve comes from any place of ego or self, it makes me pull back in fear that ego will distort the work. Then that fear touches and distorts the honest places of loving and worshipful desire to serve. It confuses me. When there's fear, although I hear Aaron, I doubt even that. Yet when there's love and the full experience of God and of that love from Aaron that surrounds me, I know no doubt. Aaron has talked about this at length with me, but I wonder if there's anything you would add that would help me to understand and balance these forces?

Q'uo: We would speak of two minds and two hearts. The first mind is the mental mind. In it there can only be mentally feared obstacles. For one who is an adventurer within the mind, the barriers of fear do not arise. However, the mind that is mental deals almost exclusively with the relativistic illusion in which each now experiences and enjoys the dance of incarnation. Thusly, although one may be mentally curious, one cannot use that mentality to plunge into the abyss that must be accepted in order to reach the second mind.

The second mind is often called the heart. In the open heart is stored the true mind, which begets wisdom and compassion. However, many things occur during an incarnation that may tend to cause an entity to erect defensive barriers in order that this precious heart may not be wounded more than it already is. Thusly, in order to open the second heart or the heart of wisdom, one must first gaze at the erected barriers in acceptance and love for the self that needed those barriers, allowing them to remain until they are no longer needed. Then the heart may open and wisdom may be fearlessly received and equally fearlessly manifested forth.

It is said in the holy work called the Bible by the one known as Jesus, "I am the vine, you are the branches."[5] Let us look at *I am.* I Am is the true name of the infinite One. I Am. Say this in your heart: "I Am. I Am with you always. I Am the way. I Am the truth. I Am the life."[6] Each is I Am. Thusly, each open heart receives, reveals, and manifests the fruit of that great root of consciousness, the I Am of all that there is. When the branches of the vine surrender their self-importance in a humble awareness that without the root I Am, their I Am would be dust and ashes, then the branches bloom, flower, and bear fruit and seed to replenish the Earth inexhaustibly.

Let us now speak of the first and the second heart. This, too, is helpful in finding and allowing the release of fear; for in the first heart there is wisdom, but there is only the perceived awareness of the nurturing constancy that is love. The first heart often attempts to bloom, to nurture, and to give simply because it is full, and those about it need replenishing and filling. The first heart, though wise, when full because of its unstinting compassion, is also foolish. This folly is beautiful to us and a testament to the incredible generosity and power of the open heart. Yet there is a second heart and that heart may be conceived to be—whether we speak of the male or female form—the womb of life. That heart moves in fullness with no need to serve and no need to do anything other than be full. The second heart is the womb, ever pregnant with love, ever giving birth out of fullness into

---

[5] John 15:5 AV.

[6] Matt. 28:20, John 14:6 AV.

that which is actually full. Thusly, the second heart responds not because of the needs of others, but because it, like sunshine, must propagate its light and give birth ever and ever and ever to its own I Am, which—as the womb of this second heart is more and more maturely experienced—becomes more and more nearly the undistorted, uncreated Logos, which is Love.

Is there a further question, my sister?

Barbara: I have no further questions at this time. Thank you, Q'uo.

Q'uo: We thank you, my sister.

Now we would speak just a moment about that which is called patience. How boring to be patient, to wait, and to watch, when the heart leaps like a deer and wishes to fly higher than the highest mountain in joy, in radiance, and in awareness of perfect love! Yet the will of entities in incarnation is made perfect, not by its use, but by the surrender of its use to the will of the one infinite Creator.

In your illusion it seems there is a passage of time. Outside of this illusion, all times are one, all times simultaneous. Yet within the illusion, darkness broods over the mind and over the heart and sometimes the night watches seem to go on forever. Yet it is in the darkness of midnight that the messenger of realization, illumination, and love comes ever so quietly, walking on feet of I Am, I Am, I Am, . . . silent feet that cannot be heard unless the heart is watching and praying and waiting.

This is the use of patience—not time to be spent quickly, but time to treasure that expectancy that the bride and bridegroom feel as they wait for the wedding day that has already been set. Within an incarnation, the spirit has many wedding days, many glorious feasts; but those feasts are punctuations—gifts, we may say—that give the commas and the periods to the long sentences of expectation. Thusly, it is well to give great respect to the practice of waiting, watching patiently in complete faith that, although the seeker does not know the next wedding day, yet it is known and it will come. In this joyful readiness lies a fearlessness that does not quail at the darkness of the hour or the solitude of the night watch. Rather, it waits in a patient faith, in a honed edge of will to listen, to surrender, and to be that I Am that is the wedding present of the consummation of the present moment.

We would leave this instrument at this time, thanking each for the beauty of your vibrations. It has been a great joy for us to be with you, to be called to your group by the intensity and beauty of your calling and your needs. We hope we may have offered helpful opinions, but as always, ask each to remember to cast aside anything that does not speak to the personal truth. We are of the principle known to you as Q'uo. Adonai. Adonai. I leave you in the love and in the light of the infinite Creator.

Barbara: Last week, Aaron, you spoke of promptings to serve coming from the emotional body. What comes to the mental body is a pure desire to love. You've previously spoken of imbalances between these two and of bringing them into harmony. This morning in meditation I began to see the opposite side of the above. I felt the mental body was the one blocking the true loving emotion, that when I enter that tabernacle it feels like the emotional body opens and any separation comes from the mind. Will you speak further about this?

(Barbara channeling)

Aaron: My greetings and love to you all. It is a joy to be with you this morning and to feel the love and light that emerge from this group. And I thank the principle of Q'uo for that which has been shared. There is great comfort in hearing the same thing repeated by different voices. It is part of trust, because truly there is nothing I can say to any of you that you do not already know. But our words reassure you and help you to trust the wisdom of your own hearts.

You ask about these bodies. You understood this morning, as you thought that question, that you were asking partially in reference to

Kabir's powerful poem,[7] where he makes the statement, "How hard it is to feel that love with all our four bodies. Those who try to be reasonable about it fail."

You are consciously aware of the concepts about which I speak and the experiences that underlie those concepts; but to some degree, perhaps, we do not share the same vocabulary. Let me speak first for a moment, simply establishing the vocabulary that I use so you can hear this without misunderstanding. Please feel free to substitute the labels with which you are familiar for the labels that I put on the experience.

There are four bodies: physical, emotional, mental, and spiritual. In your incarnation you deal with all four of them. The astral body is that which you experience when you are not within this physical body but are in the spirit plane between lifetimes and experiencing only the emotional, mental, and spiritual bodies. These two—the physical and astral bodies—are what you are used to referring to here as a third-density being.

Slowly the emotional body drops away. To say it in your terminology, you graduate from this third density. There is still somewhat of an emotional body, but there is no reaction to that body. It is merely felt as that cloud passing by that I spoke of last night. And you do not need to do anything but observe that emotional mass appear and disappear. As you move beyond the causal plane, the emotional body drops off completely and there are only the mental and spiritual bodies. Here the being is learning a sense of wisdom for which thought is still necessary.

Yes, there are two kinds of wisdom: that which comes from the heart and that which comes from the mind. As Q'uo has just pointed out, they are simply two levels of the same way of knowing. Slowly this mental body also drops away as it is no longer needed, as you move back into that core heart of the Creator of which Q'uo has just

---

[7] Robert Bly, ed., *The Kabir Book: Forty-Four of the Ecstatic Poems of Kabir* (Boston, MA: Beacon Press, 1977), poem 43.

spoken. Thus, the being moving into what you refer to as seventh density moves more purely to being the pure spiritual body, which is the soul. That is all the soul is: the spiritual body with all the rest, not discarded, because that implies an aversion, but simply fallen away, as you shed your clothes when the sun is hot on a summer day.

Coming back to where you are now, in this third density, as you begin to understand, no one of these four bodies is more mature or less mature than another. Each body serves its purpose. What you experienced this morning when you felt the heart open so completely and then experienced fear of that opening was neither the isolated mental nor emotional body.

Fear is an emotion, and fear comes from many places. It is not that the emotional body is less mature but that the emotional body is less accepted; that while at some deep levels of meditation you are aware of the usefulness of moving beyond conceptual thought, you do not condemn yourself for thinking. But you condemn yourself often for feeling, until habitually you build up a fear of the emotions. Essentially, you have backed yourself into that tunnel we have talked about so often.

I have talked in another channeling[8] of a tunnel, a very safe place. You are comfortable in this womb. Perhaps you will wish to think of it as a cave with only one end open, and across that end you have put strands of cobwebs to protect yourself from that which you feel will harm you, to protect yourself from another's anger and also your own anger, to protect yourself from the pain of feeling separation and to protect yourself from grief. And each strand that you have put up has served a purpose, because you felt you needed that protection. And yet, it is dark in your tunnel and on the outside it is light; and you have reached a place where you want to allow in that light. Can you feel the brutality if one were to reach in a hand and tear out all of

---

[8] Barbara Brodsky and Aaron, November 21, 1990; unpublished; available from Deep Spring Center for Meditation and Spiritual Inquiry, 3003 Washtenaw Avenue, Suite 2, Ann Arbor, MI 48104; archives.deepspring.org.

those cobwebs, all of those strands, and how you would cower in terror against tearing all of that protection away?

Yet gently and with full awareness, you can reach out, lift one strand at a time, and examine it. What is this fear? Have I still need of this? Whence is it arising? How long must I hold on to it? Seeing a strand, perhaps of anger or greed, one notes how that greed or anger arises out of fear and out of a sense of separation. One sees the ways that fear has enhanced the sense of separation. The self, which then perceives itself to be separate, feels a need to protect and allows the arising of anger or greed as its protection: "What if my needs are not met? What if I'm harmed?"

But this can only come from a sense of self and other self. Where there is no separation, there can be no anger. Can you begin to see how fear leads to that sense of separation that then leads to the first distortion of self-awareness? This distortion provokes one not yet fully immersed in separation but experiencing a distinction between self and other self to cultivate that distortion that first allows fears. Observing, you can begin to understand how this process works in yourself. Then as fear or separation arise, you can gently lift that strand of anger from where it blocks the light, look at it, and ask yourself, "Do I still need this or am I able now to put it aside?" Always do this with gentleness and never with force, never asking the self to be what it is not ready to be, but accepting the self as it is so that the being will always be challenged, but always simultaneously accepted and loved. In this way the emotional body is not something with which one fights, but is part of your integral, harmonious self.

You asked me to speak further about the distortion of service to others that grows out of fear in the emotional body. When there is a sense of the self's not being adequate so that there comes a feeling of needing to do something to prove oneself adequate, to soothe that pain, then the service in itself becomes distorted. You experienced this morning the love of that spirit that was known in his last incarnation as Jesus and you felt the strength of that loving energy flowing through with absolutely no distortion.

Last night I said that in human form it is impossible to allow the energy to flow completely distortion-free. This is because as soon as there is a concept of service to others, there is a self and an other. And thus, we come back to that fact that self-awareness is a distortion. Ra calls it the first distortion and I would agree with this. Excuse me, Ra calls free will the first distortion—potentiation of an active Creator whose nature is Logos or love.[9] But in order to love, there must be that which is loved; and that takes self-awareness, so in a sense we are saying the same thing in a different way.

If you will, picture a river flowing with an absolutely clean and sandy bed and with a strong current. Somewhere down the stream place one stone, just large enough to break the surface, and see the ripples that break around it. Let us call that first stone self-awareness. The current flows around it with its full force, and yet there is a small distortion in that current. From self-awareness grow so many doubts and fears: comparisons; competitiveness; and thoughts like, "Am I good enough? Am I acceptable and loved?" Suddenly we have a whole load of stones thrown into this river and now the water flows through in many ripples. There is still a current. But if you were to float a stick downstream of that very first stone, it would float smoothly down the stream. If you put a stick just upstream of that first stone and watch it, you see how it deviates around that stone and loses some of its direction and thrust. Now let that stick move downstream to where all these stones are, and see how it swirls around in little whirlpools.

Thus, when you are lost in a distortion of any sort, your energy does not flow freely. In the meditation you felt that entity known as Jesus's energy flowing unimpeded and enhancing all energy that came into it. All separating emotions, even love, create distortion and turbulence. The mental body quiets that turbulence through reason, and yet that reason separates the entity from the strength of the river's flow. It is as if one, seeing all those rocks in the river's bed, erected a

---

[9] Don Elkins, Jim McCarty, and Carla Rueckert, *The Law of One, Book II* (Louisville, KY: L/L Research, 1984), pp. 2–3, 54.

dam within the rocks, diverting the water so that there was no longer turbulence from the rocks but impeding the full flow of the water.

Each distortion must be worked with back and forth, always with gentleness and compassion, always asking the self: *What am I being offered to learn? How can I work with these fears, these forces within me, more skillfully? How can I gently begin to lift out each stone, to move to that perfect awareness so that there is no separation and so that this self that is aware is not a separate self but only part of the force of the universe?* The fully evolved soul returns to the fire whence it came. But it returns, not as the tiny ember that it began, but as a brilliant sun in itself, enhancing and strengthening the power of that original sun.

Do you wish me to speak about this further or are there other questions?

Barbara: I have no more questions about this, Aaron, thank you. I don't know if others do or not.

Kim: With regard to working skillfully with anger, I understand the concept of noticing, feeling, and allowing anger to pass as it comes up in the day-to-day life. I'm not sure what to do with the angers that have been there for many years—the angers that I can tap into at any moment just by recalling any of many situations. In each case, I suppose the anger has to do with my feeling that I have been wronged somehow. And I know that what I need to do is to be able to accept and forgive myself fully, as well as whatever other person is involved in the situation. But this seems to me to be the work of an entire lifetime, at least, and leaves me feeling pretty hopeless about dealing in any significant way with those long-term angers. Can you comment on this?

Aaron: You say that this seems to be the work of a lifetime and that leaves you feeling hopeless. And yet, this is the healing for which you took birth, because in past lifetimes you have held anger in much the same way, learning slowly to let it go, reaching an understanding that anger is just anger. And now you have arrived at a point where you understand the usefulness of moving beyond that anger, of letting it drop away, and it *is* the work of a lifetime; yet you are working on it and making progress. You are in that tunnel that I just spoke of with all these strands across. And when present anger arises, you have learned skillfully to look at that anger and not necessarily need to attach it as a strand across the entrance. But there are still all those strands from the past.

I suggest that it would be useful in meditation, as you feel the courage and readiness, to lift each strand and examine it. Do not start with the heaviest ones. Build up your strength with the lighter ones. As you recall some moment of intense anger where the self felt attacked in some way by another self and felt that it was wronged, just gently look at that strand and the feelings that came, asking yourself, "What is this anger? Why is it here? What was its function? Do I still need it, or am I ready to set it down?" Always know that if you feel vulnerable and afraid, you may put it back again into place if you need to, trusting that as you grow you will have less and less need to do that.

Each of you is here to learn to love yourself and others more fully, to learn faith and love. The anger is quite simply one of your learning tools. It is very easy to love unconditionally in a situation where there is nothing that arises to provoke any feeling but love. But how do you love when you are provoked to defend yourself, when that separation arises? Can you continue to love when noticing the fears, when noticing the separation and how anger arises from that? As you become more skillful with doing that with each small resentment that arises in your present life, you will find the faith and love to go back to loving in the moments of larger resentment.

There is one more thing here. You say you know this is what you need to do. I feel a sense of judgment in that. There is some sense of your feeling that until you do, you are not quite adequate or there is something wrong with you that needs to be corrected. You do not need to do this; rather, as you grow you allow yourself to do this. Can you see the difference? Allow yourself to be where you are, always reaching for the next step, but reaching out of a sense of love, not out of a sense of despising that which is. It is essential to treat all of this within you with love, because your contempt will only further enhance the sense of separation and further fragment the self into what is acceptable and what is unacceptable.

Do you understand and do you have further questions?

Kim: Thank you, Aaron, I think I understand. I may have more questions at a later time.

Aaron: I would like briefly to add one thing, which is to emphasize that I share the concern of what Q'uo has said about patience. Can you picture yourselves swimming up the stream in a river? You know that eventually you will come to the source of that river. But for now you are just enjoying the swimming, noticing the brightly colored fish that swim beneath you, feeling the coolness of the water and the sun on your back, stopping to rest when you need to and then swimming again. As you move further upstream the river begins to narrow a little, and suddenly you start to have a sense that this river is coming from someplace and that perhaps you will get to its source.

Now, you stop your strokes and look up, wondering how much further. But as you stop there, the current pushes you back and you lose your momentum. You start to swim again. The closer you get to the source, the fresher the water feels and the stronger the energy of that source. When you start to look around and say, "How much further? I can't wait to get there," you lose some of the joy that you had before of just enjoying the water, enjoying that life in the water and the sensations of it on your body. This happens to all beings as they come closer to the source. It is not a fault, simply something of which you must be aware so that you can begin to notice the impatience and allow yourself to return to the joy of this incarnation, knowing that yes, you do come closer and closer to moving beyond the need for rebirth, to knowing your true self in a deeper sense and connecting with the source of that love and light in a deeper sense. But that will be when it will be, and this is now. Cherish this now. It will not come again.

As there are no more questions, I wish to thank you all for sharing your loving presence with me. I cherish each and every one of you and wish for each of you that you could grow to cherish yourselves as do those loving spirits and friends that surround you. That is all.

Session 3

Weekend I, Part 3 of 5
(This session was preceded by a period of tuning and meditation.)

Group question: We all have questions about fear. Barbara has fear of responsibility she is not able to meet, fear of the unknown, and fear of going beyond her prior limits. Carla and Jim fear being unable to measure up to their own standards, ability, and potential. Kim does not wish to rely on outer authority but fears she is not equal to the task of establishing her own inner authority. Would you please speak to these fears or to fear itself?

(Barbara channeling)

Aaron: I think it would be useful for each of us to speak for some time and then to relax from that rigidity a bit so that we can speak back and forth. This is almost a ritual form of communication. I do not wish to impose this on Q'uo. If that is acceptable to Q'uo it is acceptable to me. That is all.

(A pause while Aaron waits for any objection. There is none.)

You are asking about fear, and I do prefer this idea of a dialogue to individual monologue. So, rather than trying to give you a half-hour, comprehensive view of the subject, I am going to talk a bit about what seem to me to be your deepest issues and then pass it on and let it return to me again. I feel we will learn more that way.

Each of you has different understandings about fear and questions that come from a different need, a different place, so that we start with a very basic question, "What is fear?" Not even "How does it arise?" or "Where does it come from?" but "What is it?" Essentially it is an emotion that also touches on the physical and mental bodies, not just the emotional body; and finally it affects the spiritual body. So it is a feeling that totally enfolds you.

Fear is rather paralyzing to many of you. It distorts your way of seeing. It creates confusion and chaos within you. Because of the turbulence that it creates within you, it easily moves out of control. It is even harder than anger to step back from to get some perspective because of the ways it paralyzes you. As with any emotion, it is not fear that is the problem but your reaction to it. Fear in itself is just a mind/body experience, but it does lead to all these reactions within the physical body and in the spiritual body as well.

I have left out the mental body in talking about reactions to fear, because fear does not provoke a reaction in the mental body so much as it grows out of both the emotional and mental bodies. The emotional body feels the fear. The mental body in a sense creates the fear, unless it is a purely physical fear in response to a physical stimulus, such as a fear of falling as you feel yourself falling.

The mental body originates the fear. It is then picked up by the emotional body. For example, when you are in a car about to crash, at that moment you are safe; but you move from that present moment to an image of what you perceive will happen in the future. You feel yourself skidding and suddenly you envision yourself folded against that tree beside the road—an image that comes from the mental body—or you move back to the past, to your past experiences with a similar situation. Again, fear arises from the mental body; so the mind creates that situation where fear may enter, by moving out of the present and into the past or future. Then the emotional body picks up on that fear. Fear then moves on to the physical body, this being such a quick process that I would not expect you to be able to break it down. But there is immediate physical tension and at that moment the fear enters. Fear cannot coexist with love. Along with love I also place those experiences of faith and trust. At the moment when fear is that strong, the spiritual body loses all sense of trust that this will be okay.

Let us speak about this more specifically. Firstly, fear is never in this present moment but always in the past or the future. Think about this. Put yourself again in that skidding car. It is just skidding. You may be fine. Can you see your mind moving to that tree and the collision with it, or your mind moving backward to the last time you skidded? Can you see how you have moved out of the present moment?

Let us take a purely emotional situation. Somebody is walking toward you and his face looks very angry. The last time that you had an encounter with that person, he raged and snarled at you; he led you to feel small and humiliated and so both anger and fear arise. The fear is not based on this present moment, but only on your past experience.

Let us move from this to Carla, Jim, and Kim's questions. Looking at Kim's question of fear of her own inner authority versus an outer authority, of trusting herself, I remind you again that there is no fear in the present moment. Kim, when you are feeling this, can you take a deep breath and ask yourself, *Where is this fear?* Begin to gain that perspective that allows you to know that you are creating an outcome if you act in a certain way or remembering an outcome when you did act in a certain way; but that each moment is fresh and you are not the same being who was in that situation before. You have learned not to trust your own inner authority, and now you are trying to learn to trust. And yet there is a sense of wanting to know that you are right before you claim that authority; there is that in you that says, *Maybe I'm not right,* and gets caught up in those fears and angers. Then it moves to resentment of that other being who feels more self-assurance that it is right. So you have fear and anger mixed together here: anger that you do not have that same self-assurance, resentment against that being for its assurance, and a fear that maybe you are not right. The fear itself diminishes the sense of inner knowing.

Carla, when you spoke about your concern that your work would be adversely affected by pain medicine tonight, you were not remembering that it is not the medicine that prevents clear channeling but a fear that the medicine might prevent clear channeling. Can you see that difference? You are perfectly capable of repeating the concepts you receive under almost any circumstance down to near unconsciousness, because you have trained yourself so well to do this. But you are capable of allowing it to flow through you only when there is love.

Again, love and fear cannot coexist. As soon as fear enters, and a sense of doubt, it diminishes the ability to channel clearly.

Here we come back to your question, Carla and Jim (I know I have not answered the other question in depth, but I do want to avoid a long monologue here and would prefer that all six of us speak. I will gladly speak more on this upon request.) You fear you are not measuring up to your potential. Can you see how fear itself invites such perceived failure? I believe you understand; and the question is, how do you work with that fear? There is nothing special you need to do. You cannot take that fear and fling it away from you. But you can notice it and reach out to it with love. This fear is the child that comes to you, saying, "There's a big dog outside and I'm afraid." And you open the door and pat the dog and see that it is friendly. You might reassure the child, saying, "The dog is friendly," but you don't belittle the child's fear. You do not say, "It's stupid to be afraid." But that is what you do to your-selves and as soon as you do that, the fear solidifies.

When you embarrass the child into going back out, it may finally reach out and pat the dog, but it will not get over its fear. When you hug the child and say, "I see how afraid you are. It's okay to be afraid of big dogs. Would you like me to walk outside with you?"—this is not pushing the child to pat the dog or do anything special, just reas-suring it with your love. The child will feel that calmness and begin to touch its own fear with love. As fear falls away enough, the child can naturally reach out and pat the dog.

Can you apply that to yourselves? Your dog here is your potential and all the ideas that you have for yourselves. As with the big dog, it may feel overwhelming! You are truly, each, unlimited; and there is no way that in human form you can achieve all that is possible for you. Can you accept that? You are not asked to be perfect, just to do the best you can do. But when you relate to that fear with criticism, saying, *I shouldn't feel afraid. I should know my unlimitedness. I should be able to do anything,* you can see how that solidifies the fear and prevents you from acting.

You know this. You know that love is the answer, and yet in a sense it becomes an intellectual mantra: "Love is always the answer." But what does it mean to say that love is the answer when the heart is feeling fear? How much more lovingly can you relate to the fear?

There is much more that I could say about fear here. I would prefer that others speak and come back to me. If you have specific questions about what I have said, I would be glad to answer them. If Q'uo wishes to speak now, that is fine with me; or if any of you wish to share your own ideas about fear, that would also be appropriate. That is all.

(Carla channeling)

Q'uo: It is with joy at the insights of the one known as Aaron, as well as in the love and in the light of the one infinite Creator, that we, known as Q'uo, greet you.

Let us look at fear from the perspective of deep generalization. This does not mean that the generalization always applies, but it may be a tool that the seeker may use. Fear is an intensification based on the illusion of separation. Were all beings aware that they were one, the motives and circumstances of behavior would be plain to see. If the Akashic Records[10] were known, people might well choose to enjoy themselves more, being courageous enough to accept death as an ending to an incarnation. Although death is inevitable, most entities do not reckon with this.

Much fear is caused by a need to control the environment in a way helpful to the physical animal that houses the consciousness of each of you. This animal has a need to survive, which predisposes consciousness in manifestation toward control over the environment in order to obtain comfort, relaxation, and a feeling of security. Thus, fear is a perfect example of that which we would call a negatively polarizing thought. It assumes separation and usually hinges upon gaining or keeping control of that situation.

---

[10] Akasha is the space element. It holds the Akashic Field within which we find the Akashic Records. These contain complete human experience, personal and of the entire cosmos.

Session 3

Let us examine this instrument; for though it is not aware of fear, yet it acts in fear. The red-ray center of this instrument's body is very strong. However, the instrument feared it would not remember to be kind to its animal, as this instrument is always energetic emotionally, mentally, and spiritually. Thus, through fear of a possible outcome, through fear of losing control of a vital piece of paraphernalia, this instrument restrained itself.[11] This can be called good judgment or it can be seen to be the fear of losing control of a detail of behavior that is supposed or presumed to be a life-or-death matter. Consciously the instrument feels no fear, yet there is enough respect for probable outcomes that the entity does indeed fear and reacts in as loving and helpful a way as possible to the animal that honors it by serving as its manifestation in form.

Look at fear and ask, *What am I trying to control?* It is well to know that it is only an illusion that we ever are in control of anything. Not that entities are not free to make choices, but that the reality that eludes the illusion you enjoy is that all are parts of one flowing fountainhead of an active, creative, beautiful, and living ocean of light. All flow into each other, through each other, through the self. Whatever condition the flow experiences, this condition is experienced not only as harmonious or aesthetically beautiful, but perfect. Each of you, as a spark, perceives the self as imperfect and at risk. That stops your spark of light from joining in shared heart as one.

The only control entities have is not in circumstances, but in choosing skillful actions to deal with the catalyst that has been given. Thusly, if you see, hear, and analyze mentally where the being is attempting to control and in what way, the start is made. However, it must be continually grounded in constant reaffirmation of faith and an awareness that one has no control except when one dedicates oneself to that highest and best occupation one may personally offer. We feel that we reach out to each other; but in reality we reach in to free ourselves from the

---

[11] Carla was loosely tying her hands down so that she would not damage her shoulders by gesturing thoughtlessly, as they were very flared-up with arthritic pain.

fear of an unknown, only partially manifested other self or from a condition or substance with which one has experienced loss of control previously. The true freedom is that of the devoted and absolutely faithful seeker.

We are those of Q'uo, and we open the sextalogue once again. We leave this instrument in love and in light.

(Barbara channeling)

Aaron: I find it wonderful to talk like this, in that Q'uo's thoughts expand my own, and I would assume the reciprocal is true.

There are two things that Q'uo has spoken of that I would like to take to a different space. One is the relationship between fear and separation. There is never fear in the spiritual body of a self in relation to that self. The fear is always of a perceived other self.

There are two kinds of separation that occur here. One is the illusion of being separate so that there is a self and an other, and one is the separation from the self. Let us address these separately. Let us firstly come back to that being approaching you with an angry face and the sense of fear that perhaps that being will attack or harm you in some way. There is, of course, the need to protect the self. As Q'uo has pointed out, this physical body desires to continue itself. Yet that being approaching you is not an other; it is just an aspect of the one heart and mind as you are, an aspect of the Creator as you are. Then this slips into fear because one perceives another about to harm it. One way to approach it in a more skillful and creative way would be to remind the self that this is an angry aspect of yourself and to treat that angry aspect that approaches you as you would treat your own anger. If you have learned to deal more skillfully with your own anger, you know that just as your own anger cannot harm you, another being's anger cannot harm you. It is the illusion of separation that creates the defensiveness that escalates the anger into a specter of harm.

We come back here to the visualization I asked you to make yesterday evening of love as concentric circles, and of fear and anger as sharp points emerging. When you can see those sharp points emerging and know that this is not an other but simply an aspect of yourself, that it is not that being's anger or fear but just anger or fear, you can remain enfolded by those concentric circles and send them out to that angry being. Each sharp point hits these softening circles that you send out. As soon as you pull back and begin that sense of separation that allows you to feel attacked, then you begin to send out your own sharp points. From my point of view, I simply see a sword fight of light—sharp points are stabbing at each other, and nothing exists to soften them.

Secondly, what about the separation from the self? The self, the deepest self, is love. The Pure Spirit Body can feel nothing other than love. When fear arises there is always a separation within the self. Here I am simply explaining more deeply what I introduced earlier in this evening's session—that separation from one's self creates a fragmentation, with the spirit body sending out love and the emotional and mental bodies feeling need. The feeling, then, is one of great distress to that self, because that of itself that knows oneness and knows love as the deepest truth is imprisoned in a way, torn out and separated. The being is cut asunder from its spiritual body. When you are separated from that sense of love, such strong doubt arises in you that it becomes very hard to get back to that love. You know what is happening within you, but it is so hard to stop it.

This, above any other time, is where the being must cherish itself. As soon as fear is noted, the first step must be to enfold that frightened being with love, thus reducing fragmentation so that the being can come back into the center of itself and begin to feel again its connection with the Creator and with all things and know that it cannot be harmed.

Often you think of fear as being a useful emotion in that it protects you. You are crossing a street and suddenly see a truck coming toward you. There is that instant of terror, of "What if it hits me?" And you move quickly. It is true that the physical body responds to that fear in a chemical manner that allows a fast reaction. But fear is not necessary and in fact works counter to the most appropriate reaction. Let me explain: while it is true that the being does move out of the way of the truck and that you would not want to stand there in the middle of the street and send love to that fear when the appropriate action is to move, the movement does not grow out of fear but out of love that respects the physical body enough to preserve it. Fear is paralyzing, and love is enabling. You cannot take the time to analyze danger. The physical being must act to preserve itself in a certain way. But this does not need to be a matter of fear, simply a matter of wisdom; and here again, wisdom grows out of love.

Q'uo spoke of Carla's fear and the sense of separation. The attempt to preserve the physical body through a sense of separation enhances the separation. Will you look at this carefully, each of you, in some example that suits your own needs and see that it is not necessary to respond with fear to preserve the body? When you know your oneness with all things, truly know that there is no separate self, then each time that you see separation emerging, you can remind yourself that this is the voice of fear and allow that illusion of separateness to fall away. It is not expected that the incarnate entity will always be able to keep that in its mind; and yet the closer you can come to that, the less paralyzing your fear will be, and the more freedom you will find.

There is one more thing that I would add, which is that fear can be balanced by lovingkindness to oneself and others. This is a quality in the self that can be nurtured. It is helpful to remind oneself each time one feels fear, that one is fearing a delusion when one sees part of the self as a separate self. You may acknowledge that delusion, and then send love not only to the self that is fearing but to that which is feared. Beyond that, begin to notice all the times one does not feel fear. When one is in a situation that is in some way threatening, often one responds with love to that situation. Truly, each of you do that far more than you respond with fear or anger or separation. And you do not notice that response. It goes by. But it is a small, tender sprout, that of lovingkindness; and it must be nurtured. Can you begin to bring your attention to each time you respond in a loving way to a situation that might goad you toward separation? You do this not to pat yourself pridefully on the back for that loving response but to nurture that sprout of love within you and encourage it to blossom.

There is more that I could say about fear, but would prefer to end here to allow Q'uo or any of the others of you to speak with either questions or comments, as you feel appropriate. That is all.

(Carla channeling)

Q'uo: I greet each once again in joy, love, and light.

And how shall seekers learn to bloom into adventurous and fearless citizens of the universe? One good resource is one's own imperfect memory; for fears upon the catalyst of an outer happenstance are merely the top layer, in most cases, of what could be seven or seventy times seven layers of similar and repetitive situations that ended in a perceptive judgment that this situation is frightening. The lines of genealogy of fear go back like the long listings of who sired whom in your holy works. The most recent fear can be helpfully worked with by gracefully and accurately assessing the present fear and all it connotes, and by comparing it to previous similar experiences. The pile of repetitive experiences may eventually begin to be seen as a repeating pattern. And as one peels away the onionskin layers of memory, one comes at last to the initial occasion of fear.

We may not be able to forgive the self for its present fear; however, we surely may be able to gaze upon the helpless infant and see with compassion the utter and complete dependence of this helpless consciousness. The infants have chosen parents that shall offer them the fears; that is, the unmet desires that will not be met. Talking is out of the question. Writing is out of the question. Even independent movement is unthinkable to the newly born. It routinely experiences areas of sheer terror. Since the infant is in a very small universe within the illusion, the fear is deeply rooted because of the absoluteness of its lack of ability to control situations in order that it may be clean, full of nutrition, and comfortable.

We do not encourage the exercise of moving backward to discover the root of a present fear as any kind of parlor game or diversion. When each fear is followed to its root, that root is as strong as a lifetime of distortion in recurrent patterns can make it.

When one has found the root of that fear, one is then able to become aware of the portion of the identity that has been lost. However, like wearing an old shoe that never fit, entities tend to accept fear stoically. There is far more use in full and clear communication of the self. Each self has an observer that is a portion of the self and integrated with it. It is an art to avoid doing violence to the beingness of the self when one is rooting out a portion of that identity. Thusly, it must be done courteously and honorably, as the one known as Aaron has said, as the gentle stripping away of any minuscule portion of the blockage that is no longer needed. Thusly, one is able to have spiritual cleansing without attendant violence to the integrated mind, body, and spirit.

Perhaps the greatest anguish of all to each self is the inevitable iniquity that is part of the experience of being in what you call human manifestation.

I am Q'uo, and once again we leave this instrument in love and in light, that all others may feel free to collaborate upon this most important topic.

(Barbara channeling)

Aaron: With thanks to my spirit friend and brother/sister self, I would like to speak to this idea Q'uo has raised about the infant and the terror that it feels. It would seem that a sense of terror is inbuilt into the human experience and one must then ask, "Why?" If one cannot avoid the experience of fear as a human, then one must assume there is a reason why that is given. And perhaps looking deeper into that reason will help one to accept fear in a more loving way. Come back here to the thought that it is not the fear that is the problem, but your relationship to the fear. The infant's relationship to fear is necessarily one of aversion. It has needs, and if those needs are not met immediately, as Q'uo pointed out, it has no way of expressing this pain beyond its crying. And so it learns to fear and also to perceive itself as separate, because as long as it is nurtured and never feels the rising of a need, there is no separation from the mother. But each time that need arises and is not met instantly, it begins to perceive itself in this illusion as a separate self; and that self solidifies.

Of course, my dear ones, this is necessary to the human experience or it would not be given. If you incarnated and this veil that screens you out of full spiritual knowing did not drop into place, if this illusion of separation did not happen, then you would not learn on this earthly plane. There would be no difference between this plane and the spirit plane except that you would be in a body. But to be here in a body with no illusion of separation and with full spiritual awareness would mean that you could not learn the lessons that this incarnation is meant to teach you. Can you see that?

So I would ask you to begin to embrace fear as a gift that is meant to teach you. When it arises, rather than struggling with it and hating it, say a small "Thank you" to it. Let your fear talk to you of oneness and not of separation. Let it be a reminder to come back to that core where you are part of the one heart and the one mind, rather than experiencing fear as a sword that severs you from your heart and mind. Treat your fear with love and gratitude for its teaching.

Are there specific questions that any of you have, related to anything that has been said or has not been said? That is all.

Carla: Aaron, I see myself as a perfectionist and see the fear that comes from not being able to live up to my own ideal. That would seem to suggest that being a perfectionist is not wise; however, I have found that unless one aims for the ideal, one never begins to approach it. I don't mean this in the sense of brutally urging myself to do what I obviously cannot. It is more an existential question, apart from any situation, as to the value of the perfectionism that is at once my greatest helper in living a godly life and certainly my most devastating vice: self-judgment. I see I am not flowing in the stream by asking continually to be my best, for I am always watching myself. Yet this attitude has helped me tremendously in that in disciplining myself I seem to have been able to become accepting at a deeper and deeper level of compassion. Would you wish to comment upon this, Aaron? I would be glad to hear it. Thank you.

Aaron: My dear one, this quality that you call perfectionism can come from two different places. It can be a voice of fear or of love. As you have pointed out, it helps you to realize your ideal, to be all of what you can be and to hold that in front of you. What you are holding in front of you is the soul, which is unlimited and perfect. You see the image of that perfection and know that while the physical manifestation cannot reach that full perfection, yet in the true sense it has already reached it. You are already all that you will ever be and always have been. Here we get into a question of simultaneous time, and I will not go deeply into that now. You are all familiar with the general concept of which I speak. But the self that holds that ideal in front of you is no different than the self that kneels down in prayer before an image of the Christ, understanding the depth of that being's love and compassion and ability to forgive, and knowing that one has the potential in oneself and can achieve that potential as it works at it through many lifetimes, to reach eventually—not in this density but further along the way—that level of pure, unconditional love.

Then there is that perfectionism that comes from the voice of fear. This does not hold an image up as our ideal, but rather, it is a derogatory voice. It speaks of nonacceptance. It speaks of the history of the being, both in that incarnation and in other incarnations where so many times there has been defeat; so many times there has been nonacceptance by the self and by perceived other selves.

A voice of perfection speaks of eventual success because it knows, fully knows, that it is already perfect. The other voice speaks of failure, because it sees all the places where the physical manifestation is limited. So, as with anything else in your life, it is not the quality of perfectionism that is the problem, but where that is coming from or which voice is speaking.

This is not true just of perfectionism, but of any quality in your life. A desire to serve comes to mind here. We have spoken of the concept in the past few days that this desire can come from a voice of love or a voice of fear. It is the voice of fear that distorts the ability and fragments the self, further enhancing the sense of helplessness and limitedness. It is the voice of love that opens the self, that inspires, leading the being to be all it can be and touching the deep sense of acceptance and compassion when that human can do no more because it is human.

Would you have me speak further on this or have I answered your question?

Carla: No, thank you, Aaron. This is sufficient.

Aaron: My friends, you each contain a great deal of wisdom within you. I understand that when there are these channeling sessions you are anxious to hear our thoughts, and yet your own thinking would prompt you to a greater depth as well. So, it is not only questions but also comments that are appropriate. That is all.

(Carla channeling)

Q'uo: We dwell in love and light and would sculpt the final thought of this extremely enjoyable session of working.

The ones known as Barbara and Carla this day were speaking about the concept of prayer pills. This concept was visualized as a simple recognition and respect for conditions perceived, the particular condition being the one known as Barbara's clear awareness of outer-plane contact, which is unlike inner-plane contact. Inner-plane contact is the privilege of only those teachers that have incarnated upon this planet at one time. Such contact cannot harm the self, as it is within the energy web of that particular consciousness' field. At some level inner-planes contact has been accepted personally by the self or it would not come into manifestation.

There are many outer-plane influences upon entities. For instance, the astrology that many use is a way to become more aware of circumstances, although, because the exact moment when the soul enters the physical vehicle must remain unknown, astrology will remain specifically inaccurate and is only helpful in mapping out the topology or neighborhood where catalyst is now occurring.

No matter what the personal situation may be, the tools of prayer—contemplation, meditation, inspiration, and all of those intuitional qualities—are of much aid. The outer-plane confluences are from stars, galaxies, and, in truth, any external consciousness that has been perceived.

When affirming and praying, one is able to experience fearlessness, for one is involved in worship; and all else may be put aside for that moment of worship. It has been suggested to pray without ceasing. This is excellent advice, for the outer-plane entities that speak through instruments such as this one are cosmic energies that influence the self. A continual "medication" of meditation in ceaseless remembrance, love, and praise of the infinite One places the conscious awareness in a state far more resonant with unity than an unprayerful state would. The "medication" of meditation improves its ability skillfully to perceive.

Respect and honor the need for heavenly food of the self. If positive and negative outer-plane entities rain upon all alike, like the cosmic influences that they are, and if free will is to be maintained, the self must be independent and thoughtful. For above all, fear is uninteresting.

May you each find the gentleness and tenderness to re-create and reexperience that helpless and brutalized infant whose space has been invaded again and again, whose needs are not often adequately met in some area or another. Be gentle with this and patient, and remember to remember the one infinite Creator, whose nature is limitless love and whose every manifestation is light. We greet you and offer benediction in all that there is—the love and the light of the one infinite Creator.

May we of Q'uo speak for the one known as Aaron in thanking each for the passionate love of the Creator and of service to others that has called us here and given us an incredible opportunity to triangulate upon a central question. We find working with Aaron a delight and are humble before this entity. We offer our blessings and our love, our peace and our joy, our love and our light. All that there is, is that condition in which we leave you, never truly leaving, but merely receding so that the raindrops of our positivity may not fall upon the unprepared heart. Adonai. Adonai. I am Q'uo.

Session 4

Weekend I, Part 4 of 5
(This session was preceded by a period of tuning and meditation.)

Group question: Please talk about accepting and not judging the self, concepts of what we think we should do, and how this is involved in fear. How do we accept ourselves and avoid the "shoulds"?

(Barbara channeling)

Aaron: I greet you each with my love in the beauty of this new day.

"I should" is a voice of fear. I would like to explain that further. Last night we spoke of the ways in which the "I should," that sense of perfectionism, comes from a yearning toward the ideal; but it also may come from fear. When it comes from fear there is a sense of pushing the self, forcing the self, rather than allowing the self to express its own radiance. It is rather like bringing in a flower, a soft bud, and brutally pulling the petals open, as if one could force it to blossom in that way. But it cannot be forced. It must be allowed by leaving it in the nurturing sunshine of one's love.

Yesterday Barbara was reading some material by Ram Dass. In it he tells the story of how he met with a Buddhist teacher who suggested that they do a meditation together, expanding outward. After a few minutes the teacher said to him, "You're still trying." And Ram Dass said, "Yes, I'm still trying to expand outward." The teacher said, "Don't try to expand outward, just expand outward." Do you see the difference? By trying, you create the conditions where it becomes very difficult to allow. This does not mean that no effort is required, but the effort is that which flows through the being in perfect harmony rather than the effort that comes from a distortion of self-will.

There is a piece of writing by the third Zen patriarch (Seng-Ts'an) that speaks of quieting the mind. He notes that in your effort to become quiet, you simply generate more activity. I am sure this is clear to all of you. The question then becomes, "How does one quiet the mind or move beyond the dualistic, conceptual mind to reach that state of total merging with the Eternal?" Why not allow it? Why have any "I shoulds"? You do not need to achieve or attain anything. There is nothing to attain. You are already there. What you are doing is allowing the perfect flow of energy through you until you come to that understanding of the knowledge that you are already there. You must begin to understand that you are not moving yourself from "this" to "that," but simply knowing that you have always been "that" and can be nothing else.

You have heard me say many times that love and fear cannot coexist at the point where you fully understand that you have always been "that," even though sometimes you act as if you were not. In that place there is total harmony with all that is. When you are trying to become "that," there is disharmony and there is a state of fear. We spoke last night of the correlation between fear and separation and why one outgrows that pattern. The first occurrence is a state that recognizes self-awareness, and out of that self-awareness comes the fear that there is something that one is not, something to be attained. And out of that fear arises a stronger sense of separation. Can you see that as long as there is something to be attained, the being feels some fear as to whether or not it is good enough or worthy enough of attaining that? But when the being fully trusts that it already is all that it has ever been and ever will be, then it allows that fragile bud to open so that the full beauty of the flower becomes visible.

Allow me to speak a bit more specifically here. It is fine to speak of intellectually knowing that you are "that," but how does one keep that faith that allows one to move beyond fear? You are always in connection with the Divine. Several months ago Barbara was singing a song many times, early in the morning. The words were, "Seems like such a long time, Holy Spirit, waiting, since I've drawn your breath in, silent and all-pervading." As she sang that song over and over, she began to have that deep understanding that the breath of the Holy

Spirit is always present, that the Creator is always present, and that it is she that chooses to draw that breath in or not to draw that breath in. Then she understood how fear had separated her from choosing an affirmation of holiness.

To make such a choice, to fully affirm that oneness, is a responsibility. At times you feel you are not ready to commit yourself quite that far, and in fact you are not because you are here to learn. And in a sense that fear, first learned by the infant, is a part of your learning. There is nothing wrong with fear. Yes, it does seem to prevent you in some ways from fully reaching your potential, but that is a bit of an illusion. If you did not choose that fear as a catalyst, it would not be there. Fear is just fear. Can it be met with kindness? So, as you are able to turn around and relate more lovingly to that fear, you move yourself further on this path, reducing what I have called the specks or shadows from the self so that the self becomes more transparent and is more nearly ready to reach into higher levels of light.

In essence, what I am suggesting here is that you learn to trust that when fear arises, it is okay, that you do not need to flee from that fear but just to greet it with an openheartedness that says, "Oh, here's fear," and relate lovingly to fear, allowing it to bring whatever lessons it brings.

As with last night, there is much more that I could say here, but would prefer to have Q'uo speak first and let us pass this back and forth. That is all.

(Carla channeling)

Q'uo: I greet you in love and light and delight in the infinite Creator. We are most privileged to be called to your group once more and are enabled and ennobled by the sharing of our fallible opinions with the beautiful one known as Aaron.

Fear and the "shoulds": Where do these "shoulds" first occur? The voice of "should" is learned before the small entity has gained enough experience to count as irrelevant all suggestions that do not fall upon the heart with the feeling of truth and love. Thusly, the original voice of fear does not take into account the nature of the self or of how the self might relate to these parental and authoritarian instructions toward behavior and values.

At some point within the incarnation, most entities realize that these voices of "should" are a relic of childhood teachings. These teachings are generally intended to benefit the child and to create for it a knowledge of how to move through the intricate rituals of social behavior with the lubrication of appropriate, kindly thoughts, words, and actions. Thusly, the "shoulds" are valuable in dealing skillfully with the societal group at large. It is within the self and the self's perception of the self that the "shoulds" become less than benign.

The voices of childhood come without volition of the self; however, these voices, even though forgiven and no longer valid upon the outer, manifested entity's self, may well be internalized and become the influence that seems to the self as the voice of the self. Here we may see the ultimate separation of self from self. The self needs to be aware of its inner voices and to heal, by forgiveness and acceptance, those voices of the ultimate critic that gazes upon the self's manifested works with a jaundiced eye, looking not for what is right with this picture but what is wrong with this picture. This is a form of self-torture, a denigration of the self that is done quite innocently. To become mature, one does need to see those things within the self that are not innocent or authentic but rather judgmental and full of complex argumentation.

The amount of complexity experienced by the self is a good gauge of the self's authenticity. Authentic selfhood is simple, pure, and full; not reaching, not grasping, but content to do the best one can, as one can, however one can, and where one can. These voices, then, that judgmentally denigrate the self need to be recognized, accepted, named, and then forgiven. Yet how shall one forgive? The psychology, if you will, of redemption is the choosing of a perfect symbol, which is then able to forgive the self because its very nature is love, which always accepts any gift that is given.

It is no error that the one you know as Jesus was born into a mystical Jewish tradition. This tradition is chock-full of "shoulds." It is into this milieu that the one known as Jesus chose its incarnation in order that a fully literate Jewish scholar create the firm concept of constant redemption. How greatly does the Jewish tradition emphasize the positive value of fear. Concepts of kosher, of living ethically and humanely,[12] flood the Hebrew personality. Thusly, when the one known as Jesus said, "Your sins are forgiven you,"[13] He was speaking out of a background quite full of "shoulds" and judgment. Thusly, you may see that if the one known as Jesus could gaze at iniquity and instantaneously forgive it, then how indeed can one fail to forgive the self?

This method of becoming aware of redemption is roundabout and makes use of the illusion of separation. The Jesus that forgives is easier to hear as an other self speaking from a great distance of time than if Jesus the Christ were considered to be within the self, a part of the self, and ultimately the self. So, although all religions and spiritual systems of faith have much to recommend them in terms of finding allegories between their experiences and one's own, one must at last meet the self upon the plane of inner awareness. Then when "shoulds" and guilt arise, one may experience redemption, not only from an imagined other self but in a hearty, earthy, and substantive way as part of the process of love, which includes Love itself and therefore a lack of judgment. As the one known as Aaron said, each must bloom in its own time and ripen according to its own rhythms.

Yet entities usually do not perceive themselves as either virtuous and godly seed or beautiful blossom. It seems to the self that the self is anything *but* that beautiful seed that grows and blooms as one sees flowers and living trees express. This creates an instant bias toward

---

[12] As editors, we do not feel that the Q'uo intended to suggest that all concerns of living ethically are rooted in fear, but that attempting to codify all of life very strictly and completely is an effort rooted in fear. However, we also see the logic of attempting to codify ways of treating food, especially, as being needed in those early times in order to prevent illness.

[13] Luke 7:48 AV.

judgment. How can one learn to experience the self as beautiful, as godly, as perfect? We would let this question linger in the air as we allow the thread of this message to be elaborated by the one known as Aaron. We briefly leave you in love and light. We are those of Q'uo.

(Barbara channeling)

Aaron: I would like to address the question of the fear of moving beyond one's perceived limits, how one perceives those limits in the first place, and how it presents one with a choice: to let go and proceed, or to hold on to the perceived safety of shore and to the delusion of limits.

We start with the reality that you are unlimited and that within the illusion you perceive yourself as limited. While it is incidental to my main direction, I would point out that the perception of the self as limited is not an accident, but is a gift to help you to understand that you are unlimited. If there is never a sense of being limited but only the full understanding of the reality of your limitlessness, there would not be any inspiration or provocation for growth. So you hold up that ideal and want nothing more than to reach that ideal, noting the standards of your own behavior as well as the ways that you manifest in your life.

Because you are human you constantly fall short of the ideal, and yet you constantly ask yourself to let go of that edge onto which you were holding and strike out again to cross the sea of truth. It is a very courageous act, and yet you rarely give yourself notice of the courage. You perceive the fear that asks you to hold back, and you miss the beautiful bravery and love exhibited each time you take a new step. Does a child learn to walk with a parent who says, "Don't take another step, you'll fall!"—or with a parent who applauds each new step and picks that child up and takes away the hurt from the inevitable fall? How can you learn to pick yourselves up in this way? I believe this is the question Q'uo raised at the end of the preceding talk. Can you learn to cherish that self who so bravely tries again and again? Know that in this physical manifestation you cannot reach that perfection toward which the self yearns and finally come to an acceptance that reaching that perfection is not necessary. Rather, the yearning is a tool to build the strength and faith so that one begins to understand one's inner perfection.

When you make a choice and it turns out to be an unskillful choice and brings harm to another because there was fear or anger or greed as part of that choice, there is that in the being that declines responsibility for that choice, saying, "I couldn't help it." But as you evolve to the point that all in this group today have reached, you have learned that you are always responsible. Can you see how difficult this is? You used to be able to make your choices in a less judgmental way, though they were less skillful, and there was more anger and blame. But now you truly know that you are responsible; it feels like a burden and not a joy. The question, then, becomes how to make that sense of responsibility appear as it really is, a joy and a gift, so that even your unskillful choices can be met with love and not self-denigration.

This is where we come back to what I spoke of earlier, about allowing rather than forcing. When you come to a place of choice and understand the responsibility for making a skillful choice, and yet at times do not see the fear or greed or anger until it is too late, that distorts the choice so that another feels pain from it. When you come to that place and there is a sense of fear, of "What if I make the wrong choice?"—that fear shuts out the flow of energy, shuts out the flow of knowledge within the spirit. When you can come to that place with a prayer, opening yourself to all the love coming from within the self and coming to the self from without, then the voices of fear or anger or greed are heard as voiceless echoes. Then there is a joyousness about that responsibility because you see that it is leading you into being a mature being, into blossoming into the light.

Q'uo spoke of the separation of self from self. All of you, at one time or another, fail to notice the positivity within the self, the generosity, the patience and lovingkindness—all of those beautiful qualities that are part of this beautiful being that you are. Then you judge yourself and focus on all of the qualities that you judge as negative: the impatience, the anger, the greed. I would suggest that two practices may be helpful for you. One is to begin to notice more and more carefully all those times when you are loving and patient and kind, to begin to allow this beautiful self to move into the sunshine of its own love. This is not pride. It is reality. Also, it is useful, when one perceives oneself as love and will not allow that this is so, to ask why you will not allow it. Why does one pay attention only to those qualities that are perceived as negative? One must then begin to see that there is something in the self that wants to cling to those qualities that are felt as negative, even while it begins to move on into the light. There is a yearning for that light and for the full knowing of oneness, and yet there is that within the self that feels unworthy. In the book with which I think most of you are familiar, called *Dark Night of the Soul*, St. John of the Cross suggests that the soul feels itself to be unworthy of God and yet yearns toward connection with God. And although it feels itself to be unworthy, the force of its love is what gives it the courage to seek that connection.

How can you allow the force of your love to come to the forefront of your awareness so that it can lead you into the full knowledge of all that you are and always have been, to lead you past that fear that calls the self unworthy? As long as you are human, you are not intended to be perfect. What you perceive as limitations are not limitations at all, but merely the teaching tools offered by this density. You do not have to get rid of fear or anger or greed. All you need to do is to allow what beauty is there to flourish and bloom. The fear and anger and greed will fall away, because the knowledge that was gained from them is no longer needed.

The most important tool here is awareness: knowing always what is being felt. If anger or greed are being felt, touch those, not with judgment but with an acceptance that allows the being not to need to act on those emotions. It is not the emotions themselves that are a problem. You do not harm another by experiencing greed. You harm another by taking what belongs to another.

How much more lovingly can you begin to respond to all these forces within yourself? As you learn loving response the need for fear will pass. It is as if you were swimming across a river and there were one hundred floats to hold on to. Moving across the river, you swim to one of them and grab hold to keep you afloat. And yet as you look, you say, "They mar the beauty of this scene. I don't want them." In one aspect of you, you know that if you get rid of them and your swimming ability is not yet refined enough, you will drown. So you leave them there, noticing that they mar the beauty, but also that they are useful until you have perfected your swimming so you do not need them anymore. At that time, they will simply drift away.

I believe that Q'uo has something to say here and would like to pass this to my brother/sister at this time. That is all.

(Carla channeling)

Q'uo: I greet each again in love and light.

We are attempting to offer tools and resources to the third-density entity for working toward allowing and accepting. A great resource for doing work in consciousness is creative visualization. The closer the visualization comes to resonating with the timbre of memory, the better the chance that it will aid the entity at deep levels of emotion, those levels that contain true wisdom. A visualization about the loving self might be this: within you lies the small child that is attempting to do well, and that constantly perceives the self through the awkwardness of childhood as failing to be adequate to its own requests of the self. Picture, then, the loving self. You are indeed all very loving entities as parents. Would the parent within you turn to a child and scold it when it has acted in self-perceived error, or would the loving parent take the child into the cradle of its arms and place the child's head where it can again hear the heartbeat of the womb?

The child is afraid of the vampire that it has seen in a movie, and so it wakes from nightmare. The parent moves swiftly to the child's side and offers it a sense of proportion. It does not make fun of the child. It is aware that each entity has its nightmares, its fears; but when the child is cradled, it quickly becomes comforted as the parent says, "This was a true nightmare. There are truly portions of consciousness that are terrifying. That is the way that that is. But that is only a small portion of you, my child, my beloved one." As the parent rocks and nurtures this baby child, the feelings of safety, of security, and of being loved slowly and gently allow the child to accept its own vampire and to find that it is not so scary after all; that vampires, too, fall under the love and care of the nurturing parent. Thus, one may invite into the self that vampire, realizing at last that although the vampire is a part of the self (and any other image is equally acceptable here), it is not the totality of the self. Thus may your own lovingness be shined as the light that it is into the darkness of that child that is fearful.

When this inner child becomes stronger, it is, as children are, willful. Thusly, it is well for the visualization of the nurturing parent cradling the child to become more organic, more within a flowing process. The child, newly strong now, is willful. The loving parent is wise to advise the child not to let the outer expression of new realizations become important.

It is not at all important that others know the insights one has gained, for these insights are fragile, just as the infant is fragile. They must be treasured and protected as they grow stronger. When the child is willful, the loving self gently reminds the child within that it may remember the many times that willfulness has not been a skillful choice of attitude. For in willing from within the conscious mind, there is an ignoring of the greater will of the higher self that is lost in the Creator, so that self and Creator are truly one. These tantrums of will may be gentled and healed by that nurturing parent until the child sees clearly that its will is likely not to have a very intelligent or spacious perspective.

It is not that it is incorrect to use the faculty of will, but rather, that such use of will must be seen as sacramental. When one uses the will, one needs to see that volition for the choice it truly is. One surrenders that shortsighted will of self in the mundane sense, utterly and completely, moment by moment, to the will that speaks from a vast perspective of thousands of years, shall we say.

It is written in your holy works that the yoke of Christ, or the yoke of Christ Consciousness and acting according to that level of thinking, is easy; the burden is light.[14] This may be examined as a deep truth. One within incarnation always carries baggage, always has something strapped upon its back to carry. For in finity, which the body expresses perfectly, there is always perceived effort; that is, effort perceived as effort by the self. To enable that small child that is nurtured by the loving parent within, by presenting to that child's eyes a view of a whole and unified process, is the work of faith. The child has learned that it can use its will; and if treated gently and with respect, it shall learn to choose that will that is most well-informed, that has the spacious perspective. In this way of service, one approaches such a light burden, such an easy yoke, that one becomes free. In surrendering a small volition, one is able to hear, at last, the volitions of Love itself.

Thus, one who does the will of the infinite Creator is simply listening more skillfully to the voices within. One of the many conversations one has endlessly with the self is a conversation with that Self that is the Creator. How splendid and glorious it is that this that is of the dust of the Earth may yet speak with the Deity and be heard, and then hear also what the will of that Deity is. Then one is free to do the best one can, single-mindedly and with a full and generous heart.

One aspect of the self is well encouraged by the nurturing parent; that is, the sense of humor. One may perceive oneself without humor and thus become heavier and heavier with the weight of solemnity. Yet does not any play, even a tragedy, have its moment of heartfelt release and catharsis?

And how much of life may be seen by the self as the soap opera or the cartoon? This is not to denigrate the importance of the self or of service, but to allow the sense of humor to strip outer experi-

---

[14] Matt. 11:30 AV.

ences of fearfulness. When one may undress the object of fear and see it, however allegorically, in its boxer shorts—preferably those sprinkled lavishly with hearts, frogs, or golf clubs—one then sees the vulnerability of that object of fear. It is only strong when it is dressed majestically. Thusly, in not accepting a solemn and heavy view of the present moment, one is allowing a sense of proportion, an ever-growing spaciousness of attitude. Humor is the beginning, in many ways, of full acceptance of self, which eventually very nearly silences the voice of fear within.

We would at this time move into the contributions of the one known as Aaron. We leave this instrument in love and light. We are those known to you as the principle, Q'uo.

(Barbara channeling)

Aaron: It is a joy and a delight to work in this way, with Q'uo and me stimulating each other through our ideas, and also with the sharing of each of your thoughts that you have sent to us. I wish to thank Q'uo especially for reminding me of the importance of humor and must stress my strong agreement with what Q'uo has said—that with humor comes the beginnings of acceptance. There is much more that could be said here; and yet in the interests of this session not becoming heavy, I would simply like to open myself to your questions rather than speaking on with my own thoughts. That is all.

Carla: How may one help another to begin to perceive this process? It is easier to work with the self, by far, than to create useful and persuasive inspiration for another seeker, which has its own journey, its own priorities, and its own keys. Perhaps in essence I am asking how one can serve as inspiration while completely observing free will.

Aaron: In serving another in this way there are two factors of key importance. One is that you can only learn for yourself. You can open the door for another, but you cannot push him through. To attempt to do so is a violence against that being. Thus, if you see another's misunderstanding, you may gently and lovingly point out that misunderstanding while assuring the being that he has your full acceptance and love, whether he accepts that misunderstanding or not. That is fully his choice. You are concerned that even to state that the misunderstanding is seen could be a violence. It depends how you phrase it. If you say, "You're wrong. Look at this!" and reach out to shake another to make him understand, that is a violence. If you simply say, "We have a different perception of this, and I see it differently. Are you willing and interested to hear how I see it?"—and if that being then says, "No," of course that is it. And if that being says, "Yes, how do you see it?" then you can share the way you see it, and then it is his choice to select helpful thoughts and to leave the rest behind. So that is one way you may be of service.

And the other and more important help is through the example of the self. Mistakes are corrected through constant work on oneself; and a deeper level of honesty with the self develops so that one becomes a shining example. But be ever mindful that this self that one offers as an example is also imperfect, that there will be errors. There will be unskillful choices. The example, then, is not to be perfect but to accept the imperfections in the self and in other selves with love.

Here I would like to stop, unless there is any further specific question upon what I have said, and offer Q'uo the chance to speak.

(Carla channeling)

Q'uo: We greet each in love and light once more and suggest that this be the final portion of this working, as this amount of material is sufficient for one, shall we say, meal for the heart and spirit to digest. We would not be heavy on the dumplings when offering you the good protein of thoughtful insight.

We would simply ask the self how powerful it thinks it truly is? The concept of being able to infringe upon free will with an opinion is deeply narcissistic, deeply aggrandizing the mundane self's power.

Once again, there is the shadow of control, of fear. Why would this instrument be afraid of speaking honestly with its opinion or offering itself as a channel for the opinion of one whose opinion the instrument values? Can this instrument or any other leap tall buildings at a single bound? Can this instrument or any other single-handedly destroy or create, or add height to the body or length to the life? Where is this notion of powerfulness?

You see, the true power is always in the Creator. Thus, as one stills that narcissistic concern, one allows oneself to become transparent. One becomes as that city upon the hill in your holy works, shining for all to see.

The very natural human tendency is to listen to a needy person, to accept that person's expression and then to say, "Yes, I respect that, *but*..." In that little word there lies the shadow of fear, of separation. Rather, can one be humble enough to allow this entity to express until it is done?

And if it does not ask the instrument's opinion, or ask the opinion of an entity that is channeling through the instrument, that is perfectly all right. There need be no "yes, but ..." type communication. It is only if that other self invites either one's own opinion or the opinion of the contact that one may offer the opinion in a very righteous and feeling manner.

When one hears the question mark, one knows that the seeker's heart is ripe and ready for the picking, for the aid. When each hears itself say, "yes, but ..." to one who is vulnerable and needy, one may simply observe that fear, the fear for another being as foolish and the fear for the self. Thus, one is free to ignore. Nearly perfect expression of a life lived in faith, with no "buts" but only a loving awareness of the flowing of all that is necessary to learn, moving to each one, through each one, and sweeping into infinity—that is the true nature of consciousness as an infinite Intelligence.

Allow yourself to stop being a bubble and to become the ocean. Allow yourself the luxury of being asked before speaking and of feeling no responsibility for those who do not ask questions. The skillful help one may give to the entity who does not ask questions, but is suffering, is simply to allow the overwhelming compassion within and to send, out of fullness of self, that loving and healing energy of acceptance of that other self just as it is, with all of its self-perceived imperfections. This acceptance is as much a catalyst for another— although it is not aware of that—as is the verbal acceptance. Entities prefer verbal acceptance because they do not understand the depth of their own perceptive abilities. Honor this simple holding of another in compassion, acceptance, and forgiveness. And honor, above all, that same attitude toward the one named self, that everlasting child within that is bound to make unskillful choices again and again.

We embrace you all, as does the one known as Aaron. It is indeed a privilege and a great deal of fun for us to dance together with these concepts. We delight in each other as one flowing stream. How beautiful is this service, and how grateful we both are to the dedication and love that allow this calling to come to us. We thank each as we participate in the great work that ever goes on, the work of learning to cease the striving, to still forever the child's fears. We leave you in the love and in the light of the one infinite Creator and recede from your consciousness at this time. We are those of Q'uo. Adonai. Adonai.

Session 5

Today we are joined by several additional people who come regularly to an open Sunday session. One is another "C.," not Carla.

(This session was preceded by a period of tuning and meditation.)

C.: I would like to know how to draw anger out of my son and reestablish a calm relationship with him. There is a lot of pent-up anger and it comes out in inappropriate behaviors. He is a very sensitive, bright child. He never felt that he fit in anywhere. He has never felt like he belonged anyplace that he's been. He's never been able to adapt to just functioning in the everyday world. He tends to be off in his own world quite a bit. When he can't reconcile the two, it comes out in anger that is expressed physically and that type of thing.

(Barbara channeling)

Aaron: With greetings and love to you all. It is indeed a blessing and a gift to be invited to join you tonight and speak to your heartfelt concerns.

This question of working with anger in another, of helping another truly in any way, is a difficult one. You love your son and do not want to see him in pain. Each of you wants so much for your children, and yet each of you can only learn for yourself.

You cannot learn for him. It becomes useful to begin to differentiate where you hope to learn for yourself through your son's anger and where it becomes a matter of wanting to take away his anger because it is painful to you.

I am going to start here with something that you all know, though sometimes it is very hard to accept, especially when the one involved is one you love. You cannot take away another's pain. You cannot deprive them of the experience of that pain, nor can you know why they have moved into such experience. This knowing is for the wisdom of their own soul. You can create the learning situations and the loving and accepting environment that will allow that which is not angry in your son to flourish. You can nurture all that is not angry within him, but only he can work with his own anger. I do not mean that to sound hopeless. There is much that you can do. I only want to point out here that to try to take away his anger is a form of violence to him. You say he has always been very sensitive. He, in his wisdom, has created certain situations in his life, including choosing you to be his father, so that he might work with that which most needs to be healed within the spirit.

First, try to separate your discomfort at his anger, knowing that this is work that needs to be done not on him but on you. In short, if he needs to be angry, can you simply let him be angry? Can you reach that place in yourself where he feels from you only complete acceptance, that there is not that within him that is unacceptable to you? This may help him more than anything else you can give him, because surely he already judges his own anger. If he finds that unacceptable to you, it will increase the depth with which it is unacceptable to him.

How well do you accept your own anger? This is another way that you can teach him. I seem to be saying this a lot this weekend. There is nothing wrong with anger. There is nothing bad about the emotion of anger. It is just a feeling. When you use that anger as a reason to act in an unskillful way toward another, then you have a problem. Then you are creating disharmony and adhering karma. But the emotion of anger is simply the emotion of anger. It is not the anger that is a problem, but your relationship to the anger. Moving into yourself, then, are you totally loving and accepting when anger arises, not needing to get rid of it or do anything with it but just to watch it? So many of you feel that anger must either be suppressed or acted upon, but there is this third choice, just to observe it: "Here comes anger ... I wonder how long it will stay ... There it goes. ..."

Session 5

One of the things that all of you are here to learn is to approach—not to attain but to approach—nonjudgmental and unconditional love for yourself and what you perceive as other selves. As long as there is that within you that feels unacceptable, then you judge the same to be unacceptable in others. I am not denying that anger causes you pain or that your son's anger causes him pain. But he will need to work with that pain on his own. So, the best gift you can give him is first to begin to look closer into your own anger and to reach a point where you truly can accept your own anger. Then you can begin to accept his anger, so that when he is angry he still feels love from you. In this way, he can begin to let that anger drop away, to be honest with himself about it, and to understand it more clearly.

The second gift that you can give him is to nurture all those qualities that are beautiful in him and help him to nurture that in himself. How much has his anger or sensitivity made him see himself as different and feel himself to be unworthy? While assuring him that neither his anger nor anything in him is unworthy, can you also nurture what is beautiful in him, including that sensitivity you spoke of, letting yourself feel how much you cherish that in him so that he may begin to cherish it in himself?

There is one more issue here that needs to be looked at. Why does a being choose to incarnate into a situation where he will feel different in any way, where he will become angry? Why does he choose to subject himself to those catalysts? It would seem to me that it is likely that you both have this issue of self-acceptance. Sometimes one needs the catalyst of anger in order to be challenged to look at one's feelings more deeply, to uncover the love, and to nurture that.

There is a story told about a spiritual teacher named Gurdjieff. This Gurdjieff had a spiritual community in France; and living in that community was a man who was intensely disliked by all, including himself. He was slovenly in his personal habits. He was rude and abusive to others. He did not do his share of the work. Finally, feeling the dislike that surrounded him, he packed up and left. Gurdjieff went after him and begged him to come back. The man said "no," at which point Gurdjieff offered to pay him to come back. The people in the community were aghast. They said, "How can you bring him back?" Gurdjieff said to them, "He is the yeast for the bread. How can you learn about compassion and forgiveness when you live here in a community of such perfect harmony—beyond this one man—that you have nothing to be compassionate about, nothing to forgive? You need him to help you learn compassion."

One who chooses to incarnate into a situation where one lives with anger is choosing that situation to prod oneself, one might say, to learn a deeper level of forgiveness and compassion. Of course, one starts with the self, finding acceptance for that anger in the self so that one may not judge that in others, but may love all aspects of all beings. How does one love another's anger? It is not the anger that one is loving, it is the spirit of the being itself, which is pure and holy and beautiful. The being is not its anger nor its greed nor its fear. And yet you constantly create this duality, and so much of your work is to move beyond that.

There is one more specific thing I want to say about your son. Please remember that each being is always exactly where it needs to be, regardless of surface appearances. For a parent with a child, this idea takes a high level of trust. You can open doors for him, but you cannot push him through those doors. You can do nothing with his anger but to love him and to love yourself. As you create that doorway through your own power of love, when he is ready he will walk through it.

There is a great deal more that could be said on this subject of anger and the specific question about the son. We prefer to end this teaching and allow Q'uo to speak, and listen to your further questions about this. That is all.

(Carla channeling)

Q'uo: We greet you in the love and in the light of the one infinite Creator through this instrument, with thankfulness that you have called us and the one known as Aaron to offer our opinions. Take what each feels is his own truth and please leave the rest behind.

The communications of a spiritual nature promise that the result of spiritual seeking shall be a simplified, comfortable, and easy existence. These communications are promising the direct opposite of that which is the inevitable outcome of living the life as a spiritual seeker that is eager to accelerate the rate of spiritual evolution. This situation is one good example of this truth. Spiritual awareness often brings pain, for one is now responsible for an enlarged grasp of the nature of illusory catalyst and its purpose. The more one accelerates this pace of learning, the more one is responsible for creating a way of living in faith that is the equal of the concepts that have enlightened one.

One such concept is the spiritual truth that all are one and that within each one there is all of the universe of possibilities of attitudes and biases. Thusly, when one experiences another's anger, one is, in terms of one's spiritual growth, gazing at the self. What one has not come to forgive in one's self, one feels far more keenly when the mirrors of intimate family members and friends express that attitude in any way. The son's anger then becomes a mirror held ruthlessly and clearly up to the face of the parent. The parent, in assuming that the child is separated from the self, is cheating the self of the valuable, accurate mirroring of the self to the self through the catalyst of another.

Let us gaze at anger toward the self, for this is truly the spiritual situation. Has this seeker allowed an awareness of its own anger to ripen and mature until it can look at that anger it feels without judgment? If all entities possess in potentiation all qualities, should it surprise one when a seemingly negative quality appears in the mirror? Must you turn away from the mirror because it is too painful to see the self that is that behavior and painful experience of the other self? The best teacher of accepting the negative aspect of the self is the drawing of the attention, as the one known as Aaron has so rightly said, to those many times when one is experiencing, either in one's own mirror of self to self, or in the mirror held up by another to the self, all the loving, compassionate, helpful, and wise portions of the self. The beginning of the healing of self-judgment is the awareness that the mirror does not always show the negative or negatively perceived aspects of consciousness.

Intellectually it is easy to say we are each all things. We contain all that there is. But much circumnavigation and rationalization is practiced by most spiritual seekers in order to avoid gazing into the mirror when the mirror shows that which is perceived as negative qualities that the self, of course, shares, as it contains all things and all qualities. Thus, the focus is upon the healing of the self. That healing begins simply with the self, not with the head-to-head confrontation of self with the disappointment in the self. Sit with the self. Watch what arises and departs within the mind and within the heart. Watch each transaction, not to discover how to change the self, but simply how to identify the self more clearly within the self. For until the spiritual seeker accepts itself as it perceives itself—that is, in a state of considerable error—it cannot gaze in compassion at the mirrors that reflect that self to the self.

Plutarch's injunction to "Know thyself"[15] is primary and fundamental to a life lived in faith. Again, we emphasize that as the student of spiritual principles moves further in assimilating material, the responsibility for living the spiritual principles involved in that material becomes ever more challenging. The critical observer-self seems biased toward noting not what is right but what is lacking. By this unhappy habit, many have come to the conclusion that they are unworthy and incapable of becoming that which they wish to be. This is not so. The road does not end. It is occasionally very bumpy and stony. Yet the pilgrim, when it is rested, moves on as best it can, clambering over debris and stony paths with the eye always upon this precise moment, this particular resonance of infinity as it intersects with the life-stream, perceived within the illusion as linear.

Always, infinity is at the behest of one who chooses to remember the infinite Creator and the love the entity has experienced from this

---

[15] Plutarch, *Morals.*

great source of love. Thusly, in healing the self-judgment, the parent is then able to express itself as a healed and whole entity, and is thus able to give whatever it may find possible to give out of a fullness of heart, a total and 360-degree acceptance of the self, knowing that the self is indeed all things, positive and negative, as is perceived within the illusion. When this healing is complete, then the entity may simply sit with this anger from another and see it as a catalyst that has done its job already.

There is eventually no self-perceived need to assign any quality to the other self, for that quality has clearly been seen within the self and forgiven within the self. It is in this acceptance and rest that the child may come to believe that it is possible to be miserable and yet to be hopeful, for the child knows the parent and knows the parent's version of this same negative trait, as perceived within the illusion. When the parent authentically establishes a healed awareness of self, when it is capable of saying, "Just as I am, just this much, is perfect in a way I do not understand but perceive by faith alone," then compassion flows from that womb that is the true heart, which is ever pregnant with the fullness of love and ever propagating itself in seeds of fullness out of fullness that may rain upon those about it. Thus, in finding the peace and acceptance of the self, one finds the acceptance of the unquiet mirror offered by another self.

(A pause while the tape is turned over. These sessions were recorded on audiocassettes. When we came to the end of a tape it needed to be flipped and dialogue paused. We left this one example in the text in order to give the reader a feel for how this originally occurred.)

I am Q'uo. We continue. When one is able fully to accept that self, one then becomes the healer who has healed the self first and is willing simply to act as catalyst, as the light upon the hill that gleams forth hope to those who are mired in pain.

So much between parent and child is learning based upon simple imitation. When two spirits with the same areas of perceived weakness are parent and child, it may clearly be seen that each is the teacher of each. Thus, in allowing the self to heal, one by definition has allowed the entire creation to heal.

What is concern but a kind of fear, fear lest that loved one not be happy? We ask you, can any entity create happiness either for the self or for another? The answer, as far as we know, is that happiness is like a visitor that never stays long. It brings its gifts, it holds the self in its embrace, and it shares in rejoicing and love. And quickly, perhaps before the self has even grasped the source of this happiness, the weather of the emotions becomes cloudy and the happiness is gone, leaving the self, perhaps, to brood overmuch on loss of happiness.

What baggage creates anger? What is it that is picked up and held and cherished that creates the anger of the self? Perhaps we may suggest that anger, at base, is anger at the lack of complete acceptance of the self. Thusly, to work with one's own anger, it is well to perceive the benefits of not striving to become anything, not trying to advance, but simply allowing an awareness of the full nature of the self, to be held in the gentle arms of that nurturing portion of the self. Once one's own inner child, which is often angry because of lack of control, has been clearly perceived, then the attempts of a young soul—that is, young within this incarnation—to control the environment in order to make the self heard or in some way more secure can be accepted as the spiritual process it truly is.

Each of you sees the self, unless one is careful, as a solid object; that is, a solidified being that is such and such a way. However, the present moment insists that there is no solidity of being or of the qualities of being, either positive or negative, but rather that the present moment flows from present moment to present moment to present moment. To see oneself in process and that the process is ongoing in far larger terms than one incarnation is to allow oneself the perception of the enormous malleability and plasticity of the self in process: The Creator is not done with any. None is finished. All are in process. Let this sink into the heart so that the heart feels less and less judgment; and when it experiences judgment, it accepts that judgment also as a portion of the self. When all is seen clearly, choices may be made more skillfully. Once the element of fear is removed, the loving heart is content to offer itself without condition and without overconcern for the pain of a beloved other self.

Is there at this time a following query?

C.: Both you and Aaron seem to have anticipated the further queries that I would have had. I thank you for your words, and hopefully I can begin further work upon myself. Thank you.

Q'uo: We thank you, my brother. We would at this time allow the vibration of the channeling to move to the one known as Aaron for any further question. We leave this instrument, briefly, in love and light.

T.: I have just a short question. Most was answered by the previous channeling. In my life I am looking for love, for someone to be with and to share my life with. I realize that I have to accept myself, and there are many things about myself that make me angry and that I cannot accept. I realize that I have to do this first. As I attempt to accept myself, am I being counterproductive in even attempting to find this love outside of myself?

(Barbara channeling)

Aaron: I understand your question. It is never inappropriate for the heart to seek what it desires. Yet I believe the confusion here comes from not being certain about what is desired. There is that part of you that finds itself to be lovable and loving, and wishes to share that love with another self. The fact that you have not yet been able to do that speaks to the fact that there is also that within the spirit that pushes away that intimacy. In short, when you think that you want something and yet hold yourself back from that, you must ask why.

I see a number of possibilities here, and would ask you to choose what seems most appropriate to yourself and discard what does not fit. One possibility is that while such intimacy is desired, there is also that in yourself that feels unworthy and is afraid to open itself so closely to another for fear that another would recognize that unworthiness. I spoke of this earlier today to a friend, saying that within each being there is what I call the *what-if-someone-found-out?* space. You see yourself as a loving being. You have work to do, yes, but are still a loving being, a spiritual seeker, and a good and caring person. And yet within the self there are so many emotions, so many forces that you cannot accept, that each of you cannot accept. You are each like an iceberg with what is acceptable being that small bit that shows above the surface and so much buried that you have not been able to accept. As you progress on your path and become mature and responsible and more highly evolved, you become harder with yourself. When there is anger, rage, greed, jealousy, or fear, there is a strong "I shouldn't"; but you cannot keep this separate from the self.

Q'uo and I have been speaking about fear and how it arises, and the point was made that the newborn infant experiences fear because its needs are not met. No matter how attentive the parents, there are times when that infant's needs are not met, and it knows that it cannot care for them itself. Q'uo pointed out that there is terror there.

One must then accept that fear and other emotions are meant to be, in some way, part of your experience; that one does experience emotions and that these emotions are here to teach you. When you are incarnate in a physical form, you have both an emotional and a physical body that the being who goes beyond the astral plane does not possess. These are your tools for learning. This physical manifestation, this form, and the emotions are part of the complete being in this human form. You are never going to free yourself of emotion. It is impossible while you are a human. And it is not the emotion that is a problem, but how you relate to it. You see that rage or greed or whatever it may be, relate to it with hate, and say, "This doesn't fit with the way I want to see myself or the self-concept that I want to impart to others. What if someone finds out?" I do not know to what degree this is true for you, but for many it becomes a strong factor in keeping them apart from a closeness with others, even when they long for that closeness. I would suggest that it would be worth exploring.

Another factor that often enters into one's ambiguity as to whether there will or will not be a close relationship is the learning about separation and oneness. So many beings incarnate on this Earth to experience the strong sense of separation. It is a gift to teach you. When you feel the pain of that illusion of separateness, eventually it becomes painful enough that you must truly probe and study and investigate it. Then and only then do you begin to look at reality, which is that you are not and have never been separate. The sense of separation is painful; so are the heavy emotions that we just discussed.

I am not implying that your learning must be painful. Pain does not teach you anything. Pain is, if Carla will excuse a bad pun, a pain in the neck. But pain screams, "Pay attention!" and paying attention teaches you. When you can learn to pay attention without pain, you will need far less pain to learn. You can pay attention to the ways in which you feel separate and move past that wall of pain and anger that enhances the sense of separation. You find acceptance and forgiveness for all of that in yourself that has created the illusion of separation. Then you will no longer need that illusion.

There is one further thing I would say here. So often you seem to hear two voices within you. One that comes from the heart is a voice of love, and one that we would call the voice of the brain or of reason is often a voice of fear. You have one voice within you that asks you to trust yourself and to trust others, to allow yourself to open, to cherish that beautiful self within as a bud, bringing it into the sunlight of your love. And then there is the voice of fear and it says, "Well, I have work to do on myself. Maybe I'm not ready for a relationship." Do you see the excuses there? Can you see the avoidance? There is always work to do on oneself, no matter how evolved you become. You are never complete but are always in progress. Do you wait for perfection? Can you begin to see that it is the voice of fear that suggests that you wait? Can you begin to ask yourself with some compassion, "What am I afraid of? What is this fear?"—not to track it down analytically as it grows out of this or that event of childhood, but to begin to see all the anger and lack of self-acceptance behind it and to relate to that with love and compassion?

It is so hard to have compassion for yourselves. Each of you here would respond with great love if someone else had told you your own story. But to yourselves you turn only judgment and contempt. It is not that you need to become more lovable before someone will be interested in you enough to have a relationship with you. It is not that you need to become more lovable or to have enough to offer to another so that it seems right to offer yourself; rather, it is that you need to love yourself enough and to trust.

Know that when you open and trust there may be pain. At times, the trust will not be met with the same level of love and trust. Begin to take everything in your life as a learning experience; to know that being alone and lonely is teaching you something, opening yourself and allowing yourself to be vulnerable to another is teaching you something. Finding a deep and loving relationship with another will teach you something. What is it that you need to learn? It is so hard to let go of the edge of one's current perceived illusory limitations and strike out across the vast sea of consciousness, letting go of the shore, of the safety of that shallow and safe beach, to move into deeper water, not knowing where one is going. Indeed, one often feels like those early explorers who wondered if the world was flat and if they would fall over the edge. That story appeals to many because of the depth it holds in one's own unconscious mind. How difficult to let go of the edge and proceed with faith and with the courage that one is always where one needs to be, and that the next learning offered, whether it is of loneliness or of love, is exactly what one needs. If one is able to accept that love that is offered and to move beyond the fears a bit, not getting rid of the fear but allowing it to fall away as it is no longer needed, then one finds that a world of love is offered.

Session 5

I feel that you have specific questions about what I have said, but I would prefer to let Q'uo speak now. And if those questions are not answered in what my brother/sister says, we would be glad to return to them. That is all.

(Carla channeling)

Q'uo: To continue this thought, we would bring the attention back to a fundamental concept regarding the nature and purpose of the third-density incarnational experience. Earlier this instrument was singing a phrase from your holy works, "for he is like a refiner's fire."[16] In this pioneer density, it is not expected that all the slag and dross of self shall be purified. It is expected, rather, that in the darkness of unknowing and by faith alone, one may see that the incarnational experience is a process, first of choosing the way that the self wishes to be distilled, of what essence it wishes to smell; and then having made that fundamental choice of how to love, opening oneself to the very painful process (to the self, which does not like to change) of distillation or refining. This instrument often sings a prayer, which is:

> *Temper my spirit, O Lord. Keep it long in the fire. Make me one with the flame. Let me share that upreaching desire. Grasp it Thyself, O my God!, Swing me straighter and higher. Temper my spirit, O Lord. Temper my spirit, O Lord....*[17]

The densities above your own are densities in which this refining process progresses from the point at which you are when you graduate from the third-density schoolroom. Shall we say that in third density, the higher self, which is the Creator, evaluates and grades, shall we say, using the curve, as this instrument would call it. There is not absolute

---

[16] Mal. 3:2 AV; and the text for a bass solo from Handel's oratorio, *Messiah*.

[17] This hymn, based on the poem "The Passionate Sword" by J. S. Untermeyer (1886–1970), was often sung at camp in Carla's childhood. The hymnbook used is no longer to be found.

perfection possible. Thusly, one is hoping in a relativistic way to approach nearer and nearer to a heartfelt dedication and to begin the refining process in a conscious manner. One intends not to react to the stimuli in this thick darkness of unknowing but to choose rather to live a life in blind faith and to prosecute that first choice of service to others that does begin in love of self with every possible vehemence and passion.

There is always much to forgive when the self perceives the self. We suggest that each entity may helpfully see all the dross of self, not as shameful but as inevitable—as, to use the one known as Ram Dass's phrase, grist for the mill. Thus, one can refrain from fear of one's own fears, anger at one's angers, judgment at one's own unskillful judgments, so that the process may be seen mercifully, that the self may see that the self plunges into the furnace by choice. Yet we would suggest that lovingkindness and mercy be a portion of self-awareness, so that one is able to move into the refiner's fire only when it will not do violence to the young, precious spiritual self that was born immaculately within when the first decision was made of how to serve the infinite Creator. The choice to serve others is not a conclusion. It is the cornerstone or beginning of a process of distillation that will continue for a long, long time, as you understand time.

We would conclude with a comment about emotion. Entities overvalue the intellect because it seems to the intellect that one has only the intellect with which to analyze situations. In the strict sense of analysis and linear thinking, this is so. Yet by depending upon that analytical ability, the attention is drawn from the true intelligence of the self, the true seat of wisdom, which is the mercy seat of purified emotion. It is not *your* lack of self-acceptance, it is *a* lack of self-acceptance, a quality that you now dip into and experience and use. It is not personal to you. It is an emotion felt by you and by many.

In emotion one is never alone, for the emotions run like the underground waterways that bubble up in clear springs at their own time and season. One who wishes to dig a well to tap this underground or subconscious source of the water of spiritual refinement needs to go gently, to go deep carefully, so that one rather woos or courts the earth away that lies between it and the water of purified emotion, which is a portion of the deep wisdom of the self.

Honor each emotion. Look at it as you would gaze at a gem, at a crystal. You may see it as imperfect, but it is your truth. As you turn that crystal, flawed as it is, you may see that though it refracts light unevenly, yet the refraction is full of beauty and color. Thusly, in honoring the emotions for the wisdom that they truly convey, one is able to bear the pain of self-revelation, which is the essence of conscious entrance into a safe and gentle refining fire, a fire that does not burn away that which you still need.

We would at this time allow the energy of the group to move back to the one known as Aaron. We leave this instrument, briefly, in love and light. I am Q'uo.

(Barbara channeling)

Aaron: It is with love and joy that I share this process of responding to your questions with the principle known as Q'uo. I speak for both of us when I say that it enhances our understanding as well to listen to each other and to your own thoughts, and to investigate these questions more fully. We have by no means exhausted any discussion of fear or anger; and yet, perhaps enough has been said for tonight.

Are there further questions that any wish to ask?

Questioner:[18] R. would like to know if the work begun in healing the child within, and that was left undone after discovering it, plays a significant part in his current illness.

Aaron: I am troubled by the question because of the place of self-judgment from which it comes. We have spoken with R. and find much anger within him at the self. His assumption is correct, and yet,

---

[18] Offered in absentia for R.

he must be helped to understand the desire within him to use that assumption simply to blame himself further; that it will become simply another object of anger, another source of that anger. Can you see how easily this is distorted? It is necessary to be truthful with him. And yet, if I were speaking to him in person, I would stress instead the healing that is needed and the opening more compassionately to the self. Rather than putting the focus of the attention on what has not been done, I would put the focus of the attention on what it is possible to do. Is this answer sufficient or would you prefer me to speak on it?

(The questioner indicates that this was sufficient.)

Are there further questions?

M.: My question has to do with pain and the emotions that surround pain as a messenger. One technique that I've learned in looking at the pain is to be soft with the pain, to resist not. I wonder if you could elaborate on how one learns to soften more. I think that is enough.

Aaron: I understand your question. As you know, this technique is a very valuable one. It would be useful to look deeper at why it works. What does softening around pain mean? I would like to suggest the value of investigating the difference between pain and suffering. Pain is just pain. That does not mean it is pleasant, but one can deal with a great amount of pain without it causing suffering. Suffering comes with your resistance to pain and is very different. We speak here both of physical and emotional pain and suffering. When you struggle with what is, wishing it away, hating it, you create suffering for yourselves because you cannot control what happens in your life. You have seen this countless times. You are happy and everything is beautiful, and suddenly it has been turned upside down. You are picnicking with your loved ones in the sunshine and it begins to pour. And you hate the rain! You are hiking on a beautiful trail with exquisite views and begin to rub a blister on your foot. How can you avoid pain?

Q'uo spoke earlier of happiness. As it comes and goes there is a much deeper level that one can reach than happiness. What is happiness? It is not something that comes from sunshine on a picnic or freedom from a blister on a hike. It comes from a place within that knows that whatever happens is okay. I would suggest the term "equanimity" here—a deep space of acceptance where one lets go of the need to control and where there is neither aversion to what is nor a grasping for what is not. This does not mean that one does not give energy to try to make things better. But there is a difference between preferring that something be a certain way and working toward that preference, and needing it to be that way. When you need it to be that way then you create suffering for yourselves, seeing suffering, then, as resistance to what is, even to the point of hating what is.

I would like you all to try an experiment with me. I would suggest that Carla not do this. Hold out an arm; just hold it up while I talk. I will go on to other things and allow this arm to become heavy, allow you to feel some pain.

What I want you to begin to look at is the difference between the pure physical sensation of discomfort that you call pain and that within you that hates the pain, that wants to put the arm down and that says, "This is enough," in the struggle to make it go away. As you begin to sense that struggle, whether it be with physical pain, with an emotional pain, or with anything in your lives that brings intense discomfort, when you begin to see aversion to that discomfort, that fear is what you need to soften around. First, you notice the aversion, the wanting it to be different, the hating it the way it is, and you allow yourself permission to grieve for that which could not be. In its most simplistic terms, you wake up on the day of the picnic and see it pouring. You stub your toe and feel the pain, and know that because of that pain you will not be able to continue to walk and that your life will be uncomfortable for several weeks. Then you move into a space of anger and judgment. Finally, especially those of you who are more spiritually advanced, you say, *I shouldn't be judging. I shouldn't be angry,* and that just increases the suffering.

I believe most of your arms are feeling heavy enough now to continue with this experiment. Can you begin to separate the physical discomfort from the suffering that comes from disliking that discomfort, allowing yourself the right to be uncomfortable? Experiment with this for a moment, and when you need to, put your arms down.

So there are two different things we are speaking about here. To soften around pain means to let go of the resistance to that pain. When you do that you are no longer suffering. Then it is just pain, nothing else, and is far more easy to bear in that way. Second, when you notice the suffering, you begin to treat yourself with much more love. To honor the pain and respect it gives you a great deal of freedom from hating it.

There are many other techniques that can be used to soften around pain. Visualization is a great help here, especially when speaking of physical pain. Simply think of that being whose presence connotes love to one. It may be Jesus or whatever being of your choice. Visualize that being literally sending out love and light to that part of the body where there is pain, not lessening the pain, perhaps, because that may not be in its power nor may it be desirable that the pain be lessened, as it is there for a reason, but touching the heart that fights against the pain and the place of fear that wonders, *Will this pain never end?* because there is so much fear in pain.

Another thing that may help is remaining in this moment, because so much of the fear of pain is not that it is intolerable in this moment, but fear that it will continue till the next moment and the next and the next. When you can come back to this moment you can simply experience the pain with a far less intense need to get rid of it. What is pain? When you come back to this moment, you can begin to investigate it. You will see that it is not solid, as it feels at first. It comes and goes. It moves around. Sometimes it seems to peak, then to relax a bit, and then it returns. It is not a solid object with which you need to wage a war. How much more lovingly can you relate to it?

Finally, I would suggest a method whereby one visualizes the blockage in that part of the body where the pain is concentrated. Visualize, if you will, your own inner energy as flowing through you and simply blocked at that point. A visualization that some have found helpful is to see themselves as lying in the bed of the stream, when it is a hot, sunny day and the water feels cool and refreshing and it is flowing strongly, a stream with bubbling rapids. Lying with your head upstream, allow that water to flow in through the crown chakra, not forcing its way past any obstruction, as that would be a violence to the self, but allowing that gentle water to touch the obstruction with loving coolness, to remind the self where the obstruction exists so that the self may gently allow it to dissolve, not feeling any brutality at all but just the loving pressure of water that over a time erodes even the largest boulder. Allow that same loving presence gently to touch this obstruction, one sandy grain at a time, until the energy flow is restored. When there is an injury to some part of the body or a recurrent physical ailment, this continued use of this visualization may be helpful.

One of the things that may grow out of such a visualization is a clearer understanding of where the energy is blocked. When you experience a chronic illness, it will help you to understand why there is blockage in that area. I say this because you are each aware that you have certain weak points in your body. And when there is physical injury or loss, it seems to concentrate, for one in the head, for another in the stomach, for another in the back, and so on. These are not by accident, but come from the cells' memories of past karma. One does not need to know the experience of the entire lifetime to have a brief glimpse that there was an injury there or violence to that area of the body, and that there is still holding or contraction there that needs your love and forgiveness to dissolve.

I believe that Q'uo has more to say to this, and rather than trying to answer it all myself, would prefer to share the answer. That is all.

(Carla channeling)

Q'uo: We feel this amount of material is sufficient to engage the hearts and minds of those now sitting. This shall be the concluding response from Aaron and ourselves.

In parting, we would offer to each that which is not original or new, but that which seems at this particular moment to be helpful. We would preface this by saying that each entity is far more than it realizes itself to be, yet the ruthlessly literal nature of logical processes in which the mind is so often engaged creates a situation wherein the body is indeed the creature of the mind. The body, however, in its literal hearing of the mind, expresses itself as literally as possible in response to a catalyst that has not been used by the mind, thus expressing within the body in a very dogmatic and fundamentalist way, if one were to speak in terms of spirituality, those blockages or difficulties encountered by the mind as stimulus.

Thusly, we would ask each to perceive again that there are indeed, as we have been speaking of in these last few sessions, two hearts and two minds. The mental mind is shallow, but extremely useful for dealing with the illusion. The second mind is that heart or emotional self wherein lies deeper knowledge, deeper wisdom, and true awareness. Likewise, there is that heart that is the heart of wisdom and that would give anything and everything to ameliorate or palliate pain, either self-perceived or perceived by another who comes to the self for helpful advice. This first heart strives in its wisdom ever to become more wise, more purified in its emotions and its wisdoms. The second heart is indeed the heart that needs to be worked with in softening the self to "resist not evil,"[19] as the phrase goes.

This heart, whether male or female, can be imagined as a womb that is full, soft, and pregnant with unlimited fullness. Each time that one experiences the tightening of any portion of the physical vehicle, it is well to move gently and slowly down this tree of mind and heart to the full heart, which gives a fullness without diminishing itself. Feel the tension in all of the body, but especially in this womb-heart

---

[19] Matt. 5:39 AV.

and literally in the way the abdomen is tensed. One may even push at the abdomen to feel the degree of tension and explore this as a physical sensation. Then one may guide one's breath ever deeper, breathing in mercy and lovingkindness, allowing that rigid belly to be soft, literally soft. You will find that as soon as the attention wanders from the softness of that abdomen, of that womb, the belly begins once again to tense.

The entire body, when facing the catalyst of pain, reacts quite literally in defense by tensing against a danger. Thus it is very healing to work continually with patience at the unending task of relaxing that creature of mind that is the body, and especially with allowing the breath to flow into the heart-womb, bringing its gentleness and its healing to dissolve tension. Breathe out all that tension in deep, spontaneous breathing. Do not attempt to breathe deeper than usual. Simply breathe in visualized love, nurturing light, and spaciousness in which the self may relax.

In the case of a solidified pain due to illness, there are many, many layers of tension and tightness. Thus, it is not enough to do this exercise once or periodically, but rather to honor the self by paying it the coin of attention and mindfulness that it deserves. Attend to the state of tension of the body; and whenever it is perceived, in whatever company or circumstance, allow the mind to do its visualization of softening that heart-womb of fullness and allowing that fullness to give out of fullness into fullness at the cellular level for all of the body. Then, the feedback of body to mind becomes that which the mind cannot create; that is, mercy and merciful forgiveness.

May each respect its own striving to be more and more a channel for the love and the light of the infinite One, but may each also perceive the mercy and kindliness of a Creator that is Love, and allow that love to inform ever more deeply the conscious being that often feels unloved.

You are all beautiful. The blending of your vibrations gives us enormous aesthetic pleasure. And the joining of our hearts to yours in shared thought is a more precious gift than we can convey with mere words. So allow the love of the Creator that is channeled through us and through each other to rest upon you, now and in each moment. We would leave you in the love, the light, and the peace of the infinite One. We are known to you as those of the principle, Q'uo. Adonai. Adonai *vasu borragus*.

WEEKEND 2

For our second gathering, just over one year after our first gathering together, we were again a small group. This time we gathered in Carla and Jim's living room. Outside the open windows, spring flowers were in full bloom, and their fragrance filled the room. We had some time in the afternoon for the humans to talk and relax together, and in the evening we brought forth our questions. This was a shorter, overnight visit, so we had only two sessions.

As with weekend 1, we had not planned this in any way as a formal workshop, but just a place for the gathered humans to ask their hearts' most compelling questions to Spirit. This was always our process: to spend some time asking the deepest questions we had, so as to invite the clearest possible response from Spirit.

This trip, Barbara came with a friend, Karen, who was able to fingerspell for her with greater fluency. For the formal sessions, we settled on the method we devised partway through the first weekend, with Jim typing Q'uo's words. The hum and clicking keys from the computer were disturbing to some, so Jim sat away from the group, hearing through a microphone and with a computer monitor close to Barbara so she could read what he typed.

As is always our process, we began with a period of tuning. We alternated the tuning sessions for the group, but Carla and Barbara also each did their own private tuning before the sessions. We would like to offer you this particular tuning from Aaron, which is taken from session 18.

Aaron: I want to introduce you to this tuning process by asking you to participate with me in a brief guided meditation.

Please allow yourself to follow along without concern for whether you can or cannot do what I suggest. Our emphasis here is not on getting rid of anything within you, but simply on allowing the barriers of ego-self to dissolve so that you may move into the divine aspect of yourself and hear from that place of center.

Begin by taking a few deep breaths and releasing.

Breathing in ...

There is nothing external to you. As far out as you can go into the universe, when you breathe in, you take that universe into that which you call self.

When you exhale, you exhale that which you call self into the universe.

Breathing in and letting go, each exhalation dissolves the boundaries of self.

Inhale and let go of any resistance to taking the universe into your heart or of any resistance that wants to hold on to being "somebody," just letting it go. If anything holds on, it is okay. It will go. Nothing to do, just being.

Breathing in and expanding outward, with the exhalation flowing into the universe, then breathing the universe into yourself ... open ...

The heart is weary of its isolation ... open ... allow yourself to come into the essence of who you are, let go of all the concepts of who you always thought you were, and just allow that pure, clear mind/heart to be what it always has been: Pure Awareness, Pure Being.

As you drop your boundaries, feel the connection to the joy and suffering in the universe. Be aware of the rising aspiration in yourself to be a tool and to offer your energy as a tool for the alleviation of that suffering: not my suffering or your suffering, but our suffering. Be aware of the aspiration to be a source of energy, courage, love, faith, and healing for all beings and to manifest your energy in such a way that it promotes peace and happiness in the universe. This is the primary intention: moving out of the fearful, small self; open to the Divine.

In your own words, silently state your intention to serve the universe and all that dwells therein, to be a vehicle of Love. I will be quiet for a moment while you phrase this intention in the words of your own heart.

(Pause)

Given that aspiration and intention, the next question is, "How do I implement this?" You alone cannot implement it. You, when connected to all that is, are empowered to implement joy, peace, and harmony. So the next step is to invite in whatever help there may be—each, in your own way, invoking Jesus or the Buddha and asking God's help.

Silently voice your prayer that you may become an instrument for healing and love in this world. Not for your own ego, but in service to all; not for your own glory, but that your service may be offered back to God in grateful thanks. For you are but a reflection of that divinity: divine in your own right, but taking your light from that most brilliant and perfect light. Rejoicing, you are returning that light, ever brighter, ever clearer. I will pause again, then, so that you may voice your prayer in your own words.

(Pause)

All beings on human and spirit planes contain some mixture of positive and negative polarity. None is totally negative, nor are any but those most fully enlightened masters totally positive. We do not flee from the shadow in ourselves, but aspire to touch that shadow with love and thereby to grow. In the same way we do not flee from external negative energy, but aspire to touch it with love.

If there be any being within this circle, human or discarnate, that is of predominantly negative polarity and that wishes to hear these teachings, we welcome it. It may not speak through this instrument. It is welcome to listen and to learn the pathways of service and love to all beings.

At this point Barbara will be silent with herself for a few moments. Her own process here is to make the firm statement of what she stands for and values, and that none may channel through her unless they are fully harmonious with her highest values. She uses this process, although a high percentage of what she channels is this energy that I am, simply because it is an important statement that gives her confidence in what she receives and allows her to relax into the channeling. I will be quiet now and allow you each to meditate in your own way for two or three minutes.

Session 6

Weekend 2, Part I of 2
(This session was preceded by a period of tuning and meditation.)

(Carla channeling)

Q'uo: We greet and bless each in the love and light of the one infinite Creator.

If the one known as Barbara and the one known as Aaron are sufficiently prepared, we should enjoy commencing this session of working. We would wish to express our deep enjoyment of the opportunity to share our thoughts with each of you and to work with the entities that may express through the instrument known as Barbara. As we would prefer to allow the one known as Aaron to begin the working, we would at this time content ourselves with the expression of our joy at the beauty of this circle of seeking and for the moment leave this instrument in love and in light. We are Q'uo.

(Barbara channeling)

Aaron: My blessings and love to you all. The energy of spirit, not just disincarnate spirit but of all spirit in this room, is very lovely to behold. Barbara is bursting with joy inside at the heightened frequency vibration she is experiencing; and experienced secondhand through her, that energy is still very brilliant. It is a great joy to speak in this way and share a conversation with my brother/sister Q'uo.

The last time we did this we were making an attempt to move back and forth with more frequency, rather than for one of us to talk at length and then the other to speak at length. And if Q'uo and Carla are willing, I would like to suggest that we do it that way—no long monologues, but a more flowing conversation between us. There will be no difficulty in this. I will know when Q'uo wishes to speak and will simply pause and Q'uo will know when I wish to speak.

No decision has been made as to the nature of the questions or the direction of the channeling tonight and it is not my place to direct this; but I would like to offer a suggestion that it feels relevant to me that we speak, at least to some extent, about the nature of service and the misconceptions that the incarnate being may move into about the nature of service. These create a distortion in that service and give rise to fear. I would pause here for your responses to this suggestion. That is all.

(A pause while Aaron's suggestion is considered.)

It is not necessary that you hold to this idea of service at all. It feels to me to be something relevant to all of you, but I do not wish to impose my concept on each of you. Is there a totally different area that you would prefer to explore?

Carla: Why don't we take this opportunity to form a group question on service? What is it that we wonder most about service? The thing I notice most frequently that people ask me is how to be of service to other people when they have not yet learned how to love themselves as human beings with faults, so that they can have compassion on themselves and therefore have compassion on other people. So, my first question about service would be, "How can people be encouraged to see themselves as people worthy to offer service to others?"

Barbara: I understand Carla's question. I feel a different discomfort with service. I think it's a question partly of being versus doing, but it seems more a question of the arising of fear; that as soon as I get into wanting to serve, I separate myself from that part of me that is already serving. I don't know how to get past that. I know my question is rather vague, but there's a sense, not of aspiring to serve but at grasping at service, that gets in the way of actual service. Can you speak to that distortion and how I can move past it, how any of us can?

Session 6

Q'uo: I greet each again in love and light.

> Ah, to be upon the road and
> To forget that the feet are walking,
> To become numb to the dust,
> To smell not the heat of the damp
> Of the dew upon the dust as you trudge
> In the morning light of young and unskillful pilgrimage;
> To carry your brother and your sister in your heart
> And think that they are upon your back;
> To be numb in the feet, in the heart, and
> To feel burdens that are not there.

This is one way to describe one who serves with every heartbeat, yet believes that one must carry a load, one must show weight and effort in order to serve. Is not every step an effort? Are those feet not dusty and sore? Is the heart not full to bursting with compassion and love and will? What is this fetish about the showing of burdens? About the suffering that is visible? Is this carrying of burdens what each thinks that service is?

Let us move back from this scene and think of the heart of each entity who desires to serve. Is this heart active, defined by action? Is it completely passive, asleep, and incapable of action? Or are both sleeping and waking, dreaming and acting, informed by an unsleeping and ever-living consciousness that merely and utterly is?

Any determination to be of service begins not with dreaming and not with acting, but with consciousness itself. And that consciousness is that which is purified by a fire of desire that tempers consciousness, cleanses it of the confusing, self-deprecating, or arrogant emotion so that one is neither consumed with unworthiness nor battened by pride, but merely is, as is the Father of all things; merely is, as is the Nurturer of all things; merely and utterly is, as is the spirit of love that is the nature of all that there is.

One serves because one is of a certain nature. If that nature be impure, the service shall be impure. If that nature is undisciplined and unguided, the service will be undisciplined and unguided. If this consciousness chooses negative ways of distorting itself, its service will express itself in manipulation and control of others. And if the purified consciousness has been purified toward love without any hindrance, let, or stint, then the service of such a one will be beyond description. Whatever the action, the essence of the service will remain within the being that informs the service.

No one can keep from serving, no entity whatsoever. Thinking upon this may begin to take the emphasis off wanting to serve, for that desire is after the fact. We would transfer this energy to the one known as Aaron at this time. We are known to you as Q'uo.

(Barbara channeling)

Aaron: Q'uo spoke about unworthiness and pride. These are both manifestations of ego. I would suggest the usefulness of beginning to regard service in a different way, not as a strained giving or even as an eager giving but as a gift. There is no joy that I know so deep as that of serving, and a part of the joy inherent in service is the emptiness of self that one comes to when one truly moves out of oneself in order to serve.

So much of your pain comes from the illusion of a solid self. Without that illusion, neither ego nor pride can exist. There is no unworthiness. There is no grasping. Service is truly your path beyond ego, because as you walk that path of service you see constantly how that illusory self arises; see the seeming solidity of ego as you become bound in fear.

What you see is a magnification of what exists. We have talked about this at length and I believe we spoke about it a bit last year when we were here. If you offer something 99 percent purely and I percent with the impurity of ego, you are aware not of the 99 percent but of the 1 percent and you condemn yourself for that. You so quickly forget that this service is offered by a human. The spirit is unlimited, but the human does have its limits. Thus, you tend to become lost in that small percentage of the service that is guided by ego, rather than the much greater percentage that is guided by true aspiration to serve God and the deep love for all that to which the servant feels itself connected.

As you move into that minute distortion of fear, you start to feel yourself unworthy; or in an effort to override the fear, you move to pride—the latter more rare than the former for those of you who serve in the ways that you in this room do. You are more prone to unworthiness than pride. When you can remind yourself that the path of service is a gift wherein a reflective mirror shows where ego still exists, it gives you a very different perspective on that ego.

At that point you may turn with compassion to this human being that is doing its best to serve despite the occasional arisings of fear, and use the path of service as a constant reflection of the arising of ego so that you may allow that illusion to dissolve. If you were not given this catalyst of service in the way that those in this room ask themselves to serve, you would not have the strong promptings that you each have to purify yourselves. Yes, you are here to serve others. But the wonderful gift of that service is that in the course of it, this aspect of the one that you identify as self must be allowed continually to dissolve and dissolve more fully until all illusion of separation is eradicated.

I would like to relate this thought to Barbara's question. Barbara spoke of the arising of fear and the distortion created by the desire to serve, by grasping at service. Can you see that the grasping is a manifestation of unworthiness? When you know that you serve simply by being, there is no longer need for grasping.

Last month Karen shared a very beautiful poem with us, a poem she was taught as a child by her grandmother. I do not know if I have it completely accurate, but as I recall it, the words were:

I am the place that God shines through
For God and I are one, not two.
God wants me where and as I am.
I need not fret, nor will, nor plan.
If I'll just be relaxed and free,
He'll carry out his will through me.

This is truly the essence of it: relaxed and free; not willing, not planning, just being and trusting that you will be placed where you need to be in order to serve as you are asked to serve. You do not need to set up such situations of service so much as to allow them to happen. You allow them to happen by purifying your own energy, by constant work on yourselves, by prayer, by your constant offer to be of service without grasping at that service, and by deep awareness that when you say, "I *need* to serve," that is a manifestation of unworthiness and of ego—"I need to serve so I can feel better about myself." Well, fine, but first feel better about yourself, and then all the service you want will pour through you. It really is as simple as that.

I believe the important thing here is to become aware that each time "I need to" arises, there is a sense of unworthiness behind it, a sense of fear. The first step, then, is mindfulness and deep awareness each time that sense of fear arises. The second step is acceptance of this human who sometimes feels fear: just a smile and a "Here is fear again. Come in, fear, I have been expecting you." Give yourself a hug and return to the act of loving, of worship of God, and of extending your loving energy in whatever ways you can, not just to others but to yourself. With the acceptance of that small arising of fear, it will not grow into distortion.

You do not have to get rid of fear. You only have to recognize that it is there. The fear does not interfere with your being a clear channel, for example, but your relationship with fear interferes with it. If you wish to serve others in any way—serving food in a soup kitchen, working in a homeless shelter, counseling others, or whatever ways you may choose to serve—you need not eradicate fear but recognize it and find mercy for this human who sometimes feels fear, and in that way change your relationship to fear.

Until you change your own relationship to the fear that sometimes moves through you, you cannot clearly serve another because you will always be in some amount of judgment of his or her fear and the distortions that fear creates in another. There will also always be "he who serves" and "he who is served" as long as you are not friends with the fear in you. But when you can make friends with that and thereby befriend fear and all its distorted manifestations in another, you remove the separation of self and other. And then there is no longer "servant" and "served." Both are servant and both are served.

Do you think that when you serve another by offering them food, that does not serve you? Here is the distortion of pride: "I am the servant." And again it creates separation, and such separation cannot serve anyone. When I offer you food and you offer me the opportunity to offer you food, I thank you for that. You give me a gift, truly.

I offer you my thoughts right now, and I cannot express the deep gratitude in my heart for the opportunity to speak to you all and the ways that you serve me by giving me your listening and your open-hearted attention to my thoughts, because when you listen to me, it makes me be more responsible for the purity of those thoughts and thus stretches me and aids me to grow.

So, I ask you to remove the duality in your mind between "served" and "serve" and to look closely at your discomfort with the arising of fear and see it more clearly for what it is. Truly begin to understand that the fear does not create the distortion in your service, but your relationship with the fear creates that distortion.

I feel that Q'uo would like to speak at this point. There is more I would like to say, but I would prefer to turn this over to my brother/sister for comment and allow us to move back and forth. That is all.

(Carla channeling)

Q'uo: We greet each again in love and light and apologize for the brief pause, but we were conferring with our friend, Aaron.

We hope that each has listened to these words concerning desire, for desire purified does not partake of fear; it is not separate and does not create separation. Remember two things that this wise entity has said: the path of service is a gift. The path of service is a reflection.

Let us look at these statements from a slightly different perspective and from a slightly different set of opinions. These statements can be pondered over and over.

The path of service is a gift. What is the path? Is it something you walk or is it you? Are you the path and the gift? And are you by your very nature serving and served? For if you are of love and if you have consciousness aware of itself, is this not the only undistorted transaction of which you are capable: the giving and the receiving of that great service that is loving?

Can you conceive of yourself as a gift that is perfect, immutable, whole, and complete, yet transitive—the self as a verb? Only those selves who see that they are not only *on* holy ground, but that they *are* holy ground, can move from being a "he," a "she," an "it," a noun, into being a verb—a transitive, acting verb that connects love with love, that acts as a catalyst between subject and object because it knows that subject and object are one. The subject is love and the object is love if the subject is self and the object is other self.

One who is the path and one who knows itself as holy knows that self and other self and all that there is exist in a ground of love. Love speaks to love, serving and served, loving and loved. Distortions are released; fear becomes less necessary. As this process gradually takes place, the self becomes the path, the gift, and that servant which is finally transparent to love flowing through it but never remaining, for love flows as endlessly as the sea.

The path of service is a reflection. This is simply the same statement turned backward so that one may see that one is served as one serves. We would not belabor this point but only wish each to ponder it. You are a reflection to others, just as others reflect you to yourself. What, my friends, shall you reflect to others? Is your mirror transparent? Are you love? Can you allow love to flow through you and allow the images that you reflect to others to be clear and lucid and shining with the light of a truth that is beyond you but can only flow through you?

We ask you to ponder this second statement as a corollary of the first, for it deepens and aids understanding and grasping of the nature of the self as a servant of love. When a servant is serving, he is also served. And when he accepts serving, that acceptance is also a service.

We would at this time again move to the one known as Aaron and the one known as Barbara that we may have the pleasure of listening and learning and enjoying Aaron's opinions.

As always, we ask each to know that these are opinions that we offer. We have no authority over you. Know that we are your friends and perhaps your teachers, but we do not ask any to refrain from discrimination. For you know that which is the truth. And if you do not hear truth through these instruments, we ask you to put these words down and walk on without a second thought, for we would not be a stumbling block before you.

We leave this instrument. We are those of Q'uo.

(Barbara channeling)

Aaron: I find it a great joy to share in this way with my brother/sister of Q'uo. I would like to look at a distortion of service that was inherent in both Barbara's and Carla's questions. In your human form it is so easy to lose track of what you are doing. This is natural to the human, which is not perfect and is not expected to be perfect. I am not condoning unskillful choices here, but only asking you to have mercy for this being that is sometimes unwise in its choices.

At times many of you have a fixed idea of what it means to serve, an ego attachment to one type of service or another, and you forget so quickly that, as Q'uo just explained, service is a type of *being*, not a *doing*. When you fully allow yourself to be transparent and allow light and pure energy to move through you—both into you and out of you, giving and receiving—then you *are* service. You are not serving; you are service.

When Barbara phrased her question, she had in mind a kind of distortion. Let me give you an example. On Wednesday evenings she has a channeling session. Her family comes home at 5:30. They are hungry. They have things to tell her and to share with her. She feels a need to get them fed and to get the kitchen cleaned up and to sit and meditate and prepare herself for the channeling session.

She is almost never short-tempered with them, but she sometimes feels impatience, which she does not manifest. She feels a sense of wanting to hurry them through their dinner, wanting them to get their dishes washed, and so on. If she goes in to meditate and her youngest son comes in and shares his homework with her, she looks at her watch and is aware that "A houseful of people are going to appear here in half an hour and I need to meditate. Get out of here with your home-work!"

She does not say that. She sits him down on her lap and she looks at the homework. Meanwhile she is feeling that impatience. And then she feels anger at herself and says, "Who am I serving here? Am I ignoring my family to serve others?"

She has learned that when she can let go of her fear, when she can feel compassion for this human who is feeling fear so as to allow that fear not to solidify, then it does not matter whether she is sitting in meditation or washing dishes or holding her son on her lap and admiring his homework. It is *all* meditation because at that point, as she washes the dishes or holds her son, she *is* service; she *is* love. What could be better preparation for channeling than holding a child on your lap and giving him love? But the voice of fear distorts that and says, "I must have silence to prepare," and then self-criticism arises, because she knows that to follow up on that impulse would be to hurt the child.

It would be well worth your while to look at the ways you manifest this in yourselves. No being of third density is immune to this. No matter how aware you are, it catches you sometimes.

What does it mean to serve? A friend shared a story in which he was leading a large workshop. A woman had kept talking about her family of eight or nine children all weekend and the demands they placed on her. She spoke up toward the end of the weekend and said, "Oh, I want to serve! How can I serve?"

Many in that group had been talking about working with the homeless or those with AIDS or another disease and so on. And this man, S., turned to the woman and said, "You want to serve? Get up in the morning and serve your family bacon and eggs."

What is service? It is not a doing but a being. It is an attitude and a way of approaching the world and yourself with love.

Now, I know those are inspiring words, but the reality is that it is much harder to do it than to speak of it. Each time that you fall into that trap of mistaking service for a specific kind of doing and see yourselves attached to that doing, might I suggest that instead of looking critically at this human who has made that unskillful choice, you find acceptance for that human. What is behind that grasping at service in this specific way or that specific way? Can you begin to see the layer of fear under there? And as you allow loving self-acceptance to replace that fear, then you become love again and you become service, service to all beings.

We have spoken at length about negative and positive polarity as service to self and service to others. When there is not a distinction between self and other, then service no longer takes on that direction. You become aware that when you serve others, you inevitably serve yourself because there is no self or other. And truly, even that entity that you think of as a negatively polarized being in service to self, without having the intention of doing so, does serve others because there is no difference between self and other.

Thus, the difference is not in the direction of the service so much as the intention. When there is intention of service to self, it is because fear is present; and greed, needing, and grasping. The distinction, then, becomes intention to serve fear and the solidified self that grows out of fear, versus the intention to serve love and the deep connection that grows out of love.

Perhaps this distinction can help you to clarify the direction in which you move your energy. When you think of it in terms of service to self and service to others, the whole direction becomes distorted, because those of you with strong positive polarity who think in terms of service to others find yourselves uncomfortable when you feel yourselves receiving from that service.

I would like to ask Q'uo to speak at this time, as I hear very delightful thoughts coming from my brother/sister. That is all.

(Carla channeling)

Q'uo: We greet you again through this instrument in love and in light.

In this working we have grappled long with the concepts of being of service. This, obviously, in our opinion, is one of the more misleading phrases concerning service to the one infinite Creator. Therefore, let us look at what we say to ourselves and let us look at what we feel that the Creator may say to itself.

Does the Creator say, "I should; I need; I must; I desire"? Or does the Creator say, "I create and it is good"? What is the name by which the Creator in the Judaic system of myth and culture is known in its highest form? Is it not "I Am" or "I Am that I Am"?[20] Or perhaps, "I Am always becoming"?[21]

We speak individually to each within this unified circle, for each of you has a universe peculiar and unique to yourself. It is your co-universe, your co-creation, and you are co-Creator. No one co-creates this uni-

---

[20] Exod. 3:14 AV.

[21] JHVH, Jahweh, or Jehovah is a name of mystery supposedly given to Moses on Mt. Sinai. The definitions Q'uo suggests for this unpronounceable name are some of those translations of JHVH given by theologians.

verse but you. It is the creation of the Father and of you by your responses. All that is created and realized and sensed within your creation is yours, either by being or by reflection of being. Your creation is unlike any other, and all that you feel is outside of you is actually occurring within you.

We speak of mirrors. Do you realize that in actuality your eyes, your ears, and all those things that you use to garner information are illusions also? Do you realize that the sense impressions that are filtered through to your conscious thinking have been through so many judgmental screens that they are in fact already myth and legend before you are aware of thinking, perceiving, or realizing each sense impression? The depth of the illusion that you experience is infinite. You will not know anything within this illusion. You may have our permission to stop trying.

You are becoming. You are creating. There is no "must." There is no "should." There is no "want." There is no "desire."

What is your true nature? If you are a creature of the one infinite Creator, then the answer to that for those who feel that the Creator is love is that you are a creature made of love. Here you are. We speak to you in a limelight all your own even though you are one with all in this group. You are love and you are becoming and you are creating. Rest in this bright light, the surest sign of beingness.

This is your incarnation. This is your experience of being, of consciousness. This is your chance to examine the nature of yourself. And as you examine that nature and you say, "I need; I should; I want," stop and say to yourself rather, "I create." And then look to see if you think that the creation is good! For that which is of the Creator within you will say, "It is good." And if you create and can say, regardless of all imperfections that are apparent in this immensely deep illusion, "It is good," then you are upon the holy path of seeking and of service.

Are there any brief questions at this time?

(A pause for group consideration.)

Q'uo: As we see there are no questions that those present wish to verbalize at this time, we would ask the one known as Aaron to close this session of working with our expression of profound gratitude for the delightful opportunity to share in this teaching, in this service, and, my friends, most, most deeply, in this being served by being able to blend with the vibrations of each of you the hope, the prayers, and the faith of each of you. How beautiful you are and how inspiring is your steady and persistent gaze upon truth, beauty, and love.

We leave this instrument now in the Creator's love and light, and transfer this energy to the one known as Barbara and the one known as Aaron. We bid you adieu at this time. We are those of Q'uo. Adonai.

(Barbara channeling)

Aaron: For those of you who are interested in pursuing this, I offer a bit of homework. In the coming evening and morning, watch yourself very carefully. Service is not just the big things, but the little: smiling to another, washing a plate or glass, petting a cat who is seeking affection, being love....

Watch yourselves very carefully. Watch for any arising of "I should." Begin to distinguish the movement of "I should" through the third chakra of will and determination and the "I Am" of love expressed through the open heart.[22] The more deeply you can move into awareness of these patterns in yourselves, the less control habitual pattern has over you.

You are so used simply to reacting, so deeply patterned in your responses that it takes very careful attention to break those responses. It is like a habit of biting the nails, perhaps, or scratching, pulling at

---

[22] Aaron is referring to the *chakras,* or rays of the energy body. See the Glossary of Terms at the back of this book. Aaron is suggesting that one move from the use of the will and "should" in yellow ray to the use of love in green ray.

the hair, or whatever one may do when one is nervous. In order to change that pattern, one must begin to observe the nervousness. To change the pattern of moving from a place of "I should" into a place of the open heart, one needs to observe the arising of separation that moves one back from the open heart center to the third chakra and pushes one in the direction of "I should."

So, just watch fear-based body impulses and the arisings of the mind, holding no judgment about them. As you bring increasing awareness to these expressions of your being, you find freedom from reactivity to them. You do this by simply noticing the habitual move back to "I should," moving back to separation and coming back to allow the heart to open again through loving acceptance and compassion for this being who moved momentarily into fear.

I love you all and am filled with joy at the opportunity for this sharing. I thank Carla and those of Q'uo for allowing me to participate with them in this teaching, sharing, and learning. May I suggest that we close with a moment or two of silent expression of our joy and gratitude to each other and to God for bringing us together in this way. That is all.

Session 7

Weekend 2, Part 2 of 2
(This session was preceded by a period of tuning and meditation.)

(Barbara channeling)

Aaron: My greetings and love to you all. I would like to continue where we left off last night, to ask you to consider service in still newer ways. Service is a manifestation of love. We spoke last night about being service rather than doing service and of the ways that such doing creates a distortion of self and other, of server and served. Being service is simply opening yourself and moving away from any duality.

Something I find very interesting is that those of you who aspire to serve grasp so hard at something that is innate to you. It is not that you must work in order to serve. That is natural to you. When you are not "being service" there is a distortion. Your energy is being distorted into some misconception of separation. Therefore, the ideal is not to aspire to serve but simply to pay attention to where pure "being service" is blocked by fear.

I spoke last night of intention, of moving away from the limiting concept of service to self and service to others—which is quite disorienting because service to others is service to self and vice versa—and to begin to see with clarity the ways that service to others springs from a ground of love, and service to self springs from a ground of fear.[23]

---

[23]Reference to these two orientations, service to self and service to others, may be less confusing and more easy to understand when viewed from the perspective of their essential oneness; however, the two orientations are validly distinguished from each other in any objective discussion of the choices available to the seeker. The Confederation's channels such as the Q'uo group, as well as Aaron, are oriented toward service to others, and that is what their teaching discusses.

When you begin to see the intention to offer love or to react to fear, to allow fear to direct your choices, then you can move away from the concept of service to self or other self and toward the pure experience of "being service" or the pure experience of reactivity to fear.

Once you move away from the concept and into the experience, those of you with strong positive polarity will find the experience of "being fear" is an ample check in itself. As soon as you allow the reality of that experience to arise in you, something within you stops and pays attention and says, "No, this is not the way I choose to express my energy." You then allow yourself both to be aware of the fear and nonreactive to it, so that the aspect of "being love" and expressing service through the being of love can manifest itself.

The most important point to remember here is that expressing service through being service in love is natural to you. And when you do that, you are not doing anything; you are not creating anything. You are simply expressing your own true nature. When that nature is in full harmony with the external positive energy that may move through you, your energy to serve is magnified. At that point, you do not need to ask, "How can I best serve?" You simply choose the paths that lie right at your feet, whatever they are.

I shared a story at Christmastime of the one whose name was known to you as Jesus. I told how, at that time, I was part of a group that was with this being. This is a being known for his service. I want to use this story as an example of what service may really mean.

We came to a place where there were followers of his who welcomed him and prepared a meal—an elaborate meal by their standards, simple by yours. They gave the best of what they had.

It was a poor village. There were those who despised and feared him and they also were part of this village, but not within the group that sat to eat. He was served first, offered a bowl of food. As he sat there with that bowl in his hands, ready to begin, he saw children on the edge of our circle. An elder of the village got up to shoo the children away. He said, "This child is the son of one who disdains your teachings," and went on to say, "Get out of here! Go!"

That one child hung back. He was a young boy of nine or ten years, emaciated, and with sores on his body. Jesus simply got up and walked toward the boy. The boy was frightened because he had been told to leave and here was this stranger walking toward him. Jesus said gently to him, "Do not be afraid; I will not hurt you. Do you want food?" And he offered him that bowl. And while the boy ate, he asked for cloth and water and washed his sores. And then he came back very simply to his seat and took another bowl.

There was no lecture about service. There were no words, like "You should love your enemy." There was no verbal teaching. He simply served. He was service. He was love. He took, not the universe, but one child that needed to be fed at that moment, and fed him and washed his sores. Just that. There is no teaching in my many, many lives that I have received on service that has touched me as deeply as that one.

Think, then, about what service—being service versus serving another—really means. When you move into that distortion of seeking to serve another, begin to recognize it as a distortion. See that your serving makes them the one who is served, makes you separate and unequal. See that this is a violence to another.

Is that the course you really choose? How can you learn to express being service in ways that do not create separation? We will speak further on this. I wish to pass the microphone, as it were, to Q'uo. That is all.

(Carla channeling)

Q'uo: We greet you in the love and in the light of the one infinite Creator.

The one known as Aaron asks, "Do you wish this dichotomy betwixt self and other self, betwixt servant and served?" Each would, as a beginning servant, say, "Yes, I must have someone who needs my service so I may be a servant." Outwardly there seems no falsity in this reasoning. We, ourselves, have often thanked you for the opportunity to serve you, merely noting that your allowing us to serve is your service to us. Service by this chain of reasoning seems an endless loop. Yet how does the one desiring to serve enter this loop and become part of the infinite, upward, spiraling light and love of all serving all in love and for love's sake?

Many are the seekers who feel guilty because they must take time to work within their own consciousnesses. Many also are those seekers who pridefully state that mate, family, and all the mundane aspects of life must take second place to the self's work in inner enlightenment. Whether one feels guilty for taking this time for one's own purification, or not guilty but arrogant and elite for taking time for this purification in an impure world, still the concept of taking time to work within the self always is suggested and encouraged by any spiritual teacher.

Now, is this time taken for the self, by the self, in doing work in consciousness service to self or service to others? You may perhaps see by this question itself that the tendency toward dichotomy when thinking of service arises here, at the beginning of a student's preparing to start the journey of seeking to know how to serve. The immediate thought is, "I must do this work. Am I selfish? Should I take this time? What good am I to others?" And of course, some will become absorbed in this inner process and neglect outward-gazing compassion.

The story of the one known as Jesus, told by the teacher Aaron, shows an entity who has awakened to his own inner love. This entity has done his work in consciousness. The personality is disciplined. The emotions are purified, and the response lacks either prideful humility or prideful arrogance and seems natural. We suggest that in our opinion it is part of a life lived in service to others to spend time as if it were the most precious coin or money, always budgeting a portion of finite time for work within one's own consciousness.

At this moment, do you love yourself without reservation? How can you know this? Examine your thoughts for the last hour. Were you nervous? Were you irritated? Were you impatient? Did you have any negative emotions? We speak not only regarding one's inner dialogue but also of mental responses to the actions of others. For those responses are your material, reflected to you by the mirrors provided by the presence of other selves.

That which you think of another, you think also of the self. If there is judgment, turn it upon yourself and analyze the root cause within the self. Here is material for this day's budget of work in inner consciousness: nervousness, irritation, impatience, anger, resentment, disappointment.

Make an appointment. Let all of these self-perceptions see the doctor within. Analyze and examine these responses. Let them sink into the self and find their root and their home. Then touch that home with your compassion, your love, and your redeeming forgiveness of self by self.

Do you feel that the infinite One keeps a score, has tidy books, and forgives not? We do not believe you think so, else you would not try to serve. Therefore, we ask you to do this work with the same fervor, intensity, and respect as the work you do for others, those whom you call other selves, for work upon the self and work upon the other self is all work on behalf of the infinite One whose name is Love.

To serve the raising of one's own consciousness is to worship the infinite Creator. To extend the being and consciousness of love to perceived other selves is to be the clear and transparent extensions through which the Creator's hands may actually touch another human spirit in manifestation. Simply do not separate these two activities within the mind, but do both as two sides of one coin. That coin is serving.

We would at this time return this circle's energy to the one known as Aaron. We leave this instrument in love and in light. We are known to you as those of Q'uo.

(Barbara channeling)

Aaron: There is another area of duality and misunderstanding of which I would like to speak. You identify those who bring love to others as those who serve others. The attributes of those who "are service" are gentleness, patience, and generosity. And you identify those who cause others pain in some way, those who affront others, and those who are greedy or arrogant, as those who do not serve others. I would like to explore this a bit further.

Most of you have heard me say that we are all beings of light, even those who manifest very little of that light. Even those who are very negatively polarized and in the conscious levels of self would affirm their desire to serve negativity. Even those who feed off the fear and pain of others, at some level, are servants of the light. It is well to move past the duality of seeing them in such sharp contrast as good and evil, servants of love or ones against love.

At our last gathering, I told a story about Gurdjieff and a man in his community who was unpleasant in his demeanor and finally left. Gurdjieff invited him back, saying to the people, "He is the yeast for the bread. How would you learn compassion without a catalyst for that compassion? How would you learn nonjudgment without a catalyst for that nonjudgment?" Thus, this man, in all his negativity, also served others.

Granted, there are negatively polarized entities. There are those who thrive on the fear and pain of others. There are beings that are mired in deep misunderstanding, and yet, even their negative polarity and misunderstanding is a service. How would you learn without such catalysts?

When you can begin to view such misunderstanding and negativity as another way of service to the light, you begin to view such individuals differently. For most of them, it is not their intention to serve the light, although for some that may be true. No being whose intention is to serve the light will willingly do so through causing harm and pain to others. So it is not their intention; but nevertheless, they do serve the light by offering you the catalyst that you need for your own learning.

When you can begin to find welcome for such beings, to move beyond your judgment of them and open your heart to them, to the very real pain that their misunderstanding causes for them, and to thank them for the ways in which they offer you the catalyst that you need, then you can begin to do the same for yourself in those moments when fear and other negative emotions arise in you. I have spoken often of the reverse of this, of coming to a place of nonjudgment of yourself as a way of learning nonjudgment of others. I am just offering the opposite side of the coin.

When you see yourself in a position of possible service to others and fear or any type of negativity arises, if you can remind yourself of something such as the story I just shared and allow that this fear in you is also a catalyst that may be transformed from darkness to light by your clear observation of it, by your awareness and acceptance, then you find that even the so-called negative emotions in you can give rise to purity of action, speech, and thought. Fear becomes a catalyst for compassion. Hatred and the fear behind hatred can be clearly seen for what they are: not as an intrinsic part of you, but as a reaction due to certain conditions that have arisen and led to that fear. And the knowing that there is fear within you, in itself, becomes a path to clarify your energy so that your response to this being that is feeling fear, to this aspect of yourself, becomes even more loving, more clear, and more pure than it was before.

To do this takes deep awareness, a constant awareness of the ways that patterns of connection and separation, love and fear, move through you; noticing the conditions that give rise to each; beginning to break it down into small parts to see that you do not just suddenly become afraid; you do not just suddenly become jealous; it is a process that you have moved through, conditioned by old-mind patterns. These are the patterns of the mind's old, deep conditioning, often based in fear. You can break into that process at any time you choose with awareness and love and make the choice to move into a new pattern.

This is the crux of it: choice, responsibility. The being who acts in reactivity to fear, and thus acts in what we have called service to self and with the intention of harm of others, has either denied his responsibility and his ability to make a choice, or is frightened of that responsibility and choice.

The being experiencing deep fear who watches the patterns of the arising of that fear and then makes a choice for love is acting with freedom from conditioned patterns and thus is able to make skillful choices. The more you see this in yourself without judgment, the deeper awareness you are able to have of that moment of choice: "Here I can act with conditioned mind and the old patterns of fear," or "Here I can act with awareness of the patterns in which conditioned mind pushes me; I can choose to say no to that; I can trust and move in a new direction."

I would like to take this thought around now to a very real, practical application. You are all beings who aspire to serve. You are all beings who aspire to offer love and nonharm to all else, and yet you constantly find arising within you old patterns of conditioned mind leading to fear, self-hatred, negativity, greed, jealousy, and anger.

Each arising of such discomfiting emotions that have the possibility to harm another is a gift, a chance to observe the old patterns in yourself, and a chance to practice. It is practice that you need over and over and over again. That is why you are offered it over and over and over again. As you work with these patterns in yourself and are aware that some of the response has been prompted by the negative energy of others, it gives you a chance to transcend the duality of negativity and positivity, and to begin to see the gift even of that negative energy in others and the gift of negative energy in yourself as a catalyst to learning; to moving deeper into nonjudgment, compassion, and love.

This is the wonder of being human. You are here with this emotional body for a reason. Even those emotions that you deem negative are not to be gotten rid of, but are to be used as part of a transmutation process by which hatred and fear become the catalysts for love, greed becomes the catalyst for generosity, and so on. When you really begin to know that, in a deep way within yourself, you will not have so much fear of the negativity in yourself. When you make peace with that, then you really can give an answer to Q'uo's question: "In the past hour, I have not found anything I disliked in myself. I truly have loved myself, as my friend Carla is fond of saying, warts and all."

I would like to pass the microphone to Q'uo if my brother/sister wishes to add anything here. If not, we wonder if there are specific questions we may answer. That is all.

(Carla channeling)

Q'uo: I greet each again in love and in light.

Our one addition to this examination of the service-to-others efforts and lessons of third density is a simple suggestion that may be summarized in two words, first heard by this instrument from the entity known as Ra: Go higher! Go higher!

Aaron and we have long discussed the painstaking, careful, and subtle work of removing the perceptions of duality and thereby balancing negative and positive impressions and opinions. As a balance for this careful, analytical approach, we would suggest the concept of experience as a game sphere, a ball. The instrument known as Carla has called such earthly balls "trouble bubbles." When a trouble bubble flies at you, to lose the game is to catch it and fall under its weight. To win the game is to leap toward it in joy, praise, and thanksgiving. And as the bubble meets this sea of joy, praise, and thanksgiving, it simply pops.

There will always be another trouble bubble, another conundrum to solve, another bump in the road. Leap toward them with affection and joy. If it be another self that is a decided irritant, instantaneously be that entity, and as that entity, experience all its sorrows. Then, as that entity, leap for joy in praise and thanksgiving. You are not infringing upon free will, for you are playing a game; but in this game you allow your mind to become that which you fear, and then give thanksgiving and praise for the joy of it.

Go higher! This is work best done when one is, as this instrument would say and as we trust you soon shall be, "full of beans," and not for those days when, like the cloudy, pearly skies, you feel muted and reflective. However, this technique makes a welcome and energizing change to the endless repetitions of analysis, understanding, and acceptance of experience. It is a leap of blind, pure faith from immediate experience to immediate acceptance. Only choose this option when it is honestly within your abilities.

We feel the energy waning, and therefore would take our leave of all of you. May we say with the one known as Aaron how utterly delightful your company is and how very, very much we have been thrilled to blend our energies with yours as we all move from moment to moment in ceaseless and abiding love.

We thank you for allowing us to share our opinions and, as always, remind each that we are not final authorities. We leave each of you in the blessing and peace of the love and the light of the one infinite Creator. Adonai. We are those known to you as the principle of Q'uo.

(Barbara channeling)

Aaron: I would like to make only one brief remark, as I asked if there were questions, and as the principle, Q'uo, made its last statement there was a bit of a wrenching cry from somewhere inside Barbara saying, "Yes, all of these thoughts are fine, but how do I do this?" A moment of deep pain—this is the gift of being human. It is not going to go away. It is the catalyst that constantly challenges you to purify that energy that you are, knowing that it will never become perfect; that while in human incarnation you will never become pure service, constantly and without error.

And yet, each moment given with mindful attention and love brings you closer to that beautiful ideal of "being service." And each moment of attention to the arising of fear in you brings you closer to the purity of nonjudgmental acceptance of everything within the experience of mind and body, not mine or yours, but all of ours. It is this unconditional love that you are here to learn and practice and express in whatever ways you are able.

I do thank you for the opportunity to share with you today. My love to you all. That is all.

WEEKEND 3

It was fall and leaves were piled on the ground. Carla cooked ahead of time and wonderful food aromas filled the house. Karen was again with Barbara, and Kim was there with Carla and Jim. Two friends, Roman and Dana, were also with us. The beautiful weather led to many breaks to walk and sit in the artful, stone-edged gardens that Jim had created.

Session 8

Weekend 3, Part 1 of 2
(This session was preceded by a period of tuning and meditation.)

(Barbara channeling)

Aaron: Greetings to you, my dear ones. Q'uo and I are practicing being polite and each waiting for the other to speak first. Our hearts are full of the loving energy that you send out, full of the joy of your meeting. I wish that you could see with our eyes the radiance glowing out of this room!

Barbara, Karen, and I spoke a bit in the car about what subject matter you might wish to discuss tonight, what direction you might wish this to go. Of course, the questions must come out of the deepest questions of your hearts. But I also want to remind you that what we share is not new. You know that we are not teaching you anything, only reminding you of that which you already know.

For those who might be drawn to read this work at a later time, I feel that the greatest value lies not in our conceptual answers to your questions but in this shared energy itself.

You are approaching a time when Earth will become fourth density; then today's humans who are presently third-density energy will graduate from this plane.

You are approaching a time when each of you will be fully telepathic to others, when there will be no holding back and no clinging to another but just sharing that which is.

At that point there still will be an emotional body. You will still feel emotions. However, there will be equanimity about that which arises and, thus, no need to fling emotion at another.

You will experience total compassion toward what you feel from another, with no fear or closing; no sense of being attacked by another's pain, but only compassion for that pain.

What is it like to be that way? Each of you is approaching that more and more in your life so that now it is possible for six humans and two spirits to hang out together and to enjoy each other's energy. The humans have reached a level of consciousness where, when there is some reactivity, it is noticed quickly and worked with, with love. I wonder what inspiration that might give to those who walk this path and aspire to reach the point where they can share openly with others, without the heart closing; without the reactivity that may lead to pain for beings.

Thus, while the content may be of intellectual interest and also help to inspire and teach in some ways, it feels to me that our very working together is of supreme importance. To that end, to whatever degree it is natural, I would suggest as much of a moving dialogue as possible rather than long talks. When two of you converse, you understand when the other is ready to speak. You finish that immediate thought and stop. So, if the principle known as Q'uo finds this appropriate, I would like to see our working together move in that direction as much as is possible.

We[24] tossed many topics around in the car, as I am sure you have here. I feel not only Q'uo ready to speak here, but many of you. What are your thoughts? That is all.

(Carla channeling)

Q'uo: We, too, greet you in the love and in the light of the one infinite Creator.

We approach this meeting with the greatest of joy and echo the one known as Aaron's exclamation of delight at the beauty of the energies of this circle of seeking. How much of each of you is brought together in new ways each time there is a meeting! It is a joining not only of minds, hearts, souls, and spirits, but also the seemingly

---

[24] Barbara Brodsky had driven from Michigan to Kentucky with a companion, Karen, and had joined Jim McCarty, Carla Rueckert, Roman, and Kim, who lived at L/L Research.

humdrum contraptions in which you are carried! The strong effect of physical nearness is its possibility for spontaneous communication; the combustion of spirits searching, sharing, and encouraging each other together.

We pause for enough time to elapse that all may sense and feel the connections of harmonizing energy swirling circularly about this group. Feel the aliveness of this fresh-forged unity! We pause.

(A pause for silent group meditation.)

In gratitude, we of Q'uo ask for a first query.

Roman: Would Q'uo suggest how to find a way of looking at the turmoil in one's life when that turmoil is very emotional? Is there a way to balance all that seems to be negative and pressuring and happening seemingly at the same time? Is there a general principle that can be extracted from feelings unique to me that others would enjoy too?

Q'uo: The beginning of a more friendly environment is light. When one sits in darkness, one has no perspective, no reference points. Claustrophobia surrounds the timid soul. So it is with emotional and spiritual feelings that are dark. Like the body itself, the spirit feels overwhelmed by dark emotions. How to lighten the darkness and the burden of concern? We move to Aaron. I am Q'uo.

(Barbara channeling)

Aaron: My dear ones, first you must look at the erroneous assumption that the turmoil and darkness are your enemies. When you experience turmoil, that is just turmoil. When you experience fear, that is just fear. Then there is the secondary reaction to that turmoil or fear. It is not fear that closes your heart and sends you into the darkness but your reaction to that turmoil or fear. Can you see the difference?

It takes a great deal of practice in awareness to begin to notice the process. First is the arising of fear. With that first notice of fear, you are still neutral about it. You are not frightened of the fear.

Then you move to the stage of feeling attacked. At that point, there is a change in the chemical balance of the body and a change in the vibrational frequency of the light body. I see it as a constriction in your energy field, so that the light, which was moving freely through, out of, and into you, suddenly becomes trapped in this physical vessel, bouncing back and forth, truly in turmoil. It looks a bit like a pinball machine with the ball going *bing, bing, bing, bing, bing!*

You are not here to get rid of anything in your life. If turmoil, confusion, or fear is what is experienced, you do not need to get rid of it. Rather, learn how to greet it as a friend; to allow the experience of it with your heart kept as open as it can be; no judgment if it is closing a bit, but consciously making an effort to stay open. Then the aversion to the emotion does not cause closing.

Then none of the old-mind matters; the remembrances, in this body and other bodies, of this kind of fear and all the projections into the future do not become part of the issue. You are just here with this moment of fear.

Are you familiar with those sticky burrs that catch on the legs of your pants as you walk through the field? The pants are the material of your fear. The burrs are all the added burdens of the past and the future. As they knot together it becomes an unworkable mass. That is what closes you into darkness.

Being mindful of that pattern in yourself, you find that you can ask yourself to stay in this moment with this very workable and much lighter bit of fear or turmoil or confusion and allow the experience of it. It takes courage. It takes sharp awareness.

When you do this, you come back to your connection with the light. This is not something you have to grasp at or create in yourself. You are not, for example, naturally depressed or frightened. The lightness, the openness, the lovingkindness, the generosity and patience, the energy, and the courage are all qualities that are natural to you. They are small seeds within you. But if you take a small seed, put it in a pot, and then put it in a dark closet, it cannot grow. It needs light.

Your mindfulness of your reaction to fear is a way of opening the closet door and inviting in light. You are making a statement: "Fear is not who I am. At this moment I am experiencing fear, confusion, and perhaps the outgrowths of fear, such as anger or greed. But that is not who I am."

As you learn to do this, you start to see that each of those catalysts is in fact a gift offering you the chance to practice just what you most need to practice, which is how to be with a painful catalyst without pulling the closet door closed behind yourself, without needing to seek that protection. In essence, you are practicing how to allow yourself to stay open and vulnerable.

This is your deepest connection with the light, this deep knowing: "In essence, I am spirit. I am divine and connected with the Divine. The body may be vulnerable, but I cannot be harmed if my heart is open and loving."

This is the way of opening the door: remembering your connection. Through countless times of practice, you deepen your ability to keep your heart open, no matter what comes. When your heart is open, you no longer have the illusion of being in darkness. Rather, the turmoil, the anger, or the greed is seen more clearly as the illusion that deepens the sense of separation.

I am not suggesting that it is easy, but it is workable. My brother/sister Q'uo wishes to speak. That is all.

(Carla channeling)

Q'uo: I am Q'uo and give thanks to the one known as Aaron.

As you consider his words of excellent advice, you may wonder that you seemingly already knew that which has been addressed. The question then becomes, "Why can I not put these truths into practice?"

144

Consider that you have two intelligences. Your first intelligence, and the one that you largely use, is the intelligence that came with your physical vehicle.

The second intelligence is of another order. You are one of an infinite number of stations, shall we say, that in computer language runs a metaprogram that you would call a primary distortion of the One who is all: infinite mind or intelligent infinity. The intelligence come from essences bathed in this second environment, this mind with its perfect infinity and its absolute awareness.

The hitch lies in running the answer back into the first animal intelligence. There is an excellent connection between the metamind and the individual idiosyncratic mind that you carry just for this incarnational experience. It is, however, a connection made deep within the roots of the first mind. This lies in the domain you call the subconscious. This connection has been characterized as "the still, small voice."

Still it is, and silent, to a profound level. Small it is as well, if it is evaluated by intellectual standards. For the metaprogramming, shall we say, of the love that is the Logos is that which enfolds and becomes one with the listener in this blessed, silent communion.

How often has each sat to meditate and felt no realizable touch of the great mind? Yet stubbornly, again and again, 'midst self-imprecations for being foolish and shallow, do doubting seekers such as all here go again to the table of silent heaven's fare and hold up the self like a dish, saying, "Feed me. However this works, I wish to be one with this bread of heaven that is found when least expected in the course of regular meditation."

The dark feeling from judging and fearing the emotions experienced is not easily lightened by pursuing logical, data-consuming thoughts and opinions. Far more skillful is the seeker who decides to move from the incarnational program into the overarching metaprogram.

Do you see, my brother, that you already are aware of perceptions concerning fear and are stuck, shall we say, more in how to place the truth in a position that will actually affect that dark-feeling mind?

(A pause while Q'uo's question is considered.)

We gather by the silence of the one known as Roman that he may not precisely understand our query to him. That is all right. We speak to the generality of your condition.

We also have two kinds of mind, as we have incarnations also. We share in the wonderment that all our seeming knowledge does not automatically become manifested in our thoughts and actions. It is, however, the more skillful use of the concern about dark-seeming situations to do something like that which we did to begin this session of working: We all sat and felt the spontaneous circulation of harmonizing and encouraging vibrations, each offering love to each, each feeling the love of each.

In times of ghastly turmoil, there is the incarnational instinct to cringe, to back away, or to explode into defensive action. Remembrance of an essential moment of flowing harmony moves the mind's eye to gaze and move toward that subconscious linkage into all-mind, the spontaneous, essential feeling, rather than intellectual thought processes, that yields a true moment of the joy of love itself, being placed like the light in the closet that gives you the courage to remain quietly observant, neither running away in the mind nor grasping the problem with such constrictive and fearing bonds.

The one known as Aaron would say, "View the situation with neither attachment nor aversion."

Do you wish to query further, my brother?

Roman: Yes, with my intellectual mind. I wish to give others in the circle a chance to ask questions first. I would like to thank both of you for offering your thoughts. Thank you.

(Barbara channeling)

Aaron: I wish to return to Q'uo's clear statement that your heart understands, and that your human, incarnational brain cannot follow. It is precisely this that gives you such grief, because in the wisdom of your heart you understand your connection. That which Q'uo has called the metaprogram is the reality; the brain's frantic fear is illusion.

And yet, you find yourself moving toward the illusion. At that point anger often arises at the self. At some level there is a knowing: "I am responding to this mindless illusion. I am like a mouse on a treadmill, and I cannot get off." The only way to reconnect yourself with reality is to notice the judgment that is arising and return love to the self; to have love for this being that is running around on a fear-created treadmill so that it cannot hear the deeper wisdom of that small, still voice within.

Simply put, the light is always there. When you find yourself in darkness, you must ask, "Why is it that there is this illusion of darkness? Why have I closed myself in?"

You are light. You know that you are light. Yet to fully express that in the human incarnation is a very, very difficult thing. And this is precisely the way it needs to be. If it were easy, what would you be learning?

I am not suggesting that your lives need to be difficult or painful, but if you were already perfect, you would not be here in the incarnation. If the heart was always open and there was no reverberation to the chords of fear, then you would not need to be here in an incarnate state.

When you notice the arising of that fear, it can become a catalyst to have compassion for this being that is feeling fear. Just a tiny bit of compassion begins to crack open the door, just a tiny bit of light coming in. It serves as a reminder: "I am stuck in the illusion. This is reality, this tiny sliver of light. Follow it. Trust it."

As my brother/sister reminded you, you have two intelligences. Habit has dictated to you that you follow the human intelligence while in incarnation and so you become very unused to following the higher intelligence. The physical body has built up the catalysts of so many lifetimes into habitual, unskillful patterns.

We talk about this fight-or-flight idea. As my brother/sister said, you cringe at it or strike back defensively. But that is not natural to you or necessary to you. It is learned behavior. It is precisely that learned behavior that serves as the tool for learning. You cannot simply decree, "I will not run in fear. I will not fight back." Yes, you can develop a strong degree of self-control, but that does not change the harmony or lack of harmony in the experience. That does not bring in love.

Can you have some compassion for the being who has developed this mindless pattern of fleeing or fighting? Can you begin to understand that your awareness of that pattern is the beginning of the path toward being free of it?

The pattern in itself is not a problem. Yes, it leads to unwholesome karma. It leads to hurt for others. In that sense, of course, it is a problem. But when you relate to it as a problem, you relate to it as something to fight against or to get rid of: "I am not going to act this way anymore." That is just more judgment to yourself, more hatred. You are involved in the resultant fear and not attending to the causes.

When, instead, you see this being whose fearful brain has developed this fight-or-flight mechanism and feel some kindness for the being caught in a very tight place, then you allow yourself the possibility of hearing the deeper voice within; of hearing the deeper wisdom that whispers, "You are safe. Keep the heart open."

There is something else. When we know something is good for us but we do not do it, it is logical to ask why. When I say that the fight-or-flight mechanism is not natural to you but learned behavior, I also note that it was learned many lifetimes ago, when the creature that you were sought to defend itself. To continue to survive and to do what is necessary to survive is natural to you, so you have learned unskillful behavior in order to allow the continuity of that particular life-form.

As soon as fear arose, there was a sense of separation, and you lost the clarity of the awareness that you were connected to every other life-form. Instead, armoring against the fear became a protection of the small ego-self. This was part of the distortion of self-awareness.

You have been running with that pattern ever since, each of you. Your work here is not to get rid of anything in yourself or to change anything in yourself, but to begin to know who you truly are and to allow that reality to penetrate so that you can more fully live it rather than living the illusion.

You need the illusion. It is what helps to point out the reality. It is the practice with the illusion that strengthens the reality.

By way of example, if you never knew the fear that "my needs might not be met"—a fear that leads to greed, hoarding, and clinging—then what would connection and generosity mean?

If you never had the sense that "I could be hurt. My needs might not be met," then of course giving would be very easy. There would be no sense of self or other, so you would give and give and give. It would be very beautiful, but what have you learned?

You are here to grow, so you are constantly handed those catalysts that you need for that growth. The illusion is the catalyst. That is why you have this "veil of forgetting" that separates you from clear sight of your spiritual reality when you take birth. Otherwise, the incarnate state would be simply a matter of self-control: "How strong can I be in this situation? How determined?" But you are here to learn faith, not self-control; to learn love, not the expression of willpower.

I have said that you learned long, long ago that you needed that fight-or-flight mechanism to defend the self. Now, when you are in that dark closet, seeing only the existence of the egocentric self—"me against them" separateness—then it is very difficult to see that what you are experiencing is illusion. You stay defended.

So first there must be the awareness: *This is defended behavior. This is casting me deeper into the illusion of separation.* Then you may notice the judgment arising: *I should not do that.* But, my dear one, if this were a small creature, a squirrel perhaps, and you chased after it with a stick and it turned and ran, would you think, *It should not do that. It should trust me?* Or if this small creature attacked you in its fear, would you think, *It should not do that. It should trust me?* Or would your heart reach out to this small creature whose fear was so intense that it had to flee or attack? You would feel compassion for it.

Can you look at yourself with that same compassion, simply seeing the patterns of so many lifetimes and knowing that now you have reached a level of consciousness, a level of growth, where you no longer need to follow those patterns blindly? The freedom from reactivity cannot grow out of the judgment of the self that has been reactive. Such freedom can only grow out of compassion for that self. Compassion allows the light in. It allows the remembering of the deeper reality of the metaprogram of love. That is all.

(Carla channeling)

Q'uo: As the teacher known as Aaron states, you are in incarnation to grow from the inside of the nearly always somewhat dark interior of the mental and emotional closet. You may question the probability of achieving growth. However, you cannot avoid growing. The illusion works with mechanical force—call it friction—wearing away at the sensibility. All you need be concerned with in terms of growing is that you honor and respect that which is occurring, focusing more and more lucidly on the delineated structure of the present moment.

You, in observing the present moment, are doing all you can with the incarnational mind. Once observed, the catalyst will grow acute. There need be no further action except to turn and bless the incarnation with all its meandering, winding destinies and unexpected occurrences. We ask you to cast a warm and loving attention on yourself in the incarnational closet of flesh and limitation of viewpoint.

In this configuration the inner memory opens to the light of companionship, the light of joyful memories, and the use of affirmative imageries such as the light of the sun dancing upon the water. This is how the metamind thinks. It cannot be termed logical. To this mind sunshine is a song, a poem, a dance, or a zephyr of cool air on a hot day.

So it is that many find sunshine in the midst of confusion and self-compassion in the midst of judgment; by singing, as does this instrument; reading inspired writings; gazing at visual and tactile art created out of moments of clear, visionary sunlight shining through the artist to show what love is; and more, how perfectly unified all is. As the plangent tones of a truly heard piece of music pierce the incarnational mind with sweetness, so can you use these nonlogical images and practices to enhance and multiply the effect of silent meditation and communion.

You are light to others. Others are light to you. Beyond all else you are loved. It takes the breath away to ponder the totality of this love for even an instant. It is the love of All-Self by All-Self. It merely flows through you. You need not deserve it. You cannot own it. It is your real identity.

May each smile when next each discovers the self sitting in that emotional, closeted darkness. Yes, my friends, smile and reach the finger of attention to flick on the light of nonjudgment and compassion.

We are those of Q'uo, and we leave this group at this time, rejoicing in being once again able to share the teaching that teaches us so much. With the master known as Aaron, may we rejoice that each gentle being who is here has come. How miraculous the alphabet soup of shared life! Love one another and release that terrible need to find the sunshine while holding on to the limited point of view of the incarnational mind. We leave you in love and in light. We are known to you as those of Q'uo. Thank you and farewell. Adonai.

(Barbara channeling)

Aaron: I would like to offer a few brief, practical tools for your consideration. As my brother/sister of light said, you may picture yourself in that dark closet and have compassion for this being who is afraid of the dark.

It may help to take it further, to think perhaps of a child who is afraid of a dog. You walk down the street holding the child's hand

and suddenly there is a large dog in your path and the child cowers behind you. If you push that child and say, "Now pat the dog. You must," the child may conquer his fear enough to pat the dog, but he is never going to enjoy patting the dog. He never will choose to do it if he is not pushed.

Or you may say to the child, "I see how afraid you are. I think this looks like a nice dog. He is big. I am going to pat him. We have become friends." And you pat him and perhaps shake his paw. The child watches with no pressure. It may take a dozen meetings before the child is ready to come up and pat the dog himself.

You offer patience and compassion to the child. Offer yourself that same patience and compassion. Know how many lifetimes it has taken you to build up these patterns of fear and separation. When you acknowledge your own suffering and fear, and greet it with compassion instead of judgment, then you offer yourself a pathway back to the light.

It is something that you can practice constantly in all the small catalysts of your life; all the moments when somebody says or does something that irritates or offends you or offers you just the brief moments of impatience. You do not need to practice it with the very heavy emotions. You practice with the small things. You would not ask the child to pat an elephant or a tiger before he has learned to pat the dog.

Then, of course, there are ways of bringing more awareness of light into yourself. One that I would suggest as a useful exercise for many people is to plant a garden in your mind. Think of all of those small sprouts: generosity, patience, lovingkindness; so many, many more. Some of them are strong flowers in yourself already, and some of them you see as small seeds. Choose one that you can watch in yourself.

Now, it is very hard to measure such a seed as lovingkindness. You might want to choose one that is more easily seen in its physical form, one such as patience or generosity. You notice how often you are impatient or how often you are frightened of giving. Do you notice how often you are patient and generous? I do not speak only of material generosity here, but generosity with your time and your energy.

Begin to watch just one small sprout in yourself, when there is momentum to be patient or to be generous, for example, and then you will hear that small voice that says, *No, I am afraid.* Acknowledge it. Do not think, *You should not be afraid,* but, *I hear your fear. It is okay,* just the way you do with the small child: "I hear your fear."

And then make the skillful decision, if it is at all possible: *I am going to be patient. I am going to be present with the fear that says, "My needs will not be met here," or "I could be hurt," and I am going to ask myself to be patient or to be generous. And then I am going to watch the results.*

As you move into practicing that on a daily basis, you will find that you can change the old-mind patterns. You can be present with fear and reach for the light switch. You can keep connected to that deepest truth and beauty that is you.

Another tool that comes to mind is an ancient meditation practice called tonglen, a practice of sending out the positive and good and taking in the negative and harmful to develop equanimity and compassion in the practitioner.

It is a very simple meditation. I would ask in closing if you would join me in it. First, simply be aware of yourself sitting in a cylinder of light. Breathe in. Feel the light descending through the crown chakra and down to the heart center. Exhale and release it, just the way it came in. Inhale, light descending to the heart. Then exhale and release. Feel yourself expanding with that light. Open to that light. Notice if there is any resistance to letting it in and soften around that resistance.

With this light filling you, bring to your heart and mind the image of a being who is suffering. It may be someone you know or a stranger across the globe. Think not of the whole world of suffering but rather just one person or one life-form of whatever sort you choose.

Breathing in this time, allow that light and loving energy to move to the heart center. Then, breathing out, direct it to the suffering being. Breathe in light and love. Exhaling, direct it out to the being who is suffering. Inhale light. Exhale to where it is most needed, just allowing that light and loving energy to channel through you, allowing that being's suffering to touch your heart with the wish, "You are suffering. May you find peace. May you find an end to your suffering. May you be healed." Allow yourself to be a channel for that loving energy. Please try it for a moment on your own and then we will go on to the last step.

(A pause while the group meditates.)

That being's suffering is so heavy. You may begin to see it as a dark cloud of blackness—a heavy, sticky kind of blackness. Your good wishes are felt, but the darkness is so heavy that they cannot fully penetrate.

We expand the meditation now. Inhale love and light. Exhale, releasing it to that being who is suffering.

Now, inhale that darkness that you see, letting that, too, run through your heart, but not holding it in you in any way. You are simply the channel for its release. Exhale and release it to God, to ground of Being, which is far more skilled and able to handle that heaviness than you are.

Inhale love and light and release it to the one who is suffering. Inhale the pain and release it to the Eternal.

Inhale light. Direct it to where it is needed. Inhale that suffering in whatever form you envision it. Notice any resistance to letting it touch you and come into your heart. Soften around that and then release it.

As you practice this meditation, let it bring you back into your connection with all that is. Let it remind you that you truly are a channel for love, light, and healing, and that you are also a channel through which suffering may find its release, so that those who are your brothers and sisters may not carry that weight unsupported.

I am going to be quiet now for several minutes and ask you just to practice this on your own.

(A pause while the group practices.)

When you feel alone, frightened, and in darkness, make the conscious choice to open the door of illusion that holds you confined in darkness and to bring in light. I know no better way of bringing in light to yourself than to wish to share that light with others.

It helps you to know who you are and to remind you of your connection with all that is. The serving of others in that way, the joyous willingness to serve, helps connect you to the light and divinity in yourself. It helps you express that joy that begins to move through you. With that increasing lightness, the clouds that surround you become more and more transparent, and the storm begins to blow away.

It has been a joy to share with all of you this evening and, as always, a deep gift to share energy and thought with my brother/sister of Q'uo. I thank you all for your joyous participation in this circle and for the light and love that each of you brings to your search. My love to you all. That is all.

Session 9

Weekend 3, Part 2 of 2
(This session was preceded by a period of tuning and meditation.)

(Barbara channeling)

Ariel: This is Ariel.[25] I greet you, my brothers and sisters of the light, with love and with gratitude for your willingness to allow me to join your circle. It is a grace to be here in this room from which so much light emanates.

This instrument spoke last night of sensing a very old and ancient energy, one that seemed in her senses to transcend all duality. There was/is/will be, indeed, such an observer.

Please understand as I speak that it is not the Spirit that speaks. The Spirit would be incapable of such speech. Speech must come through the mental body. While I possess a mental body, I am imperfect. What I express to you, then, is merely my opinion with as little distortion as I am able to give it. I humbly ask that you take whatever I say with that recognition. It is not offered as Truth with a capital T, but as the clearest seeing of which this one is capable. And that is all I can give you.

I once spoke to a group in another of your cities about the origins of the Earth as I had understood them and experienced them. There were those on the immaterial planes who were stuck in some way and in need of greater catalyst for their learning. It was understood that this must be a plane of love; that certainly negativity would enter, but that those who saw the need were willing and eager to give of themselves to lay the foundation of love.

---

[25] This source may be identified with the energy of the Archangel Ariel, also spelled Uriel. Aaron identifies Ariel as one of his primary teachers. Ariel is occasionally trance channeled by Barbara.

156

My dear brothers and sisters, you have learned. This experiment that we have called Earth has been successful beyond our wildest imaginings. Of course, there is negativity on this plane. There needs to be. You understand that it is part of your catalyst for learning and that there is no duality, no difference between the positive and the negative in the long run, and that, at the same time, negativity must be resisted with love because of the suffering that it creates.

What has occurred on this earth plane that has seemed so wonderful is that those of you of third density who are learning these lessons of faith and love graduate with far more depth, also, into the fourth- and fifth-density lessons of compassion and wisdom. Of course, there is no time pressure, so you may well ask, "What difference does it make if we learn the lessons ahead of our grade, so to speak?"

The difference is that compassion and wisdom are not finite skills. The being who moves into fourth density already with deep compassion and wisdom expands those qualities far beyond what has come to be expected on other planes of learning.

Our experience, then, is that those of you who move through this earth plane, working skillfully with the catalysts of this plane, have moved into an expanded sense of compassion and wisdom by the end of seventh density, and in that way expand the Infinite.

While the compassion and wisdom of that which we might call God or the Eternal are infinite, they are also ever-learning and ever-expanding. And those of you who move into seventh and finally eighth density through this plane, and return to that spirit that is your essence, bring a far deeper wisdom and compassion that expands the Eternal and Infinite.

That you on Earth are capable of this as you move beyond the earth plane on your journey, of course, makes this plane a target of negative energy. You understand that there has been a quarantine, as you phrase it, against physical contact, against the visitation by negative energy. And yet, of course, we must respect the free will of all beings. There has been effort, then, among those of positive polarity to help to strengthen as many people as we can and to teach them how to work with negative energy.

Love is a gift, but it also may become a distortion. One must learn how to balance that love with strength, with faith. I have said that the learning of wisdom and compassion on the earth plane has awed us, in a sense. And yet great care must be taken that faith and love are learned either before learning wisdom and compassion or simultaneously with it.

Distorted compassion can lead to a distortion of wisdom, which does not oppose negativity with love but rather feels the need to hear it out. In that way, negativity may play on that compassion and wisdom and manipulate immature faith and love.

We who profess to be guides and teachers can only share what we see with complete respect to your free will. We see a situation on Earth now whereby, with your own expanding understanding and curiosity, you are reaching out to the universe with "microphones," technological tools with which you hope to pick up outer-space signals. You are reaching out to take your true place in the universe. We cannot protect you any more than the wise parent strives to protect the child as he moves out of the sheltered home. We can only alert you to caution; not to fear, but to awareness.

Many watch this experiment we call Earth with a deep sense of hope because of the power of the light that comes from this plane. It is especially groups like this that draw the attention of both positivity and negativity. You know that. The question that many of us have is, are you ready for this move into the fourth density? Are you ready to deal with the onslaught of negativity that will be experienced on Earth if there is no longer any quarantine to that energy? In essence, have you developed that faith yet?

Much of the work that your groups do is the deepening of wisdom and compassion. Do not neglect the deepening of love and faith. It is harder to talk about love and faith than about wisdom and compassion. You can suggest skills, as the ones who are known as Q'uo and Aaron suggested last night—strategies, in a sense—for working with the catalysts of your density.

Do not forget the power of prayer, of connection to that light. I know I do not need to say this to this group, but there is nothing I have said today that you do not already know. I only hope to remind you of the importance of tempering your wisdom with faith and with love so that you do not become imbalanced and more susceptible to negative influence through the distortion of love that is not yet firmly understood.

I thank you for allowing me to share this with you today. I know that my brothers/sisters of light, those that you know as Q'uo and as Aaron, would also like to speak to you and to speak to your questions. With my joyous love to each of you, I leave this instrument at this time.

(Barbara channeling)

Aaron: This is Aaron. My love to you all. Barbara is still in a very deep trance. You cannot call her name to bring her out of it as she is deaf. I would ask that you direct your energy to her, simply calling her in your minds as I will also do. That is all.

(Carla channeling)

Q'uo: Greetings to all in the love and in the light of the one infinite Creator. The privilege of speaking with you is appreciated. As the one known as Ariel has said, we offer opinion only.

The difficulty of aiming for an absolute is that in your universe of relativity, one may approach but never reach the absolute. Yet still, we encourage each to comfort, protect, and give support to that pilgrim within which hungers for a more nearly pure experience of being transparent to eternity and to the limitless light of the Logos that offers embodiment to eternity and infinity.

Earlier we spoke concerning the long and difficult path of endurance. Each wonders, perhaps, why endurance would seem to call first for faith and then for understanding and wisdom.

The archetypical feature of wisdom is its ability to regulate. This is seen in the archetypes of the body,[26] wherein the Potentiator of the Body is that which controls and manages the physical energies rather than those energies being fully open and uncontrolled.

However, the need for regulation of energy cannot precede the development of a firm and persistent compassion. Compassion is a corollary of faith. Thusly the first persistence is in working with your consciousness to exhort and encourage the self to be foolishly faithful—foolish, that is, in the eyes of a pusillanimous world.

The quarrelsome world turns to one who is attempting a persistent devotion to a life in faith and says, "You have not got the picture. You do not have a clue as to the realities of the grimy situation that you call civilization and societal interaction."

However, those who do attempt living by faith are often more nearly entwined with those viny, dark energies that curl about your illusion than those who are so cynical and world-wise. You see, they attempt to regulate an unforgiven incarnation.

The seeker must first, in faith, face every encyclopedic, universal kind of being that makes up the whole self. It is this universal self, with as much of negativity as positivity experienced in its makeup, that the seeker embraces. The seeker who wishes to have faith embraces all without regulating or judging the phase or facet of the whole of nature's ways. Thusly is the incarnation redeemed and forgiven by the self.

This process is only hindered by the wisdom that says, "You must flee from spite and scorn, from the dirt and discordance of negative thinking and move instead in mental, emotional, and spiritual lands of light and joy." Wisdom would divide the self against the self if that self moved to learning wisdom before it had forgiven the whole self first.

---

[26] The Q'uo group is drawing upon information originally given through the Ra group in the early 1980s. The Ra's discussion of the archetypes of the mind, the body, and the spirit may be found almost entirely in *Book IV* of *The Law of One*. *The Law of One* books are available from your bookstore or from L/L Research.

Session 9

How can one forgive those precincts of personality that are capable of murder, theft, and a multitude of regrettable activities, except by faith?

What is faith?

Can you catch it from another?

Can you learn it, as at school?

We might suggest that it is by far the quicker entry into a faithful life to begin accepting what is, precisely at that moment. If you, at that moment when you decide to commit the self to faithful living, are in the midst of traffic, then your first act of faith is to experience the beauty of all that is seen in the hustling, bustling street. By faith you suddenly experience sitting more lightly in your car, touching with love and reverence the steering wheel and the gearshift knob. It simply needs to be deeply accepted by the self.

Then comes the long, long pilgrimage of deepening that faith of living, ever aware that faith, not words or manifestations, offers the truer suggestions and solutions to the very complex and often troublesome living environment of the incarnation. Only when the pilgrim is solidly and firmly devoted to a life in faith, so that the open heart's energies flow and flow and flow without stop or hindrance, is it time to consider wisdom.

May we, that is, Aaron and we, invite a query?

(Barbara channeling)

Aaron: My dear friends, may I invite your questions, not specifically about what has been said, but whatever question is closest to your heart this morning. That is all.

Carla: As we who have been working in the spiritual path for some time go through our days, it seems that we don't become very much more intelligent in our use of affirmations than we were in the beginning. I think that praying without ceasing is the ideal, but I seem only to be able to approach it just so far.

Dana: Carla, you just asked a question that's been on my mind for a week.

Carla: How can we get closer than that to being faithful?

Aaron: There is a difference between the concept of prayer without ceasing and the experience of it. When you move into it as concept, it becomes another "should," something else at which you are grasping. I ask you to consider in what ways you may more deeply allow the experience of it, transcending thought and concept. That is all.

(Carla channeling)

Q'uo: We shall leave you with a few thoughts and allow the energies to flow once again through Aaron and Barbara.

We may say that in the learning of faith, your greatest strength is each other. We know you value each other and we encourage each to have a light and loving but utterly persistent devotion, each to each. In any relationship, each may teach, may learn, may hurt, may heal, may do together anything that occurs, better and more efficiently than the solitary soul.

Therefore, we encourage communication by your letters when there is distance between you, so that when all come together there is already the full and loving interplay of energies that potentiate each and, more than that, the growing oversoul, if we may use that term, of the group, by focusing upon the being as part of this or other groups.

You form and re-form small beginning attempts at the life of a social memory complex. You, at this juncture in space/time, are beginning to find the company of others more helpful. This is the natural progression toward your fourth-density experience. Welcome to the beginning of the New Age.

We leave this instrument and this group, glorying in the love and in the light of the one infinite Logos. Farewell and peace.

Session 9

(Barbara channeling)

Aaron: There is only so much to be said about faith itself. I do not wish to be repetitious. Rather, I wish to speak from a different perspective, one that my brother/sister Q'uo brought up last night. After I spoke about opening the heart and being compassionate to oneself, Q'uo said, "You aspire to that but find yourself blocked."

You also aspire to a life of faith and find yourself blocked. Many of you have high intelligence, and at times you use that intelligence as a way of grasping at understanding because you feel frustrated. You want to feel faith, but you cannot force that. You cannot create faith in yourself. You can only gently remove the blockages to faith so its natural appearance may expand in you.

What I wish to point out is that you may grasp at understanding and in a sense that is a grasping at control. It grows out of a place of fear. Love does not deal with concepts but with penetrating all concepts and all appearances to get at the true nature of things.

When a catalyst in your life creates pain or confusion and you strive to understand it and to deal with it in an intellectual way so that you may give yourself a program—"I could do this and that and that"— that takes you further from faith.

When you can notice the fear arising in you, founded on those uncomfortable catalysts—when you can notice the desire to control that grows out of the fear—then you may move back to the open heart.

I cannot say what faith is. I can only speak about how it manifests itself. And perhaps the prime manifestation that I see is the open heart. This is what I would call the heart of surrender, the heart that knows, *I am not in control. I am not running this show. I do not really understand anything, but I will try to greet with love whatever is put before me. I will try to attend the fear with compassion and allow that fear to dissolve so I may move back into love.* This is the demonstration of faith, not the thinking about faith but the living in faith.

In this way, faith precedes wisdom. You do not need to know anything, just to follow the guidance of your open heart. When you follow that guidance, let go of all need to control, and are simply present with whatever catalyst is there in that moment as lovingly as you can be, then the mind ceases thinking about, grasping at, planning, and controlling. Then the mind is free to penetrate beyond thought and really understand at a level to which thought cannot take you.

If surrender is a manifestation of faith, then courage, willpower, determination, and energy are all ingredients that make surrender possible. How much harder it is to face the unknown than the known fear! Surrender does not mean saying, "I give up," and ceasing to express your energy. It means expressing your energy in a direction of love with no understanding of where you are going. You cannot foresee, in your human shells, where your path is taking you. You cannot know what it is that you or another needs to learn.

I would like to use an example here, a being that Barbara has seen as a past life, one that she has agonized over and for whom she has finally found real forgiveness and great love. This being was a Native American medicine man. He taught peace and organized a peace conference of sorts at the request of many others. Beings from many tribes and other races attended.

There was one tribe that had great fear and they came in and massacred the whole group. And then white soldiers on the hillside swept down and massacred those of that tribe, even the women and children.

This being that Barbara was survived all of that attack. He sat on the hillside and asked himself, *What did I do wrong? I brought this together. Somehow I should have known it could not have worked. Look at all the death, all the devastation. Am I responsible?* He had not yet learned the lessons of faith, and so he blamed himself and punished himself in his mind with guilt, remorse, and self-hatred. He forgave the others but he could not forgive himself.

What he did not understand was that this massacre in some way was necessary for them to learn peace. Had those beings come together and formed a peace treaty and signed it, it would have been a very fragile kind of peace. There was not a tribe there that did not suffer from the outburst of fear. There was not a tribe there who could not take those experiences home and say, "If we had peace, this would not happen."

There was no one to blame. Everyone's fear was involved in it. This was what they needed to learn. They had tried gentler ways of learning and had not been able to learn. The peace that was created some few years later was built on that experience of loss, of pain. That loss and pain were an explanation of the need to open their hearts and trust one another so as not to continue to destroy each other.

Now this Native American, this being, sat there; and he did not have faith. He thought he knew what they needed to learn, which was peace. And he was right. That is what they needed to learn. But he thought he knew *how* they needed to learn it.

You never know. You do not know what another needs to learn. You cannot take another's lessons away from them. You can only clarify your own energy as much as you can and offer as much love as is possible in any situation and then surrender: "Truly, thy will be done. I do not know anything." Can you see how your efforts to understand conceptually, to pigeonhole it all and make logical explanations, offer an escape from the far harder task of having faith?

Compassion can also be misused in this way. I have spoken very, very often with people about compassion and codependence. It is hard to have faith in a situation and give loving energy to that other being whose energy is distorted into unskillful patterns, but to say no to those unskillful patterns, that you will not aid them.

Compassion becomes distorted into, "I want to help." But as soon as you say, "I want to help," you must ask yourself, *Why do I want to help? Is their pain too uncomfortable for me, so I want to fix their pain? Can I trust the whole situation, come back to faith and love, and attend the fear in my own heart, seeing how my pain reflects their pain? What do I find when I get in touch with that fear in myself? Who is it that I want to fix—them or me? Do I want to fix them so I will not have to pay attention to the distortions within myself, because the mirror will have been removed that reminds me of those inner distortions? Can I have faith that this friend or loved one is in a painful situation and that I am in a painful situation because there is something to learn? Can I truly say, "Thy will be done," and stop trying to make anything special happen, just be present with whatever is with as much love as I can?*

I said before, this does not mean no energy, no effort. But where is effort given: to fix, or to surrender and offer love? To let go of the need to control—to see the fear that it springs from and let go—is one of the hardest of human experiences. It is only from that place of deep faith that undistorted wisdom and compassion can develop. Wisdom penetrates into the depths of reality rather than thinking about reality. Compassion grows out of connection to all that is rather than the concept of compassion, which puts a bandage over your own pain.

How do you find that kind of faith? It takes practice. That is why you are here. Remember, each of you is, in essence, an angel in an earth-suit. This body enfolds the true nature of you and allows it to move through the earth-plane situations that offer you learning. The more you can allow yourself to be aware that both are real—the spirit and the physical—and that you are learning on both planes at the same time, the more you can live your life in faith.

When fear grabs hold of you, it is so easy to forget who you are! Your prayer without ceasing helps you to stay connected.

When I hear the term "prayer without ceasing," what I think of is awareness of that flow of brilliant light, that umbilical cord, so to speak, that connects you with the Divine, so that you never lose track of who you are. And when you never lose track of who you are, you cannot lose track of who anyone else is. They are just another part of you, another part of God.

So that is one tool to deepening faith. The other is awareness. They are part of each other: prayer and awareness.

Here, awareness speaks of what blocks faith and encourages a willingness to reach out for that hand of the Divine, to take that energy into yourself. And with that opening of heart you may lovingly greet each catalyst, transcend your fear, and keep your heart open. Then you may truly say, "Thy will be done. I am not in control here. I surrender. I offer my loving energy in whatever way it can best heal this situation, in whatever way learning may best happen. But I do not know what that is. Instead of trying to figure it out with my brain, which is the seat of fear, I will try to understand it and listen with my heart." That is the best way I know to begin to live a life in faith.

I would ask if there are questions at this time.

(There are no questions.)

It is such joy to share the loving energy in this room. I thank you all for the opportunity to speak with you and offer my thoughts. And I offer thanks to my brother/sister of Q'uo for the opportunity to pass this back and forth, to learn and teach from and with each other.

I echo the words of the one you know as Q'uo: When your hearts are open, when you are in deep sharing and communication with one another, you are coming as close as the human can come to the fourth-density group experience. While you know there is no need to practice that which will be learned in another density while in this density, yet you are all making that shift. You are beginning to understand that you can keep your hearts open to one another.

And how much greater is your energy when it is shared! How much easier it is to have faith when that energy is shared!

Enough words. My love to each of you. That is all.

WEEKEND 4

We gathered again in Kentucky, just ten weeks after weekend 3. This time we had more people in the house. These sessions were so wonderful that we wished to share them, and people begged to come. Outside, it was midwinter and the cold wind rattled the windowpanes. Inside Carla and Jim's living room, we sat together in warmth and love.

This time we had three days, so we began on Friday night, and then had two sessions on Saturday and one closing session on Sunday. Once again Carla had been cooking and there was much feasting. All the bedrooms were filled and the house resounded with laughter. During the time between sessions, it was a joy to get to know each other, human to human.

While it was a larger group than previous weekends, it was still small and personal. The first questions came from the hearts of the gathered group. Our concerns were centered around the fact that we were all spiritual seekers, trying to live our lives with love, and yet we were puzzled as to how to serve others without disregarding our own needs.

Carla always said that cooking was a sacred activity and she rejoiced in having the opportunity to share the wonderful tastes of living food with those who came to make the gathering circle. She always seemed to be blissful in the kitchen and we all benefited from her offerings.

Carla's Honey Soy Chicken Wings

6 pounds of chicken wings, rinsed and dried on paper towels
4 tablespoons olive oil
1 cup soy sauce
4 tablespoons ketchup
2 cups honey
6 cloves of garlic, minced
1 tablespoon sea salt
1 teaspoon black pepper

Preheat the oven to 375°F. Oil a 9 x 13-inch storage pan.
Arrange the chicken wings in the storage pan.
Mix the oil, soy sauce, ketchup, honey, garlic, salt, and pepper.
    Pour it over the chicken.
Bake the chicken for one hour or until the sauce is caramelized.
Serves: 12

Session 10

Weekend 4, Part 1 of 4
(This session was preceded by a period of tuning and meditation.)

Group question: Concerning codependency and compassion, "How do I live more lovingly for others and still live with respect for myself?"

This question relates to the following statements from Aaron: "You aspire to perfect service and to prayer without ceasing. The being cannot pray without ceasing while it is moored in judgment and confusion. The heart and energy are not open. It can pray without ceasing when it notes the arising of fear and allows fear to be a catalyst to compassion and connection. Heartfelt prayer arises from that connection. Primary is the question of making friends with your own humanness and imperfections in the incarnate state."

(Barbara channeling)

Aaron: My greetings and love to you all. I raised this question some weeks ago because it seems to come from so many of your hearts. I wonder if it would be useful for you to offer any additional thoughts you have about this question. In the rephrasing of it as it comes from your own hearts, there is sometimes that twist that helps you see where the distortion lies. I would pause here for a moment, then, and ask if there are any additions to the question. That is all.

Carla: How can we be of service to others without dumping all over ourselves, using up our time, talent, and treasure and not having anything left over for our little special projects? Others are asked to clarify or add to this question.

K.: I think it is right to the point.

Aaron: Let us first speak about the word "codependence." All beings are, in fact, codependent. The word has picked up bad connotations in your language, as if there were something negative about being codependent. But, in fact, it is not codependence in itself that is negative. The negativity derives from fear. When codependence is acknowledged as part of your connection with all that is, it is a wholesome state.

You breathe in the air. You are codependent with the trees that help create the atmosphere. Your bodies are largely water. At your death that water in your body moves back into the soil. In your breath there is moisture. The moisture from your body helps the trees grow.

Codependence, then, is not the problem. It is simply a statement of your nonseparation, your interbeingness. Rather, what we need to address is codependence as separation; that is, that state of fear that leads you to acts and words and simultaneous resentment about those acts and words, or the fear that leads you to encourage others in unwholesome acts as a protection to the self.

When two beings interact and wish mutually to serve each other, certainly that is codependence. But it is a skillful codependence where each being learns that it is part of a greater whole and honors its interactions with other beings.

The right hand does not withhold comfort from the left hand. They know themselves as part of the same body. Yet within the extended earth-plane experience, you view others as separate from self. Then negative codependence arises.

We define negative codependence, then, as acts and words based on an illusion of separation. Within that illusion of separation, fear has arisen and also a lack of clarity of the being's highest purpose.

Each of you has places of deep fear within you. There is some preference not to look into those places, a need not to confront that fear in yourself. When another's demands upon you allow you to escape from that confrontation, a part of you says, "Oh no, incessant demands," and a part of you says, "Thank you. Thank you for the projection of your demands."

Last month I talked to a mother who wanted very much to write. That was her expressed desire. She had a baby, perhaps a four-year-old child, and that baby had a tendency to whine and to pull on her constantly for attention, which tendency I noticed as we were talking. The child's self-entertainment was that it constantly came over and interrupted.

Of course, the mother has unconsciously taught it this behavior. When you use the term "codependence" in a negative way, it grows out of this type of relationship where the mother insists that she wants to write and wants her child to become more independent so that she has freedom for her work, and yet surreptitiously encourages that dependence because it protects her from writing. At a much deeper level, the writing terrifies her. This, then, is what we might define as unwholesome codependence.

As with everything else in your life, negative codependence is an invitation. When you see a repetitive pattern that seems to hamper you in some way, it would seem wise to ask yourself, *What does the continuation of this pattern protect me from? Is there any way that I am encouraging it?* Then you may begin to look at the fear that has led to continuation of that pattern.

At first it seems almost impossible to change it, to say no. There is self-discipline involved here. At some point, as you look at the patterns that seem discouraging to you, you need to ask yourself, *What if I just say no?* And then watch very, very carefully to see what happens.

Now here is another area of confusion, of distortion perhaps, because many of you do get this far and decide, "I am going to say no." But you are not really aware what it is to which you are saying no. In your mind, you think you are saying no to the other and to their uncomfortable demands. That *no*, then, has arisen from a place of anger. You still do not see that what you are saying no to is your own fear.

For this mother I just described, she might finally say no to that child: "No, you must sit down and entertain yourself. Here are crayons. Here is a book. Here are blocks. I am not to be disturbed for half an hour."

But it does not come out that way. Instead it comes out as, "No! You sit down and play with your toys! I have had enough!" That kind of anger pours out. Who is she really angry at? What is the anger really about?

When you are very clear in yourselves that you need to do something a certain way and that your choice is not harmful to another, it is not hard to say no.

It becomes hard when there is no clarity, because you do not know whether you want to say no and end the behavior or whether you want to allow the behavior to continue. So, some of you get to the point of saying no but your no is said in anger, which escalates the tension between you, rather than speaking with love.

I have a good deal more I would like to say here. However, I feel Q'uo wishes to speak and will turn this over to my brother/sister. That is all.

(Carla channeling)

Q'uo: Greetings to all in this circle of seeking in the love and ineffable light of the one infinite Creator. It is such a thrill to blend our vibrations with your own as we allow our energies to merge with yours and become a hymn of praise and thanksgiving to the one source and Creator of all that there is.

We are most especially glad to have this opportunity to work with the one known as Aaron. This is unique in our experience of inner- and outer-plane cooperation. Perhaps you could say that Aaron and we are codependent in teaching our best for service to you, as you are codependent in sharing what we offer and in using that which you find useful!

We do not claim authority over you. Please use your discrimination and leave behind any information that does not meet with your needs and opinions. We would not be a stumbling block before you. This being said, we would like to state our opinion of the portion of this large query upon which we have begun work, for there are several portions to this issue.

Firstly, there is the portion of codependency that works with the Creator, its design, and its and your co-created agenda for this incarnational experience.

Secondly, there is the portion wherein the seeker is working to find the heart of its own self.

Thirdly, there is the portion dealing with relationships, not in the outer sense but rather in the sense of the self or the society in regards to the hook that ensnares you into so-called codependent behavior.

Fourthly, there is the portion devoted to the consideration of the seeker in relation to its central entities: the mate and the family and, in unusual occasions, a special acquaintance.

Perhaps you may see our feeling that, in dealing with the central relationships of one's incarnational experience, you are dealing with the Creator's plan, your work within this incarnation, and your generalized buttons, shall we say, or sensitive places wherein connections with the self or society are found to be frustrating in this codependent way.

Before we can consider fully the central codependency, however, let us begin with this latter, for it shall prove to be the way we move back into this series of discussions.

Here you are: you, the seeker. And although the life-mate or family member has seemingly associated with you in an unskillful way, and you with the other, there is still the full travel of free will. What force moves within your heart that causes the exchange of hurt and emotional pain?

Let us look at the force of need.

You see, my friends, you are entities who wish to be of service to others. Therefore, just as we, so you need others in order to be of service. This flavor of need undoubtedly played a role in your choice of this partner as a co-creator, and again within the illusion in manifestation. This other was chosen because this other needs you.

Now, this works very well in bringing together entities, both of which have planned to work upon changing fear to free joy. For did not the other entity also choose you because the other needed to be needed also? Thusly, a loving symbiosis, wherein each helps the other and each happily acknowledges the need for the other, becomes cramped and crushed by the seeming demands of those who express desires that will take up all of your space and time.

The need to be needed is likewise unlimited.

And, my friends, each other portion of the manifested personality also makes plans upon the available time. And that which worked so perfectly as symbiosis, when there was time enough and many fewer complexities of personality, hits the crunch of a far more complex agenda for living. Symbiosis has turned into codependency.

Fear has several flavors. Perhaps the most acute is the fear of running out of time. There are other fears here, too: the fear of not being appreciated, the fear of abandonment, and the fear of the month! These things change, but the tendency to react to your own fear does not change its flavor like the content of this month's fear, which will inevitably give way to your changing journey in consciousness.

So we ask you to begin looking at the contexts in which you live and give and love and attempt to serve others.

We move back to the one known as Aaron. We leave this instrument in love and in light. We are those of the principle of Q'uo.

(Barbara channeling)

Aaron: Jim, I can see the thought patterns forming in your mind but with Barbara's eyes closed, I cannot see whether those patterns find a continuity to your fingertips and to the keyboard. Thus, my question: Is this still too fast?

Jim: Yes.

Aaron: I will slow down as much as I am able. When there is a gap between the continuity of my energy, Barbara drifts in and out of the state needed to most clearly channel me. It will take some practice on her part to sit there for some moments with a blank and trust that the next thought is coming.

Session 10

I appreciate Q'uo's distinction between living symbiosis and codependence. Symbiosis is alive, a flowering of the energy of each to each, where perhaps codependence has its emphasis on the fear and need of dependence.

To be codependent on another there must be two. In fact, that is how you perceive yourselves. You are not your beloved friend or family member. You are not the water you drink. That is conventional reality. But in terms of a deeper reality, there is no separation.

When you care for a loved one with the sense, *When my work is done for this one, then and only then I can attend to myself,* this is delusion. This is seeing through the eyes of conventional reality.

When you see that your service to your loved one is truly also meeting your needs and that your needs intermesh so perfectly, then you are seeing with clarity and wisdom. This understanding of your fundamental connection with all that is, is essential to your growth.

We speak about love and fear. If you watch yourself carefully, you can see yourself drift in and out of various states such as fear and separation, love and connection. Observe it in yourself as you tend to another's needs. Are you looking at your watch, thinking, *How much more time need I give? When will I go and do what I want to do?*

My dear ones, what did you come to do? To build this or that building? To drive to the market? To tackle this or that goal? Is that the purpose for which you incarnated?

Even what would seem to be the loftiest purposes—to write this book, to help that friend—are they the purpose of your incarnation? Yes, the book may be a gift to many or the conversation with your friend a gift to that one. The walk through the woods may bring joy to your heart.

But you incarnated for one basic reason: to deepen your experience of faith and love; to move away from the delusion of a separate self; to move into such deep awareness of your true nature that your acts, words, and thoughts most consistently reflect that awareness.

Do you know what you need to do in order best to practice that clarity, faith, and love?

In a sense, the practice of faith deepens faith. First there must be clear seeing that you do not foster dependence to avoid your own fears. Once that is established and you are able to move from a space of clarity, much of your confusion will end. You will begin to see that what you most need to do in service to others is exactly what is most needed for the learning of the self.

I would suggest that as you ask yourself to have faith in that statement and to observe it carefully, you will find that much of the clamor, of *I need* or *I want,* simply dissolves. Did you really need to do that project? Would not a shorter walk do as well? Yes, you must attend to your own needs. You must care for this human body and nurture all the aspects of you.

But how much of the clamor to constantly be *doing* grows out of deep self-nurturing and how much from fear?

What happens within the heart when you watch the arising of *I need?* What happens when you watch that arising and smile at that solid, separate self? What do you really need in order to grow beyond the delusion of this small ego-self, to understand your true nature, and to manifest your energy in service to all, without differentiation of self and other?

When you serve the divine energy without distinction of self and other either in your divine manifestation or in human manifestation, it is then and only then that the spirit finds true freedom. This freedom is the fruit of the practice of faith and love.

That practice takes self-discipline, but not the discipline that you perceive. And here is where you often get into trouble. Your self-discipline often takes the form of *I will do this for him or her, for another.* Can you see, my dear ones, that resentment rises with that separation? With *I will do this for us,* there is no resentment. As I serve you, I serve myself. As I help you to find healing, I find healing. As I help you to understand, I learn.

Some of your projects and busyness are the ego's wild attempts to escape from this ultimate reality of connection. The ego does not die easily. It screams. It kicks. With attention we learn to hear both voices.

The contented baby, pain eased, falls asleep in the mother's arms and that mother looks tenderly at her child, so glad that she was able to ease its pain.

But there is still the small voice in that mother that says, "But I did not get to finish the chapter in my book," or "I missed the end of my movie on TV." Then she squirms with guilt and discomfort.

Can we learn to smile at that voice?

As she cared for her baby's voice of pain, can we offer compassion to our own voice of pain? Can we learn to hear it for what it is: ego making a last-ditch effort to assert itself?

Then we may bask in the beauty of a deeper level of being, of the connection that grows out of actions and words that are clearly not for you, but for *us*. As you smile at the ego-self that does not want to give up, you shift your perspective from fear to love, loving even that ego-self and letting it be.

Then the heart is free to connect into that deeper level of being, and the heart knows, "I have just done exactly what I needed to do."

We spoke about faith. You all know that in third density your prime lessons are of faith and love. In our last joint session with Q'uo, the one known as Ariel spoke of the impetuousness with which older third-density incarnate beings sometimes prefer to overlook the learning of faith and love and move into the pathways of deepening compassion and wisdom.

If faith and love are learned simultaneously with this deepening of compassion and wisdom, it works well. But when faith and love are overlooked, there is often distortion, even physical distortion of the body where the upper chakras are open and attention is not given to the blockage of the lower chakras.

One aspect of deepening faith that is overlooked by many of you is that when you watch this shift in yourself—service to other versus service to self—as you watch yourself shift in perspective, faith grows from blind faith to a verified faith. Intuitively you know that you are moving deeper into connection. Your heart knows that you are doing the work you came to do; not getting rid of ego, but allowing ego to dissolve in the light and energy of ultimate reality.

That reality knows the self as unlimited, divine, and connected to all that is. When you bring your attention back to this deepening of faith, you may simply remind yourself, *This is why I am here. This is the self-discipline that is called for.*

It is not a voice that says, *I **must** meet his needs.* It is not an intellect that says, *You **should** have compassion.* It is not judgmental in that way. Rather, it is the voice of the heart. It is the voice that dissolves all boundaries, dissolves all fear, and brings you into that wondrous knowing of your own true self, of God, and of the self's true nature as part of God.

Can you allow each arising of *What about me?* to become a reminder: *Can I observe this fear? Can I smile at the ego kicking and screaming and let go? Can I really trust that if something needs to be done there will be a way for it to be done?*

No, that does not mean you can lie back and let someone else take care of it. Effort is required. But what is the doing about? Is it an assertion of ego, at least in some part, or does it take you closer to connection and deeper love?

I thank you for your attention to these thoughts. I expect that we will be delving into this question and its many ramifications for several days. May I return you now to the energy of my brother/sister of Q'uo? That is all.

(Carla channeling)

Q'uo: I am again with this instrument.

We would leave you with one focus. The one known as Aaron asked, "Can you laugh and love the entity you are?" This query is central.

In the context of relationship, we ask you to reflect upon the persistence of desire that is not analyzed or understood. For instance, if you think, *She is so angry with me,* you may well be thinking, in truth, *I am so angry with her.* The very need that was perceived as an occasion for service becomes an affront to the waking consciousness of third density when the service is rendered and no appreciation is offered. The greater the perceived service, the greater the unrealized need, often, for thanks and validation.

Now in truth you truly wished to serve purely, with no expectation of any return. But this is the point with which we wish to leave this session: seldom can an entity offer itself so purely that the incessant, persistent, and continuing arising of desire does not make less than pure the consciousness that has come to serve. Can you love that self that continues very naturally to desire?

We shall pick this up with great glee at our next session of working. Meanwhile, we congratulate each of you and your various numb body parts and consciousness. We perceive a level of fatigue in the group. We hope that you may wash that aftertaste of weariness away with companionship, some food for your physical vehicles, and, of course, the praying without ceasing that you do not yet know that you are already doing.

How we love you, my friends. We do look forward to our next opportunity to work with your queries. Meanwhile, we leave you in the joy of the love and light of the one infinite Creator, in whose name we come. We are known to you as those of the principle of Q'uo. Adonai, my friends. Adonai.

(Barbara channeling)

Aaron: It seems redundant to add anything to that statement. My blessings and love to you all.

Session 11

Weekend 4, Part 2 of 4
(This session was preceded by a period of tuning and meditation.)

(Barbara channeling)

Aaron: Good morning and my love to you all.

In relation to the focus that Q'uo has offered, there are two areas I would like to offer for your consideration. One is as this instrument has just summarized. The other is to look practically at those places where you get stuck, to look with real-life examples so that each of you may begin to pinpoint where distortion arises.

The arising of desire to serve another grows out of aspiration to be of loving service. There is a pureness and love to that aspiration. Yet you also find yourselves in a situation where others are making unskillful demands upon you. Perhaps they are releasing their anger on you or are asking you to do that which you know they could do for themselves.

Yesterday I spoke of times where you do for others out of fear rather than love and desire to serve. That is one segment of the confusion.

A related segment grows out of the heart that truly wishes to serve but does not understand where that service lies. When you see another stumble, your instinct is to reach out and help. That is a loving gesture. What of the one who continually stumbles because he does not want to walk on his own feet?

There is a desire to serve the other. The struggle into which you move grows out of the fact that it is never 100 percent. There is still an ego and old confusion.

You see the real workings of compassion in yourself, the pure heart connected to the pain of the other as you wish to release that being from its pain. But, my dear ones, you cannot take the pain of another.

You can help another learn to let go of its own pain. You can offer the love, the support, and the kindness that gives another the strength to face its own fear. But it must do that work by itself.

Here is where compassion becomes distorted. There is deep compassion and the desire to alleviate suffering. But there is more. When you see another stumble and feel you must move to end that being's pain, to support them more than you already have, whose pain are you addressing?

Look at this carefully in yourselves. What is the desire? Whether it is to barge in and fix their life for them or simply to lift and carry them a bit, where is that desire coming from? Is it too painful to you to watch their stumbling? Is it too close a reflection of your own stumbling? Then as you see that reflection of yourself, you get just a glimpse of it and you turn on yourself as if the very pure love and desire to alleviate suffering were nothing more than your own selfishness.

So, you swing from one extreme to the other and find it so difficult to accept that both are happening: "There is genuine compassion in me, a deep empathy for another. There is also fear in me."

Compassion, my friends, is that level of empathy where you so clearly understand the fears and pains of another's heart that there is truly nothing left to forgive, for there is no longer judgment. Each of you has the innate ability, the seeds, whether sprouted or not yet sprouted, for that kind of compassion within yourselves.

Another necessary part of compassion is clear seeing. Compassion is not maudlin. It penetrates into absolute reality. It knows fear when it sees it. It does not seek ownership of that fear. It is not *his* or *her* fear, just fear, *our* fear, the fear in the hearts of every being that our needs will not be met; that we will be hurt; that we will be lost or in pain.

Codependence, in its unwholesome aspect as we have defined it, is not a problem. You have heard me say there are no problems, only situations that need your loving attention. This definition is the clue. When you pay loving attention, it allows that natural seed of compassion in your heart to sprout and blossom. With compassion there is no self or other. Loving attention allows you to see where self is brought in, where fear arises and leads you to inappropriate and unskillful choices, perhaps trying to fix another or mis-serve another so as to alleviate your own pain.

What I have done so far is merely to present the situation in which you all often find yourselves. I have really said nothing that you do not already know. Hopefully, I have presented it in a clear enough form that we may now begin to address the questions: "What do I do with the fear that leads me into unskillful choices?" "How do I, as Q'uo challenged you, learn to love myself, to laugh at the fears that arise and let them go, and to move back into that joyful connection?"

I would like to pass the microphone, as it were, to my brother/sister of Q'uo. That is all.

(Carla channeling)

Q'uo: Greetings in the love and in the light of the one infinite Creator. May we briefly say how pleased we are and how privileged we feel to work with the one known as Aaron in sharing our thoughts this morning.

This being that is you, the seeker incarnate and manifesting as human, finds itself awash in its human characteristics. The desire to control situations for an increase in comfort and security often prompts you into actions and reactions seemingly lacking in compassion. And when two together are so functioning, the term for what occurs is sometimes "codependent behavior."

We would like to focus in upon the seeker you are and begin to gaze at resources that one may find useful in dealing with the pain of that desire which is not fully grasped or well stated, which involves you so often in these feelings of fear and then anger and guilt at the beholding of the unskillful expression of humanity.

Remember that the way the seeker relates to another has its roots, first, in the seeker's basic incarnational biases; and secondly, in the seeker's more fundamental biases, which are the fruit of many incarnations. And, lastly and most deeply, in the relationship that the seeker has with its so-called higher self, or that infinite portion of self that is in common with the one infinite Creator.

From the very beginning of consciousness, whether within the creation or within the incarnation, the seeker's first experiences of compassion are those of the nurturing attention of the Creator or parent. In the beginning of life as a cosmic entity or as an incarnational manifestation of that entity, the baseline of first experience is total attention and all needs met, although as a soul and as a human being, it is soon discovered that the needs and desires proliferate too quickly and thickly for the nurturing creation to answer each need in full.

Yet still, the ideal of being treasured, cherished, and fully nurtured remains a standard hoped for in the seeker's heart.

Turn and gaze at that heart. Do you have mixed feelings about this hungry heart with its incessant desires? How does the seeker move toward the learning of compassion for its heart? How can you as a learning and maturing soul bring understanding to bear upon your own greedy heart?

We ask you to think of the infinite creation with its infinite and seemingly vastly wasteful expenditures of energy, each star blazing and consuming itself down to the smallest visible sight where the atoms move in a perfect frenzy of energy, constantly moving and constantly attracted onward. The entire manifested creation of the Father hungers.

You, yourself, are the object of the Creator's hungry heart. The Creator desires to know itself, and you have been sent outward and given free will in order that the Creator might learn of itself because of receiving your harvest of experiences.

You are here to enlarge your experience, not to control it but to fully enter into it. It is not by taking thought that experience is deeply felt, but the opposite. It is by allowing deep experiences without so much control that learning eventually occurs. The thought is well taken by reflecting upon that which has been received. Thusly, you may see yourself as a natural portion of the Creator. You are a being whose hunger for safety, attention, or comfort is not despicable but inevitable.

When this first vision of the self as being natural in its seeming imperfection is fully seated within your mind and heart, then you may begin to unravel the tangled thread of compassionate clarity that has become caught and twisted by the attempts you have made to escape your nature. Yes, each of you is quite pure, innocent, and untouched within the deepest portion of that which is you.

Now you may focus on how the relationship you have with the Creator, with your higher self, and with your incarnation can inform and guide you well toward the shining source of that thread of pure compassion that you wish to knit up into the fabric of your lives and relationships.

This is a journey from head to heart; from fear to love; from meekness to an acceptance of the eternal untidiness of catalyst, perception, and experience.

We would move back to the one known as Aaron, as we find the basis in theory that we offer is far better followed by more concrete observations. We happily yield to the one known as Aaron. We are those of Q'uo.

(Barbara channeling)

Aaron: My heartfelt thanks to my brother/sister energy of Q'uo for the wisdom with which it speaks. Yes, precisely, this is the journey from fear to love, from brain-oriented choice to heart-centered choice. But, my dear ones, you do not have to be perfect at it. You do not have to get it all at once. If you were already perfect, you would not be here in incarnation. You are learning.

This sense that it should have already been learned is the source of so much suffering for you. You struggle and there is pain. Can you begin to see that all of the situations through which you move are part of the learning?

186

Have you seen a young child build with a pile of blocks? Perhaps the second block sits on the first, but with the placement of the third, the stack topples over. There is not yet an understanding of balance. The child experiments and finally begins to understand that the center of the weight of the third block must be over the other two. Then it can add a fourth.

Your situations are the building blocks on which your learning is based. Yes, I know that when a block is unskillfully placed and that block connects with another's heart, there is pain. And I know and you know that you are responsible for that misplaced block. Here is an area of concern for many of you who are older seekers. Deepening awareness of responsibility creates a new form of fear. You know that you are responsible, and thus you become increasingly impatient with your mistakes.

I certainly do not advocate irresponsibility, nor would I suggest that it is okay to harm another. But remember that you are learning. You are all learning. And one of the things you might practice is patience, patience combined with honesty that looks clearly at unskillful choices so that they need not be repeated.

You are not a two-year-old with blocks. When the block is placed and it topples, it needs to topple once or twice and then the lesson is learned. There is no need for the self-chastisement into which error is often distorted, but simply for the observation, "I keep repeating this mistake. I need to pay closer attention. Then I can act more skillfully."

So, you are all embarked on this journey from fear to love, from the contracted heart to the open one. But it is an infinite path. I cannot speak about eighth density nor anything beyond that. I can only speak of those beings moving into seventh density by my own observation. So what I say here is conjecture. But my conjecture would be that perfect love is still being learned, even at those levels.

It is not something you have to do today. Can you be a bit more patient and kind to yourselves? Can you simply remember, I do not have to perfect it today? Not only do you not have to be perfect, but you cannot. You can only improve it a bit, understand it a bit more clearly, to take one more step.

My dear ones, on this journey of yours, this search, each step that brings you closer to unconditional love is a step taken in unknowingness. You are blind. When you believe you are not blind and think you are in control, you are walking in circles. You are not going anywhere. The next step in your growth always involves letting go of everything you thought you knew and moving out into the unknown. Can you begin to cherish yourselves for the courage and faith to keep letting go of that which is known, safe, and controllable in order to launch yourselves into deeper exploration of the Infinite?

Let us shift course here and work with some concrete examples. I do not choose here to invade anyone's privacy by using set examples from the lives of those in this circle. Let me instead use hypothetical examples, but those with which you will be intimately familiar through the circumstances of your own lives.

You are each in intimate relationships with others, or have been. This may be your partner, your parent, or your child. It may be a sibling or a dear friend. Q'uo has spoken about your being drawn to each other in part by the desire to serve one another and by recognition of the deep possibility of service.

Sometimes this service seems not quite equal and one, seeing fears arising, begins to resent another. Sometimes one is less compassionate to the other. Sometimes one is more reactive to its own fear.

To make this concrete, I will use an example of partners of either sex. But please fit this into your own life in whatever situations you find yourself. One being strives to be ready to go out at an agreed time. The other being is always late. Let us call them being A and being B. I do not want to assign the lateness or promptness to one sex or the other.

B understands that A is irritated when A says, "It is getting late. Why aren't you ready?" A sees B's need to go at its own pace and not be rushed. At first A feels anger about this because hosts and hostesses are a bit perturbed by the late arrival, and A feels, "I am being blamed and it is B's fault."

At first A may make excuses and say, "Well, I was ready but I was waiting for B." Finally, A begins to see through that fear. It needs no longer blame B. It continually asks itself, "Can I have compassion for B?" A sees the fear of fast motion in B. It sees the ambivalence of putting the self into social situations that leads B to be late. It speaks to B about all of this. It makes peace with the situation, readies itself on time, and then sits and reads a book, simply waiting for B to be ready. At that point there is no quarrel between them.

A is acting compassionately but also allowing B to dwell in its own fear. A's responsibility extends only so far as pointing out fear to B and asking B to consider what might be a more skillful action.

"Consider" is the prime word here. If A says, "You must heed me," that is a violence to B. It is attacking B's pattern, attacking B's fear. It is trying to fix or to change B. But it is responsible action for A to very gently point out what it sees to B and ask B to consider how to change the situation.

What happens when there is a bit of a shift in this pattern? As A has become comfortable with B's choice and is able to leave B alone with that choice, B begins to be later and later. B is looking for a reaction. It wants someone to light a fire under it, to get it going, and A has refused to do that anymore.

So B becomes aware, "I must do something to provoke A." Perhaps B is even later. At that point, A feels the arising of anger again.

Perhaps B has a different approach and is almost ready but then picks an argument with A. Perhaps B is the last one out the door and as they are going out the driveway, A asks B, "Did you turn off the lights?" and B explodes, "You were ready all this time. Why did you not make sure the lights were off?!" In some way or another, B is attempting to provoke A.

Here A is pulled back into the fray by B's becoming more extreme in one way or another, by B's provocation. That provocation asks A to focus more clearly on its own reaction. A has reached the point where it is okay if B is late. Is it okay if B yells at A out of guilt for its own lateness or out of its own fear? Is it okay if B is twice as late? Where does A say no? How does A say no?

Now, obviously, if you have two cars, there is no problem. A can simply be ready on time and say, "I will be leaving at such and such a time. I will see you there," and leave B to its own resources. But let us assume that in this situation there is only one vehicle. Perhaps A is aware of the feud that would ensue if it called a cab and makes the decision, "I am not willing to provoke B in that way." What options does A have? How does it say no? Can A simply get into the car at the appointed time and drive away? Is that also a provocation to B? Where is it provocation and where is it an aid to learning?

I would suggest that the line is drawn not in the act itself but in the intention behind the act. If A gets into the car and drives away in anger, that is strong provocation. If A says to B an hour before the time needed to leave, "I understand you need a lot of time. We need to leave in an hour. At eight o'clock I will be driving out the driveway. I hope that you are in the car with me. There is no anger in me as I say this. Here is ten dollars that I am leaving on the desk so that you can call a cab if you need to, but I feel a need to be on time."

In loving, nonviolent movement with another being there must be a willingness to suffer the anger of another and to ask another to consider your viewpoint. The strength of the soul speaks its truth, be it a major issue or a very small one. It does not speak it in hostility to another, but with the deepest compassion for the pain of the other. Nevertheless, it says, "This cannot continue. Your actions cause pain to other people, be it lateness, drinking, helplessness, or displays of rage with cursing or throwing."

It is not the action of saying no, but the way no is said that is most important. If there is any intention to enrage the other further or to provoke or to find revenge for past pain, no matter how that no is said, that seed of anger is still planted.

You must look deeply into your own hearts. You must also remember that it cannot be 100 percent pure, but see if it is largely pure. If you look and uncover some anger for past humiliation, for past discomfort, then you may ask yourself, "Is my real intention in saying no to seek revenge for that past by creating discomfort in the other?

Or is my real intention to serve us, the other and myself, and lead us both into learning?"

Having uncovered those subtle, unskillful intentions in yourself, you are far less likely to act on them. You may rest assured that there will be a greater amount of purity to your choice.

So what does A do here? It first must become aware of its own anger. B is abusing it. If it is able to release that anger sufficiently, it may point out that abuse to B. In some situations that may be enough, but rarely.

With the saying of no in the example we gave, saying, "I am leaving at this time. You have adequate time to be ready," A is making a clear statement of its intention from a place of nonfear.

B may be threatened by that warning and become hostile to A. Can A have compassion for the hostility it has provoked, but still not accept abuse? This is part of that willingness to accept another's anger, to ask another to consider your viewpoint when you feel so strongly that your viewpoint is more skillful and love-based.

So A might ask itself ahead of time, "If my choice threatens B, and B acts in a hostile way, am I willing to allow that hostility? To what degree am I willing to allow it?" When it becomes uncomfortable, A has the right to say, "No, I cannot allow it any further." But why is it uncomfortable?

Is there disappointment that B cannot meet A's need? Is there a feeling of betrayal or fear? What is the pain about? Again, more clarity, more honesty are called forth. It is A's learning as much as B's, because A must be aware: "In what way am I feeling attacked here? To what am I saying no?" When B understands that it cannot pull A into its issues and that A is going to act lovingly, nonjudgmentally, but firmly, then and only then is B forced back into itself with loving support from A, without hatred or criticism but with awareness, "I need to clean this up in myself."

For each of you that sees yourself as A in this sort of situation, the questions to ask yourself are:

"In what way does B's behavior threaten me?"

"In what ways do my reactions to those threats lead me back into conflict and violence with B?"

"How can I manifest my own energy more purely, with deeper awareness of which buttons B pushes, so to speak?"

"How can I move to that point where I can ask B to consider my viewpoint?"

"How can I accept that my request is a threat to B and that B is liable to react with fear?"

"Am I willing to accept the ramifications of that fear as I ask this consideration of B?"

"How do I get myself clear?"

"What do I have to do?"

This brings us back to the spiritual perspective. You are not B's teacher if you are A. You are each other's teachers. You are not in this situation solely to teach B something. B is also here to teach you. You have joined together because you recognize the possibility of mutual service to one another and, of course, the loving connection between you as well. You are always precisely where you need to be.

If the situation is very uncomfortable and makes you squirm, stop and ask yourself, "How did I get here? What learning might there be for me in this situation? What seeds have I planted in the past that have helped to create this jungle that surrounds me now? How can I transform this jungle by my loving choices, by my awareness, back into a fruitful garden?"

There is always learning in it for you. Please remember that distortions are not "bad" but merely uncomfortable. They also may be the catalyst for learning. You may come to love even these distortions.

If you find yourself in conflict and with hatred arising or bitterness arising, then you are not paying attention. If you find yourself with frustration and fear arising, that is fine. Fear and frustration do not need to be catalysts for hatred. They can also be catalysts for deeper compassion.

Fear can be a warning signal, a red light flashing that says, "Pay attention!" And as you pay closer attention and find compassion for the places in yourself that feel threatened by these choices, then you move into deeper compassion for B and into the intuitive wisdom of the open heart that knows how to say no to unwholesome demands.

As you see yourselves go through this cycle again and again, be aware, my friends, of where you wish to avoid the lessons of the incarnation. Ask yourself, "Can I embrace even this? Can I make space for it in my heart so that I can learn?"

I would like to pass the microphone back to my brother/sister of Q'uo. I also feel that there are some questions among this circle. I do know that Q'uo wishes to speak, and then perhaps we can attend to your questions. That is all.

(Carla channeling)

Q'uo: We are again with this instrument. Obviously, you did not enter incarnation and choose your family in order to become angry together. Your higher self and the Creator did not plan the emotional details of experiencing incarnation. Rather, as the incarnation was planned, the focus was upon the offering of the self as a rough-cut stone to the refining abrasion of circumstance, designed to polish and make beautiful and clear each facet of the gem that you truly are. You and your B, shall we say, planned to come together to be of service.[27]

Before incarnation and after it, it seems only vaguely humorous that all of the emotions felt are even possible. For when the veil of illusion is not in place, the differences between entities are healed with joy. Full travel is given to free will for each to harmonize with the other.

In social complexes such as ours, for instance, each entity within the complex is unique and the distinctions and dynamics are infinite.

---

[27] As did Aaron in his address above, Q'uo is using the letters A and B to describe the dynamics of relationship between two persons.

This is hailed as a great advantage for mutual support and interest, each learning from the harmonization process a bit of each other's uniqueness. We are thusly building a larger harmonious uniqueness and becoming a fully harmonized energy and essence as well as becoming infinite in energy by the full acceptance and multiplication of each uniqueness.

So, too, you enter incarnation ready to learn. It is certainly a rude shock to awaken within manifestation and discover that the veil of illusion is opaque and harmonies are not visible.

We are working in this series to uncover ways of valuing and loving the self while harmoniously loving and living with others in a fully compassionate way.

It is well to look to the intention of incarnation in general. There was no wickedness in each entity's choices of partners with whom to share learning and service. As each abrades the other by the dynamics betwixt them, it helps to lean back against the sure awareness of a kindly and efficient incarnational plan. Then each can turn to a clearer effort at communication with the Creator, the self, and the other self, B; for there are many Bs in every A's incarnational experience.

In the next working we would share further upon the clearing of communication by means of seating oneself within a faithful awareness of the intention of the self as it came into incarnational manifestation.

We would end our portion of this working at this moment, thanking each and leaving each in the love and in the light of the one infinite Creator. We turn the microphone back to the one known as Aaron. We are Q'uo.

(Barbara channeling)

Aaron: It is indeed a joy to share this speaking with my brother/sister of Q'uo. I believe I speak for both of us when I offer thanks to the humans who have made the physical effort to come together for this sharing. I am aware of questions that have arisen from what we each have said, and also of some level of stiffness and fatigue. We will leave it to you. Do you wish to ask questions now or do you wish to end this session? This instrument's energy is adequate to continue.

(There are no questions at this time.)

My love, blessings, and gratitude to you all for this opportunity to share with this loving circle of beings. That is all.

Session 12

Weekend 4, Part 3 of 4
(This session was preceded by a period of tuning and meditation.)

Group question: The topic is continued from this morning's session, which concerns the true meaning of compassion and the clearing of communication by means of seating oneself within the awareness of the intention of the self as it came into incarnation.

(Carla channeling)

Q'uo: Greetings once again, my friends, in the love and in the light of the one infinite Creator. We wish again to express our and the one known as Aaron's joy at being called to your circle of seeking to offer our humble opinions upon the subjects of interest to you at this time and place in your journeys along what this instrument calls the King's Highway.[28]

Upon this highway you are neither old nor young; male nor female; wealthy nor impoverished. You are one who journeys as the prodigal son and daughter, having been flung far from your source of being.

Now you move through illusion upon illusion in the twilight dream-within-a-dream that is incarnational experience. As you sit here, each seeker has the sorrows of unfulfilled hopes, expectations, and love. Each feels the pang of suffering. And yet, each is still attempting to find solutions to the suffering, rather than finding space and time within to allow each portion of experience, including suffering, to have a hospitable room in which to dwell while it visits you.

---

[28] The phrase is from a hymn written by E. A. Cummins in 1922. The text of the first verse is, "I know not where the road will lead I follow day by day, or where it ends. I only know I walk the King's Highway."

The illusion boldly states that you are here to find solutions to your problems and puzzles. It is our opinion that a more realistic view suggests that solutions are irrelevant to the process of journeying along the King's Highway. What is much more important is that you ask better and clearer questions concerning this journey.

This journey helps define your relationship with yourself by suggesting that there is a loving, nurturing home from which, at some point, you have departed in order to gain experience. The process of gaining this experience is, at its best, a messy one and one that persists in being contradictory, enigmatic, and unsolvable.

Your position as seeker, then, is one of remembrance of home and hope of return to this home. Between the beginning and the end of this journey, here each is.

As the moment comes for you to suffer, we can suggest that this model of beginning, middle, and ending insists that there is a nurturer, connected intimately with home, that accompanies you and is a deep portion of you. It does not offer surface comfort, but by its beingness within you it offers a context within which you may see your right relationship to your suffering self.

You chose carefully the incarnational destiny you now are in the process of experiencing, adding to your curriculum those courses or lessons concerning love that you and the Creator felt were appropriate. Thusly you have created for yourself a destiny, or rather a destination or series of destinations toward which you inevitably shall move.

Free will is maintained within this general destiny because you have the choice at any time as to how you shall travel. For instance, from this place[29] you can reach Indiana across a bridge in about half an hour. Or you can visit the Greek islands, stop over in the Orient, and return over the pole to Chicago, driving thence south to Indiana. Your endpoints are destined, but not the duration or complexity of your travel.

Knowing that your relationships are of one nature, whether they are with the Creator, discarnate entities, strangers, friends, or your

---

[29]Anchorage, KY, just outside Louisville, KY.

nearest and dearest ones, you may perhaps see that both within the illusion and within your own internal cosmology there exist many models for nurturing.

When the moment of suffering occurs, your nurturing part can say within you, "I hold you with deepest love and rock you in the cradle of my love." The parent does not only hold and comfort the quiet or good child but offers nurturing and comfort in difficulty as well. Can you refrain from self-judgment when next you begin to be out of tune with yourself, and instead allow the nurturer within to cradle you in your distress?

What we are suggesting is that living, as you know it, will always be a messy, difficult affair. And the spirit within wishes to nurture that very confused entity just as it is—spots, dabs, stains, dust, and all. Its reaction to seeing you hurt is not to ask if you should be hurt. The nurturer goes for the Band-Aid and the cleansing swab. Then that nurturer gives you a pat and sends you back to play again. Beyond any solutions to interpersonal relationships, this nurturing is all-important for the seeker to have faith in and rely on.

This being said, we would like to take a look at the ways in which one may maximize communication with others by communicating with the Creator and with the self on a continuing basis. Unclear communications are frequently as much a matter of ignorance as they are a matter of actual difficulty.

At the beginning of this series of sessions the query boiled down to, "How can we serve others without extinguishing our own needs?" Let us look at those needs. The need of the eternal being that you are is to continue to gather experience. To the eternal self, all experiences are equal.

Much difficulty has been deliberately placed before each by the self. A grounding in this aids in communicating with the self, for there is that voice of the little child-self that asks, *Why must I hurt? Why must I change? Why must I be disturbed?* When the self can answer, *This is your job. You have to be disturbed in order to learn something new,* then the attitude with which you enter into the sometimes less than joyful experience of gaining experience may be softened.

Session 12

We would at this time yield to our brother, the one known as Aaron. We are those of Q'uo.

(Barbara channeling)

Aaron: My joyful thanks to my brother/sister Q'uo for the clarity of its teaching. At the end of its words, Q'uo has chosen to remind us that you are here to gather experience. Some of that experience is painful. Some is joyful. Some is comfortable and some distinctly uncomfortable.

We have previously discussed the difference between pain and suffering. When it is painful, that is not pleasant. But there is only suffering when you become stuck in the illusion and begin to grasp at changing what is. It is not the discomfort of an arising physical or emotional sensation that causes your suffering. It is your aversion to what arises.

You are each asked to live with one foot in the illusion and one foot in ultimate reality. You straddle a threshold like actors in a play. You play a role here. And, like actors, you must play that role as if it matters. You must involve yourself in the illusion if there is to be learning. Otherwise you might as well not have chosen incarnation.

And yet there still must be awareness. Just as the actor must have awareness that he plays to an audience, so as not to turn his back on that audience and not to muffle his speech, so you must maintain awareness of your true self while performing the myriad functions of the human personality.

When you are stuck in the small ego-self, then that awareness is disconnected. That ego screams and kicks, as we spoke of earlier, fearing that its needs will not be met. If you dismiss that as illusion and disassociate yourself from it, there is the comfort of dwelling in the spiritual plane, but there is no learning. And there is still duality because, at some level, disassociation is created by a separate self seeking to protect itself.

As you straddle this threshold, there seems to be an infinite wall that divides day from night, fear from love, and separation from

199

connection. With practice, you learn to allow this wall to dissolve and begin to transcend that duality that is the product of delusion.

Then you learn to be in this discomforting situation without struggling, skillfully looking to resolve it in the ways in which that is possible, but also allowing the experience.

You watch with the wisdom of your higher self. You find the ability to smile at this ego that keeps reemerging. In short, you find the ability to be with the whole span of your being, neither preferring the physical and its sought-after pleasures, nor preferring the spiritual form, nor seeking the bliss of merging yourself in that oneness that is the spirit's foundation. Instead, there is a coming together of the whole, an integration.

In October we ended our sessions, speaking of faith and praying without ceasing. We spoke of living in faith. As you allow yourself to move beyond the limits of the small ego-self and recurrently experience, through meditation and through awareness, your connection with all that is, you stop struggling like a fish out of water with the experiences that life brings. As you relax into the incarnation, faith does deepen. Increasingly you find the ability to be more undefended when you are threatened.

It is a matter of practice. Could you catch a ball the first time it was thrown to you? Sometimes a human child is afraid of a ball; and instead of reaching out its hands to catch, it simply bats it away. It moves to protect itself. Practice teaches it the skill of collecting that ball into itself.

As you relax the struggles with the incarnation and make the skillful decision to let go of some of the fear; as you allow yourself to experience living without defensiveness, then those seeds of deeper love, wisdom, compassion, and lovingkindness within your heart begin to flower.

So much of the frantic kicking and screaming—*What about me? Will I have time for what I want? Will attention be given to me? Will I be nurtured?*—so much of that frantic activity simply winds down. You begin to see from a higher perspective. Then, as Q'uo has suggested, you begin to embrace rather than condemn this human incarnation, this actor on the stage that is sometimes caught in the illusion.

I ask you to remember that the qualities of compassion and lovingkindness are natural to you. They are your natural state. When fear arises, it blocks the natural expression of love. It is not useful either to grasp at the love or to attempt to get rid of the fear.

Coming back to a concrete example, suppose there is one who makes requests of you that seem, in your mind, to lead you to deny your own need. There you are with one foot on each side of the threshold. The foot in the illusion is saying, "I can't do this!" or "Why does he or she keep demanding this of me?"

Back to our A and B—it is simpler than constantly saying he/she, and I do not wish to assign any specific role to one sex or the other.

"B keeps asking this of me. B is so frightened. Why does not B do it itself? If I keep serving B, I will not have any time left for me." Anger arises. Fear arises and, like that fish out of water, it just flops about.

On the other side of the threshold is that level of clear seeing that says, "This is illusion. I am spirit. I am connected." Compassion arises for B. But there is distortion because there is no connection seen between the two perspectives. It becomes an either/or proposition— to give or to receive.

When fear arises, self-discipline and courage may lead you not to act on that fear and greed. Here, awareness may dissolve this wall so that the human, with its fear and greed, and the spirit, with its high aspirations, merge; so that you see the whole range of your behavior. This clear seeing allows a level of faith: "No matter how much I dislike the situation I am in, it is just where I need to be. I am safe. I can experience this discomfort without closing in my armor, without further protecting myself."

You remind yourself over and over, "I am safe. I can allow the fullness of experience." The fear of the human combines with the deep sorrow and loving aspiration of the spirit, which sees its perfection but, because of its human aspect, cannot manifest that perfection.

What deep sorrow is there! But the more you keep your heart open to all of it, the more struggle falls away.

It is here that the heart begins to notice the prayer without ceasing. As Q'uo said yesterday, you already do that. You are just not yet aware of it. The divine aspect of yourself is always in deepest connection with the Divine. How could it be otherwise?

When you allow the presence of fear and discomfort, have faith that you are where you need to be, and allow yourself to be open and vulnerable, to let go of security. Then the heavens open, and you come back in intactness of body, mind, and spirit to your connection with the Divine.

Here again is the place where the question does not need to be asked, "What shall I do about B's demands?" A simply knows from the wisdom of its own heart. I do not mean to imply that this work is simple. It is anything but simple. But, my friends, it is the work of all of your lifetimes, this steady progression from government by fear to responses of love.

Each small step you take on this, to use Q'uo's terminology, King's Highway is wonderful. You, in your race, are only concentrating your attention on the road. If you would lift your head and look around you, you would see the cheering multitudes watching your every step; indeed, throwing rose petals on the road before you. They may not cover all the jagged rocks, but they are there. Can you open your eyes and begin to see yourselves as we see you?

I would like to transfer the discussion to my brother/sister Q'uo, with my thanks for this opportunity to share my thoughts. That is all.

(Carla channeling)

Q'uo: I am with the instrument. I greet each of you in love and light.

We turn again and again to the moment of suffering in relationship, asking each to look with new eyes upon this frequently occurring center of experience that involves joy as well as sorrow and suffering. Each is A. Each is also B. This is helpful to remember when there is the suffering within relationship.

Clear communication can be of three kinds. Each is skillful. Each is useful, according to your own judgment.

The first clear communication is to sit down with your B and state each messy and confused feeling, using sentences that begin with the word "I." In this communication you are not attempting to break loose of the illusion but are expressing, with words that picture and mirror the illusion, the feelings and impressions that you have of the situation that has resulted in your choosing to suffer. This sharing ends with the request for B to express similarly its own I, its own unapologized-for ego-self.

Egos are useful things to you. They run your physical vehicle. They keep it warm, clothed, and fed and deliver you to the doorstep of each spiritually vital experience. They are to be honored and respected, both yours as A and yours as B or as any other.

Now if the B in your soap opera or drama is not willing to express its ego-self, the next way of clear communication is of the self with the self, saying to the self all of the "I" statements. Allow all of the intense realizations of this suffering to be expressed, and then respect that within yourself.

Then you can turn to your B the face of one who suffers and is willing to abide that ego-self that is respected and allowed its voice. It is a lonelier form of clear communication, but it enables As that cannot speak to Bs within the illusion to stay within the illusion in a nurtured state. One who is buttressed and strengthened by the sympathy of the nurturer-self within, so that whatever the communication of a verbal nature may be, it is not liable to the desire for destruction to which the unrespected ego-self is prone.

This leaves B able to deal with its own ego-self without feeling the pressure from A that would ask B to redeem or love A. This is helpful to both and clears the way in your future transactions for the increased possibility of open verbal communication because of the perceived lack of back-pressure.

The third way of cleared communication is that which takes place at all times and to which you may become privy as you allow time, space, and suffering to be what and as they are or seem to be. This does not mean withdrawing from experience. Rather, it turns the order of things about.

Instead of doing the various services of physical life and then having the time available in the remainder of your day to meditate, contemplate, and pray, allow the mind and heart to be more and more aware that although the illusion is being visited, is useful, is vitally important, and is interesting, your fundamental nature is at home and has never left. Communion is constant because there is identity. You are one with the infinite Creator. You are prayer without ceasing. It is not an activity. Rather, the praying without ceasing seems an activity until it is realized that praying without ceasing could well be your name. Your very nature is an unceasing hymn of love.

In the deepest sense, the key to moving from codependency to compassionate symbiosis in relationship is seeing yourself both as a being in process and as a being beyond all time and space, with nowhere to go except from love to love. In another way, this awareness allows you the luxury of not placing great importance or lack of respect upon the details of each moment's considerations.

How can you find the way to have your needs met? As usual, the solution is not present but rather is beyond the presence of illusion. It lies in knowing that much occurs that seems unfair. Yet each unfairness passes and the attention is drawn elsewhere.

Rather than attempting over and over to break a pattern, then, think of the relief of seeing, as an A to a B, "Here is the pattern again. Here it is." The reaction of B then determines the next clear communication. If B wishes to learn and act upon the lessons of the incarnation, then both can sit down together, knowing that this is the work that they have come to do together among other services. They can share the sorrow and pain that seem to be A's and B's, but are A/B's in the reality that is known in the less deep illusion within your incarnation, which is the feeling of the heart.

Now if B is not yet ready to work together with you as a mate, then there is the generosity of spirit that is the harvest of A's nurturing of B that allows B to say whatever it can without feeling the need to justify, condemn, or defend. If even this degree of communication between entities is not available, then there is the relaxation of the illusion in the mind and heart, and the allowing of the nurturer to place one in a cradled, loving space within which it is safe to become aware of the entity within, which is eternal prayer without ceasing.

None of these three modes of communication necessarily offers a solution. But the solution would be momentary anyway. Experience moves on. Perhaps that which we would leave you with before we turn back to the one known as Aaron would be simply to suggest that when suffering arises, the clear communicator will turn to the one with whom it has transacted that suffering and begin a sentence with the word "I," not allowing the suffering to sour and bleed and become the fine wine of old anger. If you can keep the utterance of the ego-self current, you are giving yourself the maximum opportunities to become more and more clear.

This takes a kind of courage born only of blind faith, the faith that communication is effectual. We hope you may nurture that faith, because it is in relationships that the most accelerated pace of learning and spiritual evolution is possible within this illusion you call living.

We know you wish to advance your learning. It is in the fire of the forging process of relationship that your opportunity for learning is maximized. Thusly, we hope that you not be discouraged and turn from the difficult relationship. If each can feel good about expressing the ego-self's feelings as they arise, there is so much of freshness that airs out and aids in the amelioration of that suffering entity that is you.

In this manner, what seems to be the display of ego is actually a generous offering of clarity within confusion to the one who is learning to give and live. Do you see how this love twines and winds about, seemingly separate but always one heartbeat from showing the true nature of union within?

We leave this instrument now and, with great appreciation for this marvelous adventure, turn the microphone over to the one known as Aaron. We leave each in love and light. We are those of Q'uo.

(Barbara channeling)

Aaron: Q'uo has offered some very useful and concrete suggestions. As I listen to the thoughts offered by my brother/sister, I am struck with the idea that to use these suggestions you must be very aware: there are three tools.

Is there anything within you that argues with the skillful use of these tools?

Let us say that it seems necessary to drive some nails into a block of wood. Let us further project that at some level this being that needs to drive the nails feels resentment about driving the nails. Perhaps every time a nail must be driven, this being must assume that responsibility and feels there is a lack of balance. Perhaps it simply hates the act of hammering because it dislikes the way it stresses the muscles. If you offer this being three hammers, it may well choose the best tool for the job. But because there is resistance to the work at hand, upon the first blow it is likely to smash its thumb, thus rendering it impossible to continue.

Thus, before you move into these three very useful steps, it would seem useful to ask yourself, *Is there anything within me as A that hopes B will not respond? What part of me uses lack of communication as a defense against knowing my own self more deeply? What fears have I tucked away to carry around with me as a burden, because I fear drawing them out of my pack to examine them?*

If I come to B with Q'uo's suggested "I," as in, "I feel hurt. I experience fear," or whatever it may be, is there a part of me that subtly twists that communication in some small way so as to provoke rejection from B? Am I therefore ensuring that I need go no further in this communication but can handily blame B, believing, *See, I tried and B has shut me out?*

In step two, know your anger, know your fear, and know your feeling. This knowing is urgent, as Q'uo has suggested. But is there any desire to twist that again into blame so as to absent yourself from responsibility because of your own fear?

Do this work with careful awareness, watching yourself for the arising of fear, for the arising of a desire to protect. Can you greet that, too, with nonjudgment? Can you smile at it as just part of the whole drama? Step back a step, remember who you are, and then dive back in with a bit more clarity. Know that this fear is okay. *I need not be reactive to the situation. I need not be reactive to B's fear of the situation, should that occur. And I need not be afraid or reactive of my own fear.* There is room for it all to float. There is space for it all.

If it is acceptable to the group, I would like to lead you in a brief guided meditation, asking you to move beyond the limits of the perceived self; to open yourself to the energy of the others in this loving circle; and, as you become undefended with others' energy, to notice the arising of fear and to touch that arising fear with compassion. Just that. Is there energy and interest in pursuing this? That is all.

(Everyone agrees.)

I would ask you first to visualize yourselves sitting in a circle of light. Experience the fullness of your own energy. Draw your hands together before you, palms touching. Feel the energy pulsating from palm to palm. Slowly separate those hands just a bit and feel your energy radiating outward. You know that you do not end at your skin. Allow yourself to feel that.

Take in a deep breath and at the crown of that breath, just before the exhalation, expand outward.

(Pause)

Allow yourself to feel the energy body, the astral body, the light body, the higher self, and all that moves beyond just this physical self expanding outward.... Inhale ... expand ... and stabilize that expansion as you exhale. Inhale ... expand ... stabilize.... Do it at your own pace for a few moments.

(Pause)

Allow yourself to feel the energy fields of the others in the room, which are also expanding. You are light. You are energy. And you are thought. Expand outward and begin to feel the overlap of the energy that surrounds you.

(Pause)

Let that energy touch your own and let your own energy reach itself out.

(Pause)

As penetratingly as possible, notice any fear, any desire to retreat back into yourself, and touch that fear with gentleness.

(Pause)

Know that you may retreat. That is not a failure. There is no "should" here, only a desire to stay as open as possible and to feel undefended in this very loving circle of friends. And yet, in that undefendedness, know that the excesses and stray thoughts that you condemn in yourself may be felt by others. Can you trust another's compassion for you as you move deeper into your own compassion for them?

(Pause)

I am with you in this circle, my friends. None of us is perfect. The fear that leads you to seek to armor yourself is not a contemptible trait but is simply the manifestation of human conditioned mind. In a sense, it is a by-product of the incarnation that may be released with your loving practice and effort.

Session 12

(Pause)

Again, I urge you to expand outward just a bit more. It may help to turn your hands upright in your lap, palms up, to feel the others' energy. I will be quiet now for two or three minutes. Watch each arising desire to defend, and touch it with gentle mercy.

(Pause)

Can you watch yourselves opening and closing, opening, closing a bit, and opening again?

I leave you tonight with this bit of homework to perform in your relationships with others: Until we resume tomorrow, will you watch for this opening and closing? Watch also for any judgment of it. In this way you may approach Q'uo's suggestions with more clarity about your own readiness to come to such communication undefended and nonthreatening to yourself or another.

I ask you here to reverse the process now. Draw your energy back into yourself and allow it to settle. If your hands were palm up, turn them palm down on your lap. If there is any surplus energy, visualize it as a golden ball, and, using your visualization or imagination, simply snip it loose with imaginary scissors and let it float. Look for the stray bits of energy of you, and gently draw them in.

This is not armoring of the self. It is skillful work with the energy within the illusion. To further draw your energy in, I would ask you to bring attention to your feet touching the ground. This is the human with its feet on the earth, which is one aspect of your entirety. Allow yourself to come back from the expanded spirit experience to the human that you also are.

I honor each of you for the courage, sincerity, and love that you bring to your seeking and your work. I thank you very much for inviting me to share my thoughts with you. I wish to return to Q'uo and Carla, who may wish to close this session. That is all.

(Carla channeling)

Q'uo: I am Q'uo and we greet you in postscript with love and light. We find we do have one more thing to say, which is so typical of grand friendships.

We would leave you to merriment, comradeship, and good food for your physical beings with the hope that each may listen to each and know that each is teacher to each. And as you rest into slumber this evening, we encourage you to visit the ego-self. There it is: you being laid to rest, yet not all of you.

Allow that ego-self to be the size it is right now. That is how much you need. As you continue to respect the process that engages ego and spirit, that balance shall continually shift. And it will happen that eventually you will find a very small need for the ego-self, for you have become independent within eternity.

This experience awaits you. It is not now. Now it is just right that you have the ego-self as you experience it now. It is you. It is not all of you. It is all you meet. Yet it does not define any of you. Then say, "God bless this mess," and go to sleep, my friends, and rise to greet another day. Adonai. Adonai. We are those of Q'uo, and we leave you in the love and in the light of the one infinite Creator.

(Carla leads a meditation for giving back to the Creator the light that was felt by the group and includes a prayer for a group member with a personal need for employment. The meditation ends with, "The image goes up. Let the rains fall down.")

Session 13

Weekend 4, Part 4 of 4
(This session was preceded by a period of tuning and meditation.)

(Barbara channeling)

Aaron: I wish you could see this room as I see it. Through these three days, more and more light has radiated out. From my perspective, this room is a small sun situated here in the middle of the landscape.

When Q'uo and I speak to you as we have done these past two days, there is only so much you can process. Obviously we could talk about this endlessly. As we have spoken, questions have arisen in each of your thoughts. For some of you there was a sense of *I have a question but perhaps I am not quite ready to ask it. I cannot phrase it clearly enough,* or *If I had been listening more carefully, I would know the answer,* or even *At some level I already do know the answer. I do not need to ask.*

This is all fine. But perhaps it would be most useful to begin today not by hearing your one group question but by hearing the extended questions or thoughts that have grown out of these past two days of work. Your questioning is a way of clarifying your thoughts, and also most clearly expresses to Q'uo and to me what it is that you most need to hear.

Some of you have some distress with what has been suggested these past two days, experiencing some vague discomfort that may be hard to articulate. I urge you to try. It is through expression of both that which is comfortable and that which is uncomfortable that the real questions may emerge. That is all.

(A period of group sharing and discussion follows.)

Aaron: Would it be acceptable to you for us to focus on compassion today more than on codependence? I think we have pretty well covered codependence. How do you deepen compassion for this being that you are who does move back into fear? Is that acceptable to you as a focus? I wonder if my brother/sister of Q'uo has anything to add to this. That is all.

(Carla channeling)

Q'uo: Greetings once again in the love and the light of the one infinite source and ending of all that is. Indeed, we do feel that the one known as Aaron and we have covered a good deal of material on codependence. It is more than sufficient for much consideration.

Words are most helpful. Yet insofar as there are words, there is the distance or lack of immediate sensation of being in union with the Creator, whose very name is love. This love is a name that has created power. Its nature has descended throughout all levels of manifestation and constitutes your pith, your very core; love that has been turned, shaped, or, if you look with jaundiced eye, twisted and bent into each portion of thought and feeling that each of you experiences.

As you listen to our words, realize that we, as you, have no way to tell or to perform the act of pure centering. Somehow the failure-after-failure that each perceives in spiritual journeying adds up to a miracle of learning to love. And in spite of every feeling of failure, and perhaps because of it as well, you find yourselves where you were not before: more capable and more sensitive to seeing your own vulnerability and imperfection.

As we come to the end of this workshop of sessions and speak of compassion, we ask each of you to stop thinking and to accept the mystery that is in front of us as well as you. And then we ask you to join us in turning to face this mystery. Gaze at it. Feel the stunning glory and majesty of the infinite mystery. In that awareness lies the protection that embraces vulnerability. There, in the shadow of the mystery, lies the infinite wealth of love that feeds even the "you" that suffers most, even at the darkest hour.

The compassion comes not from the words. It simply takes many words for the Logos, the love that is without words, to be approached by the incarnational self. So use all of our words that have aided and clarified your situations and your progress. Use the words that have helped to define the process of becoming independent within the symbiosis with the one infinite Creator.

To find the compassion, let us turn to the tabernacle of the most high, as this instrument would say, and invite the awareness of the union that already exists.

We would pass the microphone to the one known as Aaron at this time. We are those of Q'uo.

(Barbara channeling)

Aaron: Yesterday we defined compassion using a rather cold and clinical definition. As Q'uo has pointed out, words offer only concepts and not the experience itself. To speak of compassion while probing it with the intellect is not to experience compassion.

My dear ones, do you understand my meaning when I say that full compassion, full connection and undefendedness, are your true nature? Of course, you do not always experience that. You are human and to be human is also part of your nature. But you are divine. How could it be otherwise?

I have described you as angels in earth-suits. These earth-suits are necessary to the incarnate experience. Just as a space traveler needs that which protects him from an otherwise alien environment by offering him safety from pressure, air to breathe, and protection from temperature extremes, so these bodies of yours offer the spirit a situation in which it can move through those situations it needs in a semiprotected way.

The Pure Spirit Body cannot dwell on this Earth. The physical body that is home to the spirit bleeds when it is cut. The emotional body feels pain when it is attacked with hostile words. Truly, we come back to faith here: to your faith in the experience of the incarnation; to the deepening of verified faith that *I am just where I need to be,* working

213

within the illusion with awareness that it is illusion and with simultaneous awareness, *I must treat this illusion with respect.*

Perhaps "respect" is a key word. As you respect the physical, emotional, and mental bodies you become less judgmental of the retreat those bodies offer when confronted with pain.

You have heard me say repeatedly that you are here to learn unconditional love, which cannot be learned perfectly in human form but to which you may move as close as is possible for the human. You as an integrated whole are learning. But also the higher self and spiritual body are learning.

It is easy for the spiritual body to know its perfection. If it never sees imperfection, what opportunity does it have to practice nonjudgment and unconditional love? Thus, the spiritual body moves into this house of the physical. It joins together with the emotional and mental bodies in order that it may practice nonjudgment and unconditional love toward that which was previously judged and found wanting.

One of the illusions in which you dwell and that you rarely see is that all of your reactivity against another is truly reactivity against the self. This is an unqualified statement. All of your judgments against another are judgments against those faults perceived or manifested in yourself.

You may judge another's impatience while you do not portray the quality of impatience. But somewhere in your heart you feel the arising of that impatience. And so another's impatience is judged and found disturbing by you.

Is there anyone in this circle who has never felt hatred? Who has never felt greed? Can you see what a gift all of these discomforting emotions are? They are the constant catalyst that reminds you to have mercy. This does not imply condoning unskillful and harmful acts and words that are reactions to emotion. But you can only find unconditional love and nonjudgment through the repeated experience of working with the arising of that which has been judged in yourselves.

Yesterday Q'uo spoke of the value of the ego-self. Its value is not only to remind you to watch for cars as you cross the street. The illusion of self is vital to your growth, as is the reality of no-self. They are part of each other and there is no contradiction between them.

If you would attend school, there must be a school, a being to attend, and teachers. This is what your incarnation hands you. As you enter repeatedly into those situations that lead to the arising of fear, the pulling on of the armor, and the desire to defend, you do not move past that fear and those unwholesome responses by trying to get rid of them, but by reminding yourself, *Can I have compassion for this being that I am?*

There is a wonderful story about a Tibetan saint, Milarepa.[30] He sat at the mouth of his cave meditating and, as the story goes, the demons of anger, rage, fear, and greed appeared. They were hideous creatures. They exuded a foul smell. They dangled bloody knives and swords. Their bodies were made of decaying flesh and bones that rattled with a hideous sound.

Milarepa took one look at them and said, "Come in. Come and sit by my fire." They said, "Aren't you afraid of us?" "No," he replied. "Your hideous appearance only reminds me to be aware, to have mercy. Come and sit by my fire."

This instrument has asked the question of how can she retain this openness she is feeling. How can she stay undefended?

One does not stay undefended. One simply notes the arising of defense each time it appears with the arising of fear and says, "Oh, you again! Here is fear. Come and sit by my fire."

Your relationships will continue to inspire fear and a desire to defend. You do not move away from that need to defend by denying it nor by wishing it away, nor by judging it and telling yourself, *I should not feel this. I should know better by now.*

You transcend that need to defend by embracing the ego-self, comforting it, noticing the fear, and inviting it to sit by the fire. You

---

[30]Milarepa is one of the most revered of the Tibetan saints. It is believed that simply to say his name calls forth an instant blessing. A website that offers much information about this monk is www.cosmicharmony.com/Av/Milarepa/Milarepa.htm.

cannot transcend what you do not accept. To transcend ego, you must accept ego. It is only then that the true manifestation of what you are can emerge.

You are divine. Your divinity strives to express itself constantly, but is often suppressed by your fear-based reactions. As you learn to look fear in the eye and know that you need not be afraid of fear, you will find that you do not have to create that undefended stance. It simply emerges as natural to you.

You do not have to search for connection. You experience your true connection because the blockages to that experience have been, I will not say removed, but laid aside. Like a throng of people that blocks the road before you, if you stamp your feet and say, "Get out of my way!" they taunt you. But perhaps when you smile at them and say, "Please, may I pass through?" they may step aside.

It is in this way that you learn the process of keeping your heart open. Keeping the heart open is not an event but a process. Each time you do it, you become a bit more skilled at it, a bit more skilled at seeing where you have invited fear in but then challenged fear's right to be present, wanting only to be rid of it again. You become a bit more skilled at saying simply, "Here is fear. Sit by my fire. But I will not be reactive to you. I need not be reactive to you."

There is a vast difference between the experience of fear and the need to separate or defend, which is reactivity to fear. Watch that process in yourselves and you will learn how to experience it, how to invite it to sit by your fire without your needing to be reactive to it.

Your compassion for yourself deepens as you see this human submerged in a constant turmoil. One situation is no sooner resolved and comfortable than a new one emerges, creating new discomfort. How can you not embrace the courageous you that willingly moves into this incarnational turmoil to serve, to learn, and to grow? Thus, your fear ceases to be a reminder for reactivity and defensiveness. Instead, when you see the arising of fear, through your skillful work with that arising you create a new pattern, a new habit.

Seeing the arising of fear becomes a reminder for compassion. That compassion is the key to being undefended, thereby allowing full connection between yourself and the people and situations of your life. As that level of compassion manifests itself in your own relationship to yourself, it is easily transferred to others. Then, and only then, does the small ego-self begin to dissolve.

Then another's fear is seen as no different from your own. There is nothing to protect because there is nothing that is not part of you, nothing that can really threaten you. Slowly you can learn to open your heart in that way to another: it is our fear, our pain, and our compassion. At this point the brain has stopped directing your choices, and the heart, with its deep wisdom and innate compassion, does the choosing with wisdom and with love. It is a most wonderful process, a process of which I stand in some awe.

I would like to pass the microphone here to our brother/sister of Q'uo. That is all.

(Carla channeling)

Q'uo: We are with this instrument once again.

A visualization often makes clearer that which we would say. We would like you to imagine with us the house of your spiritual self in manifestation. You dwell in a culture that has a high regard for freedom. This is the highest worldly ethic: the respect for freedom of will. And so you begin by putting above the door to your house, "I have free will" or "I have my rights." However, this house has a higher floor. The upper story of this house has a different legend over the doorway. It says, "The Earth is the Lord's, and the fullness thereof."[31]

This upper story houses that "you" that knows it is in the infinite Creator and the infinite Creator is in it. It knows that all things are the Creator's. Spend time with this awareness. Climb the stairs to this second story and sit upon your own mercy seat, even if you can only

---

[31] Ps. 24:1 AV.

enter for a moment, and open to the consciousness of all. When you climb down the stairs to the ground floor of your everyday experience, you will find the sign above the front door has changed to read, "I am worthy."

You, my friends, are worthy to receive all good things. Yet if you do not receive a good thing, you are still worthy. It is only your feelings and emotions, bruised and battered by rude experience, that communicate unworthiness. This is a false communication. Do not accept this communication, but rather, know your worthiness and your loveliness and feel compassion arising naturally within the portion of you that remains in the second story.

We can only thank and bless each soul within this circle. It has been such a privilege for us. We bid each farewell in the love and in the light of the one infinite Creator and turn the microphone back to the one known as Aaron, that this wise teacher may also make his farewells. We are of the principle known to you as Q'uo. Adonai. Adonai.

(Barbara channeling)

Aaron: May I offer you a bit of homework with which to practice until we meet again? Watch the arising of fear. See the process as clearly as you can. Firstly, there is a sense-consciousness of that perceived threat. You may feel it in the physical body as tension in the belly, the throat, or elsewhere. Note it as tension. If it is a seen or heard perceived threat, know there is seeing or hearing.

From that perceived threat, a sense of fear arises. Then comes the need to defend. See that the need to defend is not the same as the fear itself. Watch it very carefully. The need to defend is a reaction to the fear. Fear is so uncomfortable that there is the desire to get rid of fear. And out of that aversion arises either the need to defend or the need to fling the fear on another in anger, resentment, or blame.

Bring this wise teacher, Milarepa, into your heart. When you see fear arise, take his hand quite literally and say, "Fear, come in and sit

218

by my fire." Just that. Begin to observe what a difference awareness makes. Note that it is not fear, but fear of fear, that leads to your defending and your being pulled into this unwholesome codependence. Watch it very carefully, even taking notes if you wish. Do it as an experiment in consciousness.

As a second step, notice that there is sometimes reluctance to do this work. Even when you have proved to yourself that you can let go of fear and stay open, at some level there may be a desire not to do so from a part of you that feels, *I am not ready to be that responsible. While I want to love and feel connection, I am not sure I am ready to do it at this time. A part of me wants to blame and to continue this unskillful codependency rather than moving into that living and loving symbiosis.*

What voice is this that wants to continue the old, unwholesome patterns? Can you see that small ego-self kicking and screaming? Can you smile at it? The more you fear the small ego-self and strive to get rid of it with judgment, the more solidity you allow it to assume. When you smile at it with that same, "Oh, you again. Come and sit by my fire," then it allows you to reopen to the spirit that you are.

I suggest and hope that you will practice with this. And I hope you will share your findings with me when we next come together.

May I also ask you to keep in your minds the image that I offered yesterday? You are all spiritual warriors. And with every step that you take, with every small step of growth upon this magnificent path, there are a great many loving beings on all planes that bow to your courage and strew flowers on your path.

That is not said to inflate ego or to make you feel that you, as an individual, are special. All beings are special, and there is nothing more valued in the entire universe than the increased opening into love of the individual spirit.

I thank you again for allowing me to share my thoughts with you. Please remember to take what is useful and to discard the rest. My love is with you. That is all.

WEEKEND 5

Once again we had three days together. It was early spring, not yet warm but the grass was beginning to show green and the yard was full of daffodils. Many friends had heard of what we were doing together and asked to participate. This was the largest group so far filling the living room to capacity with about twelve people gathered. The kitchen was filled with cooking aroma. Carla did much of it, but others had also brought dishes to share.

We had found a pattern we liked of four sessions for the weekend. With the larger group, we were a bit more structured. Before breakfast, Barbara led a silent meditation period for those who wished it. After the morning meal, we gathered for prayers led by Carla, and also some tuning from Barbara and Carla for the group. In the afternoon on Saturday many of us took a long walk through the greening Kentucky countryside. On Saturday evening after dinner, some of us watched a movie. Others engaged in spiritual discussions. Pull up a chair and join us.

☙ Barbara's Beginning Silent Meditation Instructions[32]

Invite a slight smile in the corners of the mouth, the inner smile, a Buddha smile, a feeling of lightness in the corners of the mouth. Smile into the moment and into your body. Be aware of any sensations as you smile into your body. Bring gentle awareness to the throat, smiling into the mid-area of the throat, the jugular notch.

Smile down into the chest, into the left side of the chest, left lung, right side of the chest, right lung. Smile into the whole body. Experience it. Establish mindfulness in the present moment, mindfulness of the body.

Smile into the heart center, in the area of the physical heart. Touch the heart with awareness.

Smile into the abdomen. Take a deep breath into the chest or the abdomen. Take a deep breath, hold it momentarily, and then slowly exhale. As you do, feel the chest and stomach relax. Do this two or three times, with silent, deep breaths, and each exhalation offered with awareness. Relax into the body and let the abdomen be soft, without tension. Soft belly, Buddha belly. Let go of fear.

Right now, you are breathing, a natural function of your body. With mindfulness of breathing, you simply turn your attention to this natural process that is already occurring. Take one breath at a time and simply be aware that you are breathing in, and aware that you are breathing out. Breathing in, be aware of the whole body. Breathing out, be aware of the whole body.

Focus on the breath as the primary object of your attention. Be aware of the breath at the nostrils, mouth, or wherever the feeling of the breath is clearest for you. Notice the physical sensation of the breath touching at the mouth or nostrils, the coolness of the in-breath,

---

[32] This meditation is taken from Barbara's book *Cosmic Healing* (Berkeley, CA: North Atlantic Books, 2011), pp. 216–218.

the warm softness of the out-breath. Allow the breath to find its own rhythm and flow. You are not controlling it, just observing it, trusting in the body and the breath to function naturally. Let your breath become the focus of your attention, the primary object.

Sometimes it can be helpful to extend and lengthen the breath at the beginning of a sitting, so that you begin to focus on the entirety of the inhalation and the exhalation, as well as on the pauses or apertures between the inhalation and the exhalation. This pause between the breath is the *now*, just this very moment. Noticing this aperture helps to bring you more deeply into the present moment and concentrates the mind; this awareness can also bring us more deeply into the heart center.

Experience your breath as a circle. There are beginning, middle, and end portions to the inhalation, a slight pause in the breath, and then the beginning, middle, and end of the exhalation. After a slight pause, the whole cycle begins once again. As you allow the breath to become more subtle and natural, you may not sense the entire length of the inhalation or the exhalation. That's okay. Become aware of as much of the breath as possible. Breathing in, allow the whole body to be calm and at peace. Breathing out, allow the whole body to be calm and at peace. As the mind begins to slow down, and becomes more calm and focused, awareness penetrates more deeply. The full length and duration of the breath and the pauses between the exhalation and the inhalation become more noticeable.

Session 14

Weekend 5, Part 1 of 4
(This session was preceded by a period of tuning and meditation.)

Group question: How do we open the heart?

(Barbara channeling)

Aaron: My greetings and love to you all. As always, it is a great joy to feel the energy and light in this room and to feel the purity of your desire to serve and to learn. We are offered the question: How do you, while living in this illusion, keep your heart open through the many catalysts that your life offers you?

If you will forgive the pun, may I come to the heart of this question by reminding you that the heart never closes? You may build a wall around it, but it never closes.

There is a subtle but important difference here. When you think of the heart as closing, with that closed heart you are totally separate from your deepest reality, which is that of the Divine within you. The heart is the center of that divinity. So as soon as you ask, "How do I keep my heart open?" at some level you are captured in the distortion, "How do I retain my divinity?" But the real question is, "How do I express that divinity, remembering that it is always there?"

If you think of the heart as a place of the purest light, truly reflecting that divine light, then you realize that the light always shines. When you build a wall around that light, you might think it is the same thing as closing the heart. But you have not turned off the light. You have just walled it in, out of fear. If you hold that image you will remember the light is still shining. Constant awareness of the presence of that light can be an important tool in the work to dissolve the wall.

The wall is going to be built over and over again, as you feel threatened and as you experience fear. When there is such a wall, the external

224

light cannot move into you, and you then feel cut off from that divine light. As a conscious human who cannot experience the divinity in yourself, you thus feel hemmed in by the illusion.

In knowing that the light is there, you can focus on the light instead of focusing on the fear that prevents you from experiencing the reality of that light. By doing this you avoid a dialogue with fear. You are no longer saying, "How do I get rid of the fear?" Rather, you are simply moving back in to focus on the light: "This is reality. This is what I am and what we all are."

Can you hear the difference in these two responses?

One response is, "How do I open my heart? How do I deal with the fear?" This may get you into a war with the fear.

The other response is, "Here is the light. Pay attention! It is harder to see today because there is fear. Focus on it. Let it blossom. Let it become real for me."

As you move back into the clarity that this focus on that light allows, the wall dissolves by itself. There is no self taking down the wall, nobody doing this. There has simply been the awareness: *Fear is present. It is blocking the light. I need to find that light and look a bit harder for it because of the presence of fear. As I let love in, fear naturally dissolves.*

This process opens you to a very strong statement of who you are.

You are not your fear.

You are not your negativity, although that does reside in the human form.

You are not the heavier densities of the body, although that is part of what you are.

You are divine. You are angels.

What I suggest is not a matter of denial of that part of you that is fearful and negative, nor is it an unwillingness to allow the expression of that part. Rather, it is a coming into a state of wholeness in which you know that the fear is just fear and in which you allow the full expression of all the beauty in you: the lovingkindness, the generosity, the caring, and the energy. It is the reminder of your true being.

This still leads to the question, "How do we do this?" It is fine to say that the heart is always open and that the focus is on the wall that closes out the light. It is fine to make that distinction. But what do you do with the wall? What do you do with fear?

The heart opens and closes in the illusion that you are experiencing. It does not matter how you say it. What you are experiencing is the cutting off of light and moving back into light. When you are cut off from light it feels very, very dark. What I have suggested is only one of the many tools you may use: this recollection, "The light is within me. I am an angel. Even if right at this moment I am not experiencing that angelness, I am still an angel."

I would hope that through these next days we can get into the many different tools with which you may work with fear or with whatever it is that closes you into that darkness. I wish to keep this opening talk short and allow my brother/sister, Q'uo, to speak. That is all.

(Carla channeling)

Q'uo: Greetings in the love and in the light of the one infinite Creator. It is most blessed to mingle our vibrations with your own as you sit this afternoon in your circle of seeking. We thank each for this privilege and bless each in return.

To begin speaking of tools and resources, we would first establish that we use a certain model of patterns and centers of energy in-streaming[33] and within the third-density expression, both manifest and unmanifest; that is, both space/time and time/space.[34] That model is the rainbow body with its seven centers of energy, the first being the red or base energy center. The energies there have to do

---

[33] "In-streaming energy" means that energy from the Creator that flows through our physical and energy bodies continuously in an infinite supply. This energy is love/light.

[34] Space/time is the physical world as we know it. Time/space is the world of consciousness, the inner planes of this density and many higher densities.

with the vitality of the mind, the body, and the spirit as they are working together within and manifestly.

The second energy center moves up the physical vehicle from the joining of the legs to a spot close to, but below, the navel. It is the orange-ray energy center or chakra. Energies there are expressing how the entity is dealing with the relationships of self to self and self to another entity. This is a commonly blocked or partially blocked energy.

The next center can be described as being at that position within the physical vehicle where, if you were punched, you would bend over. This yellow-ray energy center expresses how the entity is managing and using the relationships of self to groups such as the nation state, the basketball team, or the family.

Then the green-ray energy center is seen. This is the center about which the question of "How do we open the heart?" has to do. This is the first energy that may be transferred to another's aid and assistance.

Beyond this heart chakra and within the physical area of the throat is the blue-ray energy center or chakra. Its expression concerns communication, whether that be communion with the Creator and the learning that comes from this source, any communication in words to others, or the nonverbal communications of song, poetry, art, and all alternative ways of sharing the self without stint.

At the brow is the indigo-ray energy center or chakra. This is the seat of energies expressing the entity's work in consciousness, as the entity works and strives to learn how to discipline the personality in order to be a true and authentic expression of that which one is.

This energy center, though quite high upon the rainbow and upon the ambition or hope scale, is specifically the energy that tends to bring entities to call upon those like us, which may offer some opinions or thoughts that may be helpful. This is to be noted because working with the indigo ray, communicating through the blue ray, and attempting to keep open the all-loving and all-compassionate heart is an effort that greatly suffers because the lower energies are not much liked. Indeed, entities often choose to do most of their conscious work within the upper energies while choosing not to address issues that are unclear within the expression of energies in the first three energy centers.

To finish our rainbow we add the violet-ray energy center or crown chakra. This center is a reading or readout of the state of the expressing energies of the entity and does not do work in and of itself. It functions as an up-to-the-minute report of the status of the blended energies of the entity.

Seekers often dream and hope and reach without being clear with themselves or the humdrum world. Therefore, we would begin our discussion of how to keep the green-ray energy center spinning, vibrant, and brilliantly radiating with a look at the more common blockages lower than the heart. We do this with an eye to instilling in the seeker a strong compassion toward the self and toward the illusion that startles and creates seemingly outrageous insult to the self.

Have you been in a conversation where an entity wished to impress you with its skill or accomplishments? So does the energy expression of the lower chakras wish to hog the internal conversation and speak of those things it does well, so as to eliminate or at least greatly diminish the need to communicate or to focus upon those things that, if thought about, would muddy, slow, and dim the energy.

To have the patience and the self-acceptance to move in thought each day to the examination of the places where the seeker has been caught or where the seeker has been hurt is a job that seems never-ending. Yet the more one is able to accept the humanity of the self enough to look at the self's profoundly imperfect expression without blinking, the more the seeker will gain greatly.

For many people it is the hardest work to affirm one's sexuality, one's simple red-chakra self. To accept one's seeming lack of skill in dealing with the self and others is humbling. It seems as though one cannot sink into one's own persistent imperfections of expression without becoming so discouraged that one retires from spiritual seeking.

Yet the more one is able to think of this humanity, this heavy incarnational illusion, as acceptable, the more one shall be able to be balanced and clear enough that the energy of the one infinite Creator may flow upward, circulating happily in the imperfect but balanced expressions of energy that you have as a seeker created by your work in forgiving the self, forgiving, and forgiving again.

You may think of yourself in two ways. The first is to think of yourself as a prince or princess, delicate in feature and form, beautifully attired in royal robes, and seated upon a huge, lumbering, beautifully decorated elephant. In this model you are working at the indigo-ray level while leaving unaccepted the more obviously earth-bound portions of the self's energy.

Or you may think of yourself as the elephant. This large, physically awkward-looking animal contains, given that it is a human elephant, a subjective beauty that has nothing to do with form. The energies of the physical body, the mental complex, and the spiritual complex are those of no-body or no-form. Yet the form must be there within this illusion so that the spirit that is yourself may learn to serve and choose how to serve.

In the second model the prince or princess rides within the elephant and is that which truly is the accurate violet-ray readout or summation of the combined energies at any particular time. You must be of a form, of a set of limitations, in order to do the manifesting portion that brings all of its food for thought to the unmanifest portion of the incarnated self. Thusly, one tool may begin to be described as that which reckons with the outer elephant without becoming discouraged, disgusted, or exhausted.

We would transfer the microphone to the ones known as Barbara and Aaron. We leave this instrument for this time period. We are those of the principle, Q'uo.

(Barbara channeling)

Aaron: I take delight in sharing this work with Q'uo because our mental bodies are different and we each offer the same teachings with different examples. Because you are each unique, one image speaks to one being's heart while another image speaks to another being's heart.

I enjoy Q'uo's image of the elephant and rider. If I may offer a different kind of image here, you are what I call angels in earth-suits. Both aspects are real. You are in a physical body. Without that physical body and without the emotional body the angel would be deprived of the catalysts that this incarnate state so readily offers. Without the angel the earth-suit is sterile.

As Q'uo has pointed out, it is far easier to focus on the angel and look with disdain on the earth-suit. There is a sense of wanting to move to a purer level where the earth-suit is no longer necessary. In this way you grasp at graduating from this plane, rather than just being on this plane where you are and trusting that this is where you need to be. You are each exactly where you need to be.

Each of your bodies has its own frequencies of vibration, like a stringed instrument with four strings. The physical and emotional bodies have a heavier, lower vibration. And yet, a stringed instrument that is in tune plays beautifully and in harmony with itself. There is no need to rip out the lower strings because they do not play as high as the upper strings. Your entire being can express this harmony. The physical body and the emotional body are never going to be as highly pitched as the mental and spirit bodies. And that is fine.

One place where you shut out light is when you look with disdain on these emotional and physical bodies. You see the imperfections and you strive to get rid of those imperfections rather than finding love for the being that you are.

The angel is perfect. The angel is unlimited. But the angel's wings can get a bit tarnished. The angel stands on the earth and its feet get caught in the mud. If the angel does not set foot on earth, where is it going to learn these lessons of love, of faith, and of compassion? That is why you have taken incarnation. You are here to learn in human form and to serve in human form. To do that work you must begin to embrace the incarnation rather than treat it with impatience and disdain.

This is perhaps the hardest part of being human, especially for those of you who are old souls. You reach a time in your work where you see the light so clearly, and the impurities in the lower bodies seem so solid, so heavy. You aspire to the heavens and your feet are in the mud. It makes you want to cut off your feet rather than bringing a hose, lovingly hosing the mud away, and just watching for the next mud puddle.

Those beings who do not so clearly penetrate the illusion and who do not truly know their own angel do not have the same contempt for the emotional and physical bodies. They step on others' toes. They allow themselves to express their physical and emotional imperfections without self-hatred.

I am not suggesting that this way of being is good or bad. I am only saying that it is a unique problem. The being that reaches the end of third-density experience becomes increasingly impatient with its human manifestations, which it judges as lesser than the spirit manifestations. You increasingly ask perfection of yourselves. But that cuts you off from the sense of compassion for this human.

I would like to offer an image that may be of some help. You are actors in a play. As with any actor, you must read your lines with convincing honesty. They must be real for you. No matter how deep or profound they are, if you come onto the stage and just say to the audience, "Well, this is just a play and I'm going to move through these lines quickly," the audience is not going to learn or grow from that reading. It will not be convincing; it will just be somebody up there tossing out words.

In order for there to be growth, the audience must become captured by the illusion. It must become a reality for them. And yet, the actor cannot forget that he or she is an actor, cannot turn its back to the audience nor hold its hand over its mouth to muffle its words, or the audience will again be deprived of the value of the play through being shut out of it.

In terms of your incarnate experience you are actors and this is an illusion. But this illusion must be treated with respect. It must be treated as real because you are also the audience. That part of you that is "audience" cannot learn if the actor's back is turned or if the actor treats the play as frivolous.

This is where it gets so hard to find that place of balance, where you put your whole heart and soul into the illusion while remembering, *I can't turn my back on the audience. I must be aware of the spirit body and of the reality of who I am while I work within the illusion as fully as I can.*

We come back to this question of how to keep the heart open or, as I would prefer to put it, how to allow that light that is your true self to shine through. As Q'uo said, how does one keep the heart chakra spinning and the energy channels open so that you do not become lost in the illusion, nor caught in the spirit and disdaining the illusion. How do you find that balance?

You must constantly be aware. Remember that the physical and emotional bodies are gifts of the incarnate experience, not burdens that you have been asked to carry to make your learning more difficult. When you relate to the elephant, to the physical and emotional bodies as gifts, you change your relationship with them. It is this remembering why you are here in these bodies that allows you to keep focused on that light of your angel while simultaneously allowing the full experience of the incarnation.

I do not suggest that this is easy. The actor gets so caught up in its lines that it forgets there is an audience there. It becomes totally trapped in the illusion of the play. And then it remembers, "Oh, there's an audience," and turns itself to play to that audience again, to make sure that the physical and emotional experiences are offered openly to the higher self so that the mental and spirit bodies may grow in whatever ways they are offered to grow.

I have just offered to Barbara a complex thought that was not channeled with complete clarity. I wish to explain this a bit.[35]

---

[35] At this point in her life as a medium, Barbara is still conscious-channeling Aaron; he is not incorporated in her body.

The spirit body is a spark of the Divine. It is perfect. It needs nothing beyond itself. And yet it is just a spark. It is capable of infinite expansion. The divine essence of it does not change, but its power may change so that you move from being that small spark of God into being a brilliant sun. This essence of divinity within each of you is not separate from God nor is it, in itself, God. But it is a part of that infinite energy, light, and love.

If you had a vast ocean, an infinite sea, and you took a drop of water from a dropper and dropped it into that sea, no matter that it was already infinite, it would expand. You add that drop to it. Each of you is involved in this process of expanding and enhancing your own energy and light, which does not belong to you personally but, in eighth-density experience, moves back fully into the Eternal and thereby expands the infinite light and love in the universe.

So, the soul itself is not learning. But the soul within what we call the higher self is accompanied by the mental body. As soon as there is thought, there is distortion, because with thought there is self-awareness. As soon as you are aware of a self, you move into the distortion of self and other. This distortion is part of the illusion and is useful and even necessary for a certain distance on your path. But there is also the level of awareness that there is no separate self. Pure Awareness knows that this that has perceived itself as separate is truly of the essence of the Eternal.

Here is where you move into and out of illusion. The higher self then moves into the incarnate experience, manifesting form and taking on the heaviness of the emotional body so that it can work with the earth catalysts and clarify this energy that you are.

Concerning the ideas of love and compassion, what do these mean? If there were never any pain, it would be easy to feel love. You would never feel threatened. You would never close or build that wall. But what would this love mean? When you are offered the heavy catalysts that you are offered on this plane and can still forgive, still find compassion and love, can you see that you are expanding that original spark? The light grows purer.

In effect, this small spark within you is fed by the fuel of Earth's catalysts. Two responses are possible. One is that those catalysts feel so heavy that you shut the doors, thus enclosing that flame within and not allowing it to return itself to God.

The second choice is that you watch the process of closing and opening, fear and love, and find compassion for the human who is experiencing this physical and emotional pain. This growing compassion serves to add fuel to the spark so that it burns more and more brilliantly. The shadow falls away and what is finally returned to God has become a sun in its own right.

So, you are in this illusion and yet being asked to openheartedly relate to it with balance, in working with all the catalysts of the lower chakras while welcoming these catalysts and neither preferring the upper-chakra energy and the experience of being angels nor the experience of the earth-suit. This is your greatest challenge because it is so painful to keep coming back to that earth-suit when the heart yearns to be free and back on that plane of light and love where there are no distortions of fear.

There must be constant awareness of the beginnings of any dialogue you have with fear. You know of the willingness not to get caught up in that fear or react to it. Certainly you experience pain that gives you good reason to get caught up in the fear. All you can do is to remind yourself, each time fear arises, *Trust. Trust even this fear. Can I allow myself to fully enter this illusion with as much love as I can bring to it?*

In a sense, it is not the pain of the illusion that causes you to build walls and close in the heart but your fear that there will be pain. There is a difference here when you are afraid of the catalysts of your learning; that is, when you begin to shut out the lower-chakra experiences and grasp at the spiritual.

But this is precisely where you are being offered the opportunity to practice compassion for the human and to see the human, this angel with its feet in the mud, and give it a hug instead of trying to chop off the legs and free the angel.

I know that these sessions will be continued, as we will have three more sessions in the next two days and do not need to cover this whole matter now. In essence, what Q'uo and I are doing today is laying the groundwork. I want to speak at length about how you work with fear by speaking in two directions.

The first is mindfulness of all the heavy physical and emotional experiences you have while working with your anger—your jealousy and all of that which tends to close you and to create the illusion of separation.

The second is how you may nurture the angel.

This is what I started with today: the importance of recognizing that the light or angel or divinity is always there and of remembering that you may keep focused on it. No matter how severe the darkness, you will still sense the inner light that lights that darkness if you will remember what you are. I pass this teaching to my brother/sister/ friend Q'uo and will speak again to end with a brief guided meditation of bringing in light. That is all.

(Carla channeling)

Q'uo: We are again with this instrument. Greetings once more in love and light.

As the one known as Aaron says, the fuel for incarnate learning is that which affects one, usually by disturbing it, sometimes by seeming to do it injury or harm and even sometimes seemingly irreparable damage.

Life hurts. Change is painful. It seems as if the light of spirit is no more than a candle against the great elephantine darkness of living within physical incarnation. Welcome to the world that the cliché calls the School of Hard Knocks.

Spirit is not something that you can lose. It is your being and nature. It cannot be lost. Only the subjective awareness of the spiritual nature of the self is obscured. Sight of it is lost as one turns and flees from the frightening scene where pain or grievous insult seems offered.

Within every cell of your elephant, shall we say, there is spirit in manifestation. Yet it is difficult to communicate with the cells of the body that seem to be in pain or ill or hurt in this way or that.

To move in mid-metaphor to another metaphor, let us put the elephants back on stage. They rumble about in each act of your play. You are acting as well as an elephant can, yet you also wrote this play. You are also each character, hero, and villain as well as the butler, the friend, and all of the characters. You are also the critic sitting in the audience, just waiting for a poorly delivered line, a poorly developed plot, or the tasteless costuming of elephant girths. All is self. You need, then, each day, each hour, to dwell in the always chancy, often difficult concerns of the relationship of self to self, self to other, and self to all.

It is infinitely advisable to embrace this constant grounding in your own story, in your own drama, and in each facet of relationship that has caught you this day. You cannot run out of spirit in doing this work. You can only multiply the time that you have available for it by accepting that which you see this day, turning in thanks and in praise to that portion of the self that authored this play and that set this stage.

Before we leave, we would ask if there are any queries about material covered to this point.

(Pause)

We take your silence to be a sign that so far we have been intelligible. O ponderous pachyderms, proceed! Lumber on! Find a laugh in your heart. Smile at your beloved elephant that gives its life that you might learn better to be.

We leave this instrument for this session, rejoicing in your beauty and all beauty. Thank you for this great honor. We share these thoughts with but one request and that is that you toss away all thoughts of ours except those that you find useful, for we offer opinions, not authority. We leave each in the love and in the light of the infinite One. Adonai. We are those of Q'uo.

Session 14

(Barbara channeling)

Aaron: I would like to leave you with a brief exercise that you may practice.

First, I would ask you to move into the heart center and therein to find that spark of the Divine, that place of infinite beauty and love within you, that place that is undefended and has no reference point of self. Visualize or feel that light shining out of you.

If it is helpful, visualize the being who, for you, is the embodiment of truth, and merge your heart with that guru or master. As fully as you are able, allow yourself to rest in this space, empty of all self, and to radiate that lovingkindness that is the true essence of your being.

Now I ask you to turn your memory to some moment today when you felt a bit threatened. It does not have to be a big issue. It might be just a very minor slight, but some moment when you felt fear and the small ego-self moved to protect and make the strong statement, "I am here: me, ego-self."

As you remember, see if you can feel how the solidifying of that small ego-self moves you away from Pure Awareness that is empty of self. As much as is possible, allow yourself to reexperience that move from center to what would seem to be the closing of the heart in protection.

What I hope you can experience is that the light does not fade. It is simply blocked. Each time this small ego-self solidifies, it blocks the light. You are then left with two choices, both of which we will explore in depth tomorrow: how to work skillfully with that which blocks the light and how to return the focus to the light.

For now, let us leave off on working with the blockage. Just put it aside until tomorrow. What I would like you to do now is to work within the frame of your present experience, feeling the self threatened and moving to protection, and feeling the separation from God and the separation from your true being.

I want you simply to remind yourself, "A cloud has come between me and the sun. It feels dark in here. The darker it gets, the more fear

237

builds. But the sun is still shining. Instead of getting caught in the darkness, I am going to focus on that sun." A simple reminder to the self can be, "I need not dialogue with fear but may give myself permission to move back to my true self. I am not denying the cloud, just letting it be and coming back to focus on the light."

This is a skill, a learnable skill. Most of you have created patterns whereby, as soon as the cloud appears, you raise an umbrella, enclosing yourselves in further darkness. You must first notice the raising of the umbrella and that sensation of the heart's closing. And then you must remind yourself, "Every time there's a cloud, I don't need to raise an umbrella, only to look beyond the cloud and reconnect with the sunshine."

With great gentleness to yourselves, I would ask you to practice this through the evening and the early hours of tomorrow until we meet again. Each time there is closing and a wall being built, notice that it is happening. Give this small ego-self that is feeling fear a hug. Let it know it is okay that fear is being experienced and consciously refocus on the light. No judgment about the arising of fear and no grasping at the light are needed. You are not reaching for something that has fled, only allowing your focus to come back to what is always there: to this place of love, infinite wisdom, compassion, and deepest connection with God.

I thank each of you for being a part of this circle and for the profound earnestness and love that you express by your presence. May all beings everywhere open into the light of their true being. May all beings transcend the illusion of fear so that they can more fully manifest the true nature of their love in every expression of their energy. May the work of each of us help all beings find their way.

My love to you all. That is all.

Session 15

Weekend 5, Part 2 of 4
(This session was preceded by a period of tuning and meditation.)

Group question: The group continues with the topic of how to open the heart center, with a special focus on how to work with the lower energy centers in preparation for the opening of the heart center.

(Barbara channeling)

Aaron: Good morning and my love to you all.

How have you done with your homework? Did you experience those moments of separating, with window shades drawn tightly closed? It is a painful experience and not necessary to incarnation.

Let us look together at the process. When you enter the illusion in which you feel the heart closed, so that you are separated from that beloved source of light and so that your own light does not shine, what is really happening at that moment?

When there is careful looking each time the heart is experienced as closed, you see the presence of fear.

That in itself means nothing. Who is afraid? Afraid of what? There is a cycle in which you experience fear and separation. There must be the illusion of a separate, solid self or of subject and object. As you experience the self as solid, the fear becomes more solid, enhancing the sense of separation and bringing you further from your true self.

There is a poem by Rumi that Barbara encountered this morning. I would like to ask if K. or C. would read this. It is on the right-hand side of the marked page:

> *The moment I heard of his love, I thought,*
> *To find the beloved, I must search with*
> *Body, mind, and soul.*

But, no. To find the beloved,
We must become the beloved.[36]

I would ask you always to remember that you need not seek God else-where. The Divine is within yourself. To me, this awareness carried deep within you is the key to working with the heavy energies and catalysts of the earth plane. As soon as you experience yourself as separate from the Divine, then self solidifies. Fear increases and becomes stronger. Then the darkness closes in further, and you become more and more enmeshed by your sense of separation, vulnerability, and fear.

We spoke of this a bit earlier this morning. I asked those who were listening to envision an expansive, blue sky with a brilliant sun and small wisps of clouds here and there. As the winds shift, the clouds are brought together and slowly form what seems to be a storm cloud that blocks the sun. You have two choices: to react as if that cloud were solid and move to protect yourself by fetching your jacket or your umbrella, or to remember the sun is still shining, as in, *There's nothing solid here, just bits of that same material I've seen floating through the sky. They've simply come together.*

Because you are human and must function at both levels, of course, if it begins to pour you put up an umbrella. But is the umbrella to protect you from harm or is it to keep you warm and dry?

There is a difference. When you relate to the clouds in your life as threatening you personally, then fear solidifies; self solidifies and your response to those personal clouds becomes one of fighting a war with them. You believe you must rid yourself of them at all costs so that you can return to the experience of the sun!

When you can, note the existence of those clouds without feeling a personal threat and see them as just clouds coming through. When clouds do come together, it may rain, and you may note, *I could get wet and will then be uncomfortable. So I will very skillfully put up my umbrella.* Here

---

[36] Shahram Shiva and Jonathan Star, *A Garden Beyond Paradise: The Mystical Poetry of Rumi* (New York, NY: Bantam Books, 1992), 59.

there is no fear. There is no personal threat. You know that the sun is always shining above the clouds. The energy does not contract with fear and prepare to do battle.

If in some moment your own personal cloud involves another being that is angry at you, even raging at you because of a self-perceived threat to itself, your fear leads you to strike back at that being, verbally or even physically, or to move to protect yourself in a way that connotes your own anger.

When instead you can see that being's fear and pain, you may still figuratively put up your umbrella. You may step back out of its reach. You may choose to leave the room or the vicinity of this angry being without reacting with fear.

There is that one moment where the self begins to solidify and you may experience a perceived threat, such as, "I could be hurt" or "My needs might not be met" or whatever the fear is about. There must be attention to that moment when the sudden appearance of self and other is perceived as threatening to the self.

If anger arises there must be attention to its arising against that perceived threat. With strong mindfulness, that first perception of solidified self, of fear, and of any other heavy emotion becomes like a waving warning-flag that says, "Pay attention!" Can there be compassion for this seeming self that is feeling fear? "I turn to the light within me, open up to the Divine within me, and remember that the sun is still shining."

This is a tremendously powerful tool. It takes much practice to learn to do it skillfully. And before you even begin the practice, it takes much honesty to look at the places in the self that want to respond with anger, so as to get even with that which seems to threaten. Once you do that work and can pay attention to the arising of fear, and even pay attention to that which wants revenge and just treat that as more fear, you can give yourself a literal hug with the thought, *It's okay. Whatever I'm feeling is okay.*

As you offer that compassion to yourself, you begin to be able to offer it to the catalyst. Then self and other dissolve, not immediately, but slowly. The more practiced you get at it, the faster the dissolution of separation. And it is no longer my fear but our fear, our pain. In this way, the first arising of fear becomes a catalyst, not for hatred but for compassion. It becomes a reminder: "The heart is at risk of closing. Keep it open. Remember the light is still shining."

When we look at what leads to the sensation of the heart's closing and the sense of separation from God, from others, and from self, we see that need to protect. This is another area on which you may wish to focus. This is another tool for the releasing of fear. If you pay close attention, you can literally feel the closing of the fearful heart. But you remember that the light is still shining within it.

You might envision the heart as a rose. Within its core is the most brilliant light imaginable, comparable only to the light of God. Sit in meditation and feel your connection with the Divine. Visualize the opening of this rose. It cannot be forced. But the allowing of the experience of loving connection opens those petals and you experience the radiance flowing into and out of the heart center.

As you come out of your meditation and reenter the active stages of your life, watch carefully. What happens when there is a catalyst that seems to threaten? Can you see the sun seeming to be cut off and the petals closing? If you remember, *This is illusion. Fear is illusion. It seems solid, but it is created out of my own delusion of a separate self,* then you can ask yourself, *Is there a desire to get caught up in this fear?* Sometimes that is easier.

It is very beautiful to feel your connection with all that is, but it takes a great deal of responsibility to live that connection constantly without giving in to your anger. You are human. I am not condoning giving in to anger, only suggesting that for the human there is a constant struggle to remember your connection and ask yourself to express that connection rather than separation in your choices.

So, you note the illusion of fear and how solid it seems. Come back to the heart center, that place where the light is still brilliant. If the fear is so intense that, like the storm cloud, it seems totally to have blocked out the sun, then for that moment you are going to have to be the source of light. You may not feel God's presence. And although your intellect tells you, *God is still present and I am only cutting off the experience of that,* still you are not feeling it.

So, where is the light and love to come from that opens the blossom of this rose and allows reconnection? It comes from your deep practice of lovingkindness and compassion with yourself. When you see this being sitting alone and afraid, can you reach out to it with love?

What if you wandered down the street, protected by your rain gear in a heavy storm, and there was a child alone and sobbing on the curb? Would your heart not reach out to this being to shelter and protect it? Can you not do the same for yourselves when you find yourselves soaked in a storm, hemmed in by heavy rain clouds so that you cannot experience the light?

Yes, the fear is illusion. Now you are recognizing "caught in illusion" and are also changing your perspective to know that this is illusion: "The sun is still shining. I am going to keep myself open to that sun even if I cannot seem to experience it. And then I'm going to give love to this being that's caught in the storm, this being that wants to revenge itself and that wants to scream out its jealousy or its sense of betrayal or greed. I'm going to love that being."

It is very hard, but it is the deepest gift you can give, not only to yourself but to God. For to love that which is easy to love is far less of a gift than to love even the angry, jealous, and bitter parts of yourself and of all beings.

I want to speak more about different ramifications of this work, especially in connection with the specific questions you have raised. Before I do that, I would like to turn the microphone over to Q'uo so that this brother/sister/friend may offer you its own wisdom and thoughts about this work. That is all.

(Carla channeling)

Q'uo: We greet each this morning in the love and in the light of the one infinite Creator. We keenly feel the pleasure of your company and gratefully respond to your call for information.

As the one known as Aaron says so clearly, the separation of the self's consciousness is an illusion. The physical vehicle is an organized illusion within the grand scheme of illusion that is the sensory haven for all of third-density work. Each is aware that this is a dream. However, each knows, too, that this is a purposeful dream, a much-desired and desirable illusion, an illusion with which each seeker learns to cooperate, so that learning the lessons of love may become more and more harmonious and more harmonized with the spirit within.

It is easy to dismiss one's pain. We may use pain or fear to mean the whole range of defensive maneuvers and postures taken by the self as catalyst bursts upon the conscious awareness. We find, however, that the entire process is effectively weakened in its efficient functioning if the seeker looks down on its own suffering.

This suffering is not the product of weakness. It is a product that is as strong as it is weak and as informative as it is repulsive. The emotions that are negative are described as heavy, yet this suggests that there needs to be a lightening of the weight of emotion. We suggest that it is the seeker who turns to the negative emotion and allows it to remain seemingly heavy, just keeping it company for the moment, who will more speedily and comfortably find the self able to allow this weight of energy to begin its natural movement in spiraling upward from the momentary affliction or suffering experience.

We wish to borrow a tale this instrument has read to illustrate what we mean. There was once an old sage who dwelt in one simple room, meditating and praying. So this sage lived for all of its fullness of years. In the twilight of its incarnation, a young, beautiful stranger burst into the sage's humble room with a newborn child, naming the old sage as the child's father.

The sage did not spend time and energy attempting to make it known that this was not the truth. Rather, the sage took the babe and straightway began to work as a shipyard laborer so that it could feed the child. Several years went by with the old man creaking and suffering as he worked the long hours. The babe grew to be a small child.

One day this woman, the child's mother, entered again this sage's dwelling place and took the child away, saying that it was, after all, her child. Again, the sage did not argue with the woman but simply began again its interrupted life of meditation and prayer.

To resist one's pain is to intensify it. The pain is a lie, just as the mother lied about the sage being the child's father. However, when some catalyst strikes a resonance that causes the fear and pain of suffering, to spend effort and time objecting to the situation as a lie is to miss an important point.

Yes, negative emotions are a dream within a dream, a lie within another larger system of lies or illusions. Yet there is purpose here. As the one known as Aaron has put it, the moment of feeling that impulse to pain is a red flag saying, "Pay attention." Do not look away, but look attentively at that impulse. Allow that impulse its rightful focal position. Look with attentive caring. Enter into the darkness that is the small death of negative feelings.

If not at the moment, as soon as possible go down into the darkness of your own perceptions and listen to your own being. Your being suffers to change, to become new, and to move on. A portion of that which you are expressing must die. Let this be as it is.

The verb "to communicate" is extremely important in this work. Allow heavy feelings to communicate and to become intelligible. Do not swat them away or cover them up. If time must pass before this acceptance of the self can take place, then that is well. But to use the goodness of catalyst most efficiently, the intensity and seeming reality of the nuances of these dark emotions need to be remembered and respected.

This acts like a benediction. The suffering of self is thus forgiven by the self who respects these seemingly unacceptable feelings. This allows the energy in these feelings to resume the natural spiraling upward.

Denial and resistance attempt to control and abate the suffering. Acceptance and attentiveness within the very darkness is a way to allow the self to be transformed naturally. You have often, perhaps, considered how children are born into incarnation through pain. Yet the mother is, in the end, totally accepting of this pain, for it has brought about a beloved new life. In the matter of the spirit's learning the lesson of love, you are both mother and midwife to the growing child of transformed consciousness that is your continual identity within the chances and changes of illusory incarnational life.

We would at this time turn the microphone back to the one known as Aaron. We are those of Q'uo.

(Barbara channeling)

Aaron: I find deep joy in sharing this teaching/learning with all of you and with my brother/sister Q'uo, especially joy in the ways that we may enhance each other's thoughts. That which Q'uo has just expressed might be encapsulated in a specific spiritual principle: Do not dialogue with fear.

This does not mean to get rid of fear. As Q'uo has pointed out, there must be respect for the suffering. There is no "getting rid of" here, only being present with what is, with all of what is: the joy and the suffering, the separation and the connection, the illusion and the reality.

When I say, "Do not dialogue with fear," what I mean is, "Do not give fear permission to be in control." When you relate to those catalysts that lead you into fear and separation with more fear and a need to get rid of them in order to come back to some place of connection again, some place of love, then you are dialoguing with fear. Fear is controlling you then because there is still this part of you that wants to get rid of this and grasp at that. When you become able simply to be present with what is, then you are no longer reactive to it. There is just fear. There is just pain.

Yes, it may be terrible fear. It may be agonizing physical or emotional pain. But it no longer has the capacity to shut out the light. You can allow its presence. You can move with compassion to the being that is experiencing that catalyst and immediately you are in the light, suffering whatever fear, pain, grief, or bewilderment there may be, but still in the light. There is no "getting rid of" here and no grasping.

The energy in the lower chakras becomes blocked when fear assumes such solidity that you begin to fight back. For example, with the second chakra, which is the spleen chakra, there may be a sense of a self and an other self and a sense that the other is in some way attacking you. Then a need to defend arises. The energy becomes distorted at this second chakra and you begin to act, as I have just said, in a dialogue with your fear.

At some level you are aware of the distortion whereby the second chakra is no longer open and spinning freely, whereby energy is not moving through. Fear is intensified. The sense of self is intensified. And there is a grasping to get rid of this catalyst and to reopen one's energy.

We were asked about Q'uo's statement about the cells in the body. I will let Q'uo enlarge on that if my brother/sister wishes, but I wish only to say to that, that each cell reflects the whole. When there is an energy distortion that creates a sense of the second chakra being closed, that distortion is duplicated in each cell in the body. What I am saying here is not technically correct, only an attempt to provide a visual image that may help guide you. If you visualize that second chakra being blocked, the back, the abdomen, the head, and the neck all reflect that blockage.

In a sense, each cell in your body has all of these seven chakras within it. Each is a reflection of the whole. You know that there are many energy meridians through the body: organ meridians, junction meridians, and so on. They all interrelate. Each reflects the whole. You do not cure the distortion of the back or neck or head or abdomen by grasping at the release of blockage, any more than you cure that blockage itself by grasping at the release of blockage.

Each of you has a physical body and a light body. The light body is the more pure reflection of the spirit body or of the soul. Within the light body the energy is always entirely open. The physical-body energy is heavier. It replicates that light body as best it can, but is moved and distorted by the play of physical sensation and emotion. When you focus on the perfection of the light body, there need not be grasping at that perfection, but instead a reminder: "I am this light body as well as the physical. I have compassion for the mud puddles into which the physical illusion leads me. But I also remember my perfection."

You might sit in meditation with awareness of where there may be distortion in the physical body and in the chakras of the physical body, and focus on the third eye, allowing yourself to begin to visualize there the entire light body. Focus on that as clearly as you can with no grasping, only an awareness, "These are both part of all I am."

The seed of perfection is real. The physical body is very capable of healing itself of distortion, both energy distortion and the physical ramifications of that energy distortion, if it is simply bathed in love and allowed to reconnect with the perfection of the light body.

For all of you who do energy work, such as *mudra* meditations[37] or polarity therapy,[38] which are names for different and specific kinds of energy work, what you are really doing is allowing the physical body, with its distortions, to reconnect with the light body, using your energy in one way or another to help forge and strengthen this connection. You do not heal another. You invite the situation in which the body may heal itself by reconnecting with its source.

This is a large topic. I will be glad to speak further on it if there is a request to do so. I only want to skim the surface now insofar as it

---

[37] *Mudras* work with the energy meridians. Mudras in one context are hand positions. If only the left hand is positioned in the lap, the position symbolizes the female principle of wisdom. When the mudra position is two-handed, the right hand rests on the left hand in the lap, the palms upward, symbolizing meditation. Sometimes this mudra is enhanced by the two hands forming a triangle. Then it represents, among many other mystical meanings, the spiritual fire that burns away impurities.

[38] Polarity therapy is a comprehensive health system created by Dr. Randolph Stone, an osteopath and naturopathic healer. He saw the body as a system of interrelated energy fields of which some were polarized negatively and others, positively. Using systems of touch therapy and diet, the practitioner of polarity therapy works to move the energy systems of the body back into a state of balance.

relates to working with the distortions of the lower chakras and to the physical distortions of the body.

The universe gives you that upon which you focus. This is the nature of the universe. Can you see the difference when your focus is, *I must correct this physical distortion?* You are grasping at that. When your focus is the seeming closedness of a specific chakra and there is a grasping, as in, *I need to fix this in myself. I need to change this, get rid of that, or become that,* the universe hears your fear.

On an ultimate level there is no duality. To attain this and to get rid of that are heard as part of the same thing. When you shift your focus, the universe reads you differently. You may ask, "How can I get rid of my fear? I must become a more loving person, which means getting rid of my fear, getting rid of my anger," and you are dialoguing with fear. When, instead, your focus becomes, "How can I express this energy that I have in service to all beings and for the greatest good of all beings?" that focus allows the experience of fear, anger, or jealousy, if that is what is present. There is no need to get rid of anything then.

If, at this moment in time, your learning to express your energy more purely involves the experience of discomforting physical or emotional stimuli, so be it. You do not have to like that stimulus. Can you simply allow the presence of it and send love to the being that is experiencing it?

It is this refusal to get caught in a dialogue with fear that becomes the most important part of the reminder for compassion. It takes awareness, because it is a trap into which you so easily fall since your habit of dialoguing with your fear has been so constant.

I feel some confusion in all of you. I am going to give one very concrete example.

Perhaps a being wants to learn to give its energy with generosity to others. Yet when it is asked to give in a material or energy form, it becomes aware of a contraction and a sense of "What if I need this time, energy, or resource?"

It may then state an affirmation, "I can be generous," and try to remind itself and even convince itself to be generous. It may even skillfully note the arising of fear and still say, "I will be generous." But at some level there is grasping at the generous and aversion to the fear.

Instead of making the affirmation, "I will be generous," which strengthens this grasping and aversion, if the being's focus becomes, "I will work as lovingly as I can with whatever emotions are present in my experience," then the intention is very different. It is not to be "fixed" but to be related to with kindness.

Please note that I am not arguing over the use of skillful affirmation. One must ask, "Is this affirmation a way of keeping me grounded in the aspirations of the loving heart or is it a way of disguising my fears or aversions?" When one knows one's fear of giving and returns gently to the center of the open and loving heart, one touches that core space of generosity. Then, through skillful affirmations, one reminds oneself that the core exists and that one can dwell within it.

The seeds of generosity, patience, lovingkindness, connection, energy, truth, and morality are all within each of you. This is not something you have to go out of yourself to find. You only allow those seeds to express themselves. So to be generous to another, you do not have to affirm and cling to "I will be generous." You only have to attend to what blocks the natural impulse to generosity.

Here you are not getting caught in conversation with your fear, only noting, "Fear is present," and offering it the love and compassion that it needs in order to begin dissolving, so that the natural generosity may be expressed.

You will find that the same principle is true with any emotion you are experiencing. Fear leads you to a sense of shame, jealousy, betrayal, or rage; and you can offer love to the human experiencing that emotion, let go of grasping at "I shouldn't be raging. I shouldn't be jealous. I should not be giving in this situation. I should be patient."

When you can see all of those judgments and just note, "Here's judgment again," and come back to the focus, "I wish to offer my energy, to manifest my energy, as purely as possible for the good of all beings, including myself. I wish to touch each being with love. I intend to touch each being with love," this process gives the universe a very different message.

But it must be honest. You must really look into yourselves to see *Is that the message I'm ready to offer? What fear is blocking my readiness to offer that message?* And then you will need to attend to that fear over and over and over again, because each time you think fear is gone, it reemerges.

It is not a burden laid upon you, but a gift of the incarnation. Fear, pain, or whatever you are experiencing is precisely what you need in that moment to lead you more deeply to paying attention, to give you the opportunity to practice lovingkindness and compassion for yourself and all beings.

I know that there are some specific questions here. I also would like to give Q'uo further opportunity to speak. So I will pass the microphone over to Q'uo, asking that Q'uo make the decision as to whether it wishes to speak before hearing any further questions or to ask for those questions. That is all.

(Carla channeling)

Q'uo: I am again with this instrument. I greet each again in love and in light.

To end our portion of this session of working, we would ask each to move with us in visualization. Each entity please choose the situation that first comes to mind wherein you have felt your senses thrum with the running of the energy of heavy negative emotion.

Feel the first impulse hit your consciousness: this striking of the self, this violation of calm and serenity. Allow it to seem, as it does, a wrenching, tearing, and pulling of the self in a descending gyre until the body is flattened on the dust of a barren land. Taste that acrid dust. Know this dust is made of self-condemnation. Feel the body as it is flattened by this suffering moment.

Call out within yourself:

The world is a trouble and a sorrow.
The world is a trouble and a sorrow.
The world is a trouble and a sorrow.[39]

Feel the intensification of that sorrow. Feel the healing enter into this celebration of sorrowing self. Take this body into your arms, self crooning to self and self comforting self. Rock this poor, pained child. Sing the lullaby of faith, of hope:

When I can read my title clear to mansions in the sky,
I'll bid farewell to all my fear and wipe my weeping eye.[40]

Let the child stand on its own now. It hopes. It knows it is on a journey home. Homeward goes the sorrowing, healing soul.

Breathe the fullness of that naturally rising realization of the exact opposite of the original pain. Feel the strength build as the realization is allowed to bloom that this, too, is of the nature of the one infinite Creator. This, too, is of love. This, too, is holy.

And rise in spirit singing,

Holy! Holy! Holy![41]

Are there any brief queries before we close our portion of this session?

(There are no further queries.)

---

[39] African American spiritual, "The Only Bright Light Is Jesus"; passage was sung.

[40] Ibid.

[41] Reginald Heber and John B. Dykes, "Holy, Holy, Holy, Lord God Almighty," Hymn No. 107 from *Christian Worship: A Hymnal* (St. Louis, MO: The Bethany Press, 1954).

We would then leave each, until later, in the love and in the light of the one infinite Creator. We believe the one known as Aaron will also speak, not now but this afternoon, as you would say.

So for now, Adonai. We are those of Q'uo.

Session 16

(This session was preceded by a period of tuning and meditation.)

R. and C.: How do we know what it is that we need to be doing with our lives and energies in the spiritual sense? And how can we accomplish what we are to do? In our hearts we know that we are spirit. But we want to know how the everyday self that lives the life knows what to work on and how to do it.

How do the three lower chakras show or demonstrate themselves in this third density as clear and balanced, like Jesus's were?

Barbara: I am aware that no matter how clearly I offer to give my energy, my ego creeps in, and I become afraid that I can't trust what I am doing because I know there is distortion. How do we work with the distortion that humans create?

K.: While becoming aware of fearing a meeting with another, I opened my heart to that person without any defenses. And then I felt the knot of fear dissolve and energy moved up to my heart. Is there any principle for working with the lower energy centers, of which this exercise took advantage? What are the most effective ways of working with the lower chakras that will allow us to open the heart chakra? How would the same experience look from each energy center's point of view?

Jim: How do we maintain our passion for pursuing the spiritual journey after many years of seeing that things seem to happen as they will, and that perhaps the most we can do is to keep a good attitude for all the changes that come our way?

(These questions and comments are used as seeds for continuing on with the topic that the two previous sessions have begun to discuss, of how to open the heart chakra.)

Session 16

(Barbara channeling)

Aaron: I rejoice once again to be with you. As we continue these sessions, your energy level grows higher and there is great joy and aspiration in your vibrations.

All of the questions that you are asking come together. While I will not speak at length here of this honest question of spiritual vocation, I do want to begin by stating a common misunderstanding and by offering clarification.

When you consider the blockages of the lower chakras, what comes to your minds are the heavy emotions, such as anger, greed, or jealousy, as well as the desires for power or control. You wonder how you may clarify those energies in yourselves.

The common distortion among earnest seekers is that you must get rid of all of those desires and fears in order for the heart to open and in order for the lower chakras to be clear. But that very desire to be rid of this or that in your experience backfires. This reaction is what closes the chakras.

It is not the arising of fear and its attendant emotions of anger or greed or need to control that close the chakras. What closes the chakras is your movement in one direction or the other from that first sensation of fear: either into action upon those desires or angers or into the need to get rid of them. Both movements are distortions.

The arising of emotion in the human is not a distortion. It is not the fear, the anger, or the greed that keeps you returning to third-density experience, but rather your relationship with those emotions.

You are all spiritually sophisticated. Think of what you know of fourth-density experience and of what you have been told of it. This is a group energy experience where all beings are fully telepathic with one another. Everything is shared.

The learning in fourth density is so rapid because you do not need to hide your experiences from another or to defend yourself from another's experience. There is total openness to whatever is expressed, with no judgment about it.

Presently for each of you, when there is heavy emotion you feel some shame about that. So there is some unwillingness to share that with another. When you hear of another's heavy emotion, there is some discomfort with it rather than equanimity. But it is total equanimity with emotion that denotes readiness for fourth-density experience.

You are not here in human incarnation to cease experiencing physical sensations or emotions. You understand that concept for the physical body. You know that if you stub your toe, it is going to hurt. When there is such pain, you do not try to deny the pain. You do not feel it is bad that there is pain. There is just pain. You may dislike the pain, but you do not judge it. There is simply aversion to it because it is uncomfortable.

When you stub your emotional toe and there is anger or greed, you label it as bad, as in saying, "I should get rid of this or that and then I will be pure."

The emotions that grow out of fear are uncomfortable. Part of your work is to learn to relate to those emotions with the same open-heartedness with which you relate to that stubbed toe, without judgment of the self that is experiencing them and consequently without judgment to the other selves that are experiencing such emotions.

This is the foundation for the work of all beings in third density. Through the constant judgment of what you experience, the self solidifies and enhances the illusion of separation.

You are here to reconfirm that there is no separate self, that the self solidifies through dwelling in delusion. The more you fight with the presence of an emotion, the more the self solidifies, and the more sense there is of *I must get rid of this or that to purify myself.* What you have to do, then, is to change your relationship to that which arises in you.

This brings us back to the human who is living this life and feeling the closing of the lower chakras; feeling the arising of fear, anger, greed, prejudice, jealousy, or whatever the emotion may be. Increasingly you allow the perspective that finds compassion for that human who is tossed into emotions by the continuing catalysts of the incarnation.

You become less and less reactive and more able to keep the heart open. This brings us to K.'s experience, whereby she found such compassion and connection with this other whom she was afraid to meet.

When there is judgment against fear, it automatically enhances separation. This brings you back into the dialogue with fear that I spoke of earlier. Then there is a contracted self, feeling that it should get rid of "this" and grasp at "that."

When you simply notice the arising of fear and have compassion for the human caught in that situation, self dissolves. There is no longer a doer. Then all of these powerful energies that I spoke of earlier become the beautiful seeds of lovingkindness, patience, generosity, equanimity, and ever so many more emotions that have the opportunity to flourish in the uncontracted heart.

These are not seeds that can flourish in the self that grasps at them. No matter how much you attempt to be patient with a sense of "I should be patient," you cannot make that blossom grow any more than you can make a rose open by willing it to open. The warm light of love shining on it is the warm sunshine that allows the rose to open. It is what allows generosity, patience, lovingkindness, energy, and truthfulness to express themselves through you.

At this point the lower chakras are open not because you have willed them to open, by willing a riddance of the issues concerned therein, but by creating so much space that the issues simply fall away. You find the ability to smile at this being that wants to be in control. You do not laugh at it or mock it in any way, or take its pain less than fully seriously, but you hold it in love.

This is the work for which you incarnated. We have spoken of this before. The lessons of compassion and wisdom are valuable and there is no reason not to start on those lessons in third density. But you are here to learn love and faith. And if there is not a firm foundation of those lessons of love and faith, then lessons of the higher densities will become distorted.

What does it mean to love unconditionally? What does it mean to have faith? That is another seed within you. How can you allow that seed of faith to blossom? Through the constant reminder that everything within this human experience, including all the physical sensations and all the emotions, is acceptable.

Obviously that does not give you free rein to be reactive to those emotions and harm others. But the reaction to the emotion and the experiencing of the emotion itself are two vastly different things. You are not here to learn never to be angry. You are here to find compassion for the human when anger arises and to find space for all your humanness.

We are asked about the one known as Jesus. The question assumed that this one's lower chakras were open, and asked, "How did that affect the upper chakras?" This one, of course, came into incarnation with the lower chakras entirely opened. And yet, even this one did experience human emotion. Even the Bible tells that at times he became angry. Certainly he felt physical pain in his body and some aversion to that pain.

The issue is not one of keeping the lower chakras open so that the heart center can open. The heart center may be opened while there is still some distortion in the lower chakras. The issue is, can one find such deep love for this human that one can see the distortion in the lower chakras without condemnation, thereby fully embracing the human experience?

Jim has asked how one can maintain a passion about this work. Perhaps one best facilitates that passion to express itself by focusing on the full embracing of the human. I would suggest that it is judgment against the human that puts the damper on that sense of passion.

My dear ones, your earnest seeking, your desire to express your energy with more and more purity, and your dedication to the work you came to do deeply stir those of us who have moved beyond the incarnate experience. Your work is a very real gift to us, as it deepens our compassion to watch you struggle and to remember those struggles of our own. This is not only true of one such as myself, who has moved through the earth plane, but is also true of those of Q'uo and of all beings who have moved through the different densities on whatever plane they have done so. This is your gift to us, and I thank you for it.

When you wonder, "What is my work here? What is it about?" I ask only that you keep in your mind that the work that you do is on so many different levels that you cannot begin to imagine the span of it.

For now, you are human.

Allow yourselves to be human. Work with the catalysts of this density. It is fine to acquaint yourselves with what comes next, both as inspiration for your work and to help you in keeping a balanced perspective. But you do not need to use this present incarnate experience to do the work that you will encounter in higher densities.

Embrace this human experience and the human that you are. Cherish yourselves. If I could give just one piece of advice, it would be to cherish yourselves.

A cry comes up from you, "Yes, Aaron, how? How do I cherish myself?" I will move on to that question in a while. I would like now to pass the microphone to Q'uo. That is all.

(Carla channeling)

Q'uo: Greetings once again, my friends, in the love and in the light of the one infinite Creator. We join the one known as Aaron in thanks for the beauty of your seeking and for the plangent cry of your call. It is, indeed, that which inspires those such as we and offers us the optimal opportunity for our own service and further learning.

As you followed the meditation with which we closed the previous session, each of you may have felt the transformation of vibration that went from the impulse of negative emotion to its uplifting in the most sacred of healings.

We suggest that this meditation was one example of the process in which a way is found to work with one distortion at a time and to communicate, using the purest voice of openheartedness, with the suffering portions of the self.

We said earlier that communication was a great key. There are many ways to communicate with one's distortions while one is within the distortion as an entity. They all partake, in various ways, of those types of communication that go beyond words and intellectual considerations, so that the spirit within the self may speak healing to the manifested self.

If one attempts to bring each felt distortion into the heart chakra, one is violating the self by attempting to drag energy where it is not naturally rising. However, if one can see the heart as always open and can allow the heart to be moved into communication with the lower chakras, then the combined vibrations remain crystalline, with the green color shimmering upon mentally or physically voiced communication, instead of the green being muddied by portions of red, orange, and yellow energy you are attempting to make rise. This, then, looks like a living stream of the most lovely light green, which shimmers and surrounds and gradually alleviates the blockage of red, orange, or yellow, so that the two colors gradually become equal in their radiance and power.

Prayer is one way of moving beyond words with words. If one can conceive of the infinite Creator as the Father/Mother that truly listens and cares unstintingly, then one may be moved to share one's confusions in the privacy of prayer. One may, for instance, do as this instrument does in simply speaking her heart: "Dear Creator, I am at sea. I feel frustrated. I do not know what to do. He hurt my feelings. I hurt."

There does not have to be a lofty, beautiful, and aesthetically pleasing quality to the prayer. Speaking one's truth when one is in pain is not likely to be pretty. It is very likely to be the whine, the howl, or the indignant, barbaric NO of the small, small child; for that which hurts is that which is not deeply understood.

The darkness is that of ignorance. Incarnate pain or pain that blocks energy is primitive pain, no matter how sophisticated the source of that pain or the spiritual nature of its origin, which may be very far removed from basic, instinctual pain.

So in prayer, communication is best when it is forthrightly honest, even and especially when that pain partakes of pettiness, foolishness, or unjustified indignation and is full of errors in judgment. To howl your mistakes and the pain you feel is certainly to howl about that which is not so, for your pain or your self-judgment is a dream within a dream. Yet it is this exact dream that you wish to heal. Thusly, pray truth the best way you can.

There is a quality to other kinds of communication, such as the reading aloud of poems or passages of inspired writing, which, like prayer, use words to go beyond words. These communications speak to one's focus of distress and purify the heart's journey to the blockage below.

Now, in truth, each center is as the heart center, opening and functioning well; however, because the lower centers are concerning themselves with relationships, there is no independence or spirit-driven movement available below the heart chakra. On the other hand, the green, blue, and indigo rays are focused upon absolutes offered from the spirit within and do not depend upon any, shall we say, earthly relationship in order to be viable. To spend all of the time in the higher energy centers, however, with lower-chakra communication left undone, is to invite the gradual attenuation of strength available for that work because of the unattended difficulties with relationships, the self to the self being chief among these.

The one known as Aaron may now take the microphone, as we feel there is a natural shift at this point. We find this sharing of teaching most pleasant, and we thank each for allowing this combined use of these channels, for it is greatly heartening to both the one known as Aaron and to us. We now transfer. We are those of Q'uo.

(Barbara channeling)

Aaron: The relationship of the self to the self, as in how to learn to cherish this self so that one may fully cherish all selves, is the gift of your incarnation. Can you begin to see, then, that the distortion that leads away from cherishing the self is part of the gift and not a barrier to the learning of this love? If there were not that arising of sensing the self as imperfect, or the arising of low self-esteem and all of those many emotions that lead to less than the treasuring of the self, with what would you practice? What if this self always appeared to be perfect?

Somewhere on this journey of yours, you are bound to meet that which does not appear to be perfect. Without this practice, you would judge it and have strong aversion to it. All that which you judge within yourself is the gift for practicing nonjudgment and unconditional love.

As humans, you work so strongly with habit and your habit says, "Judge! Get rid of!" You are so immersed in that pattern.

Firstly, you begin to see the pattern and to bring mindfulness to bear on the arising of judgment. What is this low self-esteem? In a situation in which low self-esteem is present, you might ask yourself, "What if I really liked myself, here, despite whatever heavy emotions are arising in me? What if I really treasured myself?" When you ask that question, you may begin to see the ways that low self-esteem becomes an escape.

Unconditional love is very difficult. The human feels hurt and wants to fight back or feels betrayed and wants revenge. The human sometimes does not feel ready to be as responsible as some judgmental inner voice suggests that it should be.

You have habitually used this pattern of moving into dislike of the self as an escape from the direct experience of the heavy emotions and from the need to be responsible for them, with kindness.

It is uncomfortable not to like the self. But perhaps it is even more uncomfortable to recognize the true divinity of your nature and to recognize that you are capable of unconditional love. Here is the child pouting, "I want to get even!" The child wants to get in that one good kick. The child that is loved despite its pain and anger is far less likely to need to kick.

When unworthiness arises, ask yourself, "If I were not feeling unworthiness, what might I be feeling? What heavy emotions, which are so terribly discomforting, does the unworthiness mask?" Can you see how much ego there is in unworthiness?

Look at the patterns that you have established. If what you see is a desire to be a bit irresponsible, that is okay, too. It does not mean that you need to act on that desire. Just notice that it is there. *What if I can't really carry this off? What if my emotions begin to control and pull me into reactivity?* That is another fear. So, you back off and say, *Well, I won't even try.* And then you move into that dislike of the self.

Watch unworthiness arise. Watch the way it closes off the lower chakras and then seems to give you permission to react, because any other choice becomes seemingly impossible with the lower chakras closed. You thereby hand permission to the child-self to express itself.

Your work is not to deny the existence of this child-self, nor to allow it to have its tantrums. Your work is to hear the child-self and to offer it love. It is this continued remembering to love the self, whatever is being experienced, that provides full healing of the sense of unworthiness.

In a very real way you are each born into incarnation with a sense of unworthiness that needs to be healed. You do not need to be perfect in order to offer that love to yourself. You need to learn to forgive your imperfections.

You see this message in the life and especially in the death of the one known as Jesus. He essentially told those who died on crosses beside him that he loved them. This is that message of the Divine, who said, "This is my beloved Son, in whom I am well pleased."[42] That is a message offered not only to the one known as Jesus, but to all of you.

You are loved, not because you are perfect, not because you are without heavy emotions, and not because you express your energy with perfect purity, but simply because you are. It is that healing to which you are invited to come.

How do you begin to forgive yourselves? You cannot learn to cherish yourself until you forgive yourself for being less than perfect in this human form. You are not cherishing the perfect being, but the human.

---

[42] Matt. 3:17 AV.

There are many practices one might use. As Q'uo suggested, prayer is very powerful. Ask for help. When you feel yourself condemning yourself, give that to the Divine and ask for help with it. "Lord, this human is fallible. I have hurt others and myself, and now I am filled with condemnation of myself for that hurting. Help me find forgiveness and compassion for this imperfect human that I am."

Please notice that there is a difference between the sense of unworthiness itself and the relationship to it. When you experience unworthiness, you may then watch the arising of aversion to it and attend first to that aversion, asking yourself, *Can I just be present with the unworthiness and watch it? Can I be present with any emotions, voices, fears, and memories within me that prompted the arising of unworthiness? Can I let the whole thing be and just watch it?*

This gentleness brings in light and space. The heart opens. There may still be the remnants of the anger, jealousy, or greed that prompted the unworthiness. There may still be an aversion to the unworthiness and the emotion because they are uncomfortable. But they are attended to skillfully.

This is where Q'uo's image of bringing the heart center into the lower chakras may be seen. There is no force here, just a willingness to be present with all of the confusion without judgment and to let it all float. Then the unworthiness does not solidify, nor does a self solidify to combat the unworthiness. Instead there is a gentle love offered to the self that is experiencing so much pain, including unworthiness. It allows a shift in perspective to this angel aspect of the self that is perfect and that you know is worthy.

Within that shift, you begin to find wholeness. There is nothing left that needs to be "gotten rid of." You are just letting it all be, allowing it to be present or to dissolve at its own speed while it is offered love.

What you will find is that your increasing ability to offer love begins a new and far more skillful pattern whereby, as I suggested yesterday about the arising of fear, the arising of unworthiness becomes a catalyst for compassion instead of a catalyst for the offering of more disdain to the self. This reconnects the lower-chakra centers to the heart center. It reconnects the spirit body to the physical and emotional bodies. You come back into wholeness and balance. Here, even a sense of unworthiness becomes seen as a valuable gift for your learning, and you embrace it rather than wage a war with it.

I would like to close with a guided forgiveness meditation, which is another powerful tool in spiritual work. Before I do so, I would like to pass the microphone to Q'uo to see if my brother/sister has that which it would like to add. And then I would ask that you briefly stretch before the meditation, as many of you are feeling tiredness in your body and I would like you to be able to sit for five or ten minutes to participate more fully in the meditation. That is all.

(Carla channeling)

Q'uo: I am again with this instrument.

In communicating from the heart center to the suffering and unworthy self, perceived by the self, the seeker is healing its own incarnation, one small symptom at a time.

The infection called life is incurable and mortal. The small infections called error or sin or distortion are not fatal, merely greatly uncomfortable. When attempting to function as a healer, then, the techniques of healing that are not mechanical or chemical necessarily involve the first healing, which is the healing of the instrument of the seeker who wishes to heal.

The heart is the seat of intelligent healing energy. It is brought down firstly into the violet ray that contacts the Logos itself, as this instrument would say. It then moves through the indigo ray of intelligent energy. This indigo ray is that which is your work in consciousness.

We do not mean to be confusing, for we wish you to feel comfortable with our teaching. However, in order to teach with words, we must pretend that each voice within you, or rather, each type of voice within you, is separate and can communicate to other voices or types of voices within you.

Since the universe itself and all that exists is within you, it is inevitable that the communication skills we encourage for the healing of the incarnation or of those whom the healer wishes to serve require a splitting of the perceived self, so that communication's requirement of one to speak and one to listen may be fulfilled.

Work in consciousness is largely the moving of intelligent energy through the violet ray; then, by intention, from indigo into the blue ray of communication, which then opens the heart. The opened heart may go forth arrayed in the bright colors of love and purified emotion. There is the bringing down of pure light into an intelligible form of communication that carries purified emotion to the relationship that needs healing or, when the self is healer, to the entity to be healed.

Now, when the self is engulfed in a difficulty, the heart is defended by thoughts like *Not trouble again! I can't stand it! I can't stand me!* One cannot storm those defenses, and so one uses prayer, song, praise, and thanksgiving, which, unlike the prayers of the unworthy one, are focused upon the beautiful, the more real, and the more true.

To say, in the midst of sorrow, "Thank you, O beloved Father/ Mother. Praise You, O One who is all," may seem not only dishonest but irrelevant. But we suggest that you see that this is how the voice of the heart is reached.

The direction of the thoughts is changed by the purified emotion taken on faith and expressed in the song, the praise, the thanks, or the prayer. Thus, passion is restored to that great seat of purified emotion, purified emotion being the essence of wisdom as opposed to knowledge.

The procedure, then, is to suffer; to become aware of the suffering; to pay attention by spending the coin of time; to move purposefully into the prayer, praise, thanksgiving, and song, which awakens the heart; to allow this energy to pour into the heart; to allow this potentiated healing energy to move into the relationship that is the conscious focus of the suffering; and then to allow the healing of acceptance and forgiveness to take place.

Session 16

We of Q'uo confess our own planning ahead. It is not a good time, now, for us to address how this turning to inspiration can be aided by faith. So, we promise that on the morrow this shall be addressed. For now, we ask you to take it on faith that when you do praise and thank and sing and pray, there is a spirit of love itself that listens and responds endlessly, fruitfully, and fully so that each symptom of the infection called distortion or error or sin may indeed be forgiven.

We would now turn the microphone back to the voice of Barbara, as this entity offers those meditational thoughts of the one known as Aaron. We thank each for this joy of speaking with you. And for now, Adonai. We are those of Q'uo.

(Barbara channeling)

Aaron: I am very grateful to Q'uo for bringing in this topic of faith. It is of great importance and relevance to the subject, and it is my hope that we both will expand the communication on it tomorrow.

Forgiveness is not an event but a process. You come to a cool lake on the first hot day of spring and desire to swim and to immerse yourself in that cooling water. Yet, when you test the water, it is icy cold. With the process of forgiveness, you do not need to leap off the end of the dock into that coolness. You wade in to your ankles. How does it feel? If it feels good, you continue. If it is too cold and you cannot go any further, you stop and try again the next day and the next and the next. I invite you, then, not to forgive, but to enter into the process of forgiveness.

To begin this process, I would like you to invite one for whom you feel love into your heart and mind, just holding them there before you. No matter how much love there may be between you, you have also caused pain to one another.

Silently speak that being's name and say, "I love you and so it is hard to express my anger to you. But you have hurt me by something you did or said or even thought. Intentionally or unintentionally you have caused me pain. When I look into your heart, I see that you have also known pain. I do not wish to put you out of my heart. I forgive you. I love you, even if there may still be some anger or hurt about that which was said or done. I wish to reconnect our hearts with these words and thoughts. I forgive you. I accept your pain out of which those words or acts arose. I love you."

I am going to be silent for a minute, and I ask you to continue this process silently with the one you hold before you, offering whatever words or thoughts feel most appropriate.

(Pause)

Gently now, allow that being to recede from the center of your awareness. In its place, invite in a being from whom you wish forgiveness. Speak that being's name to yourself and say, "I have hurt you through something I said or did or even thought. Intentionally or unintentionally I have caused you pain and have led you to put me out of your heart. It is so painful to be thus separated from you because I love you. Please forgive me. I also have known pain. I do not defend my words or acts, but ask for your compassion for my pain and for your understanding that the voice within me that spoke was the voice of fear. I admit my irresponsibility in allowing that voice of fear to dominate the voice of love. Forgive me for the ways that I have hurt you. Allow me back into your heart."

Again, I will be silent for a moment and allow you to work with this yourself, with whatever words feel most appropriate.

(Pause)

Feel that one's welcomed forgiveness. Feel your energies rejoin. Gently let that being go. Into the space that is left there, please invite yourself as this human that you are, whom you have so often, so harshly judged, condemned, and put out of your heart.

It is so terribly painful to put yourself out of your heart in that way. So much anger and fear reside in this human who you are. The

268

loving heart has room for it all. It is the fearful brain that judges and creates separation. The heart welcomes the self back in.

Look at yourself standing there, perched like a deer ready to flee, because it expects the voice of judgment that it has so often heard. Speak your own name to yourself and say, "When did this heart last say the words, 'I love you'?" Can you offer that phrase to yourself? Speak your own name and say, "I love you. Yes, you are not perfect. Yes, you are sometimes reactive, frightened, and unskillful. Do not love yourself because you are perfect. Love yourself because you are. All of that which you have judged about yourself, you invite back into your heart."

Ask that judged part of the self, "Can you forgive me the judging as I forgive you your imperfections? Let us be one again. Let us enter wholeness. For whatever ways I have hurt you, can you forgive me for the ways I have judged you? For whatever flaws you have manifest and for which I have judged you, as you forgive me for the judging, I forgive you for being human and embrace your humanness. It is so painful to feel this separation from myself. May I be whole. May I be healed. For whatever pain I have caused to myself, I offer forgiveness. I forgive you. I love you."

Again, I will be silent for a minute. Please continue to offer whatever wishes feel most appropriate.

(Pause)

Can you hold this being that you are before you as one who is truly cherished and beloved? Look at yourself, at how beautiful you are, and offer yourself that love.

May all beings everywhere learn to cherish each other and themselves.

(Bell)

May all beings learn to forgive and to experience the grace of being forgiven.

(Bell)

May all beings everywhere find their way home and attain perfect peace.

(Bell)

My deepest love and gratitude to you all. I wish you a good night. That is all.

Session 17

Weekend 5, Part 4 of 4
(This session was preceded by a period of tuning and meditation.)

(Carla channeling)

Q'uo: Greetings to each of you in the love and in the light of the one infinite Creator. This instrument asks us to pause as the recording equipment is put into position.

(Pause)

We have adjusted the microphone so that more than those present may catch our hot air! The instrument says, "'Written on the Wind'[43] was not the idea."

We wish each to know of the depth of our gratitude that we have been able to dwell at some length upon the topic you have called us to your group to consider. Again, we ask that our thoughts be seen as offered without authority. Your discrimination shall tell you what is for you. Leave the rest behind without a second thought, for there is an abundance of guidance for those who trust their ears and their hearts each day as to the wisdom of that day.

We have been working with the way in which the seeker may find tools with which to understand the situation of the first three chakras as well as the pathways from intelligent infinity to the heart of each and every seeming blockage or confusion.

We have been speaking as though the seeker, by its own mental processes, was solely responsible for the carrying out of the procedures of finding the attention turned to the heart. These procedures include

---

[43] The Four Aces, "Written on the Wind," by Sammy Kahn and Victor Young (Decca Records, 1956).

experiencing the heart, moving the heart to the blocked energy, and releasing and allowing that blockage to reconform to the upward-spiraling line of light that is that time/space pathway within manifestation that combines all energy fields, as the whole spirit releases its bound energy to the limitless light, whence all energy has come.

However, although the seeker is solely responsible for the will and the desire to bring into harmony and ultimate unity all energies within the energy complexes of the self, yet still there is strong and ever-present help for the seeker whose resources include a life in faith.

Whether the tool of song is used, or prayer or praise or the giving of thanks when no thanks or praise seems to be appropriate, or whether the seeker chooses the great range of visualization techniques in order more efficiently to allow energy the pathway for movement, through faith the process is given what one could call the carrier wave that creates a spiritual gravity or mass that enhances the tools and resources.

Now a life in faith may seem to demand the acceptance of some culturally chosen holy or worshipped individual, such as the Buddha or the one known as Jesus. This is not so in that such ones as Buddha and Jesus the Christ clearly indicated that they were not speaking of themselves, but of the mystery that the one known as Jesus called Father or, more familiarly, Papa.[42]

This Father/Mother Creator has sent each inspired and inspiring historical figure into a troubled world to bear witness to the light and the love of the infinite Creator. The one known as Jesus said, "If you hear me, you hear not me but my Father who speaks through me."[43]

A life in faith is not built on objective or provable knowledge, nor must it be built from a so-called conversion experience, wherein one entity is seen in its human form as a personal redeemer.

---

[42] The word "Abba" in Aramaic is an affectionate nickname for Father, such as Papa or Daddy.

[43] John 14:24 AV.

This instrument moves within the distortions in which the one known as Jesus the Christ is acclaimed as a personal savior. For this instrument, this is the path, this is the life, and this is the personal truth. Each seeker must choose, not that which works for another but that which works for the self.

Let us move, then, to what Jesus the Christ said when this entity determined that the time was appointed for it to fulfill its destiny and depart the earth plane. Its students objected strenuously to this plan. But the one known as Jesus pointed out that unless he left this lifetime, the spirit that could move into all portions of the world scene could not come among men.[46]

So even if a personal savior is chosen, that very savior demands that the seeker move beyond the form of one blessed incarnation to seek that Spirit, that Comforter, or that which the music heard this day has called the Holy of Holies and that this instrument knows as the Holy Spirit.

We would suggest the term "guidance." Yes, each must be responsible for cherishing again and again the self; to learn to love the self so that one may, for the first time, know how to love the neighbor as the self. But there is the Comforter that moves within each life. There is always guidance available. There is always the carrier wave that strengthens the will and the desire to be and, in that beingness that is full, moves in consciousness that the fragmented self that suffers is healed by love.

At this point we would turn the microphone to the one known as Aaron and the channel known as Barbara. We are those of Q'uo.

(Barbara channeling)

Aaron: I greet you all with love and wish you a good morning. My thanks to my brother/sister Q'uo for leading us into this exploration of the role of faith in allowing the heart to remain open.

---

[46] John 16:7 AV.

You are beings of light. That is your nature. Even those amongst you on the earth plane who are of negative polarity have their source in that light and will eventually return to that light.

When the heart center is open, you experience that light. When you rest in the experience of that light, then whatever work may be necessary with the lower centers feels workable. Whatever issues there may be, they are just issues and do not overwhelm.

When the heart center feels closed so that you experience the absence of light, you feel yourself cut off from your spiritual roots. And any personal issues that may be focused in the lower chakras feel overwhelming and enormous; and there is just you, this self, to deal with them.

You know that a plant grows in the sunshine. Even a shade-loving plant must have some light. You would not take a plant, or perhaps a bulb, and put it in the best soil, offer it the fertilizer it needed, water it, and then put it in a dark closet and expect it to thrive. But you do this with yourselves. How do you bring yourself out of that closet?

Firstly, one must be aware that one is in the closet. *I am living in darkness. I have shut myself off.* Seeing that, you can make the skillful decision, *I am going to open the door. I need light in here.* No matter how dark it appears, you may then begin to pray, to seek, to read inspired readings and poetry, or to speak to a human friend whose faith is deep. This is not grasping at the light. It is simply opening the shades so that the light that is already there may come in. It does ask the skillful decision to emerge from the darkness.

This brings us back to some of the unique patterns of the human. There is this small ego-self about which we talk. It is an illusion, but within the human experience, it feels real and solid.

This illusion has one purpose as far as it knows, and that is to maintain itself at all costs. Why?

If you are that angel I spoke of yesterday and are truly connected with God, why would you want to maintain the illusion of separation? What purpose has this illusion? When you incarnate, you agree to experience this veil of forgetting as an opacity that cuts you off from the clear seeing of your true nature. Again, why? Why agree to that?

For reasons I cannot easily explain, the primary lessons of third density are faith and love. What will teach you faith? If you incarnate with full awareness of who you are and what you are doing in this incarnation, with clear seeing of the divinity in yourself and in all beings and the clear experience of God, where is faith to be learned?

That faith is a foundation. Without faith, the later lessons of wisdom may so easily become distorted and move the being into negative polarity. So these muscles of faith must be built by practice.

You know that there are many planes of learning and that this earth experience is a somewhat new experiment insofar as the entire history of the universe. Perhaps the greatest success of this experiment has been the profundity of the way faith is learned or of the experience of faith on this plane.

This veil of forgetting is a gift. Because of the veil you cannot take your divinity for granted but must always move deeper into the experience of it. You must always work to separate illusion from deeper reality. And yet, no matter how clearly you experience that deeper reality, as human you must still take it as a matter of faith. You are not given proof.

One thing that is occurring here is that you are strengthening the will to express your divinity and to be of service to all beings. If there were clear seeing with no veil, you might come into incarnation and say, "Yeah, I'd like to serve. Sure, why not?" But it would not be a strong decision from within the heart, nor a deep answering to a call. It would just be a following of the pattern, "This is what everybody's doing. I'll go along with it." Can you see the difference? Intention is all-important.

We emphasize that you have free will. We emphasize responsibility. In essence, this veil and the matter of faith offer you the opportunity to exercise that free will and responsibility without clearly knowing what you are doing, by just trusting that light within you and the way it connects you to all that is.

Through each incarnation lived in faith you grow into deeper readiness for that responsibility. You are responsible for what you know. To know and to have deeper wisdom and understanding carries deeper responsibility. Without the deep support of faith, that responsibility would seem too great a burden.

When you see clearly who and what you are on the astral plane between your human lifetimes and after graduation from this plane, then your decisions to serve, for example, grow out of a strong place only of will. Because you know who you are and are ready for that responsibility in the upper densities, there is no problem.

If on the earth plane you exercise will in the absence of faith, that will can easily become distorted so that it twists itself into judgment and self-judgment. Rather than expressing love, one would simply express self-discipline. One would move into a sense of "I came to do this and I'm going to do it and nothing's going to stop me!" But you are not here to learn that level of self-determination and you are not here to use force and judgment as guidance for your choices. You are here to learn love as guidance for your choices. To express your energy with love, there must be that sense of connection that grows out of faith.

So, you open your closet door. You experience that light. One moment, please. We will continue in a moment.

(Pause)

Aaron: Barbara and I were both experiencing the presence of some negative energy. We are comfortable that it is no longer making any effort to intrude and it is welcome to listen if it would learn from our teaching. We ask that all present send love to anything that wishes to learn from the deep love expressed in these sessions.

When you open this door and allow light into yourselves, something very wonderful happens within these lower chakras. You no longer feel alone and helpless.

You have been like a small generator that was trying to light up a large house but was also aware that there was not enough power to do so. Suddenly you are plugged into the source. The generator is still working, but there is far more current coming through. It recharges the generator and draws the current necessary to bring light to every dark corner.

Then you look at your issues with relationships, with need to control and fear, with desire for power or with survival issues, whatever they may be, and it no longer feels like a huge burden laid on your shoulders. Your relationship with it changes, not because you have willed that change, but truly because you have opened the door and allowed in the light.

There is some illusion of safety in darkness. It is a place to hide. And so there has to be a moment of decision, as in *Do I want to linger here in darkness or do I wish to move into the light? Why am I clinging to the darkness? What safety have I found in the darkness?*

I spoke at the beginning of this talk of the small ego-self's desire to maintain itself. You have grown into the pattern in your human form of thinking about the strength of this self as your protection from difficult experience. *If the self is strong and if I can be in control, then I can control the pain in my life.* But it does not work that way. These catalysts will continue to arise over and over again. You only move yourself into more negativity and fear when you allow the self to act through fear.

When you become aware of the pattern whereby self wants to be dominant in order to keep this being safe and you send love to that fear and open to the reality of that fear with no need to get rid of the fear, then you begin to rest in the faith that even the fear is offered as part of learning. You do not have to get rid of anything in your experience. Your spiritual path is right here in this relationship, in this job, or in this political issue. Each is an opportunity to draw in light and to offer service and love.

It is sometimes very difficult to remember this. Fear keeps closing in on you. In effect, all of these lower-chakra issues of physical health, money, relationship, or whatever are offered for one purpose. They give you an opportunity to change your relationship with fear by the very simple act of coming back to who you are, to affirming with faith, *there is that of the Divine within me. If I draw on that tremendous source of energy and love, then I have the ability to work lovingly and skillfully with this catalyst. I no longer need to wage war with this catalyst but can use it as an opportunity to practice expressing my energy more purely and lovingly.* Then all of these situations in your life take on such a different perspective. Faith is strengthened each time you work in this more loving way.

Picture that being in the dark room the first time that it opens the shutters, when it may not even have realized that there was light outside. The light seems so bright that it feels blinded by it and must quickly close the shutters again. But it soon learns to enjoy and trust that light. It becomes a pattern. When it looks around and sees that the room is too dark, it remembers, *I can open the shutters.*

This remembering is a major part of your work. This is part of the reason why I so emphasize mindfulness. Know when you are sitting in the dark. Know that you have the option to open the shutters. Know also that you have the option to remain in the dark. But if you do so, you have chosen that darkness.

Why are you choosing to sit in darkness? Why are you hiding in the darkness? What illusion of protection does the darkness offer as it strengthens the small ego-self? Do you really need to continue that pattern, or are you ready to be kinder to yourself and allow yourself to experience your true being?

I know that there are questions at this point. I would like to turn the microphone over to Q'uo that he/she may speak as he/she chooses or, if preferred, may ask directly for your questions. That is all.

(Carla channeling)

Q'uo: Greetings again in love and in light.

The one known as Aaron asks if you are ready to experience your true nature. The living of a life in faith is the living of a life in which you are willing to practice the presence of your true nature.

So many times you have heard us and any other spiritual counselor suggest the meditation or the sitting on a persistent daily basis. The advantages of such a practice are physiologically persuasive, and there are many who practice this technique in one form or another with no intent other than the relaxation of the physical body and the slowing of the frantic stream of thought. However, we say to you, is any silence empty in a universe that is full of the unity of the nature of love?

The information that fills the silence of the listening heart is the wordless and unknowable nature of the mystery of all that there is, in its full, hallowed sanctity. Practicing this meditation, you open yourself to your deeper, truer, mysterious self, which is the very heart of all that there is. And because this mystery has been potentiated to communicate within illusion, each time you move into this silent presence it speaks a new mystery through a new message of life and wholeness.

It does not take a specific credo to move into the pregnant, mysterious silence. It takes a desire to seek the truth that is great enough for you to choose to spend the precious coin of time in listening to the silent voice of your true nature, which guidance wordlessly enunciates to the resonating seat of mystery and holiness within you.

It is not that you choose to have faith. Rather, those who live a life in faith choose to be faithful in their practice of the presence of truth and in their practice of the presence of love.

The one known as Jesus was accosted by temptations from the voice of fear that is known in this myth as the devil or Satan in the wilderness. The one known as Jesus would not converse with this principle of negativity and fear, but spurned each temptation and said, "Get thee behind me."[47]

The conversation that you seek, then (for one must converse with the mystery), is the conversation with love. As you choose daily to be faithful, you choose not "this" and "that." Rather, you choose to believe that all is well and all will be well. You are seated and grounded in this faith by the practice of the presence of love itself, as guidance brings it to you.

---

[47] Matt. 4:10, 16:23 AV.

This instrument prays each day words that have meaning to her. We find the sentiments valuable in this context. And so we repeat this personal prayer without intending that each learn its words. Rather, we find the concept to be more accessible. This is the prayer:

Come, Holy Spirit, fill the heart of your faithful and kindle in her the fire of your love. Send forth your Spirit and she shall be created and you shall renew the face of the earth. O Creator, who, by the light of the Holy Spirit did instruct the hearts of the faithful, grant that she may be truly wise and ever enjoy its consolation.

She prays through the one known as Jesus. But we say to you that guidance is the consciousness of Jesus the Christ. This consciousness is transforming and life-giving. And we recommend to your own guidance the seed that is at the heart of this prayer; that is, that there is an intelligence moving through all that there is, which does, indeed, perfectly create each of you day by day, inasmuch as you can allow it; and that as you bear witness in a life of faith to this true nature that continually and perfectly transforms all that there is, you may see the face of creation blossom and infinitely expand in love reflected in love.

So, as you bring down into the life of faith the energy of the spirit of love that strengthens the heart, that it may move further downward into each darkened place within, so the reflection upward begins and the heart is informed by the energies originally locked in lower centers. And the heart frees this energy that it may make its return to the alpha and the omega of all that there is.

All things from the beginning to the ending of creation are implicit in this present moment. And the cycle or circle that is process and learning and growth reflects in your faithful hearts the eternal present moment in which love is the whole nature of all unified consciousness.

May you remain and abide in patient and persistent blindness, accepting and blessing each darkness, each fear, each sorrow, and each suffering unto death, that the work of creation may express through you the life of the self that is love, in this moment and ever.

May you, through this process, day by day seat yourself in loving acceptance and faith that all is well, that love itself may flow through you as light through the panes of the lantern, so that those about you may see this light and turn to this light within themselves.

You are witnesses expressing in a world that has need of witnesses. What shall you witness? My friends, love one another and for the first time, rest. You are home.

We open the session now to queries. Are there queries at this time?

C.: Q'uo has spoken several times this weekend about the flow of light, the crystalline green mixing with the lower-chakra colors, and has referred to the colors and the flow again today. Could Q'uo speak a little more to this topic of opening our hearts?

Q'uo: The use of the colors in our teachings is not only a true reflection of quanta of vibration and fields of vibration. On a more literal level, this device is an organizational tool that enables us to offer information by the use of an organized system of images that can be visualized.

We use the movement of these colors to delineate the way in which one field of energy, which is a portion of a complex of energy fields that is each entity's, may, by its hierarchical position, move into a position in which it benignly and benevolently overshadows the less strong and less true energy field that is the self in one particular distortion, whether that distortion be of the body, mind, emotions, or spirit.

By visualizing images, such as light in its coloration, we are able to offer ways in which each seeker may practice these movements of energy to the benefit of the whole person, which may be symbolized by the unbroken white light.

Would you please direct us further, my sister?

C.: I can't at this time.

Q'uo: And we would simply say, in response to a reminder by this instrument, that this kind of visualization is that which is helpful in working at the cellular level with organisms and energies and essences within those energies that may not be native to those energies.

Illness or disease is often that which is partially a product of the discontinuity or unnatural configuration of energy fields; or, to put it more simply, a system of energy blockages that manifests as disease.

It is also common that in illness there are essences not naturally found within the energy complex of the self, but that are thought-forms created by continually dwelling upon some fear or negative thought. This thought-form, then, becomes independent of the entity and returns as an enemy of wholeness, bringing with it, if enough energy is involved, other thought-forms that delight in suffering.

To visualize the flow of light to each cell of the organism in each of its energy configurations from the lowest to the highest, from the most physical to the most metaphysical or nonphysical, is an art in that each healer finds its own system of visualization that is its own language, whether it be color or other ways of visualizing the move-ment and overshadowing nature of hierarchical energies.

This is not fundamentally different from that which we have offered concerning the healing of the incarnation of the self day by day, but may be seen to be an extension that, in those who feel the call and gift to heal, may be used and through experience refined as a way of loving.

Is there another query at this time?

(There are no further queries.)

Q'uo: As this series of workings draws to a close, we stretch out our love as arms of blessing and thanksgiving to each who has moved many everyday hindrances to one side in order to be together for this working.

Our love and blessings to each, and our praise and thanks to the One who is all that there is that we experienced this beauty together.

May we all go forth to serve and to love, strengthened by this sharing.

We would leave this instrument so that the one known as Barbara may allow the one known as Aaron to offer benediction and a closing to these proceedings. We are those of the principle known to you as Q'uo. And rejoicing, we leave each in the love and the light of the one infinite Creator. Adonai, my friends, Adonai.

(Barbara channeling)

Aaron: Although it is a bit dissonant to the closing of this talk, I would like to offer one thought to C.'s question and Q'uo's answer about light on a cellular level.

You see the chakra center of the body as a rainbow. If there is distortion, perhaps in the second chakra, the orange segment of the rainbow is muddied. The light is not shining clearly, as the chakra itself is not spinning freely.

You have many energy meridians through your body. Some of those are junction meridians and some lead off most specifically from one chakra or another. Thus, when I look at your bodies I see patterns of light.

All the cells in your bodies reflect those patterns. If there is a cell in a part of your body that is physically distant from the second chakra but that is part of that meridian, which is the organ meridian of the spleen chakra, then the distortion in the spleen chakra is reflected in that cell. Each cell carries that same rainbow, but with a bit of difference.

As an example, I might offer the idea of a color overlay of the body. Firstly, color each chakra. Then with a transparent plastic overlay, lay over the whole pathway of the meridians of that chakra the color overlay related to that chakra. Do this everywhere in the body so that in some places there is the clear light of that particular chakra, in others there are overlaps of two or three or even more centers where the meridians join. Now take every single cell in that body and within it implant that same rainbow. Where there is the spleen-chakra meridian, the rainbow has an orange overlay. Where there is the heart-chakra meridian, there is a green overlay in the rainbow.

If the second chakra is blocked and that orange light is muddy, it will appear muddy in every single cell in the body. But the effect is doubled in those areas of orange overlay, which are those areas most specifically related to the spleen chakra, because you have muddy color over muddy color. The distortion from that chakra may manifest itself in any cell in the body. But it is especially prone to manifest itself in those cells where there is the double effect of muddy orange over muddy orange.

I share this with all of you in the hope that you may begin to understand the interconnectedness of your thoughts, emotions, physical sensations, cellular body, and the state of your spiritual awareness and openness.

You cannot clarify the lower chakras only by the openness of the upper chakras. However, when the upper chakras are open, there is more light brought into the whole body. You must still be willing to move into the specific center where there is distortion and to work with great courage with that distortion, to work with the specific issues that create distortion. That additional light helps this work.

All of these centers are connected. If you work to correct that second-chakra/spleen meridian distortion while ignoring the upper centers, you are merely working on a body instead of an integration of body, mind, and spirit. The more awareness you can bring, with each moment, to this being that you are as a whole and as this angel in its earth-suit of divinity and humanness, the more lovingly you can bring healing to where healing is needed.

There has been one unasked question amongst you to which I wish briefly to attend. You hear us speaking of these pathways to faith. From deep within some of you comes the memory of a pain in this or a past lifetime when the darkness seemed so all-encompassing that it felt as if prayer or song, reaching to God, were impossible.

So there is this question: "When there is a glimmer of light, I can remember that the light is there and reconnect myself to that light. What can I do when the darkness is total? Where do I find help in these moments of my deepest fear and despair? Where do I find help in these moments of my deepest immersion in the illusion of separation?"

My dear ones, I would ask you to remember in that heaviest darkness of your deepest grief or physical or emotional anguish that the night is always darkest before the dawn. This will pass. It takes only the smallest opening of the heart to reconnect to the light and to begin to allow light to flow once again.

Most of you are familiar with that beautiful writing, *Dark Night of the Soul*, by St. John of the Cross.[48] You must pass through this dark night. You each experience it in a different way. It is not offered as a burden, nor even, as some of you are wont to think, as a quiz. It simply is, as darkness, illusion, or fear. Finding yourself in that darkness, you have been offered the fullest opportunity to practice love. If it is impossible at that moment to practice faith, simply practice being, for in willingness to be, you are expressing love.

In that moment of darkness you are wont to ask, "Why this darkness?" You have a sense that if you could but understand the darkness, you could protect yourself from it. Such thinking only further strengthens the illusion of self. Can you sit there in that darkness and simply know, "Here I sit in darkness and I will wait. I need not fight with the darkness. I need not try to push it away. I need not grasp, even at faith."

My brother/sister Q'uo has spoken of prayer leading into the experience, not just of faith but of the truest knowing of yourself as the divine self and of meditation leading you into that experience of the divine consciousness within yourself. But sometimes meditation just leads to more silence. The seeker wants to reconnect with the Divine. What can one do when a meditation experience does not offer that end and the darkness seems to close in?

---

[48] St. John of the Cross, *Dark Night of the Soul*, trans. E. Allison Peers (New York, NY: Image Press/Doubleday, 1959).

Time and time again, the seeker goes to sit at the table of the Lord, knowing that sometimes a banquet will be offered and sometimes the table will remain bare. It is not the seeker's place to choose which will be. It is the seeker's place to sit at that bare table with as much love as it can give and to trust that this is the experience that is given and that it will suffice. It is not the seeker's place to cling to the banquet, only to fully enjoy that experience of deepest connection when it is experienced and then to let it go.

If you would cling to penetrating the illusion, allowing the experience of faith because of the beauty of the connection, then faith becomes dependent on those experiences. But faith exists, independent of experience. Faith resides within your heart. This is the clearest statement, of which I am aware, that the Divine is within you, that you are angels.

Just faith: faith expressed as the willingness to sit in darkness, if darkness is what is there, without a need to grasp at the light but with the willingness to open the doors and allow in the light. Do you see the difference?

There is night and there is day. If you open the door and it is still dark, can you sit and wait patiently until the dawn? I know that this is, as your saying goes, far easier said than done. When you sit in this dark night filled with anguish because of some very deep pain in your personal life, it is very hard not to want to get rid of that pain, not to want to grasp at feelings of comfort and the presence of God. True faith just sits, knowing that God expresses itself through the darkness and not just through the light, and knowing that the dawn does follow the darkest night.

Yes, there is preference for the light. It is more comfortable. But when you huddle in fear and grasp at the light and believe that if the light is not given, the self is somehow at fault, then you are truly enclosing yourself in deeper darkness. Then you are closing the doors and shutters so that when the dawn begins you cannot appreciate its arrival. Only love can know love. Only the Divine can know the Divine. When you exclude the self from the Divine, how do you hope to recognize it when it comes?

I understand how hard this is for the human. I have been through the process of incarnation and have strong memory of the pain of such darkness. I can only tell you that the route out of that darkness is your willingness to be patient and to trust: "There is that in this darkness that can serve and teach me. I will wait patiently with it, keeping my heart open, keeping the windows and doors open until the light reappears."

Q'uo has spoken several times this weekend of an upward spiral. I would ask you all to remember that all beings, not just positively polarized beings, are on this upward spiral. This is very hard for you to understand in this present third-density state. You see that of negativity in the world and feel that is a distortion, pulling away from the spiral and going downward. All beings are on this upward spiral.

Negativity is a distortion, and yet even those beings that are most highly negatively polarized are sparks of the Divine and will eventually find their way fully into the light. The darkness that they draw around them and into which they entice others may be a sidetrack of the spiral, used for that being's particular path. But it is still a sidetrack that is spiraling upward.

Remembering this allows you to find more tolerance for the negativity that is seemingly external to you in the world and for your own fear, anger, and other heavy emotions. When you create the duality of good and evil and see the darkness as a spiraling downward, it enhances not just resistance, but also a lack of compassion for that darkness. It enhances the fear that closes the heart.

When you see negative distortion in illness of the physical body, in the loss of a loved one, or in some other great grief or pain, remember, "This is part of the spiral to the light. Can I embrace even this distortion and offer love to it? Can I just be patient with the experience of it? I don't even have to understand it, just to allow its presence without hatred. The presence of negative distortion does not need to be a catalyst for hatred in me. It can be a catalyst for remembering to offer love."

(Pause)

Aaron: Remember your divinity, my dear ones, through prayer, meditation, or whatever connects you. I earnestly hope that you will allow yourself the experience of that divinity on a daily basis while remembering that if you sit in prayer or meditation and experience only this human sitting in prayer or meditation, then that is what you need to experience. For that moment, that is your experience of divinity. Trust it will unfold as it needs to. You need only be present.

I believe that in some of your gambling centers you would find a sign hanging that says, "You must be present to win." You must be present to win: present to win out over fear, present to deepen faith, present with whatever this mind/body/spirit complex is experiencing in this moment, present with as much love as is possible. And then you cannot help but win and find your way home.

I echo Q'uo in offering my deepest thanks to you for your presence with us in these three days, for sharing the deepest questions of your hearts and for inviting us to speak our thoughts. I again echo Q'uo: What we have shared is our opinion and not authority. We offer it in loving service and ask that you take what is useful to you. My love to each of you, and I bow in deepest honor to each of you for the love and purity that you bring to your work. That is all.

WEEKEND 6

After five weekends of doing these sessions in Kentucky, Carla and Jim were invited to Michigan. We gathered at Sunnyside Retreat Center, a small, private center on a lake, surrounded by woods. The meditation hall is cantilevered out over the lake. It was early fall and the woods around us were golden, reflecting all the colors of autumn in the still water.

We had a circle of sixteen seekers, plus Carla, Jim, and Barbara, and our hosts at Sunnyside. People came from Michigan, Kentucky, and other places. Some were housed in the lodge, and others were in tents. Everyone present had been asked to read the transcripts of the past sessions so that we would be together in heart, mind, and spirit as we gathered.

We had a session Friday night, and two each on Saturday and Sunday. For a change, Carla did not have to cook. Our hosts provided us with delicious meals. Between sessions there were conversation and laughter, walks in the woods, and paddling on the lake.

Carla remembers with special affection sitting in silent meditation from 5:00 a.m. to 7:00 a.m. There were only five or six attendees who were up that early, sitting in the very large room in which, later in the day, Barbara and Carla would co-channel. As the sky turned gray in predawn, Carla could see the blanket-covered shapes of the other meditators resting in the spacious flow of spirit. It is one of her favorite memories of that weekend together.

The content of the sessions gripped our attention, and conversation was very focused on what Spirit was sharing.

On Saturday night we all gathered around a large campfire and listened to shared thoughts from each other and from Spirit. These thoughts were not transcribed. The harvest moon was brilliant on the lake.

Because of the size of the group, Barbara and Carla created the focus question that began the session, "What is the spiritual path and how do we live it?" We announced this beforehand so that those who attended would be "on the same page" as we began.

Session 18

Weekend 6, Part 1 of 5
(This session was preceded by a period of tuning and meditation.)

(Barbara channeling)

Aaron: I want to introduce you to this tuning process by asking you to participate with me in a brief guided meditation.

Please allow yourself to follow along without concern for whether you can or cannot do what I suggest. Our emphasis here is not on getting rid of anything within you, but simply on allowing the barriers of ego-self to dissolve so that you may move into the divine aspect of yourself and hear from that place of center.

Begin by taking a few deep breaths and releasing.

Breathing in . . .

There is nothing external to you. As far out as you can go into the universe, when you breathe in, you take that universe into that which you call self.

When you exhale, you exhale that which you call self into the universe.

Breathing in and letting go, each exhalation dissolves the boundaries of self.

Inhale and let go of any resistance to taking the universe into your heart or of any resistance that wants to hold on to being "somebody," just letting it go. If anything holds on, it is okay. It will go. Nothing to do, just being.

Breathing in and expanding outward, with the exhalation flowing into the universe, then breathing the universe into yourself . . . open . . .

The heart is weary of its isolation . . . open . . . allow yourself to come into the essence of who you are, let go of all the concepts of who you always thought you were, and just allow that pure, clear mind/heart to be what it always has been: Pure Awareness, Pure Being.

As you drop your boundaries, feel the connection to the joy and suffering in the universe. Be aware of the rising aspiration in yourself to be a tool and to offer your energy as a tool for the alleviation of that suffering: not my suffering or your suffering, but our suffering. Be aware of the aspiration to be a source of energy, courage, love, faith, and healing for all beings and to manifest your energy in such a way that it promotes peace and happiness in the universe. This is the primary intention: moving out of the fearful, small self; open to the Divine.

In your own words, silently state your intention to serve the universe and all that dwells therein, to be a vehicle of Love. I will be quiet for a moment while you phrase this intention in the words of your own heart.

(Pause)

Given that aspiration and intention, the next question is, "How do I implement this?" You alone cannot implement it. You, when connected to all that is, are empowered to implement joy, peace, and harmony. So the next step is to invite in whatever help there may be—each, in your own way, invoking Jesus or the Buddha and asking God's help.

Silently voice your prayer that you may become an instrument for healing and love in this world. Not for your own ego, but in service to all; not for your own glory, but that your service may be offered back to God in grateful thanks. For you are but a reflection of that divinity: divine in your own right, but taking your light from that most brilliant and perfect light. Rejoicing, you are returning that light, ever brighter, ever clearer. I will pause again, then, so that you may voice your prayer in your own words.

(Pause)

All beings on human and spirit planes contain some mixture of positive and negative polarity. None is totally negative, nor are any but those most fully enlightened masters totally positive. We do not flee from the shadow in ourselves, but aspire to touch that shadow with love and thereby to grow. In the same way we do not flee from external negative energy, but aspire to touch it with love.

If there be any being within this circle, human or discarnate, that is of predominantly negative polarity and that wishes to hear these teachings, we welcome it. It may not speak through this instrument. It is welcome to listen and to learn the pathways of service and love to all beings.

At this point Barbara will be silent with herself for a few moments. Her own process here is to make the firm statement of what she stands for and values, and that none may channel through her unless they are fully harmonious with her highest values. She uses this process, although a high percentage of what she channels is this energy that I am, simply because it is an important statement that gives her confidence in what she receives and allows her to relax into the channeling. I will be quiet now and allow you each to meditate in your own way for two or three minutes.

(Pause)

Aaron: Again, my greetings and love to you all. My brother/sister Q'uo suggests that I begin this session, and I will do so briefly and then turn the microphone to Q'uo. Our topic is, "What is the spiritual path and how do we live it?"

My dear ones, you have been on this spiritual path since the moment when you, as what I call a spark of God, first came into awareness and sensed a separation, illusory but seeming to be real, a separation from that which we might call God. There is nothing you can do that is not part of the spiritual path. There are only more skillful or less skillful ways to walk that path. By skillful I do not mean evil or good, simply ways that bring suffering to yourself or others, or ways that help to free all beings from suffering. When you "walk" this spiritual path (I put that word, walk, in quotation marks), perhaps what you are really asking is, "How do I become more aware that I am a being on a spiritual path? How do I live my life with deeper awareness?"

Each of you is like a pebble tossed into a giant, still sea, an infinite sea. Each time a pebble splashes, it touches everything around it and sends out waves that affect all the other pebbles. When you send out loving energy, your interaction/interrelationship with the world is far different than when you send out hateful or fearful energy. And yet you are aware, and many of you have often heard me say, as long as you are human, you are going to have emotions. Fear is sometimes going to arise as anger, greed, jealousy ... You cannot stop emotions from arising, but you can change your relationship to what arises.

There are two main possibilities. First is the being who feels fear as the foundation for anger or greed and then either becomes reactive and acts in anger or in greed, or condemns itself because those emotions have arisen. Another being sees fear arising, sees the anger or greed or other emotion that grows out of the fear, and just relaxes and smiles at it and says, "Oh, you again. Here's jealousy. Here's desire. Here's rage," and holds a space for it in her heart until it passes. The main difference in what I am speaking of here is in the ownership of what arises.

This is the illusion we keep getting caught in: that we are a self and we own this or that emotion, thought, or sensation. Once you own it, you are stuck in it. Do you know the story of Br'er Rabbit and the Tar Baby?[49] We have used this to illustrate something different, but tonight I want to use it to illustrate this ownership.

Br'er Rabbit saw the Tar Baby and thought it was mocking him, so he punched it. His hand stuck where it punched, so he said, "Let me go," but the Tar Baby held tight. He said, "Let me go," and he punched it again. Two hands stuck! He kicked with one foot, two feet, screaming, "Let me go!" Finally he butted it with his head. All his limbs were stuck. Here is one very stuck rabbit!

---

[49] Joel Chandler Harris, *The Complete Tales of Uncle Remus* (Boston, MA: Houghton Mifflin, 1955).

When you see an emotion or a thought arising and there is aversion or attachment, and you grasp and try to hold on to it or kick and punch it to try to get rid of it, you begin to think that there is somebody who owns it. Then you are stuck in this concept.

This, too, is a part of your spiritual path. Even being stuck in it is an opportunity for learning, if there is awareness. But usually at that point there is so much fear and frustration predominating that awareness has dissolved.

It is never too late to come back. At any moment you can cut through that ownership and simply smile at yourself: "Here I am stuck in it again." Once more, "Oh, you again." Perhaps we could call this one, "Stuck in the Tar." A deep breath and a reminder, *This is not who I am. But I am human, and as long as I am human this catalyst is all going to keep arising. It is not given to me to fight with, but to learn from.* Just relax and be with it.

Barbara spoke earlier this evening about the *dzogchen* retreat and about *rigpa* or "luminous great perfection," which is just a fancy term for finding that space of the Divine in yourself and resting in it over and over and over. This is the essence of the spiritual path as taught by every religion that I have ever encountered in all of my many lifetimes. Some of them had it a bit distorted. Some of them were very clear about it. All of them aspired to that: to reaching that space of Pure Being.

We are not talking about specific religions here, but of the spiritual path itself. The essence of that path is to learn how to come back again and again to this divine aspect of you, which is what I have called the angel aspect of you, and to allow that to stabilize; to learn methods of recognizing that experience of the angel and of Pure Awareness. Until you recognize it, you cannot do much to nurture it.

Each of you is in that space far more often than you know. Without awareness, it comes and goes without recognition. So, first you need to recognize that space within you. Then, you work to stabilize it and to be able to relate to the world more and more from that space of clarity and connection.

That, to me, is the spiritual path. As to, "How do we live it?"—
that is what we will spend the weekend questioning. How do we live
with our fear, our anger, our pain, and our desires? How do we make
space for all of that humanness in our hearts and find deep love for
all of us as we exhibit that humanness? How do we let go of judgment?
At the same time, we must be aware that while we aspire to let go of
judgment, we are still responsible for our choices. Here we have a relative reality and an ultimate reality. There is much that I wish to say
about that, but will hold it until tomorrow.

At this point, I would like to pass the microphone to my brother/
sister Q'uo. I use the term "brother/sister" because Q'uo does not
offer itself as either feminine or masculine energy, but as a combination
of both. I also am neither masculine nor feminine, but I have chosen
to manifest my energy and to put on a cloak of consciousness and
being of that which is masculine.

All of you are a mixture of masculine and feminine. You are incarnated as male or female bodies and more fully manifest the energy of
that body. But you are all androgynous, a mixture of both. Q'uo very
beautifully balances that mixture, exhibiting the fullness of both the
masculine and the feminine. And so I pass the microphone to my
brother/sister/friend. That is all.

(Carla channeling)

Q'uo: Greetings in the love and in the light of the one infinite Creator.

We thank the one known as Aaron for the masterful introduction,
and would continue by noting that we are a complex made up of the
thoughts and memories of what you would identify as male and
female. We now study and serve as one. Our path to this point in our
walk on the path of spiritual seeking has included your range of present incarnational experience.

You are upon a path aiming toward an evolution of spirit, which you
may intensify and speed up. Many among your people have no wish to
learn the lessons of love more quickly. However, each of you does wish

to assist that process of spiritual evolution of mind, as some call it.

For our part, we greatly and humbly thank each for calling us to your circle of seeking, for as we share our thoughts with you, we are learning and pursuing our chosen path of service. And your assistance both inspires us and employs us.

We ask that each be continually aware that we are fallible. We make mistakes and would not ask that you hear us as the voice of authority. Take those thoughts that resonate within your heart and leave any others by the wayside, for we would not be a stumbling block for any.

So, as the one known as Aaron has said, you are here making choices. Let us examine this situation. It is our understanding that this, your density, is the first density of those who are self-aware. And in this self-aware state, you begin to examine both your inner reality and the nature of your surroundings.

Into the chaos of the untaught mind comes this illusion that you know as living. Colors, shapes, entities, and relationships shout out at the infant in incarnation. The young years are full of the noise becoming signal, the chaos becoming increasingly ordered, the environment becoming internalized, and the self painting the environment with its own personal colors of meaning.

It is our opinion that the choices you face continue to be of a certain basic nature. Each choice has to do with polarizing or gaining a bias toward either that which is radiant, loving, freeing, and expanding, or that which is attracting, pulling, and grasping. We call this dynamic a choice of service to others or service to self, and assign the term "positive" to the service-to-others category and "negative" to service to self.

(The remainder from Q'uo did not record.)

(Barbara channeling)

Aaron: There are a number of questions we will be investigating this weekend, but primarily it comes down to that which repeats itself over and over in your lives. To walk a spiritual path with awareness and love, one must be aware of when one has moved into fear and the cutting off of love.

How do we find that awareness and deepen it? Fear builds walls around our hearts. How do we dissolve that fear? Where does faith come into it? When we have made the best decisions we can, thinking that we are acting out of love, and the results seem to boomerang and cause great pain for us, does that mean we acted out of fear without seeing it clearly or does it mean that we need to have even deeper faith? Sometimes it is one direction and one answer. Sometimes it is the other answer. How do we begin to differentiate that?

Is pain always a warning that we are doing something (I hesitate to use this word, but) wrong? Or is pain inevitable? Might there be pain even in wise choices at times? What is pain about in our lives? Is there ever going to be a complete absence of pain in human incarnation or do we simply change our relationship to pain and end our war with it; certainly not inviting it in, but not hating it when it appears?

I am not offering any answers here, just raising some of the questions. One can live one's life trying so hard not to harm others. But if one becomes a "somebody" trying hard to be harmless, does not that create its own kind of harm?

In a talk earlier this week, I gave an example of a situation that I have seen many times while in incarnation, where monks or nuns in monastic situations try to outdo one another at being nobody. Who can take the food last? Who can do the hardest work? You can make a career out of being a martyr and truly enhance and solidify this small ego-self.

So, it is not so much what you do. It might seem to be very kind that you always serve others and let others go first. What is the motivation for that? When you look, you will find there are multiple motivations. In every act, word, or thought, there are multiple motivations.

For example, you have an apple in your pocket and you realize that you are hungry and thirsty. Here is a red, juicy apple. You pull it out. Just as you are about to bite into it, there is a small child with big eyes, very thin, holding out its hand, saying, "Please!" Your heart opens and you give the apple. As you give it, there is the small thought, *Didn't I do good? Did people see?* The giving of the apple is a pure, loving act. The accompanying thought grows out of a place of fear and wanting to be the good one. It is another aspect of somebodyness.

So, we never act or speak or think fully out of love or out of fear. How do we get acquainted with our multiple motivations so that we may begin to better understand our choices, and thereby begin to choose more skillfully and lovingly for ourselves and for all beings? This, to me, is the focus of walking a spiritual path. And it is not only the resultant actions, words, and thoughts. It is also the clarifying of motivation and the learning about how this small ego-self solidifies. It involves not being afraid of its solidification but each time it happens, using this catalyst as a reminder to move back into center and to move back into connection and into the Pure Mind or Pure Self.

We will explore all of this in depth through the weekend and will also have time to answer your personal questions in speaking to your personal situations.

There is sleepiness. It is late. I want to pass the microphone here to Q'uo.

I thank you all for allowing me to share my thoughts with you tonight and very much look forward to our continued sharing through this weekend. My love to you all and I wish you a good night. That is all.

(Carla channeling)

Q'uo: We would echo the one known as Aaron's sentiments and would leave you with two thoughts.

Firstly, those who seek together to learn service to others shall, in each other, see how impossible it is to serve others without serving the self. For your actions are reflected. And as each serves each, each receives illumination. In your sister's heart is your self. In your brother's heart is your self. And you were not incarnated to be calm. Your choices are made in the midst of activity.

Secondly, there is for each outburst or outlay of your energy, the time to take in that food and drink of spirit that nourishes and rests. Begin to be more aware of these dynamics. See your self reflected. See love reflected and feel the outpouring and the in-gathering, one to another and all things whatsoever to the infinite One.

For this evening, we again thank each and bless each, leaving each in joy and in peace in the love and in the light of the One that is all. We are known to you as those of Q'uo. Adonai. Adonai.

Session 19

Weekend 6, Part 2 of 5
(This session was preceded by a period of tuning and meditation.)

(Carla channeling)

Q'uo: We greet you in the love and in the light of the one infinite Creator and thank each for the blessing of calling us to share in the blending of vibrations in this circle of working. We share our thoughts as we, too, travel upon the ever-unfolding way that is the path of spiritual pilgrimage.

We were saying that your density of existence is the density of a choice. It is one great choice, upon which so much is based. We were describing this choice as that between radiant service and grasping or magnetic service; or as service to others and service to self.

To discern this choice in each moment is a substantive portion of that learning that you incarnated to pursue. The other part of this learning is simply to continue offering praise and thanks. That is the music that gladdens your walking. The choice made once in full awareness is the beginning. Each choice made thereafter strengthens and deepens the energy that you may usefully accept and allow to move through you. You see, the energy of all things is love.

When the Creator chose to manifest creation, that Thought that is the Creator was love, but love unknown, unknowing, and unpotentiated by the free-will choice to generate manifestations of love. The first manifestation that this great original Thought generated was the photon, or that which your scientists name a unit of light. All things whatsoever that can be sensed are manifestations created by successive quanta and rotations of light.

What you seek to do as you move through this school that is your illusion is to more and more faithfully approximate the vibration of this one great original Thought, which is love. Those who choose the

301

negative or service-to-self path are also choosing love. However, this choice is a path that bypasses the open heart. Therefore the energy or power that is created tends toward distinctions and control. This path of separation will eventually flow into a place where the negative choice becomes obviously inappropriate. And at that point, all entities that have chosen the negative path of seeking have the opportunity to reverse polarity and become again children of the open heart.

In your density, however, this choice is fresh and the negative path has its long and separate walk ahead of it. We realize that each within this group has chosen the path of love and service to others. And we may say that we feel that this path is the one that we prefer and ourselves have chosen. We feel it is more efficient and that it, in its use of power, is the desirable one. But we wish each to grasp that these choices are free. There is no final condemnation for any who seeks in any way, for that seeking will be gathered in ripe harvest in its own time.

This gives a foundation or a continuing of the foundation. For much has already been done upon which we, as sources talking to this group, may metaphorically stand when we speak of the spiritual path and how to walk it. The context is infinity, brought to one single moment in manifestation now, in each consciousness. And that now becomes now and now, again and again.

At this time we would transfer the speaking to the one known as Aaron. We are those of Q'uo.

(Barbara channeling)

Aaron: Good morning and my love to you all. As spirit I find much joy in every moment of my being. But I must say that a gathering such as this and the light that is being emitted from this circle bring deep joy to my heart, because I am committed as my most fundamental value to the alleviation of suffering in the universe and to bringing light where there has previously been darkness. And the light that you send out does indeed do that. So it is very wonderful to share with you and to rejoice in the warmth and brilliance of this blazing fire.

My brother/sister Q'uo is generally more poetic than I am. I must say that this dear friend inspires me to more poetic speech. Enough. Let us get back to basics. Q'uo spoke of the free-will choice each of you has. I wish to briefly expand here.

There is no such thing as absolute evil. There are those beings who are negatively polarized in service to self and who act in love for that self. The self-centeredness of that motivation may cause immense suffering for others. Yet one must still acknowledge that this being is motivated by some form of love, however distorted that love may be. Such a being may indeed even graduate from the earth plane, carrying that negative distortion. But it cannot ultimately return to the One, nor can it move through the higher densities beyond sixth density with that negative distortion. It becomes a dead end. So, it may carry its negative distortion to a very high level, but eventually it must change its polarity to proceed.

We have transcripts available that detail this process of reversal of polarity. Should that interest any of you, they can be found and Barbara can provide.[50] So I will not speak of it in depth.

The difference in path, then, seems to be that the path of service to others speaks of awareness of the suffering of all beings and the deeply heartfelt desire to alleviate suffering. The path of service to self ignores that suffering because it accentuates the separate self. It cannot ultimately carry one back to full unity with the Creator because there is still the delusion of separation. It is therefore a truly more difficult path.

Can one begin to have compassion for beings who are set on that path rather than fear and hatred of them? Their negative distortion causes as much pain to them as to others.

Having made the decision to live one's life in service to others, one is constantly confronted by that fear in oneself that leads to grasping and aversion to self-service. Service to others and service to self are not mutually exclusive. This is a misunderstanding.

---

[50] Deep Spring Center for Meditation and Spiritual Inquiry, 3003 Washtenaw Avenue, Suite 2, Ann Arbor, MI 48104; www.deepspring.org/archives.

Let us return to that imaginary being with the apple, whom we introduced last night. Seeing the child's hunger, the apple is offered. But what if it were the only food that the apple holder had and that apple holder had also not eaten for several days? Is that thought, *I also am hungry*, an evil thought? We chop the apple in half and trust that further sustenance will be offered to each.

The self is also an other. You are part of this great scheme of things. To simply become a martyr and offer yourself with no respect for the needs of the self is to make needless sacrifice. Indeed, one must begin to respect the needs of the self while distinguishing which needs grow out of love and healthy respect, and which grow out of fear. That being who has had a full breakfast and the promise of a full lunch has no need to take half the apple. Can you hear the voice of fear that says, "What if I need it?" and simply note, *This is old-mind speaking. In this present moment, I am not hungry and this child is hungry. In this present moment, I have no need of this food. I can give it freely.* But mind goes back to those past experiences of hunger or deprivation of any sort and that old-mind consciousness wants to hoard because of the very basic human fear, *Will my needs be met?*

The person who lives life in awareness will notice the arising of such thoughts and be able to identify what is the bare perception of this moment and what is old-mind habit. That same being, noticing that the desire to hold on to the apple is old-mind habit and noticing that there is no present hunger or need, will not scorn itself because that habitual reaction has arisen. It will see that reaction, not as its own greed to be hated, but as human fear that must be touched with compassion.

So, it notices the old-mind habit arising in itself. It notices its movement toward contempt for that habit and it asks itself also to have compassion for the human with those fears, thus allowing space for it all to float. It then finds freedom to come back to the bare perception and to recognize in this moment *There's no hunger. I can give this apple.*

By bringing this level of awareness to each arising thought, emotion, and sensation, one begins to move away from the boundaries of old-mind habit and to live one's life in the present, in the now. It is only in this moment that one can live with love and wisdom.

What I want you to see here is that the choice of service to self versus service to others is not clear-cut, as in, "I'm generous!" or "I'm selfish!" Rather, it is built on staying in this moment with a deep respect for all beings, knowing oneself to be part of this linked chain of beings, heart open to the needs of all, seeing fear as it arises, and making the conscious effort not to live by the dictates of fear.

How to walk a spiritual path? This, to me, is the essence of it: to notice each dialogue with fear and have the courage to remove oneself from that dialogue, not hating one's fear, but also not owning one's fear nor being controlled by it. It takes much courage. As you work with this, you come to an intersection. You find that there is what I call a horizontal practice of relative reality, living one's life skillfully and lovingly, moment by moment, with awareness that there is an illusory self who is doing that skillful, loving living.

There is also a vertical practice, which cuts through the illusion of self. Q'uo just spoke to you of this. When it is next my turn to speak I will elaborate on it. But first I would like to pass the microphone back to Q'uo, who would like to speak to us to elaborate on some of what I have just spoken. That is all.

(Carla channeling)

Q'uo: I greet each again in love and light.

As our beloved brother, Aaron, has so wisely pointed out, you are one of the other selves you serve. In fact, let us confuse you thoroughly and say you are the first other one whom you shall serve. And why is this? This is because, as the teacher known as Jesus has said, the law is to love the Creator with all of one's strength, heart, mind, and soul and to love your neighbors as yourself.[51] If you do not love yourself, how can you truly love your neighbor?

---

[51] Matt. 22:37, 39 AV.

Yes, each of you is all too aware of the missed steps, the erroneous conclusions, and the impulses that do not do justice to love. Yes, you are completely unfinished. Is this a reason not to be in love with your self? Can your self, in all its distortions, depart one iota from the truth of love?

Yes, it may seem to do so, just as all with whom you come in contact may seem to do so. Yet the heart that loves knows that beneath, above, and around all confusion, all missed steps, and all seeming imperfection lies the One, unblemished, unbroken, beautiful, and perfect. Your nature is love.

The walking of the spiritual path is an opening of the universal self within, in order to embrace, more and more without distortion, the heart of love in each entity and each moment. Your challenge is always to discern where the love is in this moment and to move, whether by attitude, thought, or action, to support, encourage, and enable that love. Giving that attempt your best effort shall occupy you well through this illusion that we term third density, and through several densities to come. For we witness to our continuing pilgrimage through longer and more subtle illusions wherein the choice we made in third density is refined, first by attention to love, next by attention to wisdom, and then by attention to the merging of love and wisdom.

These illusions to come are far different than your rough-and-tumble moment of choice. There is not the suffering, for there is not the veil of forgetting betwixt the conscious incarnate self and the deep self that is aware that all harmonizes into unity.

In your brave illusion, you face the dragons of darkness, rage, pain, war, starvation, and all the dark and monstrous forms of dread, fear, and ignorance, because you cannot clearly remember that these illusions are only that. It is intended that you become confused. You are supposed to be knocked completely off of your intellectual mountain. And in that momentous fall into the abyss, in midair, you pluck faith, undimmed by any objective proof that there is anything to which to be faithful. You choose to live your love.

This is your choice; not that you sit upon a throne, view the evidence, and choose, but that you become utterly aware that you cannot understand this illusion. And in releasing that desire to understand and embracing only your heart's desire to love, you pluck faith from that dash through the middle air.

This wisdom of the heart to abide and hope and have faith without proof is the glory of third density. And we must say that, much as we enjoy our continuing journeys, in looking at each of you and in being with each and seeing the courage and commitment of each to seeking the truth, our hearts fondly cherish the memory of that striving, suffering, and believing in love against all the evidence. What an exciting part of the journey you now are on!

We would at this time bow to the one known as Aaron and offer the microphone. We are those of Q'uo.

(Barbara channeling)

Aaron: As you rejoice in sharing deeply with your friends, so Q'uo and I rejoice in being able to share this teaching with one another. It is simply a delight to sit back and rest. Not that I need the rest. I am not tired. But each of us expands what the other can offer and brings new perspectives to it. So, it is a joy for me to feel Q'uo's energy responding to that which I have said, to hand the microphone to my brother/sister for response and expansion, and then to take that expansion back and again enlarge it.

Q'uo spoke of the line of love and wisdom, which is precisely that horizontal and vertical line that I have mentioned, and that eventually you must come to combine the two, living at the intersection of that horizontal and vertical line in the center of the cross, which is the Christ Consciousness or Buddha Consciousness or Cosmic Awareness that is God.

I would like to briefly define my terms here, so that when I use language, you fully grasp my meaning. Within consciousness there is still self-awareness and still some degree of personal thought and memory.

Pure Awareness is quite different and moves beyond all consciousness. There is also a ground between, where that which I call consciousness is still present but is not taken as self, but is known as a tool of the incarnation.

Pure Awareness is that which sees consciousness and knows it. What we may call Christ or Buddha Consciousness is found here, which is Awareness aware of its divine nature and yet also aware of the tools of the incarnation, the self-conscious mind. The Christ Consciousness finds no less divinity in the incarnation than in the ultimate perfection.

While the human cannot ordinarily move beyond sixth-density thought, which is the consciousness of the higher self, your meditation can take you truly into the experience of seventh and even beginning eighth density, that borderline between the two where all concept is dissolved, where there is total dissolution of the body and the ego, and where there is no longer any thought at all, just Pure Awareness and no consciousness. So, I differentiate these terms. I do not use consciousness and awareness synonymously. When I speak of Pure Awareness, it is that awareness beyond any conceptual thinking or any perception of self.

To live skillfully on this human plane, you need some degree of consciousness. This does not mean identification with the self that makes choices, but simple acknowledgment that the self is a tool and a necessary tool to the work of this plane. If you disown that self, learning cannot take place. So, there is a very fine line between allowing the experience of what seems to be self and knowing that the perceived self is a useful illusion as well as a tool of the incarnation.

All of the experiences that occur to that perceived self are also tools of the incarnation. Your physical sensations, your emotions, and your thoughts are not burdens that you are asked to carry. They are gifts through which you may learn.

One can learn to work very skillfully and lovingly with these gifts so that one is no longer reactive to emotions and no longer reactive to physical sensation. That being begins to live its life with great love.

Yet it may also experience deep pain if there is still identification with that which arises. The nonreactivity becomes a form of self-discipline and training, but there is not yet wisdom that sees that there is no ownership of that which arises.

One may also move into the wisdom vertical direction, focusing on a path of deepening wisdom through moment-to-moment mindfulness. Such mindfulness begins to penetrate the delusion of a separate self. It begins to know all arising as empty of self and as simply the recurrent patterns of conditioned mind.

Wisdom develops to understand the impermanence of all that arises. Ownership of that arising ceases. But without the love or compassion that grows out of acceptance of the human experience, such wisdom becomes sterile. Within such wisdom there can be desire to disassociate with the human catalyst. What you are learning, then, is to come to this meeting of the horizontal and vertical, this center of the cross, where compassion and wisdom meet.

I want to digress here a moment to speak about the words love and compassion. When we use the term "love," we are not speaking of a maudlin kind of love with attachment, not a manipulative love or a grasping love, but pure love that opens itself to all that is.

Love is a hard term to define. I am somehow more comfortable with the term "compassion," which is an outgrowth of that openhearted love, but is more easily recognized and less easily distorted than is the term love. We can use them interchangeably as long as we understand what we mean by each: love and compassion.

There are many ways to work on the horizontal practices. Indeed, you all are doing that constantly in your lives as you attempt to live with more love and skill, and as you attempt to live with nonharm to all else and to work on nonreactivity as you process the emotions, thoughts, and sensations that move through you. We will talk more specifically about such horizontal practice, offering specific tools that speak to your personal situations.

I want to speak for a moment about the vertical practice. In essence, when you work with a horizontal practice, you are using mind to tame mind. Mind moves into a turmoil of fear and reactivity and you use the relative practices of faith, of devotion, and of mindfulness to quiet that tumultuous mind. When you move into the vertical practice, you use wisdom to cut through the delusion of self and tame the turmoil with wisdom, in a sense like cracking the shell of a nut and allowing that hard shell to fall open so the soft inner core is exposed.

Now I would speak to you of a practice that will help you move into that wisdom. And later this weekend we will talk about coming to that place where compassion and wisdom meet. There are two specific practices I would like to offer to you: one to be done frequently or even constantly and one that you may do for a few minutes during your lunchtime break.

Firstly, as an ongoing practice through the weekend, when thoughts, emotions, and sensations arise, I would like you to note their arising and to ask yourself whichever question is more useful to you: "Whose thought is this? Mine? Who am I?" or "From where did this thought arise?" As you ask those questions and allow an honest answer to emerge, you are going to see that the answer is simply, "It arose from old-mind habit. I don't own this arising."

Let me give you an example. This morning at approximately 7:12, Barbara was sitting here meditating and had a thought, *Not many people are here yet. We're not started. We're going to run late,* accompanied by a small contracting and sense of fear. She asked herself, *From where did this thought arise?* And she could see clearly that it was just an old pattern marking her need to be in control as a way of protecting herself, or marking her need to allow things to be okay for others—not as a way of gaining approval for herself, but due to wanting to create comfort for others. And she saw that was a response of fear and just a conditioned pattern.

So, she came back to this moment and asked, "In this moment, is there any need for anything to be happening other than what's happening right now, 7:13, sitting and meditating?" She asked this with the awareness of how that fear had arisen and with the awareness that she did not own that fear. It is like a bubble that is popped by a sharp dart ... poof! The fear is gone.

In that moment one comes back to rest in Pure Awareness, not consciousness, but awareness. For just that one moment, there is no "somebody" doing anything. The ego is totally dissolved. There is just resting in Pure Being. It may only last for a second until the next thought arises. Each thought becomes an opportunity to pop that bubble again and come back to Pure Awareness.

As one does this persistently, one lets go of the habit of thinking of oneself as somebody doing, shaping, or fixing, and moves more into the true understanding that Self is truly this Pure Awareness, connected to all that is. One finds the ability to rest in that space. One ceases identifying with the horizontal.

I am only going to take it that far here. As I said, I will talk this afternoon about the ways that you may combine this cutting-through of delusion with the horizontal practices that relate to the relative reality of everyday living and that do require the self to participate.

The second practice I would like to offer is one that I ask you to do as homework during your lunch break. Do it with me now, but quickly, and then repeat it at your leisure. I want you to sit, preferably outdoors. Look at the lake or the trees or the sky. Meditating with your eyes open, send your awareness out. Breathe out and follow that breath as far as it goes. What happens to your breath when you breathe it out? Is there any boundary out there? What happens when it reaches the end of the atmosphere? Does it stop?

Sit and follow your breath. Looking at the sky might be most useful. Let it expand outward and outward and outward to infinity, beyond the ends of the universe.... Nothing stops it. Now breathe in. What are you breathing in? Is there a boundary beyond which you do not breathe in that substance?

Visualize the in-breath also coming from beyond infinity and moving into you, drawing in with each inhalation the core of all that is and breathing it back out into the universe, each exhalation a giant release ... *ahhh* ... releasing with an *ahhh* all boundaries of self ... breathing in.... Open your eyes and do this with me and with Barbara.... In ... *ahhh* ... sending it out ... in ... *ahhh* ... sending it out....

You may close your eyes again if you wish, each *ahhh* letting go of the boundaries of self, feeling one's merging with the universe.

Here we are talking of drawing the physical plane into yourself. After you have done that for a few minutes and really feel your self moving into the universe and the universe moving into you physically, do the same with awareness. Where has awareness picked up false boundaries or nonexistent boundaries, let us say, that you claim as "mine"? Send your awareness along with your breath out into the universe and again breathe in awareness, universal awareness, the deepest contact with all that is.

If in doing this exercise thoughts cease to arise, as they may, and you begin to move into a level of awareness of deep connection, simply rest in that connection. If thoughts again arise, ask the question, *From where did it arise? Whose thought is it?* And as it self-destructs, self-liberates, poof! goes the balloon of thought. Rest again in that Pure Awareness, once again releasing the boundaries and expanding into the universe physically and in awareness, and allowing the universe to move into you. Please spend ten or fifteen minutes with this, or longer if you like, over your lunch break. And I would very much appreciate hearing the results of this exercise.

Q'uo may have something that it wishes to add here. If not, I would like to open the floor to your questions and answers. That is all.

Questioner: How many densities are there?

Barbara: Aaron speaks of eight densities, each of which has seven subdivisions, each of which has seven sub-subdivisions, and so on. He loosely defines it as eight densities and says that some people may find it different. For example, he is dividing fourth and fifth density. Some people may group them together.

Once we move past the need to incarnate and move into fourth density, we move into a group learning experience, by which he does not mean a fixed group. There is a coming and going, still a free will. We're not drawn into something that we can't leave. But once we stop being reactive to our emotions and thoughts, we're ready for fourth-density group experience.

In this group we're all telepathic. So the equanimity with our emotions and thoughts, which marks the end of third density, is a necessity for fourth density. He uses this example: if right now we were all completely telepathic so that we all knew everything that each other was thinking, would this be okay? Have you had some thoughts this morning that you really don't want to share?

Once we get to the point where we have such compassion for ourselves and such nonjudgment of our thoughts and nonownership of our thoughts, we also have that compassion toward others, and we don't judge others' thoughts. Then we're ready to be in a fourth-density energy where there's total telepathic sharing. There's no embarrassment and judgment. We learn, then, not just from our own experience but from each other's experience, because experience can be totally shared.

As we move through the process of that fourth-density energy group, we begin to move out more on to our own, coming and going from the group. Sixth density moves into deeper wisdom and compassion and unconditional love. Concerning seventh and eighth density, again some traditions lump them as one and others divide them into seventh and eighth densities.

"The Universe According to Aaron," in *Presence, Kindness, and Freedom*, by Aaron, delineates each of those densities and what each is about.

Carla: Just briefly, first density is the elements. Second density is things that can't move yet, like plants and animals that don't have self-awareness yet. They're turning to the light. The animal knows its master and wants to love it a little bit, but it is not aware of itself yet. Third density is self-awareness. Fourth density is the awareness of love. Fifth density is the awareness of wisdom. Sixth density is the awareness of wise compassion or compassionate wisdom and the merging of those two. As to seventh density, Ra calls it the density of foreverness, where you finally take one last look back, turn your back on all that, and start gaining spiritual mass in going back to the source. The eighth density is the octave, and it dissolves into timelessness and becomes the first density of the next creation. And that's the cosmology of it. So, the whole billions and billions of years until the big, central explosion of the central sun is just one creation or just one little heartbeat.

Questioner: Extraterrestrials, as in the movie *Cocoon*, have these light bodies. Where does the physical fit in, in these densities?

Jim: Supposedly, from what we gathered from Ra, each of our chakras or energy centers has a body with a physical nature that corresponds to that center. The yellow ray that we are inhabiting now has this bio-chemical body.

Another body corresponds to the heart center. If you've been to a séance where ectoplasm is produced by the medium, it is seen as a smoky sort of substance that is used by entities to form the astral body, which is associated with the heart or the green ray. And each succeeding energy center has a finer and finer body, as far as physical mass that we can see. But it is more and more densely packed with light. So, they're more dense as far as light goes, but less dense as far as our physical matter goes. But each of the centers has a body.

Questioner: Isn't physical matter just a slowed-down vibration of light? So, how can this be? Aren't you just saying that each body is a more rapid vibration?

Jim: Yes, that's basically correct. But it has more light in it, more vibratory brilliance, more rotational speed, and more active light.

Carla: It is a heavy chemical body. And one of the things to think about is that if you heal the light body, the physical body also will be healed because it is a lower-octave vibration. "As above, so below."[52]

---

[52] The Three Initiates, *The Kybalion* (Chicago, IL: Yogi Publication Society, 1908).

Session 19

(Barbara channeling)

Aaron: You have many, many aspects. Repeated use of the single word "body" makes it difficult. Your language does not give an adequate choice of words. You are familiar with the physical, emotional, mental, and spirit bodies. You also have what we call a light body, which is the emotional, mental, and spirit body separate from the physical body. The physical body is, in a sense, a reflection of the light body, or we might say a manifestation of the light body.

To further define the light body, there is a higher light body, which, in essence, is what you know as the soul, the Pure Spirit Body. The lower light body is a manifestation of the higher light body and includes the mental body. This is sometimes called the higher self. There are gradations in between and beyond. Those beyond bring in the emotional body.

You might visualize, then, the purest light, which is the light simply of the spirit body in its interconnection with all that is. This light is absolutely pure and totally unblocked in any way.

Just the slightest bit below that is what I would call the light of Christ, Buddha Consciousness, or Cosmic Consciousness. It has just the barest, very barest, tint to it and is totally transparent. It is not blocking the pure light in any way, but is shaded with just that smallest tint of self-awareness.

One step down, one large step down (there are gradations) comes the lower light body. For purpose of visualization here, I would like you to picture the heart, which is the physical body's light center. Picture it as a ball, radiant with light. Within that ball, add black dots of the different emotions and thoughts and physical sensations. Let us leave out physical sensations now. We are speaking of the lower light body and not the full human body, thoughts, and emotions. There is still a mental and emotional body.

In the highest light body, there is nothing to deflect the light that shines out from you or the light that comes in. One moment please.... I wish Barbara to draw something here.

(Barbara, conscious and herself.)

Barbara: I am drawing a circle with the described flecks in it, demonstrating how those flecks block light from moving out from the center and in to the center. Our work in consciousness slowly allows this shadow to dissolve so that (I am paraphrasing Aaron here) we move more and more into the living experience of this circle, free of those bits of shadow. Now, getting back to Aaron directly . . .

(Barbara channeling)

Aaron: The human body takes this one step further down because it adds the physical catalysts as well, and that which creates more shadow. If you take a being such as yourselves and put it in front of that perfect light, which I would call God, you see a sharp sense of shadow. If you take a being like myself, a sixth-density being, and put it in front of that perfect light, there will still be a distinction between that energy that I am and that perfect light. I am not fully merged into that perfect light.

If you take a being such as the Christ or the Buddha and put the energy of those beings in front of that perfect light, they will be almost invisible, "almost," only because they choose to retain some degree of consciousness and have not yet fully moved into seventh density. I am not specifying now where these beings are in their evolution. A being that has moved into seventh or eighth density is not better than a being that chooses to remain at the borderline of seventh density so as to allow itself to be available to those of the lower densities. That is really a gift and a sacrifice on the part of that being, in holding back its own full merging with the light out of service to all beings and desire to offer itself as servant.

The distortions of the physical body are reflections of the distortions of the higher light bodies. Thus, as Carla pointed out, when you clarify the distortions in the higher light bodies, often there is physical healing.

There is disparity between the clarity of the higher light bodies and that of the physical body. You are here in physical form. Sometimes you create distortion for yourselves because you aspire to be something that you are not fully ready for. This is where you start to want to get rid of the heaviness of the physical or emotional bodies. You want to cling to being the higher self without having done the consciousness work to dissolve the shadow of the emotional and physical bodies. There must be harmony, or you fragment yourself. You do not get rid of the emotions or of any discomforting physical sensations. But as you find space for them as well as equanimity in nonreactivity to them, then you become able to work at the higher levels of light.

The frequency vibration of these bodies is different. They also must be in harmony, like the strings of a musical instrument. If the higher-level strings are perfectly in tune, but the heavier, coarser strings are out of tune, the instrument will play disharmoniously.

The physical body will be at a lower frequency than the higher light bodies. You tune it, not to bring it up to that high pitch, but to make it harmonious to that high pitch. You do this, not by getting rid of the physical sensations, but by letting go of fear of the physical sensations, and the same for the emotional body. Then you become a harmonious whole. And as that harmonious whole, the frequency vibration of the connected body begins to raise the frequency vibration of the whole. This can only be as clear as the frequency vibration of the lowest aspect of it. If one aspect is discordant, the whole is discordant.

So many of you have worked to clarify the energy of the mental and spirit bodies, but tend to want to disown the emotional and physical bodies. You work with the upper chakras and cast aside the work with the lower chakras. But it must come together.

There is more that could be said about this. Do you wish me to speak further, or is this sufficient? That is all.

Questioner: Today, while meditating and while Aaron and Q'uo were speaking, quite often I would go to a point where consciously I don't remember a lot that Q'uo and Aaron said. What can I do to keep that from happening? Or is that supposed to happen?

Carla: I would say let it be. If you want to hear, you will hear. But you're getting it at a deeper level.

Questioner: Yes, I do feel that I got it. But I couldn't tell someone that Q'uo said this, this, and this.

Carla: I think that sometimes you get to a point where you protect yourself from bearing it all at once. Your heart is wise. It puts you in a place where you'll feed it in, where it will come up gradually and you can deal with it better. There's a lot said; a lot of points are made, and a lot of work is done. Some of us can't bear it.

Barbara: One of the things that we suggest to people is to acknowledge some of this screening-out. Sometimes Aaron puts people to sleep. Some of this is resistance. Instead of saying, "I've got to get rid of this resistance," can you just acknowledge it? Can you say, "There's resistance here. Can I be gentle with myself about this resistance and allow it to emerge? What's the resistance about?" Don't think about it. Just acknowledge and let it work out.

I want to give an example. A couple of years ago, my son came home from college with a pile of literature about recycling. And I already recycle paper and bottles, but he wanted me to recycle everything. It wasn't a very big stack of literature. But I kept putting him off and saying, "I can't read it now." Finally, I became aware that if I read it, then I was going to have to be responsible for it and I just wasn't ready to be that responsible. I felt like it was going to be a big burden, a lot of work. *I don't know if I can handle this. Keep it at a distance. I don't want to know about it yet. I'm not sure I'm ready to be that responsible.*

We each need to work that through. If we really hear what they are saying and try to live our lives that way, it is asking us to be very responsible and there's some fear, such as *Am I ready to be that responsible?*

What am I getting into here?

We need to be very gentle with ourselves and not push ourselves beyond where we are, because we learn as we grow. We don't have to be anywhere but exactly where we are now, just moving at our own pace. There's no speed with which we do this. People get into trouble when they aren't honest with themselves. Some say, "Okay, I'm going to take all this in and I'm going to do it." And then, instead of becoming a work of love and kindness and gentleness to ourselves, it becomes just another kind of fear, such as, "I'm going to get rid of that and I'm going to be this." But that's not honest.

Questioner: So, how do we clarify the lower chakras?

Barbara: I think Aaron and Q'uo will both be talking about that at length. But let me just say, in working with this "screening it out," the first step is simply being aware there's resistance, as in, "Am I judging that resistance or trying to get rid of that resistance, or am I allowing myself to bring my heart to that resistance?" Do you see what I mean?

The other thing that I'd like to suggest is that the energy of both Aaron and Q'uo is at a very high frequency vibration that is not completely in harmony with where many of us are. It is very tiring to experience that energy. There is sometimes just a sense of screening it out because there's so much energy coming in. We need to be very gentle to ourselves about that.

Through the weekend, your ability to hear this and to take it in more fully will increase. One specific thing that Aaron has sometimes suggested to people is simply opening your eyes, not to look at us as we're channeling, but a kind of unfocused looking that helps to allow more awareness.

Questioner: Yes. I did that today. It helped.

Barbara: On the question of how to clarify the lower chakras, Aaron is saying that it is too big a subject to do before lunch.

Carla: I wanted to say thank you for one of the things that you all helped me to do. By listening and being in circles, I just get so much energy. I feel better when I channel than at any other time. And I just really thank you for the beautiful sharing of this incredible energy that goes around the circle. Yum! As someone who came to a workshop recently said, "It's yummy!"

Session 20

Weekend 6, Part 3 of 5
(This session was preceded by a period of tuning and meditation.)

Barbara: Aaron and I are discussing which of us is going to lead this session. Aaron would like me to share with you directly the process that I use, which is not with a guided meditation from him. It precedes the opening of my energy to him. This is simply my own process that I'm sharing with you. I'm not suggesting that you need to use it, just sharing this as how I've learned to work with Aaron.

The first thing I do is to focus on my breath, simply to settle my attention. This is not a matter of creating stillness. Sometimes there's stillness. Sometimes there's a body sensation or a thought. Meditation is not to be mistaken for stillness, but for deep awareness and being in the moment with whatever is predominant in that moment, whether stillness or occurrence. It involves simply coming to attention and choiceless awareness. This is coming to a place of center where, if there's stillness, there is no grasping at that stillness. If there's turmoil, with busy-mind thoughts or emotions arising, there's no aversion to that. It is coming to a deeper place in myself where I can watch all of this and move past. That place is a still point, uninvolved in any outer stillness or occurrence. So, that's the first step for me.

I'm going to be quiet now for a moment while I work with this and let you work with it, in just focusing on the breath as we did in the meditations early this morning before breakfast.

When I'm in that space, the boundaries of self come down and I feel myself surrounded by energy, by spirit. At this point (usually not with words so much as wordlessly, but obviously to share it I need to use words), I offer a commitment of my energy, using a statement of intention of my desire to be of service. If I notice any self-thought of pride in "being somebody doing something," I just notice that as part of it. That's the part of it that grows out of fear. I don't condemn that in myself but I also don't build that up in myself. I ask for help in channeling clearly despite that human fear that is part of my makeup because I am human. I recognize that it is not a big part of my motivation. I don't focus on the negative in my motivation or on the fearful in my motivation. I focus on the loving and openhearted in my motivation.

So, I simply and clearly state my intention: "I offer my energy in the service of all beings. I offer my energy for the alleviation of suffering. Please use this energy in whatever way is most appropriate." I then state the continuing intention that I offer myself as an instrument through which spirit may speak. And I speak to whatever array of energy I feel out there, making the firm statement, "I will not allow anything to speak through me and use my voice that is inharmonious to my own deepest values. I welcome any being that wants to be present to hear me. But it may not speak through me unless our values agree."

At this point I usually begin to feel Aaron's energy very strongly. I recognize it as Aaron's energy. When I'm simply talking to Aaron myself, we have a code that we use for a challenge. So, I abbreviate the challenge to that energy and ask it to identify itself. When I'm channeling with a group, I go through the full challenge to that energy.

At first I couldn't understand the reason for this because I said, "I know Aaron's energy." But then I became aware that a being that was negatively polarized to just the same degree that Aaron is positively polarized could feel very much like Aaron, with the same wavelength of negative polarity that Aaron is of positive polarity. Carla said to me a few times, "Challenge, challenge!" And I said, "I don't need to." And then once I experienced negative energy that felt like Aaron's, so I understood the wisdom of Carla's advice.

So, I offer a formal challenge to it; this, for me, being what I most firmly believe in. Each of us, in opening ourselves to spirit guidance, needs to use our own highest values and to challenge the energy, not only that which would formally speak through us in channeling, but also that guidance from our own guides that we listen to, in order to be certain it's resonant with our own deepest values.

What I ask for myself is three challenges. First, "Are you that energy that I have come to know as Aaron, that identical energy?" I get a "Yes" on that. "Do you come in service to the principle of love and service to all beings?" And finally I ask it, "Do you come as a disciple of Jesus Christ and the Buddha?" If I'm not channeling to a big group, I simply say, "Three times, Aaron?" and get a "Yes" three times from Aaron, so I don't always go through that procedure formally. When I have an affirmative answer to the challenges and am centered energetically, I say, "This body is consecrated to the Light," as a way of protecting it further from any negativity that might wish to enter. At that point Aaron usually comes into the body.

Now I'm going to be quiet for a few moments while I work with this process of tuning that I use. I would ask you each to move through much the same process at your own pace, stating your intention that what you receive be of service to all beings, and that as you lower your own boundaries and open yourselves to spirit, you also challenge that spirit by your own highest values, which becomes a firm commitment of your own adherence to those values. A few minutes of silence now, and then we'll begin.

(Pause)

(Barbara channeling)

Aaron: I call you angels in earth-suits. Your angels are undeniable. This is who you truly are. With your incarnation you have bound yourselves into these earth-suits and pulled closed the visor in the front, which prevents clear seeing. Think of it as a coat of armor you have put on.

Body armor would hamper the free movement of your limbs. And yet, in the society in which armor was necessary because of jousting and other such combat, the armor was both a burden and a necessary tool. Your earth-suits might be viewed by some as a burden, but they are necessary to your learning. This Earth is your schoolroom. And your body and emotions are the embodiments of the lessons you have come to learn, as well as the tool through which you can learn.

The angel lives only in ultimate reality. It knows itself clearly for who it is. The being enclosed by the earth-suit can become so caught up in the tightness of that suit that it becomes its only reality. It forgets what it is like to live outside the suit.

My dear ones, here is where it gets tricky. What your incarnation asks of you is that you find a balance, fully expressing the angel while in no way discarding or belittling the value of the earth-suit, paying attention to the earth-suit while aware that it is merely a covering that you put on, not owning it, but living it fully.

You are like actors in a play. When you come out onto the stage, if you look to the audience and say, "Oh, this is only a play. It doesn't matter," the audience is not going to get much from your lines, offered with no sincerity. If you become so involved in the illusion of the play that you forget that it is a play and forget that there is an audience out there, you may turn your back to the audience or speak too softly for them to hear. The good actor must live its lines convincingly—live them, be them—while simultaneously being fully aware that this is a play, that when it walks offstage it no longer is the identity of that character. This is how the audience learns from a play. And you also are the audience. You are both actor and audience.

This is what your life asks of you: to live the illusion as fullheartedly as you can, while still knowing this is illusion. Herein is the intersection of relative and ultimate reality or the intersection of the cross. You have one foot in relative reality and one foot in ultimate reality, and there is no separation between them. Some of you have understood that you have one foot on each side of this threshold, but you feel as if there were a wall, an infinite wall, dividing relative and ultimate reality so that you may only experience one at a time. It is very hard work to learn to blend them and to bring compassion and wisdom together. But that is what you are here to learn to do.

We have asked, "What is the spiritual path and how do we live it?" The spiritual path, for me, is one of awareness of the nondual nature of relative and ultimate reality and compassion for the being who sometimes stumbles, while trying to bring them together harmoniously. It is a path of love and respect for these beings who keep brushing off the mud and moving on again, always learning a bit more about this balance and always learning a bit more about the desire to rest on one side or the other side of the balance; seeing the resistance to bringing them together because that requires such deep honesty and courage; and finding compassion for the being who cannot quite do it, but tries.

There is one very beautiful song from the musical *Man of La Mancha*. I will not ask Barbara to sing it, as her voice is inadequate to the task. But one verse is the words, "To bear with unbearable sorrows; to go where the brave dare not go; to be willing to give when there's no more to give; to be willing to die so that honor and justice may live. And I know if I'll only be true to this glorious quest that my heart will lie peaceful and calm when I'm laid to my rest."[53] This is your path, a path of exquisite beauty. Honor yourselves for the humans you are, for the quest that you have undertaken and the extreme difficulty of it, and for the light not only at the end of the road, but the light that you emit with each step on this path.

I would like to change tracks now and move from the theoretical to the practical. We are looking for this balance of ultimate and relative reality and for this balance of love and wisdom. How do we follow that quest in dealing with the very real and painful catalysts of our lives? I feel Q'uo wishing to speak. I do not know if Q'uo wishes to speak in answer to the question I have just raised, or wishes to add more that relates to the beginning of my afternoon talk here. I will simply pass the microphone to Q'uo for my brother/sister/friend to speak. And then we will move back to my own talk of the practical. That is all.

---

[53] "The Impossible Dream," music by Mitch Leigh and lyrics by Joe Darion, in *Man of La Mancha*, musical and book by Dale Wasserman, 1965.

(As a complement to Barbara's description of her tuning process, Carla's own process has already been discussed in the introduction to weekend 1.)

(Pause)

(Carla channeling)

Q'uo: We greet each in the love and in the light of the one infinite Creator. Greetings, blessings, love, and peace. My fellow teacher, Aaron, kindly shares these teachings with us, and we stand humbly before this generosity.

Indeed, we wished to speak to the matter of how to conceive, if you will pardon the pun, of your physical, material selves being in the same physical vehicle with the infinite and eternal life-form that you are. For you know that you are not your body, but were before the world had been created and shall be long after it has been taken back into the unmanifest and unknown, which is the infinite intelligence that is the one great original Thought, which we label with the weak word "love," having no choice.

This instrument earlier this day spied an acorn. As she picked it up, half of the acorn fell away. The little pointed top fit nicely on the finger like a cap for a finger puppet. Consider the seed within this acorn's husk and the stature of its eventual manifestation. Can this tiny acorn conceive of holding such a seed? And can each of you conceive that your physical vehicles hold field after field of energy in articulated manifestation and move as vehicles do through time and space, delivering the precious load of consciousness, that it may be buffeted by all manner of catalyst?

As you choose to walk this spiritual path, within each of you is being born the physical vehicle, if you will, of the light that you shall grow to be. But now, within incarnation, this physical form of light is tiny, incredibly vulnerable, and protected only by your sense of its being as you go about your everyday affairs.

Each choice that you make strengthens this infant consciousness. Each of you is like Mary, mother to Jesus, in that you are birthing your spiritual self. And you shall carry this within you all your days within this incarnation. Each hurt, each abruptness that shocks, each sorrow, each feeling of solitude and longing for a more native country, causes this infant child within to cry. And you may stand confused.

How can you nurture this inner child of light? Each of you can, in every moment, imagine, dream, and intend this nurturing. And with the energy of this intention, you touch that tiny light-being with the Mother's and Father's love, seeing you are not alone.

For I have touched Love.

And all that you feel and care and reach for exists in abundance that shall wash over your sweet beingness.

Here, feel my love.

Because you, in all your dirt and confusion, have intended and dreamt and imagined this love and this abundance, this becomes truth. Thusly, the nurturing of infinite intelligence continues as the great work that rose beyond all of the seemingly independent sparks of consciousness and, in the end, feeds not only that spiritual self within, but also the more conscious, everyday self that may feel so poorly equipped to nurture and love spiritually.

Your secret weapon always is the parents' eternal secret: simple, honest love. As you love that questing spirit within, you nourish that which shall carry you into eternity.

We thank our brother, Aaron, for sensing this teaching impulse that came to us, and hand the microphone back to his teachings with our love. Greetings, my brother. How wonderful it is to be here with you in manifestation through these lovely children.

(Barbara channeling)

Aaron: I want to move into some of the specific questions that we so often hear, with the main one being, "How do I know when I'm following a path of love or a path of fear?" If you had only one motivation, it would be easy to know. What confuses you is the multiple motivations. In the giving of that apple, 95 percent of the motivation was pure generosity with no ulterior motives, no desire to be savior to one another, and no desire to be somebody who gives; just open-hearted compassion to the suffering of another and a clear, heartfelt response. But 5 percent of the motivation or 7 percent or 3 percent or 10 percent—it does not matter—was the voice of fear that says, "What if I need it?" and then judges that fearful statement and says, "No, I should give," compounding the judgment; or it was the voice of fear that wants to be somebody "good."

The difficulty, then, is sorting out these voices in yourself and learning to trust the sincerity of the loving motivation. Do not get into a dialogue with the negative part of the motivation. Simply to acknowledge that it is there. If you deny it, then it becomes empowered. If you acknowledge it and smile to it and turn back to the positive part of the motivation, you deny power to your fear. I call this not getting into a dialogue with fear.

You begin, through attention, to see how that arising fear ensnares you and draws your attention away from the angel aspect of your self. There are some very specific steps to working here. First is to know that in every human situation there are going to be multiple motivations. Like the Ivory soap ad, it may be 99 and 99/100 percent pure, but it is not 100 percent pure. Your fear is not a burden given you for combat. It is the fertile soil upon which you may build compassion. It is the garbage that you turn into compost.

So, first there must be acknowledgment that there are multiple motivations. And second, while acknowledging the fear, you refuse to get caught in the story of it. This takes practice. You are never going to do it perfectly and that is okay. But with practice, the skill grows:

"I know this is fear, and I don't have to get sucked into it." The more you practice with this, the more you trust the impulses of your heart.

What happens when those impulses seem to lead you into pain? I want to tell the story of a friend, while changing the facts sufficiently so as to render this being unrecognizable. We have a friend who was in a marriage that had its ups and downs, as many marriages do. This was a second marriage for both partners. I am going to refer to them as partners A and B so as to avoid any designation of the sex of either being.

There were both love and pain between A and B. B suggested to A that since B was living in the house A had previously owned before their partnership, it felt excluded because it now contributed to that home. It suggested changing the mortgage, changing the bank accounts, or whatever. It does not matter what they would change, but only that they changed it so as to share more equitably. A agreed to that with some hesitation, but A sincerely felt, "If I want to live my life in love and trust with this being, the first step is to trust it." So A offered to B half of its possessions.

After the papers were signed, B turned around, not immediately but soon after, and betrayed A. It does not matter how. But there was real betrayal, which led to filing for divorce, leaving A feeling not only heartbroken by the betrayal of B but also in a drastic financial situation. A said, "What did I do wrong? I followed my heart. I trusted, and all it led me to is betrayal." This is a very painful story.

Let us look at what really might have been happening here. My follow-up is hypothetical. The personal reasons why this happened are not something you need to know.

Why do seemingly bad things happen to people who are trying to follow the dictates of love? That is the question. First of all, yes, this is a very painful situation and very frightening to A, who would now be alone, and who would have lost much of the support of money. Is that bad? What do bad and good mean? Painful, yes; but there is going to be pain in your lives.

Is pain always bad? Is it ever completely avoidable? You have heard me say that pain shouts at you, "Pay attention!" When one pays attention, one's learning is still not always pain-free. There is no guarantee of that. The question then becomes, "Can I take this devastation that's been handed to me and make some useful learning of it, rather than having it send me into deep bitterness?" Perhaps that is part of what the whole issue was about.

It is possible that A is being offered the opportunity to let go of having to make things happen a certain way, in being offered the opportunity to trust not only the "good" but also the "bad" in its life. It is very hard when one must go through that. But if one lets go of trying to make it come out a certain way and relaxes into what is, then one can find love and healing even in the midst of pain. How much grasping is there to control? Perhaps A invited this situation because a deeper wisdom knew the need to relinquish this grasping and fear.

Part of this might also be karmic. Perhaps very specifically in a past life, A had taken from B. This is only one of the ways karma works. It would not even have to be from B that A took. Perhaps A did not take physically from B, but only could not share. You say it seems like a very backward way to learn sharing, to be punished for sharing, but perhaps A needs to take sharing beyond reward and punishment and to move to a place where sharing is not for reward, but only to share. Perhaps the past misunderstanding was that A held on to sharing for its rewards, and if it could not see possible rewards, it was reluctant to share. So, perhaps that is part of the karma.

I am reminded here of a story of a Zen priest. This is said to be a true story that happened in Asia sometime in the last twenty or thirty years. The police came to this being and said, "You have been accused of this wrongdoing. Come with us." And they took the priest to jail. They asked, "Can you prove your innocence? Where were you that night when this deed occurred?" And the priest said, "I was alone. I have no witness." The priest did not fight the accusation nor did it agree with it. At first it said, "I am innocent," but it did not fight.

So, that priest went to jail, was imprisoned and penalized to serve with hard labor. Six years later another prisoner, who was dying, confessed to that crime. They came to the priest and they said, "You are innocent. Someone else has confessed. Why did you not stick to your innocence that you proclaimed at first?" The priest said, "Because when I meditated that first night in jail, I saw that I had done this crime in a past life and I had gotten away with it, and another had been put to death for my crime. Now I have paid in my own way and I am free. I have lived these six years in prison with much love, serving my fellow prisoners. I am free."

So karma does enter into it. It is hard to understand that. You are not given the ability to clearly see your past lives. There must sometimes be much faith that even when life hands you difficult circumstances, you still can trust.

Another possibility between our A and B: Through A's ability to suffer this betrayal at the hands of B without moving into hatred of B, thereby allowing B to feel forgiveness, A is offering a very real service to B by opening a door. A may make it very clear, "What you did is totally inappropriate and I am very, very angry and hurt; nevertheless, I do not hate you."

"No" can be said with love. It does not have to be done with hate. Perhaps both A and B needed to learn these lessons, with B being served by A's ability to work with this painful catalyst lovingly so that B might also learn and grow beyond its self-centeredness and fear.

Finally, A may be offered the opportunity to look at the multiple motivations in itself, in that it shared its fortunes with B with a high degree of love and desire as well as aspiration to strengthen their relationship, but that there was also perhaps denial of any sense, "This being is not trustworthy," and perhaps denial of the fear in itself of letting go of a relationship with a nontrustworthy B.

So, one part of it is A's reluctance to be honest with itself about the realities in its situation. It is clinging to what love was offered rather than having the faith to say no. This is a hard one. It is about trusting your radiance, beauty, and divinity and knowing your true worth.

So many of you have a hard time saying no with love. You aspire to be "spiritual," to be good and kind and loving. But sometimes you interpret that kindness to mean being a doormat to others. When you offer yourself as a doormat, you are going to be walked on. Then rage builds in you and you erupt. And then you say, "Oh, I'm bad for having erupted," and you go back to offer yourself as a doormat once again. Thus you perpetuate the cycle. To do so allows you to maintain the belief in your badness.

When you have compassionate nonjudgment for that in yourself that is less than loving, you find compassionate nonjudgment for that in others. When you learn to say no kindly to yourself when the impulse is grounded in fear, then you learn to recognize that fearful impulse in others and to say no to it with the same kindness. Living without harm to others does not mean never saying no; quite the contrary. It can be very harmful to another to allow them to use you as a doormat.

You may resolve this in yourselves by paying close attention to the multiple reasons for your choices, and by starting to see those motivations that are prompted by love and those that are prompted by fear, not hating yourself for the fear, but not being drawn into dialogue with that fear. This is what leads you not to be drawn into dialogue with another's fear, but to say no and to trust *This is the least harmful thing I can do.*

Harming another by omission is still harm. If you allow another to step on you and hold your tongue, even if you do not hate them for doing that, you still harm them. It is a very fine line.

All of you are at times B, seeming to betray another, and at times A, feeling betrayed and offering invitation for the seeming betrayal. Within this exchange, each person has the opportunity to look deeply at the movements of fear and love, to reflect on how it habitually reacts to these forces, and to bring the balance more to love.

A related question, one of choice of work, is, "How do I know whether to stay with my present job, which is sometimes very painful to me, or when to move on to a new job? Am I 'copping out' or am I being guided by love?" One might ask the same question in a rocky relationship. "How do I know when to stay with it? How do I know when to withdraw?" The answer, my friends, is the same. When you start to allow yourself to experience the multiple motivations without needing to cling to being the "good" one nor to deny nor to hate yourself for the places of fear, then you allow yourself to move into a deeper place of knowing in your heart, which very honestly weighs the balance and knows the primary motivation. It is never going to be clear-cut.

Please understand that there are only more or less skillful and more or less painful or joyful decisions. There is never a right or wrong decision. If you stay with the job or relationship and pain increases, you always have the right to leave. You ask yourself, "Am I still learning here or has the pain increased to the point where there's so much contraction of my energy that I can't learn?"

If that is so, you forgive yourself for that humanness that creates that contraction and you let go of that work or relationship with the intention to look deeply at the places of fear when you are no longer so deeply stuck in it, and with the intention to understand it so you will not need to repeat it. If there is not that much contraction and pain, if there is still much love and much joy in the work, and if you feel yourself learning in those situations, then you go on. There is no right or wrong.

There is much more that could be said about these questions that I would like to get into. But rather than working with hypothetical situations, we would like to hear your questions. I also sense that Q'uo may wish to speak before you get into your questions. What we will do here is pause for a brief break, come back and invite Q'uo to speak, or open to your questions. That is all.

(The session is paused for group meditation and tuning through story and song.)

(Carla channeling)

Q'uo: Greetings once again in love and light.

We are happy to report that not only have Aaron and we spoken concerning the remainder of this session of working, but our instruments have also made their peace with our preferences. So all is well in hand. And this delights the one known as Carla, who enjoys arrangements!

We have looked at the walking of the spiritual path and have seen that it is based upon the awareness that, within the form that walks upon the surface of this sphere and dies and is no more, there exists a self that does not go down into the dust or in any way become corrupted, but that is infinite, eternal, and unknowable, as is the mystery of love, which shall always remain unknowable.

We have acknowledged that the beginning of this path may usefully be seen to be the first conscious choice of how to walk that path. Each here who hears our voice has committed the self to a pilgrimage of service to others on behalf of the one infinite Creator. We also have chosen this path and this is why we have been called to your group at this time/space.

We have suggested that beyond all questions of human motive that keep intellects busy attempting to discern right, there is the actual center of this quest in the very body that is corrupt. For the consciousness that is Christ Consciousness, that is Buddha Body, dwells with a faithfulness that shall not cease, short of death.

In the midst of the physical vehicle that you know as your own body, no matter how its condition seems, it carries Christ within it. And this being within, which is your deeper self, depends upon you to hope and dream and strive in faith amidst all difficulties and conditions whatsoever, to affirm this self within and to proudly bear all the perceived errors of self as scars of a warrior who strives peacefully toward that inner Eden in which all physicality and confusion pass away.

And the Christ within, well-launched from infanthood, may finally begin another voyage or another pilgrimage in a lighter body, within which this consciousness grows and has a larger weight as compared to the physical body. You see, in all of your attempts to live, whatever you may think of them, they have been your best. How can any offer more than this?

Now then, we encourage each to feel the feet planted upon the path of pilgrimage. Yes, there are times when you may sit and drink in such beauty, whether it be of the eye or of the heart. At these times you feel nourished and lovely and loving and well-equipped to do the walking toward the greater light. Yet, so much of any pilgrimage takes place when conditions do not seem favorable. And in these dry and desert times, it is central to pilgrimage that within your own processes of reasoning and consideration you remember who you are, where you wish to go, and how much you feel connected to this quixotic quest. It is when you are alone and without friends to encourage or understand that the spirit within most needs your ragged, jagged faith and any scrap or any off-key rendition of the blues that still may praise the Creator within.

Pilgrimages are difficult. But you would not find yourself upon this path if you did not hunger for that which gives meaning to difficulty. You wish to be wide awake and feel every stone, eat every mouthful of dust, and sit at the end of any hopeless, empty day rejoicing and giving thanks that you have been present at this miraculous disaster.

Of course, we can most well comfort each in these protected circumstances by using channels such as this one and by using the energy of each who seeks, so that each helps each. But the testing and trying that tempers and encourages the growth of that spirit within is greatly fed by these difficult, desert moments or hours or days or, this instrument reminds us, years.

Sometimes, yes, each shall have losses, limitations, and every discouragement. Indeed, each faces physical annihilation. One day this body shall be dust. None of this appeals or is easy to ponder. Yet each of you shall walk along this path with the truth receding infinitely before you, never reached, and always beckoning.

And each day shall be new. Each situation, no matter how time-worn by repetition, shall be new if you fully choose to be the pilgrim. For you who wish to walk this path, wish nothing short of transformation. And one who successfully transforms oneself has virtually healed at least some portions of an older self, so that the new within has the opportunity and room to bud and flower and bloom in its turn, within.

The question, "How can one walk a spiritual path or have a spiritual vocation when one must labor at world concerns in order to provide food and shelter?" becomes less puzzling if you assign the value to labor that you assign to meditation, contemplation, and all the good practices of the spiritual vocation.

We suggest to each that the spiritual vocation is to find love in every moment. And this makes no distinction between the worldly labor and the strictly spiritual practice. When an entity can gaze at the crowded day and see joy in the doing and Christ Consciousness in the very warp and woof of all labor, then a world opens up before that entity that is entirely drenched and marinated in Christ Consciousness.

This instrument has read the story of the nun who was asked how she could bear to wash the filthy, maggot-filled sores of infant children in her Calcutta that were soon to die, with the odor and the look of putrefaction being so dreadful. The nun reportedly looked up at the questioner and said, "Oh, but this is the face of Jesus Christ. If I thought this was a native child, I could never do it."

My brothers and sisters, each of you is as this one. And no matter to what purpose you lend your hand, you touch Christ Consciousness. Do you doubt that there is this consciousness in one who does the taxes, goes to the grocery, and attempts to park the car in a crowded lot with others jockeying for your place? If you do doubt, then praise and give thanksgiving to the one infinite Creator and go on anyway.

We shall speak to ways in which the spiritual vision may be tuned so as to be more fruitful in throwing out for your use tools and resources with which to meet Christ in the parking lot. But for now, in the course of questioning, we and those of Aaron would like to address specific requests from you.

We would open with the first query. Does any wish to question at this time?

Questioner: I've noticed in an experience that I had, and I've had it here today in listening to Q'uo, that as I get closer to God Consciousness I always feel a welling up of tears. I'm wondering why that is. They don't feel like bad tears.

Q'uo: We agree that these are not bad tears. You have the sensibility to weep at the beauty, my brother. This beauty is called forth within you by words that you recognize. Yet the beauty that brings your tears was within you all the time. Is there a further query, my brother?

Questioner: No. Thank you.

Q'uo: Is there another question?

Questioner: You indicated that all jobs are good. Aren't there jobs that are not so good, that are selfish and destructive rather than constructive, like developing atomic bombs?

Q'uo: The query about good and evil occupations assumes that one accepts the labels of good and evil. We would suggest that each entity that strives to polarize toward service to others has the tendency to select a job for pay that is either helpful or not harmful. Were a scientist to be put in the position of developing the atomic bomb, this entity could still invest every hope for positive use that it had and with sadness accept such an eventual development of the job. Given the circumstances in which the atomic bomb was developed, the intention of those who developed this was a sad but firm commitment to stopping a war that was engulfing your sphere.

The world is seldom pure in its habiliments or circumstances. Good and evil are so plaited up and interwoven in the tapestry of living that it is almost impossible to do that which yields all positive and no negative. Those who have been given gifts must attempt to offer them with the very best of intention. And if there seems to develop negativity therefrom, then that pain and sorrow, too, must be taken into that place where forgiveness reigns, healing is real, and the light does not waver.

That place lies within each. It is a place as clear in location as Cleveland. You may not know its position within the body, but its position within your beingness is specific. It is your heart. And in that place there is no right and no wrong, but only love. Beyond all that occurs and all that dies, there is love.

In terms of the outer appearances, each may run a sorry race, yet each time the spirit within throws that metaphysical hand up and says, "Praise and love anyway. We'll work this out eventually. But now, praise and thanks that we are here to witness, to love," that place of balance is reentered and the healing waters flow.

Does this answer the query, or is there a further query?

(Pause)

Q'uo: One final query, if there be one, then we would wish to transfer the podium, shall we say, to the one known as Aaron. Is there a final query to us at this time?

Questioner: I have a question. Is there any dharma practice or service that you would recommend that would enhance, perhaps speed up, or at least keep one pointed on the path toward getting to this place in the heart?

Q'uo: Yes, my brother, there is. For each it is somewhat different. But perhaps you can see the slant when we say to you that the teacher known as Jesus, in attempting to describe its nature, said that it thanked entities who had fed it and clothed it and so forth. And when the confusion arose because entities had not fed Jesus, it explained, "Insofar as you have fed or clothed the least of these, you have fed and clothed me."[56]

---

[56] Matt. 25:40 AV.

There are entities starving. There are entities who are naked. There is always some soup to fix and hand to those who have no home. And for those who cannot achieve a sense of this healing place within by working upon the horizontal plane, there are those commitments of the spirit to pray and intercede and assist the consciousness of the planet upon which you dwell.

For those who do not see love in soup but who abide in love and thanksgiving, thinking prayerfully of the planet, the cause of peace, any *beau geste,* or any windmill at which you may tilt may suffice. For those who thus abide, the doing of this regularly, day after day and week upon week, shall furnish the love. For this, too, is food. It is a kind of food that you might call manna or the bread of heaven.

If you cook, offer soup. If you pray, offer prayers. And if you do neither, sit down in one place and give thanks and praise. And then be quiet and feel the doors of the heart open.

We do not suggest that this is easily accomplished, but only suggest that some time, in the rhythm of your own energies, will be the time when all the waiting is over, and you will have that divine moment when Christ Consciousness thrills up your spine and through your very being.

And for that instant all is quite, quite clear. Ever after this first experience of the open heart, you have this subjective memory that can shine within you, like the candle lit against all darkness, until your next moment within the open, full heart.

May we answer further, my brother?

Questioner: No. Thank you.

Q'uo: We thank you, my brother, and all here present. And we shall most happily speak with you again. But for now we would yield the floor, in case anyone has queries that it wishes the one known as Aaron to answer. For now, we leave you in all that there is: the love that created everything and the light out of which all is created. We are those of Q'uo. Adonai.

Barbara: Aaron wants to speak for a few minutes before he opens the floor to questions.

(Barbara channeling)

Aaron: I wish briefly to expand on a few things about which Q'uo spoke. First, before the floor was opened to your queries, my brother/sister spoke about living a life in faith. I want to pick up on this idea of faith.

One of the primary learnings of third density is faith. Sometimes your life hands you chaos and pain. The first impulse is to say, "What am I doing wrong?" or "Why me?" It is very hard to have faith. I am not suggesting a blind faith that takes whatever is handed to you with no respect for yourself. This is the thinking that leads into "doormatism," if I may coin a word. I am not suggesting a blind acceptance that disempowers. On the contrary, true faith empowers because true faith comes from that part of you that cuts through the relative dualities of good and bad or right and wrong.

True faith comes from that deeply connected core of your heart and it is built on past experience of faith. It is built on wisdom, on looking back at this life and seeing that which you challenged with a bewildered "Why?" turned out to have answers and turned out to be at times your greatest teacher. It is that grounded faith that grows out of connection and love that enables you to deal with the bewilderment and occasional deep pain of your life. It enables you to cut through your war with that pain and confusion and to take the next step. Put as simply as I can, if life never challenged you by offering you that which was difficult, how would you strengthen these muscles of faith? How would you practice faith without the catalyst that asks that of you?

Taking this to another place, we will look at such a situation as the making of the atomic bomb. Of course it is possible and even likely that there were some who were involved in the making of that bomb who did so with hatred in their hearts and the desire to kill others for revenge. There were also those who acted in the service of love and caring for others as best they knew how. You may question their wisdom, but you may not question their intention. If one says to you, "I truly believe that I can best preserve peace and sanity in the world by creating a terrible weapon," their reasoning may be faulty, but their heartfelt motivation is to serve.

Is the bomb, in itself, good or bad? Is anything, in itself, good or bad? What grows out of it? There is a story of the man whose horse broke free of its barn and disappeared. The neighbors all said, "Oh, what bad luck!" The man shrugged and said, "Bad luck, good luck, who knows?" The neighbors shook their heads with bewilderment at his response. But the next day this mare came home leading a wild stallion, a strong and handsome animal. And the neighbors all said, "Oh, what good luck!" Again, the man shrugged, "Good luck, bad luck, who knows?" The next day the man's son was attempting to groom this horse and the horse kicked him, breaking his leg. And again the neighbors all said, "Oh, what bad luck!" And again the man shrugged, "Bad luck, good luck, who knows?" Later that week soldiers came rounding up young men in the area to become conscripts for the army, and they took all the young men in the town except this one with the broken leg.

Good luck, bad luck. What does "good" or "bad" mean? What are the motivations? What grows out of it? I am not stating here that it is acceptable to go out and murder people and say, "Well, there's no such thing as bad." You do live with one foot in relative reality. If you harm others, you are responsible for that harm. That harm is never all right in terms of relative reality. But nothing on your earth plane happens without a reason, and nothing is without its karmic consequences.

What was the motivation of those who created a bomb? The ends do not justify the means. It is not okay to kill people to create peace. You will have to decide for yourself, however, if it is okay to do certain work if your intention is pure.

What are we weighing here, the work itself or the motivation? There are times when the answer is clear. Consider, for example, one who goes out to hunt for sport, perhaps as a guide, killing animals, and leading others to this killing. It is clear that this is action that harms others. But sometimes it is not very clear. What of the hunter who kills to feed his children who would otherwise be hungry? We also might ask, "Harm for what?" There is honest disagreement. Do we cut down rain forest, thereby killing the life therein? If we do not cut it down, what do we use for fields to grow food?

I am not suggesting an answer here. Of course I have my own views, but they are merely my opinion. The question is, "What is the motivation?" And here we come back to faith. One can work as hard as one can to follow the path that one personally sees as relieving suffering in the world. But one also must have faith that one cannot fix other people or that one cannot grab other people and shake them out of their views. If people need to do that which seems to be destructive, one must simultaneously work as hard as one can to alleviate the suffering that grows out of that destructive path and also have faith that things are unfolding as they need to. It is not given to you on the human plane to see all the answers with foresight.

We come back to this same question, "Can I look at the multiple motivations within me? Perhaps the difficulty is being with another being's suffering. So I want to take that suffering away from them because it is so painful for me. I want to fix that. But in so wanting to fix them, I don't give them their free-will choice, nor do I give them permission to be who they are and to learn in their own way. Do I have the right to do that?"

You can open a door for another, but you cannot push them through. You can suggest to another, "I think that this is a path that will lead to suffering." But you cannot insist on another's agreement with your view. Here is where you need faith. You must speak up and act without attachment to results, where appropriate. And then you let it unfold as it will, doing what you can, then resting, and letting it open as it needs to.

A simple illustration, here, is the child that wants to touch a hot stove. You tell the child ten times, a hundred times, or a thousand times, "No, it's hot!" But the child has no concept of hot. You do not simply shrug and say, "All right, touch the stove. See for yourself!" You continue to say, "No, it's hot!" Somewhere along the line, you know the child is going to touch that stove behind your back and learn for itself, "Yes, it's hot!" But you are responsible to see the child does not scald itself to death.

You can open the door to another's learning, but you cannot know what the other most needs to learn. Perhaps those beings who built the atomic bomb and those who were involved in the bombing itself on both sides had lessons that you cannot begin to understand. We cannot judge others. That does not free us from responsibility for stating our viewpoint with love.

To shift tracks here, I would like briefly to speak to this last question of spiritual practice with two very specific suggestions. One is all-encompassing, and one is specific.

The all-encompassing: Whatever you do, do it with aware-ness—just that. Awareness is the key to all of your learning.
The second: What is your own personal stumbling block?
It will vary for each of you.

Awareness is the overall practice. There are many support practices that allow you to bring into your awareness the catalysts that give rise to that which you most need to practice. For example, the being who is very aware of the stumbling block of greed, as with the fear *Will my needs be met?* and the accompanying movement to hold on or grasp, might find it useful to move into a practice of always letting others go first, just to see what happens with that.

At a meditation retreat here last year, someone spoke of trying this practice of seeing the fear that it would not get what it needed to eat and of asking itself to always be last, to wait until everyone else had been served. In doing so, that being constantly needed to address that fear with awareness. And it also was given the opportu-nity to see that there was enough left. It began to see how much that fear was old-mind's habit and was not a fear borne out in the present moment. So, it began to find that it could let go and that it no longer needed to own and identify with that fear.

Jealousy is another stumbling block. A practice here is to notice, with compassion for yourself, the arising of jealousy at others' good fortune; and then, very consciously, to allow the arising of gladness for them in yourself. Look as carefully as you can at that being's fear and pain, and at the arising of joy in what it has been given or accomplished. As you consciously work with such a practice, you find a very real joy in others' successes and happinesses. Thereby you allow a part of you that had been confined and not allowed expression to come out and express itself. This allows for the dissolution of fear. You start to understand that another's gain does not mean your loss. You correct that misunderstanding.

Generosity can be another part of holding on and fearing one's needs will not be met. If this is a predominant issue for you, another way to work with it is to practice giving. Start with very small things, such as seeing that another needs a fork or a napkin. You are not giving your own. You are just reaching and getting it for them. It is a practice in giving. It starts to open your heart to how wonderful it feels to give and to be attentive to others' needs. It starts to open your heart to that innate generosity of spirit. Then you increase the giving, not just of material things, but of your time and your energy. And you begin to learn that you do not lose anything when you give. Again, you correct the misunderstanding, not through forcing yourself with a "give till it hurts"; quite the contrary. It is a gentle process whereby you learn that giving is a joy.

I will not elucidate with each stumbling block that each of you may have. You have the gist of it. There are a great many different spiritual practices. First you must identify the stumbling block and then you can find an appropriate practice that relates to it.

I would like to open the floor here to any questions that there may be. That is all.

Session 20

Questioner: Aaron, do you have a practice for arrogance?

Aaron: First we must look at, "What is arrogance?" Can you see that arrogance is simply the flip side of the coin of unworthiness? To be arrogant is to presume oneself "better than" or to feel the need to express a superiority and, inversely, to put another down.

Do not concentrate on the arrogance. That is dialoguing with fear. Move your focus instead to the sense of unworthiness. When you see the impulse toward arrogant response arising in you, let it be a flashing red light, saying, "Fear is here," and then move that loving heart immediately to the fear. Ask yourself, *In this moment, am I unworthy?* Your answer is going to be no. *Have I ever been unworthy at those times when I experienced an impulse toward arrogant response? No. It is simply the way that this mind/body construct has dealt with the fear of being inadequate or unworthy. I don't need to do that.* From this you might derive a spiritual practice to allow the arising of arrogance to be a reminder to be compassionate to this illusory but seemingly real self that is experiencing fear.

The person who experiences that which seems arrogant in itself undoubtedly also frequently experiences arrogance in others. Here is where a valuable practice comes in, which is of seeing the arrogance in others as their fear. You may also begin to work with a forgiveness meditation, really trying to see their fear as manifesting that arrogant reaction. As you forgive them, you forgive yourself. Is that a sufficient answer or have you a further question?

Questioner: Can Aaron hear Q'uo or hear what Q'uo is saying? Is it communicated to you so you can pay due attention to Q'uo?

Aaron: I hear Q'uo's thoughts but not Q'uo's words. In other words, I hear the thoughts, but do not know the choice of words with which Carla has framed those thoughts, because Carla is not thinking the thoughts. They are simply emerging.

Interestingly, last night at a point when the tape was being changed, Q'uo's thought was *We now will pass the microphone to Aaron.* So I told

Barbara, "It is time to speak." But Q'uo had not yet said that. It was simply the thought. Thus, this instrument held back.

I can hear all of your thoughts. I will not tell Barbara those thoughts. Barbara is karmically responsible for her deafness and responsible for the consequences of the isolation and limited communication that it forces upon her. And I will not simply remove that burden from her. She must live with it. I understand that it then places a burden on others to communicate with her. Perhaps that is also part of the whole karmic cycle of it.

I will tell her when there is something that could be dangerous. For instance, in a car, at one point she had begun to move from the left lane into the right lane because there was a car behind her that wished to pass. As she began to pull into the right lane, the car that was behind her speeded up and started to pull beside her into that same right lane to pass her on the right, the driver driving erratically, angrily. He honked his horn, but of course Barbara did not hear that. Here I did step in, simply saying, "Left, left," and Barbara trusted my voice enough not to pull into the right lane but to swerve back left again, and the driver sped past.

So, I will help with that which she does not hear when it is a potentially life-threatening situation, but I will not step in simply to supply the ears she has lost. That is her responsibility.

Questioner: This morning Aaron was telling us about what happens when we die and it was very interesting. And we said, "Let it wait until everyone can hear it," about the transition period and so forth.

Aaron: This answer will take at least ten or fifteen minutes. May I suggest that it be my contribution to our fireside stories? Will that be acceptable to you? That is all.

Questioner: Do you mean you are going to tell ghost stories now? Wouldn't it be fun to hear some Christmas stories.

Session 20

Aaron: That's another kind of ghost story—Holy Ghost stories.

(Group laughter.)

Is there one other short question?

Questioner: Should we guard our socks when we go home?

Aaron: It is my firm belief that socks are given to you in pairs for the sole reason of offering you the chance to practice at nonattachment and to practice offering other beings a free will. I have told you before that on our planes we gladly take your cast-offs and have no preference as to whether they match. Perhaps eventually we will be able to finally tell enlightened beings on this Earth because they will randomly wear socks that match or do not match, with no great attachment. That is all.

(More group laughter.)

Questioner: Is that how we get lint in the drier?

Aaron: The lint in your drier comes from the material of your clothes practicing dissolution of form. That is all.

(After another round of laughter, the session is paused for a period of group meditation, singing, and poetry reading.)

Barbara: So many of us get trapped in the idea that being spiritual, being good, means never saying no, never being angry, and never having emotions. Aaron says that it is harder for those of us who are old souls, as all of us here are, because we so much aspire to purify our energy. This is an intention that works against us, because even if there's a little bit of negativity in us, instead of just taking it in our stride as younger souls do, he says that the closer that we get to getting ready to graduate from the plane, the more perfective we get. And that's one of the last lessons that we learn: finding love for our very fallible human selves.

Questioner: What kind of being is the Q'uo? Is it a sixth-density social memory complex? And for what purpose did it become one; that is, a joined group entity?

Carla: Before the Ra contact began, I was channeling mostly a fifth-density entity named Latwii. It was a social memory complex of fifth-density wisdom. I really liked Latwii. After Don died, I did not channel Ra anymore, at Ra's request, and went back to channeling Latwii and others.

I got a contact from Q'uo six months after that. We thought, *Q'uo, what an odd name.* A couple of years later we finally developed enough wit to ask who Q'uo was. And Q'uo said that they were a principle made up of Latwii and one of Latwii's teachers, who was also one of our teachers, by the name of Ra.

I could no longer channel the narrow beam that required trance, but I could channel fifth density. And Latwii could talk to those of Ra and be somewhat better able to focus on the question than they were before. So, Q'uo is a sort of new, improved Latwii and Ra. The purpose of their contacting us is because we asked for it. The purpose of their joining was to contact us.

Questioner: Have they ever identified themselves as to where they're from?

Carla: No.

Questioner: Have you had much contact with Pleiadian entities?

Carla: I have worked with people who have been channeling the Pleiades. I have not accepted that contact.

Session 20

Questioner: Have you turned it away?

Carla: Yes.

Questioner: Why? Is that a personal question?

Carla: No. It is a question having to do with my judgment that the contact is mixed.

Questioner: Yes. That fits with what we've heard about the Pleiadians. There are different purposes at work coming from that system.

Questioner: Could someone speak to what they are? I've never heard of it.

Questioner: The Pleiades are a star formation, aren't they?

Questioner: Yes! And it's one of the oldest civilizations in the galaxy. Aaron gave some talks about how a lot of our culture was seeded from the Pleiades and that a lot of us came from the Pleiades.

Carla: It's very strong energy, but it's also capable of a good bit of delusion.

Questioner: Can you pick and choose?

Carla: I don't think you can as well, once you accept contact. You're going to get what you get.

Barbara: Last spring Aaron talked about the Pleiades, but I have not yet seen the transcripts from that. Does anybody know what he said? Does anybody remember? Can you share a little bit with us?

Questioner: As I best recall, the Pleiadians were a very ancient civilization that was made up, not of one race, but of many different kinds of beings who came together—physical beings and nonphysical beings like water beings, air beings, more ethereal beings. And they had a governing council made up of beings who were incarnate and discarnate. That council and those beings were aware of the distortions that were happening on Earth due to extraterrestrial, negatively polarized contact with the Earth. And there was a debate about whether or not to intervene.

So, some of the beings from the council (it is not a governing council but a voluntary council, like a service group) came to Earth. They came, not as incarnate beings, but as shape changers, which is a way of simulating incarnation here in the physical but being able to leave at will and not be subject to the karma here. So, they were hoping that by simulating the negatively polarized extraterrestrials, they could give a different message of love instead of a negative one of fear. But what they didn't realize was that by taking the form of these negative beings, they had to copy them so precisely that they had the capability even to emulate the emotional body to such an extent they could not separate from the negative polarity as well.

Thus, they fell into negativity because they also, despite their very good intentions, had a very small amount of mixed motivations or negativity within them. They were very loving beings with very good intentions, but they overestimated their own ability and their own need to learn from the negative half to understand negativity within them. So eventually many of them took incarnation. And as the years and incarnations went by, many of the lessons from their civilization became seed-points of our own great civilization. They were bringers of culture and light.

So, they came to teach, but also ended up coming to learn. And many are still here working out their karma. There is still contact going on from the Pleiades, as Aaron has told us, but there is still a debate about this contact and whether beings from other planets should actively intervene.

This was an echo of previous history in which the makers of Earth had seen the negative contact with their creations—the people of Earth. And they tried to protect them somehow, not trusting people's ability to learn from this negative contact. And this protectiveness by these beings who founded Earth became itself a negative catalyst, and further.... Yes!... It was the birth of fear on Earth!

This was long before the Pleiadians saw the contact of extraterrestrials, which was far more negative by then. So, now I think some of the contact that Carla is talking about is some of these beings come to do good, but not to intervene. There is a law or agreement not to come to Earth unless it is by incarnation. But what about those beings who do not follow the law? Do you enforce control or allow those beings to go ahead with breaking this law?

Barbara: Aaron says two things. He says, "Thank you!" to you. (I'm paraphrasing here.) He's saying that there is a force field of sorts around the Earth. They cannot use fear. They use love as the energy of this force field to prevent encroachment by negative energy. There's a force field of love that prevents highly negative energy from encroaching, because they're repelled by this force field. But energies such as the Pleiadians are not negatively polarized, but simply, in Aaron's viewpoint, have misunderstanding that the end justifies the means, and thus have intervened rather than trusting and having faith in those on Earth to work it out on their own. But they are not repelled by the force field because they are positively polarized beings. That is all.

Questioner: Has anyone here read (title omitted)?

Barbara: Yes, I have. And I asked Aaron about it and he said to read it very selectively. It is both clear and fear-based.

Questioner: It does tend to create fear of a major DNA change in another twenty years. That sounds pretty fearful. But there are some things in it that I think are interesting topics of discussion.

(The group offered topics for the next session, which include:)

"How do we move into the space of being unselfconscious?"

"Do we connect with each other vibrationally, for the most part?"

"Is there reincarnation in groups? How does that work? How do we find each other?"

"Did Christ and Buddha 'hang out' together?"

"It seems that unworthiness really goes deep, like it is genetically encoded, almost like a catalyst. Is it genetically encoded? What is the origin of unworthiness?"

"Is it better to take it slow or to try to complete this density in this lifetime?"

"Can you comment on Hopi prophecies?"

Session 21

Weekend 6, Part 4 of 5
(This session was preceded by a period of tuning and meditation.)

(Barbara channeling)

Aaron: Good morning to you all. I want to share with you how much I enjoyed the spirited energy that rose from this room last night with your joyful gathering. Some of you forget that laughter is also a part of the spiritual path. We are asked please to open the shades. Laughter is one of the most effective ways, as are joy and lightness. This lightness is that which comes with deeply sharing your energy and opening your hearts to one another in playfulness.

There is no other plane that I know of where beings limit the natural playfulness of their light as much as they do on the earth plane. It is part of your illusion of separation. So it was very beautiful to us, as your spirit friends, to feel and to share in your joy.

There are a number of questions that were offered last night. While understanding the importance of each question to the seeker, it is the mutual agreement of Q'uo, myself, and those through whom we channel that it is best to maintain the focus of the original question, "What is the spiritual path and how do we live it?"

Since our time is not unlimited in these particular sessions so that we cannot answer all the questions within each of your hearts, it feels most relevant to the entire group to limit ourselves to those questions that first drew you here, because we have by no means covered that topic. This does not mean that we do not value the other questions, but that we must answer them at a different space and time.

One thought in my mind is that in a future gathering, rather than starting with a specific focus, we could simply come together as curious seekers with questions. We can explore that route.

Q'uo and I would like first, then, to continue some of our discussion of "What is the spiritual path and how do we live it?" by returning to the question, "What is it?" and then to the second half, "How do we live it?"

Speaking to the particular distortions and confusions that offer themselves as catalysts in your lives, we come together here with a number of religious biases. I do not mean bias as a negative term, only in the sense of persuasions or beliefs. A bias might be considered a bend in the clear stream of light, such as the bend that light makes when it hits the water. The light is bent by the mass of that water so it appears to the eye to have a crook in it. Your individual values, experiences, and beliefs serve as a deflector to the true light, so that the expression of that light becomes individuated into your own personal bias.

Your religious persuasions are not to be mistaken as synonymous with a spiritual path. Rather, they are the tools that you use to help you walk your path. There are hundreds of different religious beliefs in the world. We do not wish to favor some above others. They are all of value. In some way, even those that have been viewed as negative provide a value to the seeker.

Time limits us from speaking to the myriad religious persuasions of your many cultures, nor would that be relevant to you. We have here a group whose religious understandings are predominantly Judeo-Christian and Buddhist. There are those among you who have been influenced by the Hindu or Sufi understandings, by Islam, or by Native American cultures and beliefs. These are not any less valuable.

The other reason why I choose to speak predominantly to, let us say not even Judeo-Christian, but Christian and Buddhist beliefs, is that the essences of these can be simplified into qualities of mercy and wisdom. The beings who were the masters of these two faiths have become in your hearts and minds the personifications of mercy and wisdom.

If we look into other religious streams, we will find that those streams offer some balance in these qualities of mercy and wisdom. Judaism, in its purest form, makes a very beautiful balance. Hinduism leans a bit more toward the qualities of love than of wisdom, as do the Sufi faiths. The Native American traditions come to a beautiful balance.

While I speak of balance, be aware that a balance need not be 50/50. Each of you has been in incarnation so many times that you move into religious bias because of what speaks most eloquently to your heart.

Mercy is one wing of the bird, and wisdom is the other. Call it wisdom and compassion or wisdom and love. The bird cannot fly without two wings, but always one will be the stronger. Through only the quality of faith, one can find liberation. Through only the quality of precise and finely tuned, awakened wisdom, one can find liberation. Could you see that bird struggling to fly with that one wing while the other wing is at least held out for balance?

Your spiritual path lays before you the ways in which you find that personal balance. There is no right or wrong here. One cannot offer a recipe, such as 17 percent of this and 19 percent of that and 3 percent of this and so on. What do you start with? The stew that is too sour may need more sugar. The stew that is too sweet may need more lemon.

So, you must know yourself, know your strengths, relish those strengths, and build on them. But also you must not be afraid to know the places of lack of strength and be willing to strengthen those muscles that are weak. The runner who works only on strengthening his muscles will lack wind in a race. The runner who works on his breath and lungpower and ignores the muscles will find the legs cramping and weak. And yet one runner may know the great strength of her legs and that it is what will put her ahead in the race. So she wisely strengthens her lungs so that they may endure through the race while the legs do the pumping and pushing.

What do you need to strengthen in yourselves? What are your weaknesses? It is always easier to strengthen that which feels most natural to you and to which you are most deeply drawn. But I beseech you to look at your resistance to strengthening that which is more difficult to strengthen.

So, what are these paths of lovingkindness, mercy, and compassion? And what are these paths of wisdom? I spoke sometime this weekend about using love to tame mind and using wisdom to tame mind. When I say "mind," remember that I do not mean the brain, but the mind and heart in totality.

I want to speak here of stories of these two basic teachers, the Buddha and the one who is known as Jesus, and of their teachings. I have shared with you many stories from my own heart. They are from my personal memories of Jesus in that lifetime in which I was a shepherd and knew this being in the flesh, and they explain the ways that he affected me deeply as a teacher. Predominant in those memories were the stories of his deep lovingkindness to all beings, his deep sense of humility, and his unwillingness to see another being suffer. And yet his deeds were tempered with wisdom.

I have shared with many of you the story of a visit to him soon after that being who was my wife had died and my heart was breaking. That being who I was, was injured on the way and my leg was broken. I knew that he had the ability to heal it. But in his wisdom he saw that my broken leg was not what needed healing. My heart was what needed healing. I was angry at him at first. I said, "I have to go home. I have children and sheep to be tended." "No," he said. "Your son can tend the sheep. Your neighbors and family can tend your children. You must stay here until you are healed." In my ignorance I thought he meant until my leg was healed and it felt to me that he was withholding his healing. But I was forced to remain there for some months, being tended lovingly, carried from place to place, fed, and my soul nourished, until that deep grief within me had healed and I was ready to go home and be both mother and father to my family.

He was not maudlin in his mercy. It was tempered with wisdom. But he did heal because he could not bear to see another suffer when it was within his power to alleviate that suffering.

The balance to the story is a tale of the Buddha. This is not a personal memory, but a story that has been handed to me and is known in the literature of Buddhist stories. A woman's young child died and she was heartbroken, as it was her only son. The Buddha was camped nearby with his followers. And some said to her, "He can help." So she carried the child there and said, "Lord, can you revive him?" The Buddha looked at this dead baby and said to the woman only, "I can help you. But first you must go out and find [a certain kind of spice that was familiar in that country in India]. You must bring me a pinch of this spice." "Oh, that's easy," said the woman. "But," said the Buddha, "there is one thing. It must come from a household that has not known death."

The woman was cheered by the prospect that she could help her dead son. She went out and knocked on a door. "Can I have some of [this kind of spice]?" "Oh, of course," they said. "But," she said, "it must come from a home that has not known death." "We're sorry," they said. "Our uncle died here last month." She knocked on the next door. "Of course you may have the spice." "But it must come from a house that has not known death. Have you known death?" "Yes," said the woman sadly. "Our daughter died here last week.". . . "Have you known death?" "Yes," the father died last year. . . . "Yes," the grand-mother died three years ago. . . . "Yes," the infant died in childbirth. . . . "Yes," the mother died in childbirth. . . . "Yes," the father drowned; and so on, door after door throughout the day until she finally under-stood that death is part of the continuum of life. We cannot change what is. We must open our heart to it and continue to move on.

As dusk fell she returned to the Buddha, with her tears dried and her heart open. She held her dead son one last time and bade farewell to him. And the Buddha helped her to bury him or to cremate him as the case may be. This woman then ordained to become a Buddhist nun and a follower of the Buddha's, that through her new wisdom she might share her understanding of the Way with others.

What is "merciful" here? Was it any less merciful to help this woman find an end to her suffering through teaching her about the continuum of life and death and the suffering of holding on to that which cannot be held on to? Perhaps the child's birth and death were offered simply as a gift to the mother to help her move through this learning. Who are we to judge that?

What I want you to see is that the path of mercy contains wisdom and the path of wisdom contains mercy. And yet, each predominates in one direction or the other. Those of you who are drawn toward the Christ as your spiritual master are drawn more directly toward these teachings of lovingkindness, mercy, and forgiveness. Those who are drawn more toward the Buddha as your spiritual master are drawn toward these teachings of wisdom tempered by mercy.

What does this mean in your own lives? Because each of you has strengths and weaknesses, it is easy to adhere to the strength and then hide the weakness, thus losing the opportunity to enrich yourselves and expand your path. Where there is firm adherence only to wisdom not tempered by mercy and compassion, is there some fear of that mercy or some fear of letting your heart speak for you and following the whispered messages of that heart? Where there is attachment only to the teachings of the heart, is there some fear, stemming from an awareness that the brain cannot lead and is only a tool, that if one moves into wisdom one will also move into the dictates of the conceptual mind?

Perhaps you swing to the opposite extreme at times. There may be some, who in past lives have misused the brain and followed its dictates while screening out the messages of the heart and who have now become so wary that they have swung to the opposite extreme, and vice versa.

In the fullness of your being as human, you are offered this beautiful mind/heart combination. They are one, not two. Both deep wisdom and the ability to love are offered you. May I challenge you to find the appropriate balance for yourselves and to see where fear blocks that balance?

I want to expand this heart/mind, wisdom/compassion talk by speaking a bit further about the relative and ultimate practices and the coming to this intersection of them. This is not quite the same intersection as wisdom and love. All relative practices are not heart practices and all ultimate practices are not wisdom practices. They are both a mixture of the two. But I want to make sure that you understand what I mean by relative versus ultimate practices.

You are faced with great suffering throughout your world. Those of you who are aware and openhearted are attuned to the suffering around you and have a deep desire to work to alleviate that suffering. This is the suffering of those who starve or are homeless or suffer great disease or hardship; or the sufferings of the Earth due to the polluted rivers and lakes, the dying forests, and the species of plants and animals endangered and facing extinction. You know that you must keep your heart open to this suffering and work in whatever ways you can to alleviate suffering. And so you become involved in these relative practices, both spiritual practices such as meditation and prayer, and quasi-spiritual practices such as volunteering your time to help others. When I say "quasi" I do not mean that it is any less a spiritual practice, only that one moves inward and one extends the energy out into the world. They are both important. Unless one moves deeply into the meditative space where one recognizes the emptiness of self in the doing and in the offering of one's energy, one can solidify self by one's very work to help others because there becomes a doer and a receiver. If I am helping you, we are separate. Can I serve you without trying to fix you and without any attachment to fixing you as long as we are separate?

It is the inward practices, especially meditation, that help cut through the solid "I" and that bring in the wisdom aspect that there is really no doer or receiver, that there is really nothing that needs to be done on the ultimate level. This cuts through and allows help to be given without helper or recipient.

Does not the helper benefit as much as the recipient? If I am starving and you give to me, of course you save my life. But what does my receiving your gift give to you? As long as you see yourself as the fixer, you solidify ego and prevent moving into the depth of wisdom. Or are you that being with deep wisdom and a closed heart that denies the reality of suffering on the relative plane, and thus refuses to help me? Can there be balance?

There are stories told in traditions where there is a deep belief in karma, of children who fall off of a boat and cannot swim. No one reaches out a hand to help them. The teaching is simply, "It is their karma." They flounder, scream, and drown. What kind of closed-hearted being can allow such suffering? What is the denial happening there?

Ultimately we are not responsible for one another, because there is no "one another." We are all one. But the wisdom-mind also sees that we are all always responsible for this one. And if an extension of this one is drowning, then its own hand must reach out to save it. Wisdom must always be tempered by compassion. Compassion must always be deepened by wisdom.

What is your own bias here? In which directions do you most need to open yourselves in order to best live this center of the cross of wisdom and compassion-mind or mercy, of love-mind and wisdom-mind, of relative reality and ultimate reality? Think of it as a cross with a small circle at the intersection. You may rest on the horizontal or vertical leg of the cross, but can you keep yourself within the circle?

I thank you for giving your thoughts to this, my dearest ones, and challenging yourselves as to how you may reside in that circle. I now pass the microphone to my brother/sister, beloved friend of Q'uo. That is all.

(Carla channeling)

Q'uo: Greetings in the love and in the light of the one infinite Creator. It is a great blessing to be allowed to blend our vibrations with yours and to be asked to share our thoughts with you. As always, we ask that our words be subjected to your personal powers of discrimination, for we are often in error and would not present ourselves as any final authority, but only as those with relatively more experience.

As the one known as Aaron has said, it is well to come to a self-awareness of how one's inner makeup is configured. Whether the way of the heart or the way of wisdom beckons more, each may be taken. Each intersects with the other at every turn. The difference between them is that of the two sides of one coin. And of this coin, one cannot have too much. Yet every day the supply is newly infinite, freshly minted in infinite intelligence and liberally sprinkled into every waking consciousness by the graceful hand of Spirit.

Your need for this manna of love and wisdom is yours due to the circumstance of the veil that descends upon those in the third density, leaving each seeker in a relatively dark and subtly lit environment that has been called the shadow of death. Yet still, the spirit within remains moonlit and the spirit's walk is one wherein virtue must be worked out carefully, at length, and with great patience. This is not unintended, but is specifically meant to be the case. For in the rough-and-tumble daily world in which you enjoy experience, innocent sleeping young-sters still play, unawakened to the beauty and mystery of the call to faith and service.

There is a time that recurs cyclically within each seeker, during which the seeker is plunged into a primary awareness of this moonlit landscape of the archetypical awakening mind, which is both mind and heart. These are desert times. During these times the bitterness may seem so great that there is no possibility of healing or redemption into innocence.

Yet these are the desert sands that scour away that very bitterness that has plunged the seeker into this period. The going down into the darkness and the experience of spiritual death, of profound and sudden death, and of slow and stealthy death, are rich, not only in pain but in the fertility of new birth.

Enlightenment begins in this so-called dark night of the soul. And as you, the awakened seeker, move through this moonlit time, you drop away pain or begin the process of dropping it away precisely in order that your dearest wish may be followed.

And as you emerge from this deep darkness, your new and trans-formed being is able to see more light, more beauty, more meaning, and more of love. Then the sunlight is again yours, for you are a new and innocent child. And it is your time to gambol and romp and rejoice with your brothers and sisters.

There is no one spiritual mood and no one best situation. Rather, the path wanders into the lightest as well as the most profoundly dark, into the most joy and increasing wisdom, and also into the most profound and sorrowful unknowing.

You have been forever and you shall be forever. And yet you are not only you. You are the love that sent you, as a spark of love, out into materialization that you might experience and process that experience with your own peculiar and unique distortions, creating your unique beauty and your unique harvest of experience.

How rich, then, is the Creator as it gathers more and more of experience into Itself, becoming more and more richly known to Itself. You cannot walk off of the spiritual path, for all experiences will be gratefully gathered by the one infinite Creator, who seeks to know Itself.

We would at this time turn the microphone to the one known as Aaron. We are those of Q'uo.

(The group pauses and joins together in song.)

(Barbara channeling)

Aaron: I want to attend now to some of the questions that were raised last night. These were especially referring to the catalysts of this earth plane and to the question, "How do we walk this path with love?"

There are two different issues here. One is, "What is love and what is fear?" And having determined what love is, how do we choose love? What pushes us into the distortion of fear, even though we recognize it as fear?

You cannot "should" yourself or force yourself into taking the path of love when fear feels overwhelming. It is natural to the humans that you wish to defend yourselves. Such defense is so often thought to be a movement of fear, but to act in care for the self may also be a movement of love. Thus, the question is not about what you do, so much as what is the primary force behind those acts or words? When you focus on the already present loving motivations, they will be reflected in the acts.

The ends do not justify the means of using force. If we are going to choose love, we must be consistent. Love is natural to you and becomes apparent when there is not fear.

You do not need to create love in yourselves. It is already there. Fear blocks it. We do not look, then, at these two paths, fear and love, and say, "I will choose love," even though we quake with fear. Rather, we say, "What is this fear?" and lovingly attend to the fear so it dissolves. And then love is natural and open. I am not suggesting that it will not still take courage and determination, commitment and energy, to choose love. But there is no force involved, just a loving aspiration.

You must, then, begin to see who you really are, that fear is an illusion and that you are Love by your very nature. When you penetrate through the illusion of fear, it self-destructs like a balloon popped by a dart. This is the dart of penetrating awareness, which sees the illusion of fear each time it manifests and refuses steadfastly to be caught in a dialogue with fear; and yet does not disdain that fear, but bows to it in respect for its presence and smiles to it, without dwelling in it or believing its stories.

So, how do we do this technically? There are so many possible areas that we could look at, such as relationships, work, and all the various paths through which your life leads you, that we would need weeks to explore it all.

I prefer to look at basic emotions that distort your clear seeing, to look at two specific emotions that seem to offer the greatest degree of distortion and to talk about how you may more skillfully work with these. You have a wide gamut of emotions, but they can basically be broken down into fear and love. Within fear there are two basic kinds of fear: that you will be hurt and that your needs will not be met. The fear that you might be hurt brings up emotions of anger at that which might hurt you. This is a kind of defense. The fear that your needs may not be met brings up greed, sometimes seen as jealousy or grasping anger and desire. Both are offshoots of fear.

Of course, there are many other emotions, and they each can be fit into different places. Grief is a mixture of love and fear. There is fear that your needs will not be met and that you will be hurt through this loss. There is also a sense of deep sorrow that grows out of love for that which has been lost. Part of grief is not fear, but an expression of the depth of your love. It does not manifest itself in wishing to hold on, but it is an expression of the depth of joy that was there in the connection with that which seems to be lost. So, we want to be careful not to pigeonhole too rigidly here, not to simply say, "This is love. This is fear." There is always a blending of the two.

Another kind of emotion, one that has been talked about here and about which we have written questions, is unworthiness. This is also some blending of fear and love. We were asked, "Is unworthiness genetic?" No. And yet, it is hereditary in a different way. It is, let us say, culturally conditioned and is especially prevalent in your society. Last year there was a gathering of western Buddhist teachers in India with the Dalai Lama. One of the teachers shared this story: The group was sitting around the table and one teacher asked, "What about those beings who despise themselves, who truly find themselves unworthy and inadequate?" (Remember these were all western teachers, the only easterners there being the Dalai Lama and his assistants.) The Dalai Lama was a bit puzzled. He said, "Do you mean people in mental hospitals?" The group of teachers turned and looked at one another. And the one who had asked the question said, "No, those who are sitting around this table."

Much of your sense of unworthiness is culturally conditioned. One would need to ask why—not only "Why does it happen in this culture?" but "Why did you choose to incarnate into a culture that is conditioned into the distortion of unworthiness?"

What is worthiness or unworthiness? You are divine. How could you possibly ever be unworthy? Unskillful at times, maybe; afraid or angry; a bit dull in your minds at times and creating illusory bound-aries for yourself—but unworthy? Where does this story come from?

On the other hand, one might also ask, "If there is no such thing as unworthiness, is there such a thing as worthiness?" There is no duality. Can there be one without the other? Ultimately there is no worthiness either. Worthiness is a meaningless concept because all beings are worthy. It is only your conceptual mind of duality that creates the concepts of worthy and unworthy in balance to one another, assigns yourself to one realm or the other, and assigns other beings to one realm or the other, often assigning yourself to the unworthy category and everybody else to the worthy category.

How did you move into this pattern of distorted illusion, and why? Let us explore some of the reasons behind it, perhaps as a way of providing some form of freedom from the ensnarement of the illusion.

Those of you who are old souls, which is true of all in this circle, have a very clear understanding of the Divine; of that perfect, unlimited light, which you may call the Eternal, the Absolute, God, or Q'uo's term, the one infinite Creator. It does not matter what you call it. The name is but a label for that which is not limited by the labels we give it. We each have an understanding of what we mean by that which I prefer to simply label God.

In this dark night of the soul, we see the perfection of that energy and our own seemingly futile attempts to reflect that perfection. We despair. And out of that despair arises a sense of unworthiness. We despair that we can never fully merge with that light and love toward which we so deeply yearn. We despair of our own self-perceived limits and fear our inability to transcend those limits, so that a sense of unworthiness seems almost to become a necessary part of our path. Why?

Well, on the ultimate plane there is no worthy or unworthy and never was. On the relative plane, you must come to know your worthiness. And one of the best tools that can be offered to aid that learning is the pain of feeling unworthiness.

Here I am asking Barbara if I may use her as an example. At one time she spent some weeks at a meditation retreat in which she was looking at the residual feelings of unworthiness within herself. I asked her to use this analytic approach when a thought arose, which approach I introduced to you yesterday.

For example, simply seeing the being next to her immersed in meditation, the thought of her own unworthiness arose. There were many senior dharma teachers at this retreat, by which I would mean highly experienced teachers in her tradition. So, the first few days as she sat next to these famous teachers, there arose in her mind a sense of comparing herself. And then she would look at that thought: *What is this thought? Where did it come from? From my old-mind patterns of unworthiness.* And then I would ask her to ask herself, "In this moment, sitting here, all of us in this room, all seventy of us, is there anyone here who is unworthy? No. Am I unworthy? No. Have I ever been unworthy? No. Then what is this arising of a sense of unworthiness?" And in asking that question she could see that it was old-mind's way of handling a sense of separation or aloneness, perhaps as an arising of anger because she could not hear or some other discomfort, and as a way of old-mind's explaining it to itself. It was a way of dealing with her pain and a story of the conditioned mind. The story seemed to allow her space from the direct experience of some pain. She could see that it had been more comfortable to simply put on the cloak "unworthy" than to look at the awareness of the pain. Unworthiness became an escape from that which was more painful to be with than the sense of unworthiness. It was very clear to her each time she looked that in that moment, looking with bare perception of the sense experiences of that moment, unworthiness was illusion. And yet, it yawned before her as a giant chasm.

As she looked, she could see in past lives and in this life the millions of times that she had enacted that process. She began to see it as likened to a bare plain, just slightly inclined, onto which drops of rain fell. A drop of rain that could not soak into the ground ran off, creating the faintest scratch in the earth. The next drop of rain hitting in the vicinity of that scratch ran into the scratch, carving it a tiny bit deeper. Ten drops and you have an eighth of an inch of earth worn away. A thousand drops is followed by a million drops and then a river, and eventually the Grand Canyon.

It is all an illusion that is heightened by each occasion of buying into the illusion. When it was clearly seen as the illusion, that there has never been unworthiness and that in this moment there is not unworthiness, and when it was further seen that the process of clear seeing was not one of an hour or a day but of week after week of deep meditation and constant mindfulness during the process of this retreat, then suddenly something clicked into place: "This is all illusion. There has never been worthiness or unworthiness. I don't have to be caught in this anymore. It is just habit and has nothing to do with reality. Skillful or unskillful might have to do with reality. Patient or impatient and selfish or generous may reflect the actual movements in our hearts. But were any past aspects of myself unworthy?"

You must work with this process over and over and over, each time cutting through the illusion of unworthiness and seeing how it has arisen. There must be a courageous readiness to deal with those emotions that unworthiness has masked. (I will get into that idea in a moment.) There must be a readiness to give up unworthiness, which means touching on the deeper pain that unworthiness has hidden. The reward is the awareness that there is no worthiness or unworthiness; there is only God.

What happened for Barbara, then, was that as wisdom cut through the illusion and as mercy tempered the pain that had led to grasping at the illusion, the thoughts of worthy and unworthy simply ceased to arise. The habit was broken.

I am not suggesting that she will never experience a sense of unworthiness again. But after she left that retreat, each time that sense of unworthiness has arisen, it has been clearly and immediately seen as an illusion. This has been self-liberation, whereby *pop!* goes that balloon. She is able to come back again to the clear perception that transcends worthiness and unworthiness, and then to ask, "What emotions have given rise to this illusion?" and to tend lovingly to those emotions.

Let us, then, look at what unworthiness does mask. There are many possibilities, and I cannot cover the full range of them. I want to speak to two of the most common. One of the main catalysts that leads many of you into a sense of unworthiness is parental neglect or other abuse in your early childhoods. This does not need to be monumental abuse. Even the baby that is loved may be greeted by a grouchy parent at 3:00 a.m. The baby may feel the difference between that parent that greets it with love and dries it and feeds it, and that parent that stumbles in yawning, feeling a deep irritation because it is exhausted and its sleep is interrupted. The baby will feel the withholding of love at that time. Feeling the anger directed at it, the baby will often return a sense of anger.

So, we are not just talking about what you term abuse, but the distortion that occurs with the infant's or child's anger. The child is helpless and fully dependent on the adult. It needs to form a bond of love with that adult who parents it, singular or plural. It learns early that when it responds to the adult with anger, the adult, who was often less than fully cognizant of its own reactions, reacts with anger.

Returning to the child, it needs to be loved. That is its overriding need. So, it quickly picks up the messages, "What can I do to be loved? If I play your game, you'll love me?" That game varies from family to family. In the worse cases, the child must allow itself to be a recipient of real abuse and the only way it can do that is by denying its own rage. It learns that its own rage runs contrary to its overriding need to be loved or to receive an imitation of love. How does it deal with that rage? If the child is right and expresses that rage, it casts itself out of the boundaries of the adult's acceptance; therefore, the adult must be right.

Unworthiness becomes the tool by which a child suppresses the rage. It tells itself, "I deserved this abuse" because the alternative is unthinkable: "I did not deserve this abuse; therefore, this adult is wrong and I must contradict this adult, putting myself out of the reach of its acceptance and love." The child simply lacks the strength to do that.

So, unworthiness becomes the armor over the rage. Even in those cases of nonabuse, the same pattern is true. But it is harder to see. The child does feel rage toward that adult and it is usually not permitted the expression of that rage. It is told, "Your anger is bad." That is a pattern and a distortion of your culture.

When you are feeling unworthiness, then, a helpful tool for working with that unworthiness is to simply ask yourself *What might I be feeling now if I were not feeling unworthy? Can I give myself permission to get in touch with that emotion? Can I forgive myself for feeling that emotion? I do not need to fling my rage at another and I do not need to deny it. If I was seriously abused and I feel rage at that abuse, it is okay to feel that rage. It is not unspiritual. It is just feeling rage.*

You cannot get rid of rage by denying its presence. The open admission of your emotions is the beginning of allowing yourself to transcend those emotions and to cease your ownership and identification with them; to begin to view them simply as passing thoughts that need no special reaction, only compassion for the pain they cause.

If you were not seriously abused, you may have learned unworthiness for other reasons. Perhaps you were raised by a very judgmental parent who always said, "This is bad. That is bad." Well, that is a kind of abuse, perhaps less serious than sexual molestation or hitting. But it is still a kind of abuse. Or perhaps you were lovingly raised by a nonjudgmental parent, but there was still rage in the self and shame about that rage.

Another reason for the arising of a sense of unworthiness is the fear, "Will my needs be met?" teamed with the solidifying of the ego-self, the arising of jealousy or greed, and the harsh self-judgment that arises when one experiences that jealousy or greed. This, too, has been learned from the adult who said, "You shouldn't be selfish. You should share." Is there anybody here who did not hear that as a child? Yes, of course, it would be good if we could all share. But to force on the child, "You shouldn't be selfish," is to tell the child that its feelings are bad. How much better if the wise adult can tell the child, "I know you're afraid that your needs won't be met. I know you feel anger and fear about giving this." Then, the child can make the decision, with support to move beyond its fear and without judging its own fear.

But this has not been the pattern of your culture. Again, why? Because you have all chosen this sense of unworthiness as a catalyst to your growth. You have all chosen birth into this culture and into its particular distortions. You choose the conditions for birth that will offer you the best opportunities for learning. You do not choose incarnation for comfort and convenience. Yes, it is painful. So, what else is new? Are you here to learn or are you not here to learn? You are not incarnate to stop feeling emotions, but to find equanimity with those emotions and compassion for all beings who have emotions.

Instead of waging war with those incarnate experiences into which you have moved, can you begin to embrace them? They are not garbage to be gotten rid of. They are perhaps the waste products to be turned back into the soil to become the nutrients for growth. They are not garbage, but compost. How can you make your sense of unworthiness into compost instead of trying to throw it out? How can you transmute your anger so that it becomes the catalyst for compassion?

So, you have heard the parent or adult say over and over, "You should share. You should not be greedy." But greed arises. Desire arises. Here is where we again move to the tools of meditation and the nurturing of wisdom-mind. Awareness begins to see how greed and desire arise, thereby cutting through the identification with greed or desire as "mine" and allowing them to arise and dissolve without dwelling on them or owning them. This wisdom becomes one of the nutrients for the growth of compassion toward the human that keeps getting caught in patterns of greed or jealousy. Gradually you cease to hate yourself when negative emotions arise. They cease to become a catalyst for unworthiness, but become a reminder for compassion.

I could speak to each of you in this room for an hour or more about how these principles apply to your specific situations. We, of course, do not have the time for that, nor is it necessary. You are each very capable of understanding it for yourselves. Please know how fully you are supported in this work. It is truly the work for which you took birth and will lead you to the healing for which you took birth. I would pass the microphone now to Q'uo. That is all.

(Carla channeling)

Q'uo: Greetings once again in love and light. We ask your cooperation at this time.

(The group is asked to shout, "Ha! Ha! Ha!")

Group: Ha! Ha! Ha!

Q'uo: We thank each for the instant rise in energy.

How does this organ of reason you call the brain work, which you so desire to work to your spiritual benefit? We have described the birth of consciousness of light within as the little Christ-child, nurtured in the manger of your heart. Now let us describe this same situation using other ways of description.

The analogy of the computer is also fruitful. You see, you are not one but two life-forms that cooperate to offer this rich experience you call the incarnation. The first creature is your physical vehicle. This instinctually driven creature is at one with all that there is, for it is a second-density being. Each cell within your physical vehicle vibrates with the love and light of the infinite One, and its instinctual desires are for all energies to harmonize.

The intellectual organ of this creature is driven by distinctions, the basic program being very much the 0/1 binary operations of the dynamics betwixt the characteristics. The mind, which you could realize as a biocomputer, has its priorities. These priorities are fixed by the computer within, based upon experience.

Of the complete range of catalysts that assault the physical senses, perhaps 2 percent of these sense impressions are used first. These sense impressions that have been given priority have to do with survival, comfort, and finally what may loosely be called preferences or happiness. As you gain experience, these priorities may settle and change somewhat. However, they remain logic-driven.

You carry within you what could be called an operating system that works only with expanded memory. Its programs are deeper than the programs of the biocomputer operating system of your second-density creature.

Within the programs of this operating system lie archetypical structures that only flash into the normal biocomputer like the haunting, with a melody that can so easily be missed. Yet within this expanded operating system's programs lie truth and virtual reprogramming aids that do far more to reprioritize the biocomputer than all the earnest study and effort you can galvanize to life within your increasingly reluctant self.

Now, how to trigger—this instrument would say, boot—this expanded operating system? Each of you knows the answer. It is triggered by your meditation and contemplation. The key is silence.

We ask each to become aware of the preciousness of the moments of silence you carve for yourself out of the all-too-preciously-short material you call time. It is self-loving, indeed, to create these moments of touching into that bottomless well of silent listening, into which is poured light without measure, and from which you may drink until you have no thirst.

The expanded memory's gift is at once unique and utterly intimate, expressing your deepest authenticity, as well as being completely impersonal. For, just a tiny bit beneath the surface of your uniqueness, lies your universality. This is the second life-form that you now seek to nurture and that now seeks to nurture you.

For even from the cradle, this Christ-child reaches out and loves you, for the Creator loves first. Your love of any entity, including the Creator, is a reflection. It is love reflected in love.

How this baby consciousness loves to love! Let the cradle of your heart, then, be made soft and your breathing deep as you rock this consciousness to more and more vigorous life within you. This is the being that marries, even melds with this second-density creature to produce that unique being, the human—which is both of the earth, born and dying; and of the universe, loved and loving forever.

This unlikely combination is perfectly suited to beholding a life and to assigning increasingly meaningful values to the impressions received as you go through that life.

The biocomputer is very useful in going to the grocery, in attending to the errands, in becoming a scholar, and in furnishing you with the knowledge necessary to begin and to continue ways of making the living and taking care of personal responsibilities that you have chosen to undertake.

At the same time, the sense impressions received by this biocomputer are also useful in expanded ways to one who has become aware of this expanded Christ Consciousness that has sprung into life within your flesh, so that you become also a spiritual animal complete.

Even within the flesh, this transcendence is utterly complete. And the energies that are finite to systems run by logic may become infinite as the larger system is more and more accessed, until it is up and fully running, fully integrated into the biocomputer.

In addition to the use of silence, we encourage each to examine the self for its gifts, whether they be of the arts or the sciences or any gift whatsoever. For all things may be used to spiritual good in those whose gifts are dedicated to the infinite One.

And lastly, as the expanded system becomes comfortable within, and when things begin to be seen with new priorities, that long and level plain that is the routine day may begin increasingly to be perceived in more and more of an upraised and joyful posture, until this level plain becomes full of the foothills and amazingly craggy mountains that are so interesting, and that so rest the weary eye.

Going to the place of employment, working through the day, coming home to do the chores, and putting the weary self to rest may well be all of the room you need in which to create the accurate perception of heaven with all of its glorious houses and mansions.

Here is high romance as well as greatest difficulty. Here is light inexpressible as well as spiritual moonlight. And as you walk the paths of your days, you may move up and down the scales of perception with increasing ease as you begin to find the pure freedom of that logic that transcends distinction and partakes more and more of the values of love.

We would speak more upon this in the final session. For now, we leave this instrument in the love and in the light of the one infinite Creator.

Session 22

Weekend 6, Part 5 of 5

(This session was preceded by a period of tuning and meditation.)

Barbara: I'm going to share my tuning process out loud and then invite you to join me in it, substituting whatever differences you wish in order to make it personally appropriate for you.

Moving attention to the breath, coming to center, to that level of awareness that is aware of awareness itself ... not caught in any of it, just watching it come and go, resting in that space of Pure Awareness ... feeling this that I call myself connected to all that is, opening, expanding outward, dropping away boundaries, breathing myself out to all that is, and inviting it back in to me ... I offer my intention for the session: to manifest my energy as purely as I can in service to all beings for the alleviation of suffering and toward the liberation of all beings. I invite in spirit that would like to speak through me in harmony with that intention.

Feeling Aaron's energy, I challenge it: "Are you that which I have come to know as Aaron?" "Yes." "Do you come with a principle of love in service to all beings?" "Yes." "Do you come as a disciple of that which is an embodiment of truth for me, which is that energy that I have come to know as Jesus, the Christ?" "Yes."

(Barbara channeling)

Aaron: With that collecting of our energies and mutuality of motivation and commitment, I return the microphone to my brother/ sister/friend Q'uo, who wishes to offer you some closing thoughts. Then Q'uo will return the microphone to me to answer some of your questions and to offer my own closing. And finally we will join together in a very brief and simple Sufi dance. That is all.

(Carla channeling)

Q'uo: It is time, now, to greet you for the last time in this weekend of sessions of working in the love and in the light of the one infinite Creator.

We who are of the principle of Q'uo cannot express to you how grateful we are for this extended and exhilarating opportunity to share our humble thoughts with you. Your service to us is extreme, for as we teach you, we learn from how you hear us. And this represents our means of growing in love and service to the infinite Creator.

We of the Confederation of Angels and Planets in the Service of the Infinite Creator have been called the Brothers and Sisters of Sorrow. For we were inspired to come to this planetary influence because of the great cry of pain and sorrow that you have been sending out during especially these past two hundred years, and more especially the past fifty.

We have seen how your factories and technology have encouraged in your culture the opportunities for leisure, through the blessing of time that is given beyond that time in which you must make your daily living. We have seen how this same factory and technology-driven cultural system has thrown up for you a culture that attempts always to distract and to trivialize the day-to-day leisure. This is, indeed, in its own kind of balance.

(The last sentence of this paragraph did not record.)

We do not condemn, nor suggest that you condemn, technology or factories, or your media programs, newspapers, magazines, fashion, and all the culture based upon artificially produced renown. But we suggest to you that you are in possession of free will in all matters. We encourage you to make judicious use of all your time, all your space, and all your relationships, leavening all earnestness with high spirits and the light of sarcasm, irony, puns, and bad jokes. Be reckless with your laughter and generous with your sarcastic comments. The seemingly trivial moments of self-parody and parody of others are like yeast, lightening the whole of the texture of your living.

We hope that you may practice the art of the spiritual vocation, realizing that whatever you do in your living to create the energy of money may or may not be an obviously spiritual task. Yet this is irrelevant to the living of the spiritual vocation. For within you is the heart's eye, the eye of that great consciousness that you are nurturing into strong and vigorous life during this incarnation. This eye sees with care and compassion, moistening the dry duty with the living waters of spiritual significance and context. The spiritual vocation is that which puts into a context all of one's experiences within incarnation.

Do not attempt to haul yourself into some discipline where you will be spiritual, but simply attempt in each present moment to be yourself and to respond as yourself, not being defeated by the thoughts of "I should ... I ought to ..." but looking within for where the love is and finding that thread opening to more of that material within, so that you are constantly finding new springs in the topography of your mind.

The Creator lies before your face and in your face. You open your eyes and see the creation of the Father. You gaze in your fellow human's eyes and see the Creator. It is a wonderful masked ball. We hope you enjoy the many dances of life.

And lastly, we wish you to know with assurance, beyond any doubt, that we are with those who call to us, not to channel as through this instrument, for that would be an impingement, but to be as the carrier wave of love so that you need never be completely alone.

(The remainder of this session did not record.)

WEEKEND 7

We returned to Kentucky a year later; again, autumn colors embellished the landscape. This was our largest group to date. Some were sleeping in the house; a few were housed in local hotel rooms. Many people came from Michigan, but some came from as far away as Toronto. Many of this group were aware that they are wanderers, and had come to explore this topic.

Wanderers are mentioned often in the Confederation channeling. Wanderers are those who have chosen to incarnate on Earth from elsewhere in the universe in order to help lighten the consciousness of Planet Earth at this time—the dawning of the fourth density. Thus, they come to do service. And they incarnate because it is the only way that they can enter into the harvest[55] at the end of third density, in order to graduate into fourth density, in a personal way. According to the Confederation channelings, there are millions of wanderers here, and they have in common the feeling of loneliness and isolation because the vibration in third density is different from what they remember of their home density. It is at gatherings like this one that

---

[55] Q'uo uses the term "harvest" to speak of the situation of those souls ready to graduate from the earth plane (or third-density) experience into fourth-density positive or negative polarity.

wanderers often feel "at home" for the first time as they meet others of like mind.

Session 23

(This session was preceded by a period of tuning and meditation.)

Group question: What is the true definition of a wanderer?

(Barbara channeling)

Aaron: My greetings and love to you all. I would simply like to ask that as a group you offer the intention that the work of this group is for the benefit of all beings.

Each of you has your own areas of pain. It is fine that a part of this motivation is to alleviate your own pain. But it is important that you not become stuck there. Thinking of all beings who wander in darkness and confusion, may the work of this group be a lantern in that darkness, helping all beings to find their way. May each one's energy help to brighten that light. That is all.

(Pause)

It has been decided that I will begin. We begin with the question, "What is a wanderer?" I heard you ask before, "If I am of a higher density and come back to Earth, what is my role here? Am I both teacher and learner? Why am I demoting myself or accepting demotion?" My dear ones, it is not demotion. Let us get this concept straight. You are in an open-classroom school. Each of you begins as what I call a spark of God, which is just a small bit of that energy and light moving into self-awareness. I will not explain how you move into self-awareness. Simply, it happens. You perceive the illusion that this self that is aware is separate from that of which it is aware, and you begin to believe, "God is out *there!*" And thus begins your journey. The

381

only way out is through,[56] which is through the illusion of separation. This illusion is not a burden that you must carry, but a gift. Would you remain that small spark forever, or would you blossom into a brilliant sun in your own right? The passage must involve a journey.

That first self-awareness is part of the gift. At some point awareness notices itself being aware. And with that first notice there is a shift. There is something that feels itself to be aware. At that point awareness chooses a direction in which to begin evolution. I emphasize *begin*, because nothing is ever fixed. You do not move into a path and stay on that one limited path until the eighth density. There is always choice. Some of you will choose material planes and some will choose nonmaterial planes. I will explain later in this weekend some of the factors in that choice. For now, it is sufficient to know that there is a choice.

There are innumerable planes, both material and nonmaterial. In some planes you have only spirit and mental bodies. In other planes there may also be an emotional and, if it is a material plane, a physical body. The earth plane is the only present material plane that has a foundation of positive energy and love, and in which all four bodies are brought together. As such, it is a very powerful experience.

Time is not the factor that leads one into the emphatic learning experience of the earth plane, but rather a deep aspiration to learn. Some beings choose to move into that earth plane immediately. Others, for one reason or another, are led in different directions. Later in the weekend we will talk about some of the material and some of the nonmaterial planes where beings evolve.

What is a wanderer on the earth plane? As simply as I can put it, it is a being that has begun its evolution on a plane other than the earth plane and at some point in its learning has made the decision to incarnate on Earth. It may have been in a physical form before on other material planes, or it may have existed previously only on nonmaterial planes.

---

[56] Robert Frost expressed a similar thought in his poem "A Servant to Servants," in saying, "The best way out is always through." Frost, "A Servant to Servants," in *North of Boston* (New York, NY: Henry Holt, 1915).

To say material and nonmaterial, in itself, is a bit confusing. Light is energy, so one tends to think of the light planes as nonmaterial. But all material substance is made up of bits of energy or molecules of energy. What we are speaking of here is simply the degree of tightness or cohesion of those molecules. At a certain point we call it solid and maintain the illusion of that solidity.

You are not solid. You only think you are solid. It is the illusion that establishes a material body. Thus, the difference between the material plane and the light plane is less in the form itself than in your belief that the form is what you are. All of you are simply energy and light with enough density of molecules that you may become convinced of your form. At a certain level, the physical and emotional bodies are illusions. They are the gifts of the incarnation.

Moving into Earth incarnation, you become actors in a play. The unprepared actor who walks onto the stage says to the audience of which it is also a part, "This is illusion. It is just a play and not real life." That actor deprives the audience of the opportunity of learning from the script or from the play. The actor must believe in the play if the audience is to feel the meaning with its heart. Yet that actor must not be lost in the illusion to the point that it turns its back to the audience and forgets that it is a character in the play.

This balance between relative and ultimate reality is what allows the deepest learning on the earth plane. Some incarnate beings become lost in relative reality and blind to ultimate reality. Others find it very difficult to stay in the body and live the relative-plane experience. Wanderers have an edge in this respect, because you have dwelt on other planes on which there was no veil of illusion. Many wanderers, then, are able to penetrate both realities. The difficulty many of you find is that there is some aversion to the illusion or some attachment to resting in that ultimate reality, which is so spacious and joyful.

A helpful tool in learning how to more fully enter the incarnation is to understand why you came. Each being that moves to the earth plane is both teacher and learner. This is true of every being, not just the wanderer but also those who move directly from that first self-awareness into the earth plane. Even those small sparks are teachers, which I will explain at a later time.

The wanderer is not set apart, then, in being both teacher and learner. This is true for every being. What more clearly sets the wanderer apart is the clarity that it has entered the illusion. This clarity may manifest simply as the awareness, "I came here for a reason. I don't know what it is, but I came for a reason." Eventually, every being breaks through the veil, wanderer and nonwanderer alike, and awakens to the spiritual truth of its being.

The wanderer is far less likely to be lost in forgetting. It is far more likely to feel a sense of frustration and confusion, and to ask *Who am I, and why am I here?*

I said that every wanderer—every being, but we speak here of wanderers—is both teacher and learner. I also said at the start that this whole process of evolution, these eight densities, is an ungraded classroom. On the earth plane there are clear distinctions between first, second, and third density. At present, when you graduate from third density you cease to incarnate on the earth plane.

There are some planes where third-density experience is minimal. The lessons for each plane remain the same. The foundations of faith and love support the learning of wisdom and compassion in fourth and fifth density, but they are not necessary to that learning. The process can be reversed. Some of you, for example, at some period evolved on a nonmaterial plane in which there was essentially an open classroom with third, fourth, and fifth grades. The material was learned in whatever order one was ready to learn. There is no upper limit to how much faith, love, wisdom, or compassion can be learned. This school offers these lessons. That school offers those lessons. If you wish to study music and your school has no orchestra, you join the band or choir. You may still wish to go somewhere else to learn to play the violin.

Thus, some of you evolved on planes where you moved into deeper lessons of wisdom and compassion before fully penetrating the lessons of faith and love. You learned much that could be brought as gifts to the earth plane, and each developed special skills. Feeling stuck in some way, you made the decision to more fully enter the illusion through human incarnation. Another way to phrase this is that your karma drew you here. Because you learned to play in a band and sing in a choir does not put you ahead of your neighbor. You simply have a different background. You have highly refined certain skills and understandings. There is still much that you need to learn or you would not be here. There are very few beings in the history of the Earth's evolution who have incarnated only to serve. And even those few, of course, have also learned. The difference—here I think of such a one as Jesus—is that this teacher did not need to come to the earth plane for his own evolution. Being here, of course he learned.

I would suggest a figure of 98 percent of wanderers need to understand something for their own learning and choose the earth plane as catalyst for that understanding. The other 2 percent is comprised of beings who are fully evolved, usually into high sixth density, and who incarnate simply with the desire to serve and to return with fourth- and fifth-density beings. They are past the need to incarnate. For those who come seeking learning, the third-density lessons could be learned elsewhere. But because there is something they could teach on this plane and they could learn the lessons as well, they might as well come here.

The sixth-density being has completely shed the emotional body and is not attached to the mental body. It understands the mental body to be a tool. This is the being that has no need of the teachings of the incarnate experience, but will wisely make use of the teaching when offered that opportunity.

Those that come as wanderers are most likely to be of third or fifth density. Fourth density is occupied with its group learning experiences and is less likely to move back into incarnation, although it may occasionally choose to do so. The lower sixth-density wanderer has shed the emotional body, but it may still have some attachment to the mental body. This being will be helped to release this attachment through its incarnate experience. Only the upper sixth-density energy is completely free of the illusion of ownership of the mental body in making the skillful and loving decision to incarnate solely as servant. As I said above, it will also learn.

I want to emphasize, then, that the wanderer may be highly evolved in some areas. Metaphorically speaking, an outstanding French horn player with great understanding of musical theory still must learn the correct hand position to hold the bow or to place the fingers on the violin. He or she brings to the incarnation an advanced skill for which a need is perceived. For example, a wanderer of our acquaintance who is in his first human incarnation is what you might term a computer wizard. He is offering skills and understandings gained on other planes, and for which it was clear the Earth was ready. There are two ways to bring those teachings to Earth. One is that they be channeled. The other is for a being to incarnate into human form and teach. Neither way is better than the other.

I have no need to return in incarnation to the earth plane. This is not to say I would not learn in incarnation. But I have no need, so I teach through an instrument. This friend of whom I speak was drawn to the idea of incarnation because it was clear that he had lessons that could well be learned on this plane. He has incarnated now, rather than fifty years ago, because now the earth plane is ready for what he offers.

In summary, a wanderer is a being who has evolved on other planes up to a certain point of high second density or beyond. Beings below that level of density are not yet evolved enough to make the decision to move into the earth plane. Wanderers are beings of high second density or beyond, including third, fourth, fifth, or sixth density, who make the decision to move into the illusion of the earth plane to teach and to learn. That they thus choose, indicates that they are spiritually awakened—not fully so, but enough to choose. Regardless of what density they have been, as soon as they move into incarnation they are third density and they are fully human. They may think they do not wish to be third density here on Earth, once they are here and wake up here to the fact of their decision. But some higher wisdom within them has agreed to it. Whatever skills they may have had, whatever wisdom and understanding, there are still compelling reasons why they have chosen incarnation. There are necessary areas of learning. We have barely touched the surface. I lay this before you as background.

I wish at this point to pass the microphone to my brother/sister/friend of Q'uo, that they may offer continued thoughts on what I have presented. As always, it is a great joy to share this teaching. That is all.

(Carla channeling)

Q'uo: Greetings and blessings to each in the love and in the light of the one infinite Creator.

May we thank each for calling us to your group. The privilege of blending our vibrations with your own as this circle sits in meditation is great. We encourage each to discriminate in choosing those thoughts that may seem to be of interest and of value to you. These thoughts and opinions are our service and our gift to you. We make many errors and are not infallible. Consequently, it is well that each lay aside those thoughts of ours that are not recognized as a portion of your personal truth, for we would not be a stumbling block to you in your seeking.

This instrument knows a song, "I Wonder as I Wander,"[57] and each of you has wandered into this precise situation, wondering, seeking, hoping, and yearning for love, for truth, for beauty, and for peace. We, too, have wandered. We seek with fervent hope the truth receding before us always and infinitely.

Each age, each culture has its wandering spirits. Within the framework of your present civilization, the scope of wanderers may be seen to have been extended, as the consciousness of the vast universe as native land and home becomes more and more a portion of the cultural ethos or setting of mind. Once, the wanderer was one who literally walked, being upon a path of seeking and moving from one wise

---

[57] John Jacob Niles, "I Wonder as I Wander," Appalachian folk song collected in *Songs of the Hill Folk* (New York, NY: G. Schirmer, 1933).

teacher to another. Within your present experience, the wandering is often that only of the mind or of the heart and not of the weary feet.

As the days of your millennium grow short, the seeking and hungering for truth has increased, activating a great process of transformative birthing. Each who seeks may now rest in the knowledge that he is no longer alone, for many awaken now to wonder. And in that wondering, in that searching—first intrigued, then fascinated, and finally transformed—the nascent seeker of truth arises from the peaceful condition of acceptance of consensus reality, shakes the dust of sleep from foot and eye, and starts the journey, the wandering, and the leaving of one home that is no longer home. Upon this dusty path lie oh, so many marvelous and frightening events! Adventure is the companion of the wanderer. Joy and sorrow aplenty rest within its quiver.

What is the definition of "wanderer"? Beneath all specific details, the wanderer is one upon a journey without an ending, seeking a home in a land where there is no home, and sailing upon a sea that has no port and no land, but only infinite voyaging.[58] Upon this ocean, the rudder that stabilizes and steers the ship is the spirit within. Within this inner heart or spirit lies home. How to skillfully move through this vast ocean of sense experience is always hidden within the very air you breathe, and within that which you hear and sense and think. To the seeker who pays attention come myriad clues and cues. Listen! Hark! The call has gone out.

There are many beings with each of you, hoping and wishing to serve by strengthening each servant of the light. When each goes into that inner sanctum in prayer, in meditation, and in contemplation, we ask each to rest in the knowledge that those who seek to serve the infinite Creator wait to support and nurture by sharing vibrations within

---

[58] The reader may wish to know of the poem by Walt Whitman entitled "Aboard at a Ship's Helm." This poem suggests a journey of infinite wandering in its last verse, which reads, "But O the ship, the immortal ship! O ship aboard the ship! / Ship of the body, ship of the soul, voyaging, voyaging, voyaging." Justin Kaplan, ed., *Whitman: Poetry and Prose* (New York, NY: Literary Classics of the United States, Inc., 1996).

meditation, by sharing that seeker's own meditative energies. We have no complex scheme to offer you so that you may know more about yourselves. We are here as companions in this wandering. We, too, seek and hope and wander still.

We thank this instrument and this group for asking for our service. We look forward to working with your queries throughout this series of sessions. We salute our brother Aaron and once again bless each of you. How we love you, you who are in the fog, in the mist, wondering, "Is any of this worthwhile? What is this for?" Thank you most heartily for your attention.

We leave each of you in the love and in the light of the infinite Creator. We are known to you as those of the principle of Q'uo. Adonai.

(Barbara channeling)

Aaron: I will be brief. Time is an illusion but your energy is not. The spiritual energy and love that you bring to this session is very high, but the physical bodies are tired. I wish only to offer a metaphor suggested by Q'uo's speaking of the mist that beclouds your journey.

Last month Barbara spent several days on a canoe trip in a very remote wilderness chain of lakes. In early morning's light, she emerged from her tent each morning and found the lake covered with such a dense mist that one could not see beyond eight or ten feet. This was a big lake, perhaps eight miles long and a mile across. She found much joy paddling out into the mist where she sat in her canoe and meditated, drifting in that opacity. There was no sense of direction. Since she had only visual balance, even up and down lost meaning. Except for her weight sitting in the bottom of that canoe, there were no visual cues at all. She experimented, first paddling out into the lake with some vigor, then stopping and sitting, looking around, and seeing the slight arising of fear when all was obscured around her. She knew she was safe. There were no motorboats on this lake to run her over. If for some reason the fog did not lift, she could call out for help and one of her sons would come in another canoe. Knowing she was safe, she found it wonderful to rest in this illusion of total obscuration. She found much parallel to the illusion of incarnation, with the sense *I don't know where I'm going. Can that be okay? Can I just rest here and enjoy the wonder of watching the mist rise off the water?*

As the canoe drifted in total silence, occasionally it drifted into the field of a loon, duck, or goose, as there were many waterfowl on this lake. Since Barbara does not hear, she had no auditory warning that their presence was immediate until they entered that ten-foot circle around her and she could see them. At first there were fears, such as, "What if I drift into something?" Slowly fear was relaxed and she thought, "I am safe. I don't need to see far ahead or far behind. In this moment I am safe and the wonders of the universe will unfold right here in this small circle of vision." What intense joy she felt as fear relaxed and she allowed herself to be fully present in this small circle where the illusion was penetrated and where the water and mist met.

She found that each morning as the sun rose, it burned off the mist and the circle of clarity expanded. But it took several hours before the sun got high enough to do this. She watched herself grasping at that clarity at first, wanting the mist to rise, and wanting to be able to see. And then as days passed, she let go of that desire and found that she could be present with the mist without hurrying it away. Can you hurry it? Can you force the sun to rise? When the sun finally got high enough, the mist quickly burned off. Within a quarter hour, the horizon expanded all the way to the shore, with mist still dwelling at the treetops but the lake now visible.

I ask you each to draw this metaphor into your own lives. Part of your incarnation is agreement to this veil. It is wonderful that you come here to seek answers for yourselves and all beings. I deeply honor you for that. But I ask you to ask yourselves, can you metaphorically sit in the bottom of this canoe and trust that the mist will rise when it is ready? I ask you to trust your lives and not to struggle in fear within the illusion that is meant to teach you.

You also wish to penetrate the illusion but not to deny the illusion. This relative reality *is* illusion. Those of you who are wanderers tend to want to deny that illusion, to return to shore, and to return home with a clarity. But you entered the illusion with your free will. And with great wisdom you opened your heart to the illusion and asked to become teachers and learners in that illusion. Trust that illusion, my dear ones.

I echo here Q'uo's statement: I am not infallible. What I offer you comes from my heart and I offer it in loving service. If it, in any way, is not harmonious with your own deepest truth, please put it aside. My deepest love to each of you and my gratitude that you have joined together for this teaching, learning, and sharing.

May I ask you, during whatever meditation you may enter tonight or in the morning, will you literally visualize yourself in that canoe? Note the arising of fear as your canoe moves away from land and you cannot see. Sit there in the bottom of that canoe, arms and paddle at rest, and allow whatever drifts into your presence to be there, neither grasping nor pushing away. Sit with this simple reflection: *How can I more fully open my energy to the incarnation, complete with its illusion?* That is all. I return you to Q'uo, should Q'uo wish to speak.

(Q'uo recognizes the group's fatigue and the session is ended.)

Session 24

(This session was preceded by a period of tuning and meditation.)

Group questions: What can a wanderer do if he or she wants to remember lessons? Are there preplanned services? Is there a difference between lessons for a wanderer and for third-density entities? How do we connect to the earth and ground ourselves, instead of using only our higher energy centers?

(Carla channeling)

Q'uo: Greetings in the love and in the light of the one infinite Creator. We are most privileged to be with you this morning and have enjoyed those humorous and yet profound considerations that your group has offered. Truly, for those who seek to serve, the way becomes far less severe and difficult when there are companions upon that dusty path. To serve together is to serve far more ably and effectively than each one separately. We see the instinct toward cooperation developing within your numbers. This instinct is an art and a skill that is key in the creation of the enhanced being. It is offered within what is so often called the New Age.

Fourth density is not separated from third by a great chasm, but merely by the resistance of third-density entities when faced with the need to become a part of a unified and euphonious group. Know that each of you is most valuable in your unique way. And if there is never the opportunity to function steadily with a group, yet still, the service provided by living a life of faith is infinite in value. When the opportunity arises to serve the Creator as a portion of a circle or group, we encourage each to seize that chance with glee.

We find the term "wanderer" to be one that has many layers of meaning. Certainly those upon the earth plane who have come from other earths or other densities have wandered far. Yet consider how each entity in incarnation has come not from Earth but from that mystery that lies behind all appearances and substances. The Earth cannot breed spirits, but can merely offer a home to the spirits' physical, mental, and emotional bodies during the processes of incarnation.

O dear souls, each of you has a native land far from the earth plane. This home lies beyond space and beyond time. And each is, indeed, a wanderer. For most entities there is a degree of comfort and a great ability to enjoy and to feel at home within the earth experience. Those who call themselves wanderers or are drawn to that term are those whose natures are such that the present environment of third density simply does not feel comfortable or native.

Let us look at the shape of a wanderer's story. There is the rising into an awakened awareness of difference from the normal run of people. Often, even within early childhood, there is for the wandering spirit a feeling in the heart that, "I do not belong here." And so the wanderer sets out upon a trek. Whither, she knows not. Why, he cannot perhaps say. "What shall I take? What shall I leave? What are the rules of the road?" each questing spirit wonders. The answers fade and evade precise capture.

Yet always the inner nature calls the wandering spirit onward into the unknown, ruthlessly asking the personality who seeks to lay previous structures aside to become uncomfortable and discordant in emotion, upset and overwhelmed with change and transformation. And with this, all the goods of the earth plane fly away. The traveler has no luggage.

Sore, weary, and puzzled, the wanderer oftentimes may sit by the side of that road. Finally, with all resources spent and with no end in sight, the wanderer turns and is no longer reaching, having given up. This is the moment when it becomes so clear, so apparent, that the wanderer is incredulous in asking, "How could I have missed this signpost?"

This signpost points inward.

It is also necessary to move outwardly, to wander and travel and reach in order to hone the desire and to temper the personality. Yet at the end of each trail there is the bare signpost that says, "Go within, . . . go within. . . . Enter thine own heart and know for the first time that you are at home and one with all that there is, all that there was, and all that there will be."

As our esteemed and beloved brother, Aaron, and we speak concerning various aspects of the experience of discomfort and alienation, isolation, and hunger, yet always keep within the heart our reassurance that you truly are at home within. The roads to infinity, to greater reality, and to opened awareness of love are present as gifts within each being. To them you shall always come at the end of the day's sorrow and struggle.

There is joy. There is comfort. There, within, may each tear be dried. And from that hearth of home and love and wisdom may you wake refreshed in order to move into the dance of divine play that you experience as life.

We would at this time offer the microphone to the one known as Aaron. We are those of Q'uo, and leave this instrument in love and in light.

(Barbara channeling)

Aaron: My love to each of you.

What is the difference between the experience of the wanderer coming to the earth plane and the third-density being who has evolved fully on the earth plane? Is there any difference besides the recognition that you have been someplace else and a seeking of that someplace else, as my brother/sister/friend Q'uo has just described it? For all of you, that someplace else is carried within you always. For all of you who are fully evolved through the earth plane or have passed through other planes, a keynote in your evolution is to come to discover that you need not seek home, because it is within. God is within, not the entirety of that unlimited light and energy, but your own personal piece of it.

Picture a child's drawing of a sun as a round disk, glowing and gold. The child puts assorted triangles on that disk. That is its drawing of sunbeams. One may say that the sunbeam projects from the sun. Take that sunbeam with its pointed tip and push it inward. Is there anything there that is not of the same nature as the sun? Wanderer or nonwanderer, once you discover that your true nature is divine and never separate from all that is, then you are ready to live on any plane with love, wisdom, and compassion. The earth plane offers all beings the opportunity to discover their true nature.

Each being on any plane has its own particular skills and experiences that it brings to the next moment. I ask you here to enter into an envisioning with me. Let us visualize a somewhat primitive farming culture, with people living in great harmony with the land, creating the food that they need out of the earth, and feeding themselves and each other. There is not a scientific understanding of such subtleties as crop rotation. But there is a feeling for the Earth and a sensitivity to the vibrations that the Earth emits, so that the Earth is treated as a companion and not as a slave in the venture of creating food.

This first culture finds itself in some trouble at some point because there is a lack of rain. Within this extended drought, crops are poor and people are starving. Word of this drought comes to one who is part of a technologically advanced culture across the sea. This one of the second culture desires to serve and also feels that it could benefit by learning the harmonious ways of the first culture. This second one is disturbed, perhaps, by the ways its peers treat the Earth as slave rather than as a companion and co-creator. So, the second one sets out on its boat with a plan in mind: "I will teach them the technology to bring water to their fields and I will learn how they live in harmony with the Earth." For the second one's highly advanced technology, combating drought is simply a matter of harnessing power and of pumping water through conduits. It cannot bring thousands of miles of conduit with it. It cannot bring electricity or atomic power with it. So, it arrives barehanded, with an understanding of how this may be done, but without the tools. It must fully enter into the culture to which it has come and must fully accept the culture's limitations.

It knows that it is possible to bring water to these fields. How does it do this in a manner that is consistent with the first culture's knowledge and values? This is a challenge, but it knows that it can be done. To do this work it must fully immerse itself in the culture. It must pay attention. "We cannot make copper pipes. What will we do?" In paying attention, it notices some of the vegetation in the forests and that some trees can be hollowed and connected. It notices the windmills whose power can be harnessed to draw the water up into the fields.

In a sense, this is what a wanderer must do. Before your incarnation you have clarity: *Here's the job ahead. I will help to teach this.* What would be a simple matter on the astral plane vastly changes when you enter the illusion. To teach what you came to teach, you first must fully ground yourself in the illusion. You must accept your humanness.

This being we have used as an example will find that the Earth does provide everything that is needed and that it did not need the technology to create copper pipes. Hereby, it comes into a deeper respect and harmony with the Earth. What could better teach it what it came to learn about working in partnership with the Earth? When you separate yourself from your experience by dismissing the Earth as mundane and even disinteresting through your reluctance to work with the lower chakras and with the emotions and survival mechanisms that are part of the earth plane, you cannot learn. If you cannot learn, you cannot teach. It is as simple as that. You must fully enter the illusion.

We began with the question, "What differentiates the wanderer's experience from the experience of that being that has fully evolved on that plane?" Let us reenter the metaphor. A traveler from across the sea may move through these forests, watching and looking for something to carry water, but may be unaware of the nature of this particular tree—that it is hollow. If he keeps his quest to himself, the conduit may never be discovered. When he tells his friend who has dwelt in this place, "I search for that which can carry water," and draws a pipe, then his friend may say, "Aha, *this* tree!" and then cut one down and show him. "Do you see the hollow space within? We can connect them up." This is a matter of cooperation. The wanderer does not come to the earth plane and simply hand information to the earth plane on a silver tray. The wanderer must come in cooperation with the Earth and all that lives there.

Those of third-density Earth who have fully evolved through the earth plane have their own deep skills and understandings. The wanderer may bring skills, insights, and energy from another place. Pooled together, learning grows. And within the experience of that pooling-it-together, prior boundaries fall away. To work together you must look at the fears that arise as you let go of your separation. To look at those fears and begin to evolve beyond them is the essential process of your growth. It all comes together perfectly.

The wanderer may be of sixth density and have great wisdom and compassion. But no matter how advanced, this wanderer still must learn as well as teach. To learn, it must fully enter the illusion with one aspect of awareness, while knowing with the other that it is entering an illusion and that this illusion is not to be taken as the sole reality. I spoke of this yesterday with a stage metaphor and will not repeat it here.

Perhaps the greatest pain for the wanderer is the pain of fully entering the illusion. It wants to maintain its separateness because it has the misunderstanding that in clinging to the being it was on some other plane, it is strengthened or wiser. I am not suggesting that it does not want to get its feet dirty on the earth plane so much as that there is a sense of fear of losing its clarity, as when an actor steps out on the stage and is so deeply moved by this part that he or she is afraid to fully give itself to that part for fear the heart will break.

I wish to return you here to Q'uo. Thank you for your loving presence and attention. That is all.

(Carla channeling)

Q'uo: We thank the one known as Aaron.

Yes, each has the sorrow as well as the joy, and the heartbreak as well as the elation of romance. Each may often wonder whether there is profit in relationships. We say to you that, in our opinion, it is for relationship and all that this discipline teaches that you have come into the earth plane.

Please gaze within now. Look at the energies of what this instrument calls chakras, appearing as red, orange, yellow, green, blue, indigo, and violet. Can you feel the difference in the present balance of these energies within your being from the configuration that they were in when each arrived at this gathering? Perhaps each may see that the accepted presence of each to each has been the support necessary to come into a new and more harmonized configuration of energies; not merely the higher centers and not only those gifts of heart, of communication, and of work in consciousness, but also and equally those energies of survival, of self-to-self, and of relationships, one to another.

Rejoice, then, in that golden net that grows daily upon your planet's surface as those seeking to lighten the consciousness of the planet called Earth reach out to new entities, forming networks of networks that, in turn, may reach out to find more and more threads of this wonderful net to weave together until all of the sphere upon which you enjoy life is wrapped and sheathed in an embrace of love and acceptance.

This planetary consciousness and its creation are the primary vocation of each spiritual seeker. There are many possible ministries or vocations that may seem more vital or important in the eyes of the world. The wanderer may look at a healer and feel insignificant in comparison, for she may not have a gift of healing or of speaking or teaching. He may only be able to be who he is. Yet this one ability to exist whole and complete within the cradle of the present moment becomes paramount.

We would move aside to welcome back the one known as Aaron into this discourse, with most great pleasure, my friend. We are those of Q'uo.

Session 24

Barbara: Before Aaron talks, I just want to say I am in awe of and very much enjoying feeling the shift of energy, reading this on the computer screen from Q'uo and feeling the thought in their mind from Q'uo, "Do you want to talk about this?" and Aaron's "Yes," and the shift of energy. It's beautiful.

(Barbara channeling)

Aaron: Q'uo just spoke of the evolution of a planetary consciousness as a primary vocation to all seekers. This does not mean that the evolution of planetary consciousness is more important than the evolution of individual consciousness, but they are a part of each other. This Earth was created with a highly positive vibrational frequency. Its foundation—the foundation of the Earth, the soil itself, this first-density energy—is permeated with love.

As Q'uo stated, there is no barrier between the third and fourth densities. As you find more spaciousness around the judgments and opinions of the emotional body; as you find equanimity within your-self when fear, anger, or greed arise; and as you find a lack of judgment of others when such states arise in others, then you lower your barriers. With the barriers lowered and judgment falling away, you are ready to enter the fourth-density experience.

Earth is in process of becoming a fourth-density planet. The beginning of a fourth-density Earth does not mean that there will be no more fear. You are still going to have emotional bodies. You are still going to need to work with fear; rather, there will be a spaciousness around fear as a sense of compassion that allows fear to be touched with lovingkindness rather than judgment that would seek to shut it out.

You are learning at many levels. The one I spoke of before was not only finding ways for the more primitive culture to bring water to its fields. At another level it was learning and teaching respect for the environment as well as full communication with and participation in the environment as a partnership. Those of you who are come to Earth with some technical skill to share, and with healing skills, deep wisdom, and deep lovingkindness, can know that these are what you may share on one level. On a deeper level, you bring this energy that helps all beings to release boundaries, to come to the direct experience of God within each, animate or inanimate, and to live in loving reverence of the God in all that is.

The force that will be generated on an earth that has moved to this degree of highly positively polarized energy will exert tremendous influence throughout the entire universe. It will serve as a source of immense energy and of love. While you ask yourself, then, *How can I be a better healer or teacher, a better mechanic, or a better friend?* do not neglect to ask yourself, *How does the learning of these skills help me learn more fully to love? If I keep myself separate in any way from the incarnation, in what ways is that a disservice to this deepest aspiration to bring love and light where there has previously been fear and darkness?* When you ask the right questions, my friends, you will find the answers appear in your heart and the strength to act upon those answers. You will find the clarity of your path.

I pass the microphone here to Q'uo, with much joy in this sharing. That is all.

(Carla channeling)

Q'uo: We would at this time thank the one known as Aaron. We are Q'uo and greet each once again in love and in light. This greeting is not merely a courtesy. We repeat and repeat it because it is our humble understanding that this is all that there truly is: love, the one great original Thought or Logos that created all and creates infinitely; and light, the love made visible that has built all that is manifest in all densities of the infinite creation. In this love and in this light we open the communication for queries. Are there any questions to which we may offer a thought in an abbreviated manner at this time?

Questioner: Q'uo, if I might ask, you spoke of the archetypical pattern of the hero's journey. Is that a pattern that is found reserved for a more initiatory level of experience or is it a pattern that can be found in our daily lives as well?

Q'uo: We feel that this circle of experience, this moving outward and returning inward, is a cycle or circle that may be found in many, many ways. There is the circle of the seasons: the sprouting of new life in spring; its flowering and blooming in the heat of summer; the maturing and ripening and gathering of the great autumn harvest; and the time of bare trees and brown grass, which is the time when all life sleeps, rests, and reconstitutes the vital energies by acceptance of the limitations of the darkness, the innerness, and the contraction of the cold and the winter when all seems dead or dying.

Once the circle is seen the first time, it appears again and again to the seeker who has eyes that may see and a heart that may understand. The seeker's work shall always be given to the circle and will often seem to be a loss, gaining nothing for that seeker. Yet this offering comes to another, who offers to another. And in the fullness of the circle, that seeker who first gave until he was poor shall become one who has received tenfold, a hundredfold, and a thousandfold.

May we answer you further, my brother?

Questioner: Thank you, Q'uo. May I ask you to comment on the idea of the holy breath?

Q'uo: In one of your holy works it is said that man's life is but a breath. So it is when a spirit leaves the plane of physical existence. Your doctors call the event of death an expiring. This, perhaps, may be seen to be humorous, as your culture most often says that subscriptions to magazines expire, and we realize that you are more than your present current issue. However, it is so that the incarnation, seen before and after, is a breath, a moment: one glorious, intense moment when the soul has the opportunity to choose to serve the infinite Creator with all the heart, all the strength, all the mind, and all the self. Beyond this moment there is no need for breath. Within this moment of incarnation, breath is all. So deeply, gratefully, and lovingly breathe in life and breathe out life; and the devil take the hindmost!

May we answer further, my brother?

Questioner: No. Thank you very much, Q'uo.

Q'uo: Is there another query at this time?

Questioner: I have a question. What sort of initiatory experiences are wanderers likely to have?

Q'uo: Ah, my sister, initiation! How painful. How awkward. Anyone who has gone through puberty knows the anguish of initiation. In fact, your peoples would do better with this initiation of the physical body if they allowed the suffering involved to be ritualized, so that each who became an adult experienced sharp and keenly that pain of piercing. It is not considered a good idea to abuse the body, yet those who are considered savages, who ritually cut or pierce the chest or some portion of the anatomy while becoming the full-grown man or woman, are far more able to know and accept the burden of responsibility and suffering that go with full adulthood.

Initiation, in general, is the occasion of sleeplessness and inner disquiet. The self seems to have become "other" somehow. The way seems lost and there is no light. There is within each initiation a fire that burns and a source that hollows the pipe as it passes through. Initiation is anguish. Yet at its end lies the beginning. So, when the self becomes full of this anguish, we ask each to meet that anguish with resolve and good nature.

The gift of faith is that it does not have to make any sense. When one decides to live in faith, one can be silly. One can be foolish and one can say, "I haven't slept. I can't eat. My head hurts from all the confusion. But thanks be to the infinite One and all praise for this anguish, for this pain, for this teaching, and for this time." Does this make sense? No. Is this fun? No. Is this necessary? Yes. Will you be glad when it is ended? Oh my, yes.

We ask each to be sensitive to each other's times of awakening and birthing of self. Reach out the hand to the grumpy bear. Reach out the heart to the nagging pain of complaint. Accept the variant behavior of one who suffers, for you see as in a mirror that side of yourself that you shall, and you may count on this, one day be inflicting upon your environment.

The more you desire to seek and serve, the less comfortable your life shall be. We offer no softening comfort except that it is just the acceptance of this hardship, emotionally and spiritually speaking, that finally opens the tempered soul to a joy and a peace that is not happy but joyful, so that you are companioned with joy and can truly give thanks and praise with the awareness that this is the deeper ground of being and that this is the truth of being. May we answer further?

Questioner: This is the truth.

Q'uo: Is there a final query at this time?

Questioner: Is the mirror the answer to finding the other wanderer? And what is going on there?

Q'uo: My sister, you are most perceptive. This is so. The mirror shows you the gift you give yourself. And you and the other self are the gifts you give each other. How infinitely precious.

We shall rejoin you, Aaron and ourselves, soon, and look forward to that with joy and happiness; for we, too, enjoy happiness as well as the truth of joy. For now we leave each in love, light, blessing, and peace. We are those of the principle known to you as Q'uo. Adonai. Adonai.

(The group sings.)

Barbara: This is Barbara, and at Aaron's suggestion I want to tell a very brief story that my son told me. At a church gathering, a young parent stood up and told this story. She was expecting a baby, and her three-year-old said, "When the baby is born, can I have some time alone with it?" And the parents said, "Well, we'll see." And she kept asking. They talked to the pediatrician and the pediatrician said, "It certainly seems important to her for some reason. I would try to monitor what goes on for safety, but give her time alone with the baby." So the baby was born, and after a few weeks the little girl asked again and they said yes. They left her alone in the room with the baby. They closed the door but they had turned on a walkie-talkie so they could hear, and they went and sat in the living room. They heard the little girl say to the baby, "What is it like to be with God? I'm already forgetting."

Session 25

(This session was preceded by a period of tuning and meditation.)

Group question: Everyone seems to want to go deeply into how to do the work that we have come to do, especially as it pertains to wanderers. For example, do wanderers have more issues of forgiveness? And perhaps tomorrow, if not today, we would like to know how we can take the energy that we have here, as a group, back with us to our homes and continue that work there. We are interested in how we gather our information as individuals and use it, together and at home.

(Barbara channeling)

Aaron: Regardless of where you came from, many of your reasons for being incarnate are the same: to learn deeper compassion and deeper love; to move beyond judgment; to move beyond attachment to your opinions and to the small ego-self and to come more fully into the group consciousness; and, as one of you mentioned earlier today, to learn forgiveness. The learning of these things takes you into working with the many catalysts of your life, such as experiences with loss, with relationships, and with work. Q'uo and I would like to know how much you would like us to go into these questions.

"How do I do the work I came to do?" This has been the subject of many of our other meetings with Q'uo, as well as of our ongoing teaching. It is never a waste to repeat it. And yet, you are here to focus on questions pertaining to wanderers. Please decide amongst yourselves how much you want to stay with that narrower focus and how much you want to move into this question of "How do I do the work I came to do?" That is all.

(The group engages in further discussion and tuning.)

Aaron: You have joined me here, coming out of the sunshine of a brilliant day. I enjoy seeing that the sunshine you carry indoors is in your own hearts.

You ask, "How do I do the work I came to do?" and "What differentiates the work of the wanderer from another?" Each of you has come with different work, but related. And there is one area of work that is true for all beings: You are here to learn how to love more fully, moving beyond judgment and beyond the illusion of your limits and of separation into self and other.

You are not incarnate to get rid of the emotional body but to learn equanimity with the emotional body. When there is a sense of spaciousness that sees how emotions arise when certain conditions are present for their arising and that also sees how those emotions pass away, you no longer need to dwell on those emotions. You no longer fear them, so there is no need either to deny them or to be reactive to them. When you have learned that degree of nonjudgment, you may move deeper into the learnings of compassion because the open and nonjudgmental heart can truly hear your own and another's pain.

What does compassion mean when there has been no judgment? Some of you have moved into the higher densities before coming to third-density Earth. Supposedly you learned compassion. Now you come into the earth plane and find heavy emotions arising, which lead to judgment of one sort or another, such as to fear or to the desire to protect. My dear ones, can you see that this arising of judgment is not something to be met with disdain and hatred, but to be embraced and used as catalyst for learning?

The wise gardener does not cut away the dead growth from the garden and throw it into the garbage, but turns it into the soil and uses it as nutrient for new growth. You do not want to throw away your emotions, but to make space for them so that you may move more deeply into love and into compassion. This work, of course, is true for all beings of third density. The question is, "How do I work with judgment and the various emotions carried by fear?" Here is where there is a distinction, not only for the wanderer but for any "old soul." But it is certainly experienced differently by the wanderer.

Many of you suffer from what I call "old-soul syndrome." When you are a young soul, you excuse yourself for treading on others' toes. You shrug and say, "Well, everybody does it." As an older soul, you so deeply aspire to oneness with God and are so deeply motivated by the desire to come home, that you have the erroneous idea that to do so requires that you must be perfect. You believe every arising that does not manifest itself as lovingkindness must be demolished. And so you become more and more judgmental of yourselves, as well as more perfectionist and more judgmental of others.

As with every catalyst on the earth plane, this increasing judgment and push toward perfectionism is both painful and useful. When there is a minor discomfort, you squirm a little. When you begin to feel yourself bashed by the proverbial "four-by-four," you finally need to pay attention. The very pain of your judgment of self and others pushes you to pay attention. It is only then that you become truly ready to see that what you have viewed as imperfection is another side of the perfection of your being. This does not mean that you practice greed, reactivity, or anger toward others, but that when these feelings arise within you, you begin to treat them differently. You understand that what is needed is not a hard-heartedness that would drive them out so that you can be perfect, but rather a kind acknowledgment of "Here is human fear manifesting itself again. I offer it my love." It is this constant practice, of offering love to that which you have judged to be negative, that frees you.

I said that this old-soul syndrome creates more discomfort for wanderers. This is because many of you have memories of being largely free of the emotional body. It was not there, so you could not use it as a tool for learning, but you also did not have to worry about it. Some part of you wants to deny this emotional body of yours and to say, "Let's throw it in the garbage and go back to where we came from!" The beauty of the incarnate experience is that you cannot do that. You must attend to it and you must learn to attend to it with love.

The being who has moved solely through the earth plane has memories of being on the astral plane between lifetimes, but still with an attendant emotional body. It may suffer this old-soul syndrome, heeding its judgments, striving ever for more and more perfection, and finding itself feeling deeply unworthy because it cannot express the perfection that it wishes to express. But it is not haunted by memories of being free of the emotional body.

This is not a problem for you as wanderers. There are no problems, only situations that ask your loving attention. For those who have an aversion to the emotional body and to the arisings of the emotional body, and who have an attachment to being free of emotions so that you can feel more "perfect," I ask you simply, can you begin to offer some mercy to this spirit essence that you are, which has so courageously entered into an illusion of form and emotion so as to learn? Instead of saying, "It's too hard; when I saw the ground, I didn't realize that it was going to get muddy when it rained. Now, I'm knee-deep in mud. I want to go home where there is no mud." Instead, just know within, "Yes, here is mud. I'm going to get muddy. Can I allow that to be okay? My deepest truth is not expressed by being clean of mud, but by the deeply loving and courageous ways that I work with the mud that I am given."

Later in this session I would like to hear your specific questions. Some examples might be, "How do I work with the mud I am given? Is it different for wanderers and nonwanderers? How do I open myself to my emotions? How do I learn nonjudgment?" Please offer whatever questions you may have. We could spend a session on each of these areas, but we do not have that time. So we would like to know the area that is of greatest interest for you.

At this time I pass the microphone to my dear friend, Q'uo. That is all.

(Carla channeling)

Q'uo: Greetings once again in the love and in the light of the one infinite Creator.

We shall continue our brother Aaron's discourse upon mud. You see, wanderers gaze with a more jaundiced eye at that mud because it is not as familiar and it seems unnecessary to that witness within. If the wanderer is of fourth density, the mud will tend to be along the lines of what is right and what is wrong, what is moral, and what will help. There is a kind of desire to battle the forces of negativity.

When the wanderer has come into the cycle of reincarnations from fifth density, the mud is likely to tend toward sticking in the area of life dealing with intimacy, for the wisdom density has the hard-won opinion that the war of good and evil is not necessary. Whereas the fourth-density wanderer will speak in terms of relationship, the fifth-density wanderer will speak in terms of self and Creator, which is certainly a relationship beyond all others but not a relationship easily practiced upon the family and acquaintances one meets at first glance.

If the wanderer is of sixth density, the likelihood of mud tends to be in both of these areas: the right/wrong issue that so often polarizes relationships between entities, and the issue of lack of ability to allow intimacy. These energies of compassion and wisdom are being balanced in sixth density. So the wanderer who comes to the third density to aid brings unrealistic expectation through the veil of forgetting, both in the areas of relationship with others and relationship with the Creator.

Now, the wanderer is also a convert in that the wanderer did not have to come to this party. The wanderer chose to come here. So that entity who is a wanderer has outsized, larger-than-life feelings that she came here to serve; that he must find the service, whether the scope and direction of this service is in finding the Creator in other people or finding the intimacy of family with the self and the Creator. These desires will be exaggerated beyond that which is normal for those who "have to be at this party and have to pass this test *now*."

The wanderer, indeed, is in a precarious situation until he can lay down his armor, his differences, and his pains and until she can lay down the grievances that bind her to her body and her situation with the ribbons of "should" and "must" that tie us in knots.

So the first step in constructing a life in this alien camp is the creation of a safe place where you can lay all your burdens down, even if you have to prostrate yourself on the floor where you can weep until you are dry, where you can ask and wait until you have an answer or until you die.

When this place exists only within, then it is more difficult to do the work. It is desirable that there also be a physical location for this safe and sanctified place. Some feel the need to lean upon the truth found in beauty. These entities will most harmonically and resonantly vibrate with a place in which there is ritual; whether it be the ritual of a tea ceremony; the ritual of creating a bonsai plant; the ritual of meditation, prayer, and contemplation; or the spare ritual of *zazen*, the sitting or walking, merely that: sitting, walking. For some this is quite sufficient to alter and transform into that being that is self-forgiven.

This instrument has a high opinion of one close to her who merely gardens. The instrument's needs place her within an elaborate community of worshippers of the myth of the Christ known as Jesus. This instrument spends time and energy treating that congregation of brothers and sisters as the Christ, whereas this gardener accomplishes all and more by turning the earth, by gazing at the sky, by being one with each flower and each planting, and by feeling the changing needs of this kingdom created of tree and shrub and stone and water that has become a built entity holding personality, purpose, and passion.

There is no best way. But the wanderer has, along with the many aggravations of being unfit for the climate of Earth, many, many wonderful things that are treats not often given to the natives. There is within wanderers a sharper ability to grasp the truth when it is felt. Therefore, once the wanderer has developed a safe place and is using it conscientiously and regularly, the potential for true self-healing is actually greater than for the native who has not yet experienced anything "better" than the current world scene.

Once this sacred, private, and inviolable space has been created, there is much self-to-self work to accomplish. The tools for learning more about the self include the study of dreams, the keeping of a journal in which the thoughts of the day are faithfully recorded, the seeking out and giving of time and energy to what this instrument would call birds of a feather. For as the wanderer reaches out to help another and as that other expresses its tale of suffering, who is helped more—the sufferer who hears a little comfort, or the healer who is given the great gift of hearing, being heard, and being able to be present with such a precious gift as the confidences exchanged?

It is no mystery why those who are willing to teach learn twice as much. For when the hand is stretched out and the ear is opened, the invaluable and incalculable treasure of trust and faith is given. What beauty there is in this! What strength we can draw from each other! All beings suffer, wanderers as much as or more than most. Yet those who wander and those who wonder are also those who receive.

The asking that is so vital comes naturally to a wandering soul. She is uncomfortable and she must speak up. He is lost and he must ask direction. There is also the tool called "practicing the presence," which is most helpful to some. In this practice, the wanderer may simply move through each moment, not attempting to solve it or to understand it fully, as much as to bear witness and to remain with that witness no matter how the picture might change. For the center is again and again called into being by this practice.

When there is joy, the wanderer may speak of it to the infinite One. When there is sorrow, the wanderer may speak of it to the infinite One. Anything whatsoever may be experienced. And the response of praise and thanks to the Creator remains relevant for each and every possible situation.

The wanderer's edge is this very discomfort coupled with the typical, enlarged certainty that this is not the way it has to be, that this is not necessary. The wanderer can pull from its subconscious those gifts allowed through the veil of forgetting, accompanied by the heightened sensitivity that so often erupts as allergies and food sensitivities, asthma, and other illnesses. These manifestations are the shadow and flip side, as it were, of the ability of the wanderer to trust that remembrance of a life made of light in more harmonious configurations of energy betwixt beings who are more obviously beings of light.

We would at this time pass the microphone back to our brother Aaron. We leave this instrument for the present in love and in light. We are Q'uo.

(Barbara channeling)

Aaron: Q'uo has just spoken to you of the importance of finding a clear place to rest in the deepest truth of who you are and has pointed out that there are many paths to that clarity.

There are two aspects to your incarnate work. First is the work with that which you perceive as shadows arising within yourself. These are shadows of anger, desire, and fear in all of its manifestations, as well as the judgments about those manifestations. The greatest gift of the physical plane is that you must learn to work skillfully with this arising. No matter how much you may wish to deny anger or greed, you cannot do so. To deny it is to bury it and torment yourself to prevent its re-arising someplace else. To act it out is not a viable option past a certain place in your spiritual path. You forget that you have a third choice, which is to find a spacious presence with this difficult energy, neither denying it nor manifesting it further. In making that third choice, you can see the difficult energies arising and bring attention to the causes. You thereby bring attention to fear itself and to the delusion of separation, but with compassion for the human who knows fear and who is caught in the illusion.

There are many ways of working with this discomforting arising. They all have one thing in common, which is the opening of the heart. Eventually you may become quite skilled at making space for that which arises in the emotions and at making space for physical sensations and thoughts as well, without reactivity or fear of any of these.

You are still caught in the illusion. You are busy being somebody who possesses sensations, emotions, and thoughts. And you are also busy being somebody who works skillfully with them. Eventually you

412

must let go of the illusion without denying the illusion its place as a catalyst for learning. You must come to know who you truly are when you are not somebody who is being busy learning to be skillful. This opening to your true being is the second aspect of your work.

Here I want to show you something that your eyes can take in. Would someone please hand Barbara an unwrinkled sheet of paper and may I have your visual attention for a moment?

We have here a perfect, unwrinkled sheet of paper. Look at it. This is symbolic of the perfection of your natural state. I ask Barbara to crumple it and then uncrumple it. Wrinkled, yes?

Questioner: Yes.

Aaron: Wrinkled. Let us call them wrinkles of anger, greed, jealousy, and impatience. These are all the familiar wrinkles of your lives. Can you see that the perfect, unwrinkled sheet still exists? It is right here. Where would it go? Your perfection is not something that you find when all the wrinkles are gone. Your perfection is something that is constantly within you as your divinity. Look once more before you settle back down and be sure that you can see the perfect, unwrinkled sheet that lies within the wrinkled sheet.

There is a balance in your work. This balance is found in working to learn to deal skillfully with the wrinkles and in learning to rest in that divine perfection. That divine perfection is what you truly are. Those who are not wanderers tend to work hard at dealing with the wrinkles, but it is harder for them to recognize their innate perfection. Those who are wanderers find it easier at times to rest in the innate perfection, and yet want to take an iron and eradicate or un-crease all of the wrinkles and pretend that they did not exist. Both exist. Relative reality exists within ultimate reality. You are perfect. You have always been perfect. And there are wrinkles. . . .

A very helpful path for many, then, is to use whatever practices are useful in learning to work with the wrinkles without reactivity and simultaneously to find what Q'uo has just spoken of: that safe place where one may rest in one's own deepest truth and where one may know its intimate connection with the Divine. From this space you have a different perspective. You relax and open to those wrinkles as the compost of the incarnation. What is compost, but that which is composed literally of shit, of garbage, and yet containing the needed elements to support new growth? When you are certain of this, you no longer have a need to get rid of it. You no longer fear it or push it aside because you think it will stink, but become more able to embrace it with a merciful presence.

You must not hide in ultimate reality and fear the physical, emotional, and mental wrinkles of the incarnation, which is the temptation for a wanderer. Another way of phrasing this would be to say that you must work with the lower chakras and not just the upper. Many of you have a clear sense of yourselves as spirit, even if you cannot fully acknowledge your own divinity because you see the flaws in the human manifestation. At least intellectually you recognize your perfection. Come down to earth. Ground yourselves. Play in the mud. Forget that your mother told you, "You are bad," because your hands were muddy and you must scrub them clean. You are not bad or unworthy. You are gardeners, and a gardener does get muddy. But the gardener also remembers that its purpose is not simply to turn the soil or to make mud pies, but to grow the greatest blossoms of creation.

I do not wish to repeat here what on the one hand would take weeks to teach, and secondly what has already been taught. Past transcripts, both as loose pages and books, are available that would talk of these teachings of balance, of relative and ultimate reality, and of the energy and meditation practices you may do to help you move more fully into both relative and ultimate reality.[59]

I want to pass the microphone back to Q'uo. When it comes back to me again, I would like to hear your specific questions. My

---

[59] For more information, please contact the Deep Spring Center for Meditation and Spiritual Inquiry, 3003 Washtenaw Avenue, Suite 2, Ann Arbor, MI 48104; www.deepspring.org.

friend of Q'uo has that to add which will enhance this teaching. That is all.

(Carla channeling)

Q'uo: Greetings again in love and in light.

Indeed, we call each wanderer away from perfection and away from ultimate reality. We call each wanderer to service on behalf of the people and the planet of Earth. You have suffered much, sacrificed all memory, and lived through many years in a strange and foreign land. You had to want badly to come here.

Your intention before coming into the earth plane was clear. It was to lend your vibrations to the lightening of the consciousness of Planet Earth at its birthing into that fourth density that moves steadily through the process of fecundity, growth within the womb, and manifestation. How upset you would be to discover, after an entire laborious incarnation, that you had spent your time complaining about not being a native and expressing disappointment in the quality of people and concepts.

Dear ones, you came to be servants of Earth. You came to lay all aside and give yourself fully to the cause of love. You came to suffer, and to manifest throughout your suffering your faith and persistent devotion concerning the Creator and those other selves that you know are the Creator. Your biggest stumbling block is that veil of forgetting that causes you to repine at these discomforts rather than rolling up the sleeves and pitching in to a very unsanitary and untidy but wholly natural process of growth.

No natural function is tidy or clean. Think of the act of love: sperm lubricant, strange postures.... Was there ever a less dignified or more earthy way to create the opportunity for a human soul to come into this sacred Earth? How could it have been made more low, more basic, or more messy?

Think of birth: the open, yawning gate of the womb, the spread legs, the pain, the blood, the water, and the worrisome, mumbling medical personnel. Where is there dignity, cleanliness, or neatness in birth?

Consider death if you can—the getting old, the failing health, the vomit, the urine, the excrement—all going wrong until you praise the Lord for a good dump and thrill at relative ill health because you are still alive.

This is the world you came to change. You cannot do it if you think you are doing it. Your only hope of being of service, as you meant so wholeheartedly to be, is to embrace this messy, untidy life and to take in each and every portion as that which is accepted and known.

You are servants. This will weigh heavily upon you, for you feel as though you were somewhat superior, as you have faith in better things. You can see further. Give these gifts away. Learn humility. Ask for suffering. Ask to be the last one served, to go hungry, and to cry. Allow the pain of living to be real, acceptable, and even lovely. Get dirty with this boisterous, bubbling, and infinitely energetic process of breathing in and breathing out, seeking always to serve love within situations, truth within falsity and people, regardless of how they present themselves. Await the order, the command, from those unto whom you came to be slaves. Bow before these commands and lean your shoulders to the work.

What is your work? The first work for a wanderer is to engage in the process of life as it is. When you attempt this beginning, again and again you shall fail. This is how you shall learn. Rejoice at each perceived failure. Rejoice at your failings. Rejoice at that portion of you that would kill, that would steal, that would rape, or at least have as many as possible, if not by force, by seduction.[60]

---

[60] One may rejoice insofar as such portions of being are used as catalyst for loving thought and action. It may also be helpful to reference Aaron's remarks in session 20: weekend 6, part 3 of 5, concerning the question, "How do I know when I'm following a path of love or a path of fear?" and including the statement, "Your fear is not a burden given you for combat. It is the fertile soil upon which you may build compassion. It is the garbage that you turn into compost."

When the pride falls, rejoice the most. For truth, beauty, justice, and mercy are learned only in the dust. Suffer, and praise the infinite mystery for the opportunity. And when you can do nothing but give up, rejoice, for now you have the idea. Now you are onto something good.

We have such love for each of you! How noble are your aspirations! Know that we are here for you and that our presence is ready to support, to comfort, and to accompany any who call upon us. We will not speak words. We will not attempt to be obviously there. But lean into the silence and the solitude when you have called upon us and feel our love and our total and complete support.

For each of you is the infinite One, experiencing and harvesting for the mystery that created us all. Harvesters of Earth, Brothers and Sisters of Sorrow, place the crown upon your head, then throw it and you into the dirt and do your best. *That* is perfection.

We would at this time transfer the cynosure to the one known as Aaron. We leave this instrument and this beloved group in the love and the infinite light of the one Creator. Adonai. Adonai. We are Q'uo.

(Barbara channeling)

Aaron: Q'uo has just suggested the importance of learning humility and of learning to embrace the messiness of incarnation. While you embrace that mess you must also not deny that there is pain in it. How do you learn to embrace that which is painful? Ask to be served last, Q'uo suggested. What do you do with the voice that says, "What about me? If I am last, will my needs be met?" You must not throw away fear, but allow it to dissolve when it is ready. The very arising of this fear is the compost for growth.

We are left, then, with the major question: What do any of you do, wanderer or not, with the threatening experiences of the incarnation? I am not going to seek to answer that at this time in a generalized way. I would prefer to hear your specific questions addressed to me or to Q'uo, or simply tossed out at random to whichever of us would choose to answer. Are there questions? That is all.

Questioner: I have two questions. My first question has to do with the frustration of wanderers regarding the veil of forgetting of the subconscious memories of greater unity and of the apparent separation experienced on Earth. It has to do with how we humans tend to treat each other and of course with the need for compassion and understanding. So, I would ask for any comments about that and also any instructions in particular Q'uo might have, or perhaps Aaron, on penetrating the veil as much as possible. What do we do to remember why we are here, or to seek guidance?

My second question relates to the material that Barbara brought. It is a question I've always thought about because I identify very strongly with it, as some information about it has been channeled to me directly. And that is on how wanderers are trapped in earthly karma. We have talked here about how we're volunteers, but some of us also get the sensation of doing time. And it might be useful to know what common things such as spiritual pride tend to entrap us, how to work with them, and how to support one another in that feeling of entrapment, which I personally find to be a very strong experience. Thank you.

Questioner: Is this directed to Aaron or Q'uo or either?

Questioner: Either and both.

Aaron: The veil is also a gift of the incarnation. You do not want to become lost in the forgetting. But do not forget, my friend, that you are here to learn faith. If the veil is entirely torn aside so that there is absolute clarity of who you are and why you are here, then your work on this plane becomes more a work of determination and willpower rather than the learning of faith that was your intention. Thus, the veil serves a purpose. Your quest is to punch holes in it, not to tear it aside. You may learn to punch holes in it by paying more attention to those moments when you are truly resting in a space of egolessness, which is a space of deepest connection and Pure Awareness. Each of you has moments of this, such as the times when you are listening to a symphony and there ceases to be symphony and listener. In those moments there is no self or object, just symphony happening. Another example is when you see the sunset and suddenly there is nobody watching that sunset, just Pure Awareness with the barrier of subject and object fallen away.

To use a simple example, if you wake up and your stomach hurts, you notice that experience of discomfort. But when you awaken pain-free, you fail to notice the natural space of "no pain." Similarly, you do not notice when you rest in Pure Awareness, which is the natural state of your being. You notice when you are shunted off into a separate self, because it is painful. The practice, then, involves paying attention to these arisings of Pure Awareness and connectedness. As you more frequently recognize this space of total connection, you begin to allow that experience to stabilize. You come to a deeper, ongoing awareness of who you are. When you are not busy being somebody else—being the doer, the observer, the wanderer, the friend, or lover—who are you?

There are many practices that can be done so as to come to rest more fully in that space of Pure Awareness. Two of the simplest that I know, I will teach you quickly. We will not take the time to practice them here in this room, but you may wish to try them on your own after our session.

The first is a breath exercise. Breathe in ... breathe out ... in ... out ... in ... out.... Begin to notice that there is a pause between the inhale and the exhale, and again between the exhale and the inhale. Just a *(Clap!)* small break when the first part of the breath is complete and the next part has not yet begun. When you are breathing in, you are moving into the future. When you are breathing out, you are letting go and looking for the next breath. This space between the breath, often called an aperture in the breath, is *(Clap!)* now. Try it just for a moment here. In ... *(Clap!)* ... pause ... out ... *(Clap!)* ... pause ... I am emphasizing the pauses. You will find that one is more comfortable for you than the other, either between inhale and exhale or between exhale and inhale. I suggest that you not try to notice and to rest in both, but only in one, whichever feels more natural. Let us try it this way for one minute. In ... pause ... out ... in ... pause ... out.... Do not hold the breath so long that it becomes a strain. Let there be just enough pause to be fully in this moment.

(Pause)

When you are experiencing that within relative reality that is discomforting to you, try this breathing. This is not to escape from relative reality but to make more space for it by allowing yourself that shift of weight, balanced between relative and ultimate, coming back more fully to that Pure Awareness that never has borne a veil.

The other practice I would have you try is a very joyful one. Go and lie on the grass or on a porch or terrace where you can see the trees and the sky. Breathe in, breathing in the infinite space that surrounds you, and feeling yourself filled with all that is. Breathe out and allow your energy to expand outward. Feel the borders of self that you have set and just gently relax. You are not trying to expand outward. You are *allowing* the experience of a deeper truth that is that natural outward expandedness, simply letting go of borders and moving into the infiniteness of the sky. These are simply tools that can help reconnect you to a deeper truth of who you are. From that place of truth, as it stabilizes, you are more able to punch holes in the veil.

Do you wish further elaboration on this question from either of us, or is this sufficient? That is all.

Questioner: I have a question, which I offer to either Aaron or Q'uo. In the earlier portion of this life it seemed to me that doing something of value was the primary purpose of existence in this body. Over the decades I have shifted my opinion to where I believe that it is relationships that are, in fact, the treasure of this life. My question is, is this a factor of maturity or age, or have I simply stumbled onto what is already so?

Aaron: May I reply quite briefly here? And then I will pass this to Q'uo, who also has an answer.

Questioner: Please.

Aaron: I would raise this question, my friend. Is there any difference between doing something of value and establishing relationship?

Questioner: Doing connotes the creation ...

Aaron: To establish relationship and enter into it fully is to let go of your boundaries and fully merge your heart in beingness with others. It seems to me that what you have learned is the real value of opening the heart and that this is the greatest gift. I pass you here to my friend Q'uo. That is all.

(Carla channeling)

Q'uo: We are with this instrument. We believe we may say a bit upon this point.

The seasons of the year have much in common with the seasons of an incarnation. The early creations of mind and brawn—will and steel and thought—are often used with most efficacy by the younger, less experienced entity who does not yet know that life is vain, work is empty, and all is passing in an instant. Knowledge of this kind greatly cuts into that "eager beaver" mentality necessary for creating whatever dam or distortion might seem desirable.

In the summer of a life, the being expresses the epitomes of youth—the physical beauties, the keen sensing, the indefatigable energy, the beauty of form, the excellence of learning—like flowers. The summer's children, embracing each other and life, create the seeds and in the blossom create the bait that catches the forces of procreation, inner creation, and creation with others.

The prime of life is an autumn season where the entity reaps, harvests, winnows, and then goes back to the threshing floor, seeking yet again until all has been harvested that was seeded in the youth of years, leaving the winter of life a seeming cold and undesirable time. Yet to the mature entity this is the time of realized being, the time when the sense of proportion is most informed. It is the time when the most plain and skeletal truths may be seen, shared, and preserved. The winter sees the ripening of doing into being, the ripening of solitude into willingness to go in any direction in order to form bridges between the self and anyone who wishes to learn from and give to the entity. All of these seasons have their wisdom. They all have their drawbacks as well.

There is a good partnership in most entities between the inevitable lessons of time and those lessons learned about love that are special just to you. This great gift of self is most easily seen when the fire of ambition has been quenched by achievement and when the imbalance of ambition has been balanced by inevitable loss, so that each choice, in season or out, is, in a sense, precisely equal to all other configurations of thought or priority. The genius of all seasons is the inner awareness that this, too, is the Creator. May we answer further, my brother?

Questioner: No. I thank you both very much.

Q'uo: We thank you very much, dear brother.

Questioner: I would like to ask Aaron if he could speak on the practice of dissolving that he mentioned, using the emotional judgment as an example.

(Barbara channeling)

Aaron: I hear your question.

Emotional judgments will arise. It is a necessary element of the incarnation. These will be judgments of good and bad, right and wrong, or wanting and aversion. These judgments do not arise by chance. Consciousness moves into contact with an object or with a thought. It finds that thought or object pleasant or unpleasant. The quality of pleasantness or unpleasantness is not inherent in the object or thought, but is contained in the relative relationship with that which has arisen. For a simple example, to plunge into a cold lake on a hot summer day is quite pleasant. To plunge into the same water in midwinter is quite unpleasant. It is not the object that changes but your relationship with that object. When attention is brought to each stage of this process, you will find that while the emotional judgment may still arise, all identification with it begins to dissolve. Then you no longer become caught in the stories of these judgments but see them simply as passing, conditioned objects.

Questioner: Does Q'uo have a response to that? ... because I have a question.

Aaron: I would speak a bit further. The move from pleasant/unpleasant to like/dislike is common. If you carefully watch, you can begin to observe how your energy reaches out to grasp and hold on to that which is pleasant and to push away that which is unpleasant. There is nothing wrong with this. It is very natural to you. If, in that grasping and aversion, you are pulled out of the present moment and into old-mind condition, then you are no longer free to respond directly to the object, thought, or emotion with which you have been presented. For example, consider that as a child you often experienced rejection by your peers. There might have been a situation where you came into a coffee shop and saw friends sitting together at a table, and then you walked to the table and they said hello but did not invite you to sit down. In experiencing this, old-mind conditioning might move you into gear and into a sense of being rejected. Anger may arise, judgment at that anger may arise, and you may become ensnared in all of these heavy emotions.

Using various relative-reality practices, one can begin to see how those emotions arose without a need to deny the emotion, nor a need to be reactive to it. Nevertheless, the emotion still has arisen and it contracts your energy field. The first part is to be able to recognize the arising and to know this is old baggage, as in the awareness, "I don't have to carry it around anymore. I don't have to be reactive to it or discomforted by it." Seeing clearly this is old baggage, one can do practices such as the in-pause-out breath, which is something to bring you back into a space of Pure Awareness and a space of resting in your divinity. From this space you see the contractions of your energy field as the illusion that they are.

Each of you has a light body that is perfect. We spoke earlier of a child's drawing of the sun and the projecting sunbeams. The light-body template is and always has been perfect and undistorted. The distortions in your energy field are these wrinkles in the sheet of paper. They exist in relative reality. They have never existed in ultimate reality; therefore, you are given the combined work of handling those distortions skillfully on the relative plane by acknowledging aversion, seeing any desire to be rid of them because they are discomforting, and knowing this is all illusion. You must come back—not hide in ultimate reality nor deny the pain of the relative experience, but simply recognize *This is old-mind condition. In this moment I am not being rejected. And even if I am, I need not fear it.* You do not get rid of the illusion of contraction of the energy field. You simply release that which is clearly no longer needed. On the relative plane you recognize old baggage and then you make the skillful decision to come back to that truth of who you are. This allows you to reconnect with the perfect light body and to release that contraction from the energy field so it may no longer create the illusion of distortion.

You have been practicing the distortions over and over and over. Releasing the illusion of distortion is not the work of an instant, but a continued practice. As a continued practice, it must be done cautiously. There is no getting rid of the distortion. If there is aversion to the distortion, then one must move back into their relative practice, finding mercy for that being that is feeling the pain of rejection, for example. But when there is clear seeing, *This is old-mind, just old habit, and*

I don't need to carry it around, then you release it. There are many practices that are useful here. They all center on releasing of boundaries, expanding energy outward, and coming back into that place of your own divinity and perfection.

I would offer one more image to help clarify some confusion in the group. I would like you to visualize a perfect, brilliant light shining on a piece of paper. Let us call this light the perfect light-body template for your being. Let us call the piece of paper the physical body. If you take a sheet of clear cellophane that is similar to the sheet of paper we crumpled and hold it in front of that light, the perfect light will still fall on the sheet of paper. It will not appear distorted. If you wrinkle the cellophane and hold it in front of the light, the wrinkles will man-ifest on the sheet of paper. Then you think, "Oh, I've got to get rid of the wrinkles," and you begin to try to unwrinkle the sheet of paper. But the sheet of paper never had wrinkles. The wrinkles are an illusion of the incarnate process. Finally, you turn your attention to the cello-phane and try to iron the wrinkles out of the cellophane. Eventually you come to the truth: "The perfect, unwrinkled sheet of paper is still there. What I am seeing on the white paper of the physical body is simply the illusion of wrinkle. Skillfully attending to it on the relative plane, I must look at the light of the incarnation and find the perfect, unwrinkled sheet of paper and allow my identity to rest there." Then the distortions that are no longer practiced will go, just as the wrinkles will fall out of a piece of cloth when it is left alone. But if you keep picking up that cloth and giving energy to the wrinkles, they will become more solid. This is the teaching in capsule form. I would be glad to expand on it if you have questions. People are becoming tired. If there is a brief question now, we will attend to it.

Questioner: This may be a real simple question, and if it is I would appreciate it if it were agreed upon just for the sake of the group. I just wanted either a clarification or a correction of my understanding of emotion. And I was wondering if Aaron could give a brief descrip-tion of emotion. Is emotion strictly the relation of one's reaction, either positive or negative, to an object? And is it strictly a tool, or are there other qualities in emotions that are possibly helpful to our awakening to our distortions?

Aaron: I hear your question. Each of you has an emotional body, distinct from the physical or mental bodies. All three bodies are connected to what we would call consciousness, which I will not attempt to define in this brief explanation. When there is a physical or mental catalyst that is perceived by the small ego-self as something that will enhance or diminish, help or harm, there may be a contraction of the energy field toward or against that catalyst. The experience of this contraction, not the contraction itself but the relationship to the contraction, is what I mean by emotion. Does that sufficiently answer your question or would you like me to speak further? That is all.

Questioner: I may need to think on that.

Barbara: Aaron asks if there are any questions to be considered later.

Questioner: Okay. First of all I have a question still on the table that didn't get answered, which is about "stuckness." And I'd like to hear from Q'uo. And even more so I'd like to hear from Q'uo about the harvest. What will happen? What we can do to help people prepare, if anything, and maybe some more technicalities and specifics about that.

(The group offers comments that it will be a good session tomorrow.)

Questioner: I think my last question is personal, but I'm interested in the phenomenon of physical contact with our brothers. Maybe I can formulate a more specific question tomorrow.

Questioner: I might have one for tomorrow: A commentary from both Q'uo's point of view and Aaron's on what is actually going on when

426

a group such as ours gathers, that is not visible, involving interactions between and among the group.

Carla: And I have a final consideration. It's not a question or an answer, but it's a consideration. And that is that because of the schedule of L/L, we will be having a meditation at four o'clock tomorrow afternoon in addition to the session in the morning. Probably Barbara will have to leave. I don't know. But you all are welcome to stay. Barbara of course, if she stays, will co-teach as channel with Jim and me. So, if things don't get wrapped up and if you are going to be here longer, panic not. We will be glad to dedicate the four o'clock session to working further with questions that you came with and don't want to leave unanswered in some way.

Questioner: Well, I've got one from out in left field. In Santa Fe we get all the strange and wonderful ideas like changes to the DNA, including that there's some evolution going on in the DNA and that kind of thing. I want to hear about that and see if that's true, and ask how that might come in with the harvest question.

Questioner: DNA/RNA … you can modify it to DNA/RNA.

Questioner: Yeah, what kind of modifications and what we could do about it, if anything.

Barbara: Aaron would like to say something very briefly.

Aaron: One of the questions just raised is, "What's happening here under the surface, beyond these sessions?" Each of your vibrational frequencies has been considerably raised since you came yesterday, because of the nature of these sessions and your own inner work. Rejoice in that energy. Share it joyfully and please be as aware as possible. None of you is here by chance. Allow each to be a catalyst and to serve you as you serve each other.

A catalyst is both joyful and painful. Embrace both the joy and the pain. My conjecture is that there will be far more joy than pain in your presence with one another, but that others' questions and issues may raise some pain in yourselves. Embrace this opportunity for deeper learning. With this in mind, much later this evening I would like to offer a brief ten- or fifteen-minute guided meditation before bedtime for any who would like to participate. It may be a lovingkindness or forgiveness meditation. It may be one of letting go of boundaries. I will wait through the evening to feel the energy I am receiving from you and note what would be of most use. If none of you choose to participate that is fine. Any who would like to is welcome.

Once again, I thank you. *(Clap!)*

Questioner: What timing!

Aaron: Know the movement of love that has brought you to this gathering and enabled you to participate. I express my deepest joy, for the sharing between Q'uo and myself and all of you. That is all.

(The group pauses and engages in song. Later that evening, the meditation session resumes.)

Aaron: I have been reading your energy tonight. I have the idea of two distinctly different kinds of meditation. One, to generate a deeper sense of lovingkindness toward yourself and all beings. The other, to work with the boundaries that arise within you. While I see the value of either to most of you, I think we will work with the falling away of boundaries, as it is more directly relevant to what we have talked about today.

Visualize yourself walking through lovely woods. You come to a small clearing where there are wildflowers growing, and just beyond the clearing, a stream. To the opposite side from the clearing there is a rocky wall, a cliff side of ten or twelve feet. As you contemplate the beauty of this scene, suddenly someone across the stream starts throwing rocks at you. The first whacks you on the shoulder and you turn and look to see a large, menacing person. You have noticed there is a cave in this cliff side, so you retreat into it. This is an unusual cave, more like a bowl—a soft, lined container. It is very dimly lit, enough so it is not total darkness, but not what you would consider light. It is shaped like a large balloon. The mouth has the quality that when you push it aside, it remains as open as you desire it to be until you take your touch away; and then it contracts, closing completely—a magic cave. Allow yourself to enter. Feel its softness. Feel the sense of safety within. You can hear the rocks still bouncing off the walls, but nothing can harm you. After some time, the rocks stop. Minutes, hours, years, and centuries pass.

I said this is a magical cave. You are fed. There is air. Your needs are met. You are enclosed. You spend eons dreaming in this softness. Finally the light comes to your awareness. A very dim light within this cocoon touches memories of a brilliance you had known. There arises the desire to remember and reexperience that brilliance. Tentatively you reach out to the mouth of this cocoon, remembering how the walls will expand with your touch and hold that expansion, but with the magical quality that as soon as you say, "Close," it snaps shut. Reach out from this place of utter safety. Touch that doorway and allow it to open just the smallest amount. Allow light to stream in. It is springtime. Allow the sweet smell of the air to enter. How long has it been since you have opened yourself to that freshness? What made you close yourself off here in the first place? There is the dim memory of danger. What if that being with his rocks is still there? But it has been an eternity.

Acknowledging any fear or resistance, ask yourself if you can open this doorway just a bit further and come out into the light and the fresh air, not moving out of your safe spot but allowing an opening big enough that you can truly look out. Here is the meadow, just as you remembered it, filled with wildflowers. There is the bubbling stream with small waterfalls over rocks and lovely pools where one could sit. The trees sway in the breeze and are alive with songbirds and their own whispered melody of the wind. You are safe. Open the armor just a bit more.

Can you see how terrifying it would be if someone were to slice into this cocoon with a magic sword, cutting it in half so that it fell apart? You would be free but you would be in terror. It would be a violence to you. One is not freed by being forced into freedom, but by choosing freedom when one sees that the armor that was chosen for its safety is no longer needed. We honor that armor. It served a purpose. But we recognize, "I do not need this anymore. Whatever illusion of danger there was from which I sought safety, it no longer exists. I am safe."

The memory of the man with rocks does not die easily. The dim memories of the many horrors you have experienced through your many lifetimes do not die easily. You are not attempting to rid yourself of those memories, but to allow them to take their place as part of the catalyst that has brought you to where you are today. The armor served its purpose. Now it is old habit.

I am going to be silent for a few minutes. What I would like you to do is to enlarge this opening as much as you feel comfortable. Remember, a light touch of your hands will ask it to grow bigger. Simply the thought, "close," will lead it to snap shut and you will be enclosed and safe again. Here you can experiment. You can look into your fear in a safe way. You do not need to emerge completely. You may choose to open the doorway enough that you may sit in it, like a doorway, knowing that you are still within. Or you may find that you are ready to come out and smell the flowers and to play in the pools of the stream.

With great gentleness and kindness, allow yourself to move out of this armor and to be touched directly by the world around you. There is no right or wrong way to do this. Simply emerge as far as is comfortable and investigate the nature of the fears that hold you back. We will be silent now for five minutes.

(Pause)

As you open to the world beyond your armor, you become aware that there are others emerging, each from their own armored shell. At first you may startle at the presence of others' energy and want to withdraw. If there is any sense of needing a shelter, allow yourself to withdraw a bit until you feel safe. See that the others do not threaten you, that this is old habit that wants to pull itself back in. Then you can simply acknowledge old habit and old conditioning: "I do not need to do this anymore." Touch the walls and come out again. As your armor falls away, you will find it natural to make contact with others. If it is appropriate to your own emergence from your shell, reach out your hands, feet, or whatever limb can make contact to one or more neighbors sitting beside you in this room. Very carefully and mindfully, see how it feels to allow yourself to be fully vulnerable and open to another's energy field and to release your own energy field out to them. I ask you to do this now quite literally, if you feel it appropriate, reaching out hands or feet so that you contact at least one other person. Gently explore the nature of this opening. Know that there is no force. You may retreat at any time. This practice is to help you experience the nature of that armor as old baggage, to more fully experience the nature of the presence and that you are safe and may continue without your armor, without the illusion of limits and boundaries.

You may wish to drop the hand you touch and then take it again, to feel how it feels to separate yourself from the other's energy and then rejoin. I will be quiet for one minute.

(Pause)

It is quite late, so we will end this meditation here. But I would like you to carry this practice with you to bed and through tomorrow. Each time you feel threatened, notice the contraction of your energy field and the way that pulls you back into a sense of armoring, perhaps seeing two people talking together and feeling rejected by them or hearing something that threatens you and asks you to look deeper at fear. Watch each contraction and the way you pull into your armor and then ask yourself, "Is this old habit? Can I allow these boundaries to reopen? Can I allow myself again to emerge? And again and again …?"

May all beings everywhere come to know their infinite nature and their limitlessness. May all beings everywhere emerge from their self-made prisons and find the true freedom of their connection with all that is. May that knowledge of your freedom and infinite perfection bring you home. I love you all and bid you a good night. That is all.

Session 26

(This session was preceded by a period of tuning and meditation.)

Group questions: Should we begin with all or one of the questions that we came up with at the end of the session yesterday? The feeling is to put all the questions on the screen and let Aaron and Q'uo speak to them as they will.

M. would like to hear from Q'uo about the quality of the harvest, what will happen then, and what we can do to help to prepare for it, if anything.

There is information about DNA/RNA changes that are occurring, and we would like to know if there is information on this topic that would be helpful to know.

What is actually going on that is not visible when a group such as ours gathers, as interactions among and between everyone in the group? How do we use that energy when we go home to continue to grow and serve?

(Carla channeling)

Q'uo: We are known to you as those of Q'uo. Greetings in the love and in the light of the one infinite Creator.

Upon this morning dedicated by your peoples as a Sabbath, we embrace each in holy joy and thank you for calling us to you in these sessions. You have made it possible for us to offer the service that is ours to give. There is no greater help to us than that precious call for information. Without this we could not serve in the way we have chosen to offer service. It is only in the work of serving you that we may learn those lessons that are before us as a people at this time. Therefore, we most humbly thank each for the enormous service you have done for us.

As each relaxes about the circle, we ask each to pause and simply look within, asking to see in some symbolic, mental visualization your energy nexus. How do the harmonics, resonances, and balances of this present moment compare with that system of energetic displacement with which you came to these sessions of working? We suspect that each may see the brightening, regularizing, and balancing of energies far beyond the system of energy with which each entered this environment.

Each entity is as the radio. There is the ability to vibrate at various speeds and levels of rotation or vibration to send out to other receivers. And there is the receiver that may take in those vibrations sent by other senders. When a group such as this converges for a united desire, the energy available to each in the group exponentially skyrockets because each is as the flower turning to the sun. Each basks in the others' radiant warmth. Now we realize this work is done for the most part without conscious intent; however, the conscious awareness of this process is not necessary in order that this adjustment process occur.

Now, to each entity there have come new faces and new personalities. There has been the opening to that first meeting of the mind and heart. In the natural way of third-density beings there has been the instinctual movement toward groupings. Amongst these groupings, shifting and further harmonization have taken place as each spirit deepens the lines of communication with the various other entities, so that over the period of these few rich hours of companionship and heartfelt love, a community supporting each has evolved, complete with stories to tell of laughter and of tears.

For wanderers, this gathering of like souls is especially poignant because of the extended spiritual families or clans that make up the chosen groupings of entities into community in higher densities. When each departs this crystallized new entity of light, each may carry this supporting and enabling group ethos or spirit within the memory of the heart.

You wish to know how to use this incalculable, priceless gift. Firstly, we ask each to gaze often into this memory, for there is comfort and validation in this group, each for the others. This simple remembering is potent and is one occasion that maximizes the development of faith. For each has the faith for the others.

Each falls down in faith when the gaze turns inward. Therefore, this community of seeking, devotion, and faith that has been born here may withstand the plangent, painful doubts and fears that will come to each. Further, when this memory is seen as that crystallized gem of offered and accepted love that it is, that gem may be scried as the seer's glass. And within its light the Creator itself lives, accessible in that intimate, personal way in which family members all have the same remembrance of loving parents, loving father and loving mother. So, each may see the memory both as invaluable in itself and as a clear glass in which each may become transparent to the one great original Thought, which is Love.

Now, each has its own network of friends who also walk upon a path of faith, attempting to live a life of devotion to the Creator. Thusly, each may link this group with others. In this way, that golden net of which we have spoken is more and more finished, with the strands covering more and more of the globe's inner spheres.

This is a time of beginnings and the dawning of a new millennium. In this new day, your riches shall be each other. How much you have to give each other, my friends! Yourself, you cannot save, for another must reach the hand. Yet, what you are not able to do for yourself, trust and know that you—imperfect, broken, and sorrowing; yes, you, just you, only you—can do great service for others. Just, merely, only you, as you are, are of infinite value to each other.

This is the way of salvation for all peoples: love reflected in love until your entire environment moves as though to one great music, even the flowers and trees swaying to that dawning, enhanced consciousness that is gradually coming, even now, to each questing spirit.

We would at this time turn the microphone to our beloved brother, the one known as Aaron. We are those of Q'uo.

(Barbara channeling)

Aaron: My greetings and love to you all. My beloved brother/sister of Q'uo has spoken of the ways you may draw your energy together to deepen love and faith as you reside within this illusion. That foundation of love becomes a strong source to draw upon as you work with the sufferings of the third-density experience.

I wish to speak to these sufferings a bit more specifically, especially as they occur for wanderers. Each of you is unique. I do not wish to categorize you and in that way minimize your pain. What I describe, then, is a map; and you will need to fill in the details yourselves. But I offer the map as guidance through your confusion.

I see three basic areas where wanderers find themselves struggling. The first is the physical distortion. When you enter a density that is disharmonious to your own frequency vibration, it is not only discordant with the physical body's frequency vibration, but often has the illusion of discordancy with the emotional and mental bodies' frequency vibrations. Each of your four bodies has its own specific frequency vibration. You can retune, but must also acknowledge the heavier vibrations of the physical and emotional bodies and not try to force a higher resonance before the human is ready. The second area of struggle comes at this point. Rather than trust your situation, you may use grasping and force of judgment to attempt to penetrate the veil.

The third area of your discomfort lies just on the other side of that veil: "Home. I want to go home." You cannot say it more simply or poignantly than that. Let us speak to these three areas and begin to explore how the discomfort itself may become a tool for learning and enrich your readiness to serve on this spaceship we call Earth.

I said that each of these bodies resonates to its own frequency vibration. When you strum one string of a stringed instrument, sometimes the nearby strings will vibrate as well. While each has its own vibrational frequency, the harmonics involved set up accompanying patterns of vibration. Many wanderers come into the incarnation out of tune with the vibrational frequency of third-density Earth. The feeling is as if you were a giant violin string wanting to sing out your music to the world. But every time the string that you are begins to vibrate, something clamps down on it, preventing the fullness of that vibration. The more you fight against that which stills your string, the greater the illusion of discordancy. The hand that touches the string and the string itself can come into harmonious interaction. The earth plane and the physical vibrational frequency of the wanderer can come into greater harmony when one relaxes into the environment into which you have incarnated.

It is common for wanderers to suffer from allergies or asthma, reacting to both the natural substances of the earth and the distortions of those substances. I do not suggest that such allergic reactions are mental. Certainly it is the physical body that is finding disharmony. But part of the disharmony comes from your fight with the incarnation.

I want to go into some specific detail here. There is not a specific vocabulary to discuss this. Let us use metaphor. I return to that example I gave yesterday. We have the perfect light or the perfect light-body template shining down on a white sheet of paper, which is the physical body. Let us adapt a term that we will call "sub light body." This is not sub "dash" light but sub light body, which is slightly lower than the light body.

Let us envision, here, a piece of perfect cellophane. The light that shines through onto the paper of the physical body is perfect. When you wrinkle the cellophane and unfold it, the reflection of those wrinkles shows up on the piece of paper. When you identify with the wrinkles and start to believe they are real on the piece of paper, you act in certain ways as if they were real. When you remember that the perfect, unwrinkled sheet lies within the wrinkled sheet, your attitude toward the reflected wrinkles on the lower page, which represents the physical body, will change. You look at the wrinkle and you say, *It's there or appears to be, but I don't have to act as if it's the only reality.* When you can dwell more fully in the ultimate reality, what happens is that your energy field does not contract around each wrinkle. There is spaciousness around what has arisen.

Let us bring this picture back to the situation of the wanderer with physical-body discordancy on the earth plane. The light-body template is always perfect and in full harmony with all that is. Here sitting in this room is the ever-perfect physical body that carries an experience of distortion. Focus on that pain or discordance, literally seeing it as a reflection of a wrinkle in that sheet of paper. The wrinkles may represent the painful back, the stomach problem, allergies, or whatever pain or discordance may be. I am not suggesting that it is not real within the relative reality in which you dwell. If your stomach or back hurts, your stomach or back hurts. If there is allergy and watering of the eyes, that is happening. You are experiencing it. But it is not the only reality. A higher reality is the innate perfection that is also there.

We move into the same two steps I discussed yesterday, which involve acknowledging the real, uncomfortable experience and finding openheartedness for the discomfort, wherein there is no longer such strong aversion and no longer such fear of it. The pain and/or aversion themselves are part of all that is. Do not create a duality here.

The second part is to move back into this perfect light-body template. Instead of allowing the physical body to reflect the discordancy that mental and emotional bodies have created and in which you have pain, come back to your perfection and rest in it. In a sense it is a kind of wordless affirmation. You are not denying the relative plane of reality, but choosing to more fully ground yourself in the ultimate reality of who you are.

No, you will not wipe away all your physical ills with this practice. They are gifts of the incarnation. Through your own pain on the earth plane, you learn a deep sensitivity and compassion for the pain of all who suffer. You are meant to fully experience this as a third-density human. So this practice is not going to get rid of all physical distortion, but it will considerably lessen the intensity with which you experience it. All you need to do is to sit for a few minutes in meditation when this physical distortion feels strong, send deep compassion to the human who is suffering its throbbing head or back pain, and then allow yourself to connect to the light-body template and relax into the perfection of your being. Remember, the light-body template is not disharmonious to this density. You create the body disharmony through the contractions that arise out of your struggle with the heavy-density experience. When you relax and rest in the spaciousness of the ultimate, the disharmony resolves.

Work with the emotional and mental bodies is much the same. I will not repeat the details of the practice. When I look at you I literally see light streaming down from this light-body template. This light surrounds you, not just as your aura but as the entire energy expression. The silver cord is a metaphor for what I see. Of course, it is not a silver cord in ultimate reality. But there is this seeming silver cord that connects through all the energy chakras of the physical body up through the sub light body and into the light body, and through that perfect light body into that which is the source of the light body. Here is that child's sun and triangular sunbeam of which I spoke yesterday. The energy comes from the sun through the sunbeam and through the reflection of the sunbeam, which we called the sub light body, and down into the physical body. The energy field radiates out, not just from the light body and physical body but from this whole connected cord.

When your energy is open and relaxed, there is no hard edge to it. Picture it as billions of dancing molecules of light, denser toward the cord of the physical structure, and more dispersed as it moves out. The energy of that which you contact moves in because there is no skin and no edge. When you freeze up inside, as wanderers especially are prone to do, this has a different vibrational frequency and it is going to hurt. You put a shell or hard edge around your being and move into an illusion of separation. But my dear ones, how can you help but smack into the various illusions of this plane when you create a hard edge against which they will smack?

We keep letting go of that edge, then. First, you must see that you have built it. Each time you feel the edges, you ask yourself to let them down. Then you will no longer feel the physical, emotional, and mental densities of the Earth as a hand clamping down over your string that wants to vibrate. You will begin to experience them as sister strings; for example, perhaps no longer a violin, but a bass and a cello. But you can begin to vibrate in harmony with them. First, you must allow them in.

Finally, we come to the deepest pain of many wanderers: *I want to go home. I feel so alone, so isolated, and so abandoned. I want to go home.* Earlier this weekend I said that all wanderers, 98 percent of you, come equally to serve and to learn. We cannot specify and say this and that and that are what each wants to learn. You are each unique; however, a common chord in your learning relates to that of which I spoke yesterday. I called it old-soul syndrome. It is not something that applies only to wanderers. But because wanderers generally are old souls, we find that it does very deeply apply to most wanderers. It might be expressed as, *God seems to be out there and it is perfect. I am here, separate from that divine energy, and I am imperfect. I can't go home until I become perfect.* That is the misunderstanding. You strive to become perfect instead of simply looking deeper into yourself and understanding that you are and always have been perfect. What you seek is not out there. It is right here in your own heart. The Divine is every place, but needs to be sought no place else than right here. This is the greatest misunderstanding and threshold to the greatest gift this incarnation can offer you: to begin to know your own divinity.

If you were already perfect you would not have come into the incarnation. The relative human is never going to be perfect. The light-body template of which you are a seemingly imperfect reflection is and always has been perfect. That light-body template is none other than a projection of the Divine, in which sunbeams beam back into the sun. There is nothing there that is not of the same nature as the sun.

You are trapped in the illusion of the wrinkles. That is not a problem. It is your catalyst for remembering your divinity. Allow it to teach you. When you finally understand who you are, you understand that you have always been home. How could you leave that which fills you always? How could you have ever been separate from that? What a joyful moment it is when you understand what you truly are. The healing of that delusion of separation and flaw fulfills the learning for which you came into form and frees you to offer your energy with a greater focus and a greater clarity to the service that you came to perform.

I pass the microphone at this time to my brother/sister Q'uo, with much joy in this sharing and in the way we may elaborate on each other's thoughts. That is all.

(Carla channeling)

Q'uo: My Brothers and Sisters of Sorrow, long ago, as you measure time, we and others came among you. When we left, we had salted away within your planet's inner worlds the fair fruit of some of our peoples. These "salted" people loved so deeply and heard the cries of Earth so clearly that they were willing to sacrifice their present pleasantness for the difficult and painful, challenging and worthwhile mission, if you will, of sowing within your peoples' awareness those seeds of harmonic understanding that might hopefully assist those of your sphere and the sphere itself, your beloved Planet Earth, to weather the crossing of that channel of birth. At that time it looked as though it would be a difficult birth. Now the time ripens and the fields of the Earth's spirits are white with harvest. Now the harvest of Earth begins.

Wanderers, sorrow's own folk, you have come here to serve. We call you all to service now. Take up your crown of thorns. Lift the burden of your humanity and walk forth unafraid. We encourage each to trust destiny. Your basic vocation is devotion. Work with your moments of conscious awareness in your own way and at your own speed, taking rest and comfort as you need that refreshment. Allow each morning's light to form its own agenda within you for your day and your night.

And study patience; for in addition to this great central vocation that even now regularizes your planet and its steadying light, you will come into those apparent and overt services that have been prepared for you.

To many, the service of devotion is the complete service required. If this is occurring within your life, come to an informed understanding of the value of being. For it is because your ground of being is remarkable that this lonely job of keeping the lighthouse burning has been given you. Tend, then, to this light within, hollowing the self through anguish, pain, and initiation until you are transparent to the light. This may be your destiny: to act as radiator and regulator of the light of Planet Earth. To others shall come ministries, as this instrument would call them. We encourage those who begin to develop as channels of some form of healing to move along the path of your gifts. Look always to the true shape of the gifts within.

Perhaps, in addition to being the light that shines upon the hill, you may also have what the world and its illusions know as vocations. Entities such as this instrument, the one known as Jim, and the one known as Barbara have developed such vocations. And there seems, perhaps, a glamour or desirable charisma emanating from these services. Yet in truth, these entities are but channels. The glamour and the charisma exist within the channel, which is the space these entities have created by their faith.

When such an opportunity arrives for you, you may embrace it, being completely unworthy in your own eyes. For in such service the actual job requirement is willingness to sit with that light that has been given, reaching not and striving never, but ready to accept the souls given into your care. Never accept the opinion of others when praise is given, but always know and offer credit to that which has flowed through your channel. This is so difficult: to remain open and accepting when it appears that you are successful in helping. What a difficult trap to avoid. Yet each shall keep the other's balance through communication and mutual support. Each may encourage each to true humility, true servanthood.

You have sacrificed much for this opportunity to serve. Take, seize, grasp this opportunity, not to rush forward with it but to sit embracing it, asking it, *Change me as I must change to do the will of the infinite One. Humble me. Comfort me. Give me companions along my way. Give me persistence, stubbornness, and courage. Let me love insult and misunderstanding. Let me embrace criticism and shame. Let me become empty.* These are the prayers of the Brothers and Sisters of Sorrow. These are prayers of tears and joy beyond all knowing.

We would at this time transfer the microphone to the one known as Aaron. We are Q'uo.

(Barbara channeling)

Aaron: I want to speak to this term "harvest" and what it means. This is a word that is often used. Perhaps you flinch at the term and your energy quails because the word implies force to you, in that someone goes out into a field and harvests the grain and fruit to take it for its own, as if the grain or fruit were being used or manipulated. Think of the small energy that moved into that stalk of wheat and into that apple or bean. When energy moves into that which is used on this plane as food for others, its greatest will, at whatever level it is conscious, is to learn how to offer its energy to others in becoming part of the greatness that is universal consciousness. When you pick an apple from a tree and express gratitude for the nourishment and sweetness of that fruit, it honors the apple's greatest joy, which is to serve. Its free will is not being violated by being plucked to be eaten. If it did not want to be eaten it would have invented blemishes of one sort or another that would make it unappealing. The richer it appears and the more vibrant its energy field, the more it wishes to offer itself and to make itself attractive.

Just so, the evolving human that has become ready to move beyond this density becomes vibrant in its desire to be a tool of the Divine. It becomes radiant in its selflessness. Its greatest wish is to be of service and, as my brother/sister Q'uo just said, to allow its will to be offered to the greater will of the Infinite, as in saying, "Not my will, but thine be done;[61] not for my glory, but for thine. It only comes through me. I am simply a channel."

---

[61] Luke 22:42 AV.

Think you of this. Barbara, here, is a channel. She channels this energy that you have come to know as Aaron. Do you not think that I am also a channel? What I offer you does not originate with me. I offer you divine wisdom and tell you nothing that you do not already know in the depths of your own divine wisdom. I am a channel. I am empty. When you come to what Q'uo has referred to as the harvest, it is not that your being is snatched up with no accord to your own will, but that the greatest gift that you can offer is to allow your energy and light to evolve to the point that you are ready to move beyond the limits that you have previously believed. From thence you may be harvested into the next step of your evolution.

It may help you to think of it with this image. Within each being is an intense light, unlimited in its power. Around each being are many layers of shielding, like an onion. Place that intense light in the center of the onion. With each giving up of fear and with each bit of clarity of the truth of that inner light, layers of the so-called onion fall away. You become translucent. At a certain point you emit so much light that you are ready for the so-called harvest. You are ready to move into another plane where further layers may fall away. With higher densities, more and more layers of shielding and separation fall away until finally that brilliant and intense inner core is exposed and offered into the service of the Infinite, of God.

What is this harvest about on the earth plane? I spoke yesterday of the move of Earth from third to fourth density. In fourth density you are part of an energy group. You are not forced into that and not fixed in your placement, but desirous of that deepening contact. In a sense, the connection between you this weekend is rehearsal for fourth density. When you let your barriers down and allow yourself to be both more telepathic with each other and very open in your energy fields, with thinned shielding, you are practicing for fourth-density experience. The illusions of separation will fall away.

Fourth-density Earth may appear not much different in some outward aspects. There will be seas and mountains and forests. Yet, there will be a new understanding of the deepest interconnection of all that is, both upon the Earth and outward from the Earth. You will be co-creators with the soil in the creation of your crops. If you choose to eat solid food rather than to dwell simply on the light and energy, that which you eat will be thanked graciously. And as Q'uo thanked you for the opportunity you give him to serve, your food will thank you for its opportunity to serve by nourishing your body. You will understand your codependence on others in a positive sense. You will not be ashamed of that which arises in you. Since there will be no shame over the arisings of the emotional body nor any need to fling those emotions on others, you will deeply share your joys and sorrows, much as fourth-density energy does now.

Fourth-density energy now is fully telepathic within its group. The learning of compassion is so profound because you fully experience the unshielded emotions of another, as its pains, its sorrows, and its joys. You no longer are limited to learning from your own experience but become able to learn from everyone's experience. And because you no longer guard your own experience out of shame, you offer it to others for a source for their learning. This is what Earth is in process of becoming.

People ask me, "Is this really going to happen? What about the arising negativity I see on the earth plane?" My dear ones, if you fear and hate that negativity, you simply add to it and it will become the source of your own stagnation. This process is much in the ways a child learns lessons in school and asks, "Am I ready to go on?" If he or she does not study for an examination and does not pass the test, he may not go on. The focus is not on progression but on understanding. The work must be reviewed until it is understood. There is no time pressure. If you continue to return fear to fear and hatred to hatred, you have not understood and the work will be repeated until it is understood. The Earth will continue to offer you catalyst. When enough of you understand the lessons and can return kindness and love to fear by allowing fear to become a catalyst for compassion rather than hate, then you will be ready to shed the illusion and move into fourth density.

Many of you will continue on fourth-density Earth. Others will move back to nonmaterial planes from which you came and find whatever other ways you may choose to serve and to learn. The radiant fruit that you have become will find its next place in the universe, which is its next place to serve, to grow, and to love. I would like here to pass the microphone back to Q'uo. That is all.

(Carla channeling)

Q'uo: The time has come for us to bid each dear spirit here farewell. We cannot sufficiently express our humble thanks for calling us to you to share our opinion with you. Even as we depart, our most deep wisdom, my friends, remains. It is to love the Creator; to know that the Creator loves you and brought you into being to delight itself; and to dance as the child of the stars that you are, always knowing that the key is to love one another, to share each other's joy, to bear each other's burden of sorrow, and to bring each other home.

We of Q'uo leave each in the love and in the light of the one infinite mystery that created all that there is in unity and harmony. Adonai. Adonai. Adonai *vasu borragus.*

(Barbara channeling)

Aaron: I would like to close by teaching you a very simple meditation practice, drawn from the Tibetan Buddhist tradition, which may be used to open up your own hearts and to more deeply offer your energy and service to another. It has two parts. I am going to teach them to you one at a time and then we will put it together.

Feel yourselves seated in a cylinder of light. Breathe in, feeling that light enter through the crown chakra and coming down to the heart center. As you breathe out, feel that light stabilizing within you and filling you. Breathe in, visualizing some person or place of suffering. It may be used with a friend, or perhaps when you are watching your television and see the victims of war or famine. It is best to hold one image in your mind here, and not to scatter your energy. So you have breathed in that light and breathed it out, letting it fill you and especially letting it move into the heart center. And then you have breathed in and visualized suffering. Breathing out, allow that light to move out and to be directed to that place of suffering. That is part one. Let us practice it several times. Breathing in the light ... exhale, feeling the light expand within you ... breathe in, visualizing the person or place of suffering ... breathe out, sending that light out to suffering ... breathe in light ... exhale, expand the light ... inhale, visualizing the suffering ... exhale, sending the light out ... inhale light ... exhale ... inhale ... send the light out.

Now we add the second part. After you have sent that light out to the one who is suffering, visualize that suffering as a heavy, black, tar-like mass. Breathe in, allowing yourself to breathe that heaviness into your heart. Breathe in ... exhale, feeling the weight of it ... breathe in, opening your heart and awareness to God ... breathe out, releasing that heaviness ... just let it go ... breathe in light ... exhale, expanding light ... inhale, visualizing the suffering ... exhale, sending the light to that place of suffering. Visualizing that suffering as a heavy, black mass ... breathing, feeling the weight of suffering in your heart ... breathe in intention to release ... breathe out and release. That is it. I ask that we do it for two or three minutes. I ask that you do it at your own pace.

(Pause to do the meditation.)

This practice may be done at double the speed, simply breathing in light with the inhalation, sending it out, breathing in the suffering and darkness with the next inhalation, and then releasing it. Or it may be done at half the speed with a full inhale and exhale for each step. Suit the speed to your own temperament. It may also be done with yourself as subject and object when you are in much pain. You may become a channel of light, bringing light into your heart. And you may become a channel of release of your suffering, reminding yourself through the offer to take that suffering from yourself and release it.

It is a way of expressing your energy and of truly becoming that servant of light. It is a way of expressing your willingness not to hold onto that light in service to self, but to offer it out to where there is pain. It is also a way of expressing your willingness not to bar yourself and separate yourself from pain, but to be a channel through which that suffering of the world may be released.

I thank each of you for calling us to speak with you this weekend. I thank each of you for the beautiful being that you are. Each of you I see as a rose opening into the sunshine, with each new day or each new incarnation of your being more fully expressing your glory. Please know how deeply you are loved by beings of all planes and that you are never alone, but are surrounded by loving energy that would assist and nourish you on your path. That is all.

Carla: I want every single one of you to know how privileged we are to have had you this weekend. It is such a blessing to us that you are here. This is what we are here for and it really feels wonderful. If there are times in the future when you need to come back, don't think twice. Just give us a call to let us know you're coming. We know you will bring your healing with you when you come. And we are always here to welcome you and to answer any questions we can about the mechanics of living, while you have the healing that you came to have. We hope you will keep in touch with us, whatever happens to you, because we love every one of you very much. Thanks for your company. It's wonderful to suffer with such great people. Perhaps Barbara would like to say a word or two.

Barbara: Just, thank you.

Questioner: I don't know how my, and I'm sure shared by others, sense of gratitude can be expressed to Carla, Jim, and Barbara. But thank you for holding this space and time apart that we might come and sit together with you and listen and be filled. Thank you so much.

Group: *(Sings)*

> Love one another. Love one another, as I love you.
> Care for each other. Care for each other, as I care
>   for you.
> And bear each other's burdens
> And share each other's joy.
> Love one another. Love one another
> And bring each other home.

WEEKEND 8

Once again we were a large group. We gathered in Carla and Jim's garage again, fourteen months after weekend 7. Jim had hung material on the walls to insulate the space and make it more attractive. Outside our door, late fall had turned the earth brown. Trees were almost bare. But it was a surprisingly clear autumn weekend, warm enough to enjoy the outdoors during our free time. By that point, most of our group had come to know each other and rejoice in the opportunity to spend these weekends together.

The group expressed a variety of needs. Again, Carla, Barbara, Aaron, and Q'uo had a prearranged topic that was large in scope: "What is the devotional life and how do we live it?" People had been thinking about the question for months before our gathering, so there was a great richness to what was shared.

Part of devotion is opening the heart. Barbara and Aaron led a meditation on lovingkindness.

A Lovingkindness Meditation from Aaron

Find a comfortable position, body relaxed, back erect, eyes closed softly.

Bring to the heart and mind the image of one for whom there is loving respect. This person may be a dear friend, parent, teacher, or any being with whom the primary relationship is one in which you have been nurtured.

We often take such a person for granted, seeing what is offered to us, but failing to see deeply into that being's situation. Look deeply at that being, deeper than you ever have before, and see that he or she has suffered. He has felt pain of the body or the heart. She has known grief, loss, and fear. He has felt loneliness and disconnection. She has been lost and confused. Along with the joy, see the ways in which this dear one has suffered.

Speaking silently from the heart, note this one's pain, offering first the person's name.

> You have suffered. You have felt alone or afraid. You have known pain in your body and your mind. You have known grief and loss. You have felt alienation, and the constriction of the closed heart. Your life has not always brought you what you might have wished. You have not been able to hold on to what you loved, or to be free of what brought pain. You have suffered.

What loving thoughts can you offer to this dear one? Let the thoughts come with the breath, arising and moving out.

> May you be free of suffering.
> May you find the healing that you seek.
> May you love, and be loved.
> May your heart open and flower.
>
> May you know your true nature.
> May you be happy.
> May you find peace.

Please continue silently, repeating these or alternate phrases for several minutes. Go slowly. Allow your heart to connect with this dear one, to open to his or her pain, and to offer these wishes, prompted by the loving heart.

Now, let this loved one move aside, and in his or her place invite in your own self. It is sometimes hard to open our hearts to ourselves. What blocks this love? Just for the sake of experiment, please try to follow the practice and see how it feels, even if it is difficult; but always proceed gently, and without force.

Look deeply at the self and observe that (just as with the loved one) you have suffered. Speaking to yourself, say:

I have suffered. I have felt pain in the body and the mind. I have known grief, loss, and fear. I have felt loneliness and disconnection, felt lost and confused. I have not been able to hold on to what I loved, nor to keep myself safe from that which threatened me. I have suffered.

See the ways you have suffered. Without engaging in self-pity, simply observe the wounds you have borne.

Speaking silently from the heart, this time to your own self, say your name.

What do you wish for yourself?

May I be free of suffering.
May I find the healing that I seek.
May I love and be loved.
May my heart open and flower.

May I know my deepest connection with all that is.
May I be happy.
May I find peace.

Please continue silently, repeating these or alternate phrases for several minutes. Go slowly. Allow your heart to connect with your deepest self, to open to your pain and longing, and to offer wishes prompted by the loving heart.

Session 27

Weekend 8, Part 1 of 4
(This session was preceded by a period of tuning and meditation.)

Group discussion: *(The group agreed upon the topic of living the devotional life in all of its variety and dimensions. Thoughts from the group are presented below.)*

We had originally thought that we would talk about living the devotional life.

R. says he is thinking about the fact that he takes himself too seriously.

G. is thinking about the oneness of all and yet feeling different as well.

Barbara said that many in her group were experiencing the "two-by-four" between the eyes to learn lessons. When we don't pay attention to the gentler nudge the "two-by-four" comes next. I. says that this is not always the case.

Carla says that just deciding to live the devotional life is the only way to do it.

Incarnation as the devotional body is a statement that I. would like either Aaron or Q'uo to speak on. This life, this job, is devotional, no matter what we are doing. Do we have information on being too hard on ourselves? Or could we focus more on that as well? The devotional life is not so much what you try to do as what you are able to do. And we get angry with ourselves for failing time after time.

G. enjoys reading what Barbara has to say about living her normal life, because that is practical.

(Carla channeling)

Q'uo: Greetings in the love and in the light of the one infinite Creator. It is both a blessing and a great privilege to greet each of you this evening. We are humbly privileged to be called to share our opinions and thoughts with you. We would ask, as always, that you use your discrimination as you hear what we have to offer. If the thoughts ring within your resonant heart, then we offer them freely. If they do not ring true, then simply leave them. Put them aside and move on. For truth is a personal and intimate matter and each person will recognize her own truth.

We are blending our vibrations with yours. And as we weave our way through the ribbons of your thoughts, we sense the energy of birth and transformation within each who sits in this circle of seeking. Each seeker sincerely wishes nothing more than to find truth in the self, in the environment, in the thoughts, and in each other. Each has a burden that is carried at some cost and each has a yearning that cries within and yet is deeper than tears can express: to love, to be loved, and to be of true service.

Each may well and justly consider himself a devotee and an adorer of that which is of ultimate truth. The level of anguish that has been experienced as each walks along the path of seeking is sometimes quite high. Concerning the living of a life in faith—that is, the devotional life—we cannot promise that any of you will find in our words or in any others the goal that you so desire. For within the classroom of earthly life the questions are far, far more important than the answers. In the life of the seeker within your density's journey, from head to heart and from knowing to loving, the emotions of yearning and hope are in themselves more highly to be regarded than any knowledge that can be expressed in words.

Nevertheless, much in the way of tools and resources that may aid in seeking can be expressed. But as we move through many considerations and details, please remember that your keen thirst for an inner reality that pierces the illusions of earthly life holds within its invisible field a strength and a truth that shall, one day, be a revelation. And in that day, knowing no more than you do now, you shall yet be satisfied.

At this time we turn the microphone over to our beloved brother Aaron. We leave this instrument in love and light. We are those of the principle of Q'uo.

Session 27

(Barbara channeling)

Aaron: My greetings and love to you all. I ask your forgiveness for my intrusion on your planning session. Of course, this is your human choice, because this concerns your human experience to which we properly respond.

There are many of you with slightly different needs. I will attempt to extract the commonality of need from the expressed needs. You all wish to lead your life in love. And yet sometimes incomprehensibly to you, you end up living parts of it in fear. Sometimes you judge that fear and say, "I am no longer living the devotional life. How do I get rid of my fear and return to love?" Others of you understand that both the love and the fear are expressions of devotion. But still your strong choice is to live your life in love and there may or may not be subtle judgments about fear.

I do not want to go too far here, only to express my perspective that simply to incarnate is a devotional act. It takes tremendous love and courage to move into incarnation. To live the devotional life is not to be rid of fear, but to trust that holding space for fear is part of the devotion; to learn that everything is an expression of God so that the love is found within the fear, for fear is merely a distortion of love.

My brothers and sisters, if it feels appropriate to you, my brother/sister Q'uo and myself would choose to focus on the question, What does it mean to live the devotional life? And how do you run askew of that meaning when fear prevents you from seeing the truth of fear and you find yourself moving into a stance of self-contempt for the fear-based actions or the need to get rid of fear?

I make this statement in an attempt to pull together those threads of commonality that are not only in your verbal questions but also in your thinking. Please feel free to redefine the question and to put aside my suggestions if they do not feel appropriate. Please take my words and consider them within your own heart. I thank you. That is all.

(Pause)

First we need to ask *who* wishes to live the devotional life, because there are many aspects of your self. The soul knows that it always lives the devotional life. It does not live behind a veil, so it sees clearly. But once you walk into human consciousness, it is a struggle to live the devotional life. You struggle with that which seems inconsistent with that life.

I wish to offer you an example. Be a fish with me, twenty yards down underwater. Feel the heaviness of the water and the darkness below you. Look up and see the light. Seen through the density of water and then through the atmosphere is the sun. It is hard to see this orb. Certainly there is something called light, but there is no clear perception of the source of that light. Now, please emerge from the water. And when you arrive at those last inches, suddenly, "Ah! There it is! The sun! This has been the source of light."

This act of looking through the surface, this moment, is akin to the spiritual awakening that each of you has experienced in your lives. Some of you clearly perceived the spirit realm as children, so there was no moment of awakening to the truth of the spirit realm. But even for those of you who experienced that realm as children, there was a time when suddenly you understood, "This isn't concept. This is real. This is the deepest root of my being." There are some of you who were further underwater and had the precise experience of looking through the surface, seeing the sun, and coming into the belief, "Now I am seeing clearly."

But my dear ones, what about Earth's atmosphere? You still do not have a direct experience of the sun. Your meditation and other inner work bring you into that space where finally there is nothing to distort the direct experience of the sun. But still you are seeing at a distance. Then you must go into the heart of the sun. *I will be burned up, destroyed,* you say. Yes, "I" will be destroyed. The self cannot exist except as a concept in the brilliance of that sun. Self is seen only as the tool, having no existence other than as the tool. And yet it must be cherished because it is the tool of the incarnation and you need it. But you wear it only as a cloak. There is no identity with it. It is a tool!

When you come to the readiness to release even ego-self, then you are ready to dive into the heart of the sun where there is no water, no atmosphere, and no distance. Here, at last, is the direct experience of the sun. And what do you find there? One has to laugh as one enters that moment because you find that you have always been there, that you have never left, and that the rest was all illusion.

The soul knows that it always lives the devotional life because it knows the reality of itself as spirit. Those who live in the heaviness of Earth's atmosphere (never mind those underwater, who are not yet aware of the sun) become caught in thinking there is something they need to do to experience the sun. And from the relative perspective, indeed there is. Here is where confusion lies.

The doing is not to wage war with the ego, which solidifies the illusion of relative reality. The work is to bring even the ego-self into the Divine, to bring it to the divine self. You cannot transcend ego until you accept ego. The work is not to wage war with ego-self until the higher self wins, for that is an impossible task. The work is to embrace the ego-self so that it becomes transparent and becomes seen as a serviceable tool of the incarnation.

You, as human, have a challenge, which is to move in both places at once: within the relative structure in which ego seems solid; and within the ultimate structure, which sees with absolute clarity. Relative reality lies within ultimate reality.

My friends, think of a carton. Set yourself down inside it. The lid is closed. Here is your relative reality. You think that is all there is. May I ask you to take a finger and poke up the lid. Slowly raise the head just enough so that the eyes can peer out. Aha! There are a thousand; no, a million; no, ten million and more cartons that beings inhabit. And around them is this infinite space that we call ultimate reality.

You can never leave ultimate reality, and so you can never cease living the devotional life. And yet the relative human must, in part, give its effort to the living of the devotional life, not because that effort is needed for the devotional life to be lived but because the offering of effort is part of the teaching tool of the incarnation. I wish to turn the microphone over to my beloved brother/sister/friend Q'uo. That is all.

(Carla channeling)

Q'uo: We wished to wait until the competition for sound value went a little more toward our favor, as the sound of sirens somewhat over-masters the human voice.

It is in just such moments that the pilgrim soul identifies the sound of a passing siren and thinks, "What an intrusion it is into my peace." And yet you also dwell within that siren's wail. You are the entity in the ambulance. You are the child trapped in the fire. And the siren may be equally and justly seen as the aid or the tocsin that rings to remind the heart of the love it bears for that portion of the self caught in pain, in fire, or in the ceaseless athanor[62] of the alchemist's lore.

"Who seeks the devotional life?" asked our brother Aaron. Who, indeed, should stand up and say, "I am the real person"? What portion of self can represent that seeker?

We ask each to look within and estimate how much the self has been included as an object worthy of devotion. Those who seek along the path of service to others can more easily see and recognize those efforts poured out upon friend and stranger—far more so than they can look within and see there, those portions of the self that need support, comfort, reassurance, and that ineffable quality you often call mercy.

Why is the self so often not an object of devotion? Perhaps in part it is because the seeker hears its own thoughts and sniffs the seeker's own dark side that some dark thoughts suggest or even reveal. And how righteous is the self in judging that dark side and that "hue-manity"?

---

[62] An athanor is a furnace used by alchemists that feeds itself so as to maintain a uniform temperature.

Now, it is our perception that it is entirely appropriate for the self to be more and more aware that this dark side of self exists as it goes through the incarnate experience.

We ask you not to flinch away from that portion of your human nature you perceive as dark. You are a whole and completed entity, bearing all that there is within the mystery of your consciousness. The illusion that you enjoy presents the night and the day, the dark side and the light side, just as the entire globe of your Earth turns again and again: light following dark, following light, following dark. This is the nature of the dance you now are enjoying to a greater or lesser extent.

Perhaps the greatest single stumbling block to the self's perception of how to live devotionally is this vein of judgment that the human lode contains. As in all ore, you are miners, digging through useless rock as well as precious. Do you judge the material surrounding a vein of valuable metal because it is not that valuable substance? Or do you simply process the ore to refine it and to purify it?

Truly, as that precious metal of pure consciousness within you is refined in the furnace of incarnation, it is very helpful for the self to learn to minister to the self within that is undergoing transformation. What age are you within? What age is the shadow side of self? Is not your isolation, which encompasses your feelings of alienation and this whole constellation of painful lacks and perceived limitations, the product of a young child's agony as it attempts to grow into that which it was not?

We suggest to you that when you begin to turn to self-judgment, you perhaps turn again and take up that self within that you perceive as misbehaving, and embrace that being, showering it with compassion, for it does no more than express its nature.

You judge not the slag nor the dross. It simply does not make it into the ring, the ornament, or the coin. Just so, love all of the self. This seemingly imperfect instrument is in fact perfectly created to give the seeker the maximum degree of potential for learning. Sometimes lessons come hard. But it is precisely your confusion and perceived lack of understanding that place you in so exquisite a rightness of position to meet and to learn to embrace and cooperate with the destiny that you have planned for yourself within this incarnate experience.

We would at this time turn the microphone back to our beloved brother. We leave this instrument in love and in light. We are those of Q'uo.

(Barbara channeling)

Aaron: Q'uo picked up the words, "What aspect of the self is the real self?" Have you seen a small child playing in costumes? Perhaps it picks up its mother's briefcase and pretends to be a businessperson. Or perhaps it picks up a cooking spoon and apron and pretends to be a cook. It is very easy to see that each masquerade the child moves into is an expression of the true self.

Just so, in incarnation you wear many masks. Is one the true self? They are all expressions of the true self. Which true self is that which is no self at all, but empty of ego identification in expressing the transcended self that rests fully in its own Pure Awareness and in its own divinity?

You are familiar, of course, with the lines in your scripture known as the Bible that God created man in his/her image. I ask that you look for a moment at that sentence. This which we might call God is infinite love, infinite wisdom, and infinite intelligence, always thinking to expand itself and to express itself. The individuated awareness is one expression and furtherance of the Divine. It also moves into myriad experience, like the child who masquerades. It is all part of its coming to know itself.

My brother/sister/friend of Q'uo has spoken eloquently of what happens when that which is being expressed in the self is that upon which judgment arises. For example, when that which has arisen is anger or fear or greed, Q'uo has suggested that you feel you are pulled out of the experience of living the devotional life. When fear solidifies as judgment and in effect closes you into the box that I described earlier, a place from which you lose perception of your divinity, then you cease to see the larger self and the emptiness of it. You cease to see how self is offered these myriad expressions as part of its learning opportunity. And instead, you move into a pattern of fixation on what arose in experience, and into a relationship with that expression that you must either call good or bad and judge as something to be kept or to be gotten rid of.

There is nothing wrong with the discriminating mind. In fact, you need such a mind for this incarnation. The judgment that flagellates the self is unnecessary to the discriminating mind. Discriminating mind can simply observe, "This is unskillful." But the energy field need not contract around that discernment. It is made from a place of Pure Awareness that sees the human slipping into fear. *What* slips into fear? Fear slips into fear. Do not go with it! It is only a problem when there is no awareness that one is slipping into fear. Then the energy field contracts and it is as if the box lid were shut. Then you forget who you are. You begin to believe the masquerade and to think, "I am the bad one who's feeling cheap and who's been cruel," or whatever else may have arisen. You forget that there is a soul and that this moment of feeling fear is simply one expression.

It is not fear's purpose to bind you into a box of hatred. The purpose of fear is to teach you compassion. The whole reason for your incarnation was to move into a situation where you find those catalysts that help to open your heart. You do not have to get rid of anything. When you do not need it, it will go. As long as there is an attack on what has arisen in the human self, there is separation from the self and from the Divine of which that self is an expression.

I want to ask that you begin to observe this contraction of the energy field. When an emotion arises, such as anger, desire, impatience, or pride, then, as Q'uo pointed out, judgment arises that says, *I shouldn't be feeling this*. And with that judgment you move into a space of strong self-condemnation, as in saying, "Fix it. Get rid of what's broken." But, my dear ones, nothing was ever broken.

Does a mathematics teacher put a hard problem on the board to convince you that you are inadequate, or to help you learn how to solve the problem? Does incarnation hand you the heavy emotions that give rise to judgment in order to confirm your inadequacy, or to teach you compassion? The question is not that these heavy emotions arise, but rather, it is wherein identification lies.

With the emotion and then the clarity that can observe the emotion arising without ownership of it, there is a hole poked through the box so that you can see the space and see the angel you are. "Ah, yes. I am here, experiencing this heaviness, for a reason. I don't have to hate myself for experiencing it, only love and respect the experiencer of it. My aversion, then, is against the unpleasantness of the experience. But I don't have to attack myself that it came into me. Instead, can there be greater compassion for this one?" This clarity is one essence of living the devotional life.

On the ultimate plane you are always living the devotional life. But on the relative plane, in order to live that life there must be a willingness to stay in touch with the divine aspect of the self. There must be a willingness to create that spaciousness wherein the true self can be seen through the clouds of delusion.

To live the devotional life is to be willing to not become attached to fixing the self, but rather, to aspire to loving the self. There is effort involved. It is the effort to learn that the box is transparent. As long as the box seems solid, it provides both barrier and safety. It provides a barrier to protect the small self as well as safety from that which is "outside," and may seem to be threatened by the negative thoughts of the ego-self. And so you hide in the box.

To live the devotional life is to love the Divine so much that you are willing to put holes in that armor, to give up your fear or at least your ownership of that fear. When you poke holes in the box, you cannot help but see the brilliance of the light that shines beyond. This light shines through, even into this expression that we call the small self. Can you love this small self that falls into mud puddles? It is easy to love God. But can you love this one that quakes in fear and that sometimes lies, grasps, or abuses as expressions of that fear?

Session 27

(Carla channeling)

Q'uo: We are those of Q'uo and are again with this instrument.

In closing, we would ask that, as you lay your frail barque of flesh down between the soft, cool sheets of your bed, you think on all your attributes and shower them with your affection. *Ah, sweet feet and legs that have carried me where I chose to go this day! Ah, dear, strong back, bent under the burdens of the day! Kindly stomach, hardworking heart, sweet tongue spouting such folly! Ah, dear, dear pride, lovely vanity, elegant sloth!*

Do not fear these attributes. They are yours to command and to use in understanding more. They all are yours as precious, precious gifts. Without all of your attributes you could not swim so well in the sea of confusion that is breeding new life within you.

Tuck yourself in with love this night and cast all your burdens into the powerful and compassionate arms of the Creator, whose nature is love and whose love is nearer than your breathing. The Creator does not care that you perceive yourself as imperfect, for the Creator knows your heart and dwells therein in perfect contentment.

Good night, each weary spirit. Our joy at being given this opportunity to share with you this weekend is too great to express. We love and bless each of you and, for now, leave this instrument and you in the ineffable mystery of the love and the light of the one infinite Creator. Adonai. We are those of Q'uo.

(Barbara channeling)

Aaron: You are weary and I will be brief. No more words or thoughts. But I want to bring your bodies into this because you learn with these bodies. Both Q'uo and I have raised the question, "What do you do with this judgment? What about these contractions of self-condemnation or of heavy emotion?"

There is an exercise drawn from tai chi called "pushing hands." In this exercise, two people stand face-to-face, one foot behind the other and arms resting, forearm against forearm. A pushes sharply. B's usual reaction to that push is that its body's energy contracts. If it is deeply aware, it may go only as far as that contraction; otherwise, it will push back or resist.

A is not just another person. A is all of those conditions of life that push at you. When life pushes you, you have two choices. The traditional choice is to push back. But you can also learn to dance with that force and to absorb it. And when the force releases itself, take it back. It is quite powerful to practice this, to watch that which wants to resist arising and to see, *I can't just will that the resistance fall away. I can wish it would go, but I can't make it go. I can pretend it's not there, but that doesn't mean that it no longer exists. But when I soften around that resistance, not trying to make it go away any longer and not acting it out, but just making space for it, then I become able to dance with that which pushes at me, be it internal or external. And with the worst hailstorm falling on my head or an emotion arising, I give it more space and become able to dance with it.*

I want Barbara to demonstrate this to you that you might practice it tonight and in the morning, so that we may talk a bit about the exercise and what it means to dance with life.

It is such joy to rest here in this circle of sincere and loving seekers. I express a gratitude that you have invited me into your circle. I love you all and wish you a good night. Barbara will show you this exercise when my words are concluded. That is all.

Session 28

(This session was preceded by a period of tuning and meditation.)

(Barbara channeling)

Aaron: Good morning and my love to you all. I hope you have had a restful night. A few of you are aware of dreams in which you were observant of the movement between two states, about which we spoke last night. This movement is between the state of contraction and opposition to catalyst and the state of dancing with catalyst and with the resultant contraction. We have been talking about this balance between the ultimate being and the relative being. The ultimate being is whole and knows its wholeness. It therefore experiences no veil separating itself from the reality of its wholeness. The relative being perceives itself to be less than whole and is struggling to become whole.

You are not incarnated to get rid of that struggle, but to live it out and learn from it. You must cherish the experience of the incarnation without getting lost in it. This, to me, is another aspect of the devotional life: the willingness to work in an ongoing way to keep the doors of both relative and ultimate reality open, while cherishing and living the incarnation from a perspective that sees it clearly.

You are the mother tying the child's shoes before it leaves to march in the parade, straightening its collar, adjusting the outfit, and smoothing its hair. And you are simultaneously on the tenth-floor balcony observing not only the whole parade but the infinite landscape through which the parade marches. From that perspective you cannot see whether the child's shoe is still tied. But if it is not tied because you had not given that care on the relative plane, then the child might stumble and fall, disrupting the entire parade behind it. And you would see that disruption from your balcony.

467

So, you must attend to both relative and ultimate reality. You must attend with infinite care to the details of relative existence. And that attendance is what I name as devotion, which is not shown by attending with fixation but with the spaciousness that sets you up on that balcony. You might even move to the sixtieth floor, where you can see all the neighboring villages and all the other parades.

I want to invite you to do a small inner exercise with me. Walk into a bathroom with me. Turn on the faucet and observe the water filling the sink. Suddenly it threatens to overflow and the faucet that turned it on does not turn off. It seems to turn in only one direction. The water is up to the top lip now and here it comes over the top, running down onto the floor. Try to turn it off again. It will not turn. Feel the tension building in you. It is streaming over the top, now, as a literal waterfall, and you know that this bathroom is directly above the living room. It will leak through. Quick, gather towels. Mop up the water. Toss the saturated towel into the bathtub and take another and another. If you go fast you can keep up. Can you feel the tension of that? It is the tension that says, "Me against this water." This is the relative human. And now I walk into the bathroom and pull the plug. *Whoosh!* The water goes down the drain. Feel the tension relax?

Life constantly hands you its barrage of overflowing sinks. It constantly hands you problems to be solved. And your energy contracts into a self that will handle those problems. This, my dear ones, is not devotion. This is control. This is fear.

Even if that sink was above not your own but your neighbor's living room in an apartment and your desire to stop the water was so that no harm would come to your neighbor, implying focus on service to another; even so, when you are meeting the issue with that contraction of fear, you are simply moving into a perpetuation of an old pattern that believes that the ego-self must be in control. If it must be in control, then there is something "other" out there, of which it must be in control.

So, you move into the myth of strengthening the self, being the powerful or capable or good one. There is nothing "other." In the moment when you symbolically pull the plug, you shift away from the fear track to the love track. You come back into harmony. The universe is not throwing mud on you in order to make you feel small or inadequate. If the universe does fling mud on you, then in some way you have invited participation in that experience because the soul sought the experience. It is that familiar cliché of being beaten over the head with a four-by-four. In some way the soul attracted the experience, because therein was the higher area of learning that it sought but it did not know how to open up to that level of learning.

I want to offer a brief example of Barbara's experience here. She did not ask for the tendonitis in her shoulder or the hernia in her belly *(speaking of physical ailments Barbara was experiencing at the time of this weekend)*. The conscious self did not want these distortions. The conscious self wanted to be healthy and free of pain. The higher wisdom sought the experience of moving into full harmony with the universe and was aware of the usefulness of drawing to itself the catalysts needed to make evident the areas of delusion, so as to allow the fullest possible expression of this intended harmony. The personal self agreed, without knowing the details, *This learning is the highest priority. Whatever it takes, I agree.* It was offered milder lessons of the truth of harmony and was unable to pay attention to those. It truly needed something either life-threatening or physically painful to catch its attention.

And so, the body began to manifest these symptoms. And they were these symptoms rather than other symptoms because these grew out of a karmic stream; because there had been past injuries to the body in these areas, and there is a cellular level of memory that perpetuates the original distortion until it is released. My intention here this morning is not to explain how karma works in depth, so I will leave off that particular track and be glad to answer any questions about it at another time.

Simply put, here was the human frantically mopping up the floor. And it needed to be reminded that the water is not "other." You need not attack it. Instead of perpetuating the practice of finding yourself in opposition to catalyst, stop. Use whatever practices are necessary or useful to release the tension of these old patterns in the ways that you practiced in the dance last night. That is one type of practice for coming back into this sixth-floor perspective. And then you see all of the other possibilities and that there is nothing in opposition to you. Pull the plug or open your heart or whatever is appropriate in that circumstance, with the awareness, "Nothing is against me."

To do this over and over and over is to live the devotional life. This is coming back to the memory, "I am divine and everything is divine. And I do not need to live my life in fear and disharmony." To do this seems so difficult because the personal self is so attached to its fear and to the perpetuation of a belief in its mythical separation. It has felt safe, albeit alone, in that separation. And you are constantly asked to give up that mythical separation that has held you alone but safe. You are constantly asked to offer your fear of your divinity, not getting rid of it but just releasing it. It is the opportunity to offer and to release your unworthiness, which is another illusion, and to offer and release the myth that you are bad or broken.

My dear ones, all of those myths served a purpose to the personal self. You come to one and then another and you ask, *This one, too? Must I let go of this?* Yes, all of it. With each letting-go there is resistance. When you learn to greet that resistance with a gentle kindness to yourself, it is not so hard.

After some time, you find that you can be observant of the parade on the ground level from a basement window, watching the feet go by and seeing all of the untied shoes. And you can watch the parade from the sixtieth floor at the same time, with a spaciousness that reaches out and ties each shoe as it passes by, but without any fixation on any of this passing parade as "self" and without any self to protect. There is just love that comes up to the highest floor and watches the whole process.

At this time I would like to pass the microphone to my brother/ sister/friend Q'uo. I want to state here that it brings me much joy to share with you in this dialogue pattern, each adding the richness of our own perspective. I speak for myself, here, but I know that Q'uo would echo my words. We speak as two souls in addressing this gathering of souls, which includes all of us together. I thank you with a loving and grateful heart for wanting to share with this circle in this way. That is all.

(Carla channeling)

Q'uo: And we, too, greet you with love, light, and joy in the infinite Creator.

How pleased we are to be exploring with you that great mystery that is the ground of being. To us it remains an inimitable and ineffable mystery. And at the same time, as we become more ripened as spirits we become ever more deeply in love with this mystery. We know not at what point we shall move beyond distortion, but we care not. For the delight of consciousness is like the odor of remembered flowers. It is a scent of supernal beauty that stays with utmost clarity in the memory.

We have been talking about the core of the art of living well, shall we say, that core being the establishment of a truly peaceful and non-judgmental attitude with regard to the self in all of its human vagaries. We have encouraged you to have mercy on yourselves and to allow healing, to touch the jagged edges of the wounds that the self's reactions to catalyst have caused.

But how to do that?

We are not speaking of releasing the self from the processes of self-determined ethics. We do not discourage the seeker from creating personal standards or from attempting with a whole heart to fulfill and to honor these ethical commitments. But rather, our concern is that the sense of self not be diminished in the self's regard by the straying from the subjective structure of perceived righteousness or justice. This work is important to the emerging metaphysical being.

It is difficult for many to enter into these processes of healing due to the self's disappointment with itself. As a tool to be used in moments of self-judgment, we might suggest the visualizing of a scene upon the stage of consciousness in which the Creator's hand is out-stretched, open and palm upward. That hand is as tall as you and you are just able to reach into the palm to give to this outstretched hand of love the gifts of your humanity. For we assure you that the Creator finds these gifts precious. Here is the thing not done. Here is the thing done in error. Here are the omissions and commissions that you per-ceive as erroneous. Give them up. One by one, let them tumble into that palm, one upon the other. Here are envy and pride and all the sorry gifts of the undisciplined self.

Now look upon these bits of colored stone that are the form of these metaphysical gifts. To you, when you gave them, they were gray, ugly, and broken pieces of self, fit only for the trash. Look now and see the beautiful colors of these shards of a broken life as they gleam and shine in being blessed, accepted, and transfigured by the love of the infinite One. These are gifts indeed.

When these gifts have been given and when you see these colors, retreat from the visualization a step at a time and come back to the self that is forgiven, blessed, and renewed. You are loved in every tiny iota of the fullness of your being. There is, then, the opportunity to begin anew.

And truly this chance is always real, not a mirage. For metaphysi-cally speaking, the one who turns over its perceived errors is doing substantial and blessed labor. Take deep breaths of the light that dwells as plenum in all that there is and know that you are made new.

We would at this time turn the working over to our beloved cohort, that prince in monk's robes, our Aaron. We leave this instrument in love and light for the moment. We are those of Q'uo.

(Barbara channeling)

Aaron: As there will be further sessions, my choice is to keep the next body of material separate and offer it this afternoon, and to focus our attention here for now. Barbara has spoken to me of the questions of the human as teacher and learner. Each of you is always a teacher to others. At times, that which teaches is the personal ego-self. At times, that which teaches is the Pure-Awareness Self. It would be ideal if all who taught could teach from that highest level, but of course you cannot. Thus, your teaching of another is a process of discovering and analyzing that highest awareness in yourself.

For many of you, because you are aware that the teaching comes from the ego-self, you become frozen and afraid to offer that, because of your abhorrence that you will offer distortion and thereby defile another. I bring this up as one area about which we would like to hear your concerns. Please offer any other questions that come to your minds and to which you would have us speak.

M.: In the exercise that Aaron described last night, is there a way to do this without anyone else with us?

Aaron: I hear your question. You may constantly do this. There is always a partner, although often not a human partner. There is the sink that overflows.

This instrument showered this morning and found some water on the floor. Immediately her energy contracted against the water. It is then that you must offer that small, whispered, *Dance with it. The water on the floor is not my enemy.* If you stub your toe and there is pain, you can fight with that pain or embrace the pain and soften your energy field around it. If the letter that you sought was not in the mailbox in the incoming mail, feel the contraction of wanting and grasping, and remind yourself, *I am not in opposition to the universe nor is the universe in opposition to me. That letter not coming is the catalyst. This is the water on the floor by the tub. . .*

What is your relation to the catalyst? You will see it constantly at every red light and at every wait in the supermarket line. Noting the contraction, you make the skillful and loving decision to move back into harmony, to observe the contraction with a certain spaciousness and kindness. You are not getting rid of the contraction. If you are late getting across town and hit a string of red lights, you may note at each one that there is contraction.

If you walked across a graveled driveway strewn with rocks and your feet were bare, many of them would prick your feet, and there would be pain and contraction. You would not say, *There should not be contraction*, but you, out of kindness to the body, might feel anger toward the driveway. *Why does it have to have sharp rocks?* You might think, *Next time I will bring shoes to cross this road*, but you do not think, *I shouldn't feel pain*. You do not think, *My body should not contract. My body should like the pain*. There is kindness to the body.

With emotional catalysts, such as the red lights as you drive across town, the energy contracts in the same way. Just come back to asking, *What is tense?* Come back to harmony with the universe. *The universe is handing me precisely the catalyst that I need. With each light, can I sit here on the ground floor with the squirming human who wants the light to change, while remembering that from the top floor, awareness is observing how much tension this human is feeling and is offering it love?*

As you nurture that higher perspective, you begin to keep the door open so that you can come into contact with a painful catalyst, observe the painful contraction, and not fixate on doing anything about the contraction—not getting rid of it or flinging your anger about it on another, but just noting, *Here is contraction*, and dancing with it.

As Q'uo just pointed out, this does not stop you, for example, from putting on shoes and going out and removing the sharpest rocks from the driveway. You learn to act skillfully from a place of love; to relate to the world in ways harmonious to the human's value system; and to bring about change, but from a place of love and not from a place of fear.

May we hear others of your questions directed either to Q'uo or to myself, or else simply thrown out loosely for us to decide who will answer?

Carla: Usually when I channel I can feel that the energy of the circle is upholding me perfectly. Occasionally I can tell that in addition to this energy, my essence is somehow being tapped, and I am spending a lot of my own energy. Can you give me any insight into whether this is random or whether this is as it should be?

Session 28

Aaron: I believe we would both like to speak to this question. May I speak first?

This is not random. It is the place where the ego-self has become more solid and where there is tension. Perhaps it is internal tension about the answer or some thought that the self should know the answer, so that the self ceases for that moment to be a perfectly clear instrument and offers also its own opinion or need or fear into the workings. And this is fine, although uncomfortable and perhaps less clear in the resultant channel. But it is your catalyst and your opportunity for learning.

There is a level of mind present in you that is observing this tension. My sister, may I suggest that when you experience this tension, you simply begin to note it as tension. I would suggest that you use a very nonjudgmental label. To say, *Ego is present*, becomes a judgment. Your observance of this situation in yourself simply points out the presence of some tension within you about the question or about the receiving of the answer. And when you note it as tension, you find an infinite spaciousness opening to that tension and you find yourself coming back to the clarity that is your preferred way of channeling, both for the clarity of the answer and in order not to drain your self's energy. I believe Q'uo would also like to speak to this. I pause.

(Carla channeling)

Q'uo: We are with this instrument.

We would say to this instrument: My child, you remember the parable of Peter in the boat at night on the Sea of Galilee[63] and how Peter saw his teacher walking upon the waters to him. Recall how Peter leapt from the boat and walked to meet his beloved rabbi. Only when Peter became aware that he was doing an impossible thing did he begin to sink. And then Peter remembered to reach out his hand to grasp his teacher's.

[63] Matt. 14:25–32 AV.

Always, your Beloved's hand awaits your reach. Always, the turning to trust will not be in vain.

We are those of Q'uo. May Aaron and we have the next query, please?

I.: When Barbara and I danced a bit last evening, there seemed to be several stages of release as we did. The final stage caused a different sort of contraction because I seemed to perceive flashes of some immense, bright space. But the sense of personal "me" couldn't find itself there, so it kept retreating. Are my experiences accurate perceptions of stages of release?

(Barbara channeling)

Aaron: I hear your question, my brother. It is harder to think of it as stages than to think of it as a continuum from utmost involvement in the personal ego-self with no notion of the expanded self, to total resting in the expanded self. Therein lies a vast continuum. Because the mind cannot experience the subtleties of that continuum, it may see it in terms of plateaus. But in the reaching of each plateau, there is a continuum.

Ultimately you open into that space of light. There is no personal self there, and there need not be a personal self there. But that does not mean the personal self has ceased to exist. On the ultimate level it never did exist. It was simply one expression of the Divine. But on a relative plane it does not and will not cease to exist.

If you have a screw to set in a hole and you go to your toolbox and get the screwdriver, turn the screw, and then put the screwdriver down, five minutes later has the screwdriver ceased to exist? It does not exist in that space/time, but it still exists. When you reach that place of infinite spaciousness and innate clarity, the personal self simply has no need to exist in that space/time. You will come back to it when you need it.

There are very valuable meditation practices that teach you to rest stably in this infinite space and Pure-Awareness Mind, to rest in the divine self and to reopen skillfully to the personal self when you have need to do so. You cannot take out the garbage merely from the soul self. Your humanity is needed. I would pass the microphone at this time to Q'uo. I pause.

(Carla channeling)

Q'uo: My brother, we ask: What now remains as the direction of your seeking upon this planet within this pattern?

(Pause)

We are those of Q'uo. And in your silence lies a gift that you give yourself. For skill can wane and heart can fail. Yet upon the sea of consciousness there is that spirit which abides, moving over the water to create and to destroy. It is in opening to this overarching energy that the seeker will find answers that have no words. These answers open the door into that purity of emotion within which lies personal truth.

We are those of Q'uo.

I.: Thank you, Q'uo and Aaron.

Q'uo: Is there a further query at this time?

G.: I have been working with the anger in my partner. I understand his pain and why he lashes out at me, and yet am hurt by this. That's my question. I don't understand why it is that I can be hurt, if I can see with compassion that his road is different and I can learn from him. But I am hurt. When I think about this it makes me sad and teary.

Q'uo: My sister, was it the immortal Bard that asked, "If you prick me, do I not bleed?"[64] It is appropriate to hurt or to be hurt when there are negative emotions directed upon your hapless head.

This is his gift to you. To the world it is a kind of abuse to be tolerated. To the spirit it represents, as do all catalysts, an opportunity to respond rather than react. It is an opportunity to allow the self to feel mourning, grieving, returning anger and resentment, and every iota of reaction.

At the same time it remains a viable option to decide to create a response that bears feeling from the heart and that turns from pity of self to peace in the end. Anger toward the sender of these errors can be turned into an embrace of the arrows that wound and the anger that smites.

Until that entire energy is seen as the self, confusedly striking out at its own self, this friction seems hot and very physical. Yet the issues underlying this catalyst are old and cold as stone. The challenge is to warm that system of karmic friction by your honoring of pain and with your utter willingness to allow and to suffer until all is balanced.

We are those of Q'uo.

(Barbara channeling)

Aaron: I would also speak to this question. Amongst those of you who place high value on lovingly offering your energy to others, and who look with abhorrence on the possibility of offering your energy in ways that will hurt another, there is a popular misconception that when you are abused, you must be a doormat to that abuse.

The partner offers its anger in seemingly inappropriate ways. There is indeed real compassion in seeing the fear, the pain, and the tightness

---

[64] William Shakespeare, *Merchant of Venice*, Act III, Scene I. *"I am a Jew. Hath not a Jew eyes? Hath not a Jew hands, organs, dimensions, senses, affections, passions? Fed with the same food, hurt with the same weapons, subject to the same diseases, healed by the same means, warmed and cooled by the same winter and summer, as a Christian is? If you prick us, do we not bleed? If you tickle us, do we not laugh? If you poison us, do we not die? And if you wrong us, shall we not revenge?"*

out of which the partner's hateful words have grown. There is the understanding that the partner's highest intention is not to hurt you but to defend itself, and that it simply does not know how to defend itself without hurting you. As Q'uo has clearly stated, of course there is hurt, especially as you grow in understanding and in ability to control that which would fling out of yourself in harm to others. The hurt is in the fear that the partner is not willing or able to grow in that way and so perpetuates its own pattern of offering hurt to you.

There may even be compassion about that, seeing that this partner is stuck there. So, there you are with your compassion and your sense of hurt and a stoicism that says, *I will abide. I will tolerate.* And, as Q'uo has said, to be willing to suffer as the karmic threads work themselves out is an essential part of this.

But also, there is a time to speak your own truth, not from a place of fear that would defend in the same pattern that the partner defends, but from a loving place to both of you that says, *This is enough.* The statement is not offered in condemnation of the partner, but is offered in the same way that a loving parent picks up the crying two-year-old who is having a temper tantrum and who has begun to pick up items, such as pots, and fling them. The parent does not condemn the two-year-old. It understands that the child is exhausted. But it wraps it in its loving embrace and prevents it from doing further damage. It lovingly holds the child until its energy has quieted.

It is important that the parent does not say, "You are only a two-year-old." It respects the force that is moving through the other, but recognizes that it is neither skillful nor appropriate to allow that force to fling itself out at the world. Sometimes the two-year-old will cry all the harder for a bit.

When you say to your partner, "I understand that you are angry, but your statements do cause pain. Is that what you want to do? Is your priority here to defend yourself and cause pain in me, or is your priority to help us learn to communicate better? You see that neither of us knows how best to allow that communication at this time. If your real wish is to communicate, can we wait until your anger settles itself a bit? And can we then attempt that communication?" in such a way you begin to allow the partner the right to its anger and the right to its fear. There is a certain respect for its processes. But there is a clear statement, "While you have a right to your own processes, you do not have the right to pour the energy of those processes on me in hurtful ways."

Of course, it is more complex because sometimes the partner does not seem to be ready to hear that statement. I do not pinpoint the question here. But in certain circumstances you will find that the other wants to perpetuate the pattern of its fear and cannot tolerate your invitation to move beyond its fear, and so it becomes necessary that you part ways. In that situation you will have to ask yourself, *Am I willing to allow the continuance of this pattern of fear and to continue to participate in it in order to have that which I value from this other person? Or am I no longer willing to allow the perpetuation of those patterns?*

It will not happen all at once, but if you are patient through weeks or months or even years, most often the other will open to your invitation. When I say patient, it is not that you will have to wait years for the beginning of opening, but for the fruition.

Both instruments are becoming a bit tired. May we ask for just one more question? And we will continue your questions in the afternoon session. I pause here.

I.: In the bathroom meditation Aaron was speaking about, he said that when we move from a place of control, we contract into a self that can handle an overflowing sink. He also called this moving from a fear track and not a love track. Obviously this is not truly effective. But there is the habitual thought that to be effective in a situation that we find overwhelming, we do have to take personal control. Love is unlimited. Why don't we find it easy to trust that?

Aaron: I hear your question. You say there is a habit, moving from a place of fear, that you do have to take personal control. What does personal control mean? The small ego-self is one piece of personal control. The higher self is a different aspect of personal control. This is partway on that progression from enclosure in the small ego-self to resting in the Pure Heart-Mind or the Pure Spirit Body that is the ultimate level of your understanding and is unrelated to the personal. The higher self includes the mental body, but it is a place that is free of fear.

My friends, you like your problems even though you claim to dislike them. You invite them back over and over and over. If you do not have a problem in yourself, you go out and find a comrade whose problem you can solve. To be a problem solver helps you to feel strong and safe. You repeat the same patterns over and over and over.

If indeed there are infinite solutions and if in fact there has never been a problem, only a situation that needs loving attention, then you must begin to ask yourself why these myriad solutions elude you. What is there that does not want to find the solution, because to do so is to give up being the problem solver and to give up studying the problem?

I would ask you to begin to work from a very different place. Here you are in the bathroom with the sink water rushing over the sides of the sink. Your final goal is a dry floor. You had a stack of a hundred towels, but now there are only four or five left. Clearly this is not going to work. What if you stop this mad rush to be in control and begin instead to visualize just what it is that you want to have happen?

What if G. were to begin to visualize a loving and harmonious relationship with her husband? What if she sees how that experience of mutual fear can become two people treating each other with respect? Several things may happen. She may begin to have insight into why she is at some level attached to the perpetuation of the pattern of disrespect. And she may begin to have insight into the ways that this pattern keeps the ego safe, even though the heart-self longs for communication and light. As she comes into awareness of the ways she has perpetuated the pattern, the heart's deepest wisdom intuitively will provide the pathways leading into harmony. I said before and I repeat, you must be willing to offer up that which holds to disharmony for ego-centered or defended reasons.

As Q'uo pointed out, you must be willing to take that hand that offers to you the strength, the courage, and the love to follow in the path. It is not easy. But consider those two movements, which are to offer up that which has so long been held and to seek the Divine without and within. Within those two movements is the doorway to growth, to healing, and to peace.

At this time I would pass this microphone to my beloved friend Q'uo for final thoughts and the conclusion of this session. I deeply thank you all for allowing me into your circle. And also, on behalf of all who live for the greater opening of love in the universe, my thanks to you for the courage with which you continue to seek those openings of love in yourself. That is all.

(Carla channeling)

Q'uo: Dear ones, the vampires and vampiric energies or those spears that assail and wound seem to come from the enemy. Yet you are always wounded by your very self. You cannot go around such energy. You cannot escape from this energy. For like an ill wind, it will blow where it will. Yet you can enfold such wounding energy in an embrace that accepts the energy, honors it, and takes it in without fear. Love does abide—not your love, but the Creator's love.

You cannot overspend the love that comes through you. The task lies in allowing the self to become transparent so that the love flowing through creates that glow that re-creates the face of the Earth. You tremble on the brink of miracles. Lift high your hopes and live by faith.

We shall speak again soon. Meanwhile we leave each of you, with great thanks, in the love and in the light of the one infinite Creator. We are those of the principle known to you as Q'uo. Adonai. Adonai.

Session 29

Weekend 8, Part 3 of 4
(This session was preceded by a period of tuning and meditation.)

(Barbara channeling)

Aaron: Good evening and my love to you all. With much joy I rejoin this circle of light.

We have been speaking of different aspects of the devotional life. We come to a large aspect, which is the ego's desire to blame. Somehow that which recognizes itself as an entity may have experienced pain or felt a sense of humiliation or experienced a heavy emotion. Any of these arisings are uncomfortable and make the ego squirm.

If there is a perceived threat, there is a desire to pinpoint the cause of that threat so as to feel safe. If there is shame, there is a desire to explain the self and cast blame elsewhere. If there is hurt that has come to the self through another's words or actions, there is a desire to raise the shielding of anger. These are all natural responses of the human. They are not necessary responses, such as the response of the body to bleed if the skin is punctured. But still, they are natural accompaniments of the emotional body.

To feel anger is not the same as to hold on to that anger. To wish to defend is not the same as to attack another as an enactment of that defense. To hold another out of your heart ensures the continuance of the karma around which the issue revolved. To live in devotion is to be willing to reflect upon your fear, your anger, your pain, and the ways that the holding of these have served to solidify the ego-self and allow it to feel safe.

To reflect upon the attachment of maintaining the anger is the beginning of the consideration that anger or blame might be released. To release that blame and anger is to forgive. To live the devotional life is to learn how to forgive. Forgiveness cuts karma and dissolves it entirely.

At the place where that karma was formed, we always find an energy contraction. The karma is not about *A did this to me*, but it is about the way self solidifies around *A did this to me*. It is about the misunderstandings that *I must angrily confront A or be a doormat to A*.

G. spoke earlier about the arising of compassion for her husband. She spoke about seeing deeply into his fears and into what drives him to rage. She spoke of the fact that, although she understands the roots of his rage and feels compassion, she still feels pain. When we feel pain, there is a natural desire to return to safety by moving into the illusion of control over the catalyst for that pain. To forgive is to become willing to suffer that hurt and to acknowledge, *I am human. I will feel hurt. But I do not have to hold myself separate because of that hurt.*

Then you change your relationship with the entire catalyst. Compassion is there. The ability to skillfully say no to abuse is there. And the compassion touches your own condition, your own hurt, as well as the pain and fear that encompass the catalyst. This relationship is neither based on your compassion to him for his pain nor your compassion to yourself for your own pain. The pain of each is a part of the other, and compassion is just compassion. It opens your heart and allows the possibility of forgiveness.

Ultimately, with deepening compassion, there is no need for forgiveness, for there is nothing left to forgive. But until that point, forgiveness is a very powerful practice. And, as I have said, it cuts through karma by totally changing your relationship with the catalyst.

Forgiveness is a process and not an event. You enter lightly into the forgiveness. Liken it to the way you enter the cold lake on the first hot day of spring. The air is warm, giving rise to a desire to swim. But the toes touch water that is still frigid from the winter's ice. In just such a way, the heart may still be frigid from the winter's ice. Kindness does not ask you to go to the end of the dock and leap in. Wade in slowly. If it feels good or even possible, go in. At the point where the feet are numb and there is discomfort, it is time to get out and wait until the water may be warmer. Tomorrow the heart may have thawed just a bit more. So, forgiveness is a process.

To consider the possibility of forgiveness is to touch the deepest hurt places in the self with an honesty that acknowledges the wish to enact pain in return for pain and acknowledges the enormity of the desire to be safe and comfortable. And it is not enough to acknowledge these forces. One must do so without judgment. Thus, the process of forgiveness begins with the self.

Fear is an illusion. It is an illusion to which the small ego-self has become attached. It is a habit. To live the devotional life is to love the Divine enough to take that hand that is offered, to offer up those brown stones that Q'uo spoke of, and to allow the Divine to turn them into shining gems. It is a process that leads you to release fear, to observe, and then to release attachment to fear. It is a choice to look deeply at the ways in which the illusion of fear has been used as protection.

You then come to the truth of your being, which is that the divine self has no need of protection. You may cut yourself loose from this illusion of fear and have the love and faith to come back and rest in that divine truth of your being, which is fearless. This is not a statement of condemnation of fear. It is simply a statement of a higher truth.

When you practice forgiveness, let it come from a place of opening in the heart that aspires to approach ever closer to that truth. Let it not come from a place of judgment that says, *I should not fear. I should not blame.* To do this takes much practice, including practice at noting judgment as it arises and the practice of simply opening the heart in the myriad of small ways the universe invites you to open the heart.

At this time, I wish to pass this session to my dear friend of Q'uo. Later this evening I would like to lead you in what I term a forgiveness meditation. I thank you for your attention. That is all.

(Carla channeling)

Q'uo: Greetings once again in the love and in the light of the one infinite Creator.

Perhaps you have noticed that we have not given you a set of instructions or a doctrine of things to do in order to live the spiritually directed life. This is because it is our opinion that there are as many ways to live a spiritually directed life as there are people who wish to do so. We cannot tell you to spend this number of hours in meditation or that number of hours in prayer. This is because for one seeker, two minutes would be the conservative estimate of how much is necessary to maintain the attitude desired; whereas for another, the time would be twenty or thirty or sixty minutes. Indeed, we offer you our thought that there is a very real danger to those who go overboard, as this instrument would say, with spiritual disciplines.

The Creator is not tame. The love that ignited creation is also that which destroys. Intimate contact with Deity can be fatal. And there are those mythical and also very physical and real entities throughout your history whose difficulties and deaths tell their own story. The custom of coming together in order to worship and to focus upon Deity is a most practical safeguard. For the dynamics of the conversation between the mystery and the group is universal and touches each unique psyche gently, with the energy of contact being buffered by the group of like-minded seekers. We do not wish to frighten you but only to express to you our bias that it is well to be moderate in spiritual discipline and to make haste slowly. For you have an infinite amount of time to progress, whereas you have only minutes, hours, or just a few thousand days and then you are through this incarnation. Although there are as many incarnations as are needed in order for each density's lessons to be learned, it is our sense that this life experience is precious and it was not any entity's intention to come to this illusion in order to ignore it or to preserve itself from social contact.

Work in consciousness is something that the spiritual seeker tends to think of as working with the higher energies. And certainly this can be true. However, the most common mistake of the spiritual seeker is that, in its eagerness, it moves into the higher energy centers to do its perceived tasks without maintaining the health and balance of the all-important lower energies.

Faced with weakness, blockage, or stress in the energies involved in the self's dealing with the self and with others, the spirit rushes head-long into communication and work upon the inner planes. It is as if the owner of a house with cracks in its foundation set about building another story onto the house. The foundation not being secure, the loftier and heavier weight might very possibly crack the foundation further, and the entire structure might end up in pieces.

We would encourage each of you to view the work within these lower energy centers, including work with those close to you in relationship, with great respect and with the awareness of what this instrument has called the 180-degree rule; that is, if something feels or seems right to the wisdom of the world, it very probably is wrong. If you yearn to back away from dealing with something, it very well may be time to deal with it. If the seeker cannot wait to have an outcome occur, the wise seeker may take that heady desire as a sign that more time is required to evaluate the situation in spiritual terms.

The core of devotional living is an attitude of mind and heart. One word we could use to describe this attitude is "remembrance." For the one who remembers who the self is—that is, a child of the infinite Creator—will respond to catalyst within the structure of that identity. To the one who has the attitude of devotion, all moments alike are moments that take place upon holy ground.

The 180-degree rule applies also to those things that the world feels are important. The world does not value the laborer who washes dishes, but rather, values the surgeon who successfully excises diseased flesh from a patient, thereby prolonging life. And yet if the surgeon has not love within its touch, there will be curing but no healing; whereas if the seeker who does the dishes has that remembrance of the holy nature of all life, it shall be lightening the consciousness of the planet as it lovingly cleanses, rinses, and appreciates each dish. And the very dishes themselves shall lift their tiny voices in praise.

It is the small things of every day or, as this instrument would say, the "chop wood, carry water of life,"[65] the chores and the repeated tasks, that hold the most potential for being part of the training wheels for the seeker who is striving to learn to ride the bicycle of devotional life. Things that are done daily are those things that the seeker can practice daily. And it is the nature of the human mind to form habits. That which is done daily becomes habitual. And through repetition over your years such homely routines can become permanent.

This instrument is having trouble voicing our concept. The closest word we can find is "ganglion" or "node," which acts as a memory jogger, bringing that remembrance of the holy nature of all life before the attention many times in each day. Each of you has had much mental enjoyment contemplating times when the life can be made simpler. And we would encourage such thoughts. For what this instrument has called the "little life" is that life of obscurity and modest attainments in which the quality of daily remembrance is more possible, whereas the seemingly brilliant life can often be the husk with no seed within.

The world thinks in large terms and is ambitious for gain, for power, and for authority, whereas the most fruitful path for the seeker does not contain the great ambitions. Those things that create the large or brilliant life sometimes are that which one has incarnated to do. But in the case of the well-oriented spiritual seeker, such a worldly success will simply blossom, developing naturally and without the contraction and push inherent in ambition. For ambition in the worldly sense and desire to seek the Creator are polar opposites. For one who seeks the Creator, the refrain of all the facets of living is, "Not my will, but thine."[66]

---

[65] Rick Fields, Rick Ingrasci, Peggy Taylor, and Rex Weyler, *Chop Wood, Carry Water: A Guide to Finding Spiritual Fulfillment in Everyday Life* (New York: St. Martin's Press, 1984).

[66] Luke 22:42 AV.

It is into the heart that is not being shoved about by ambition that the consciousness finds itself bubbling up with joy. We do not mean to suggest that anyone run away from success of a worldly nature. For it is not success but the drive toward success that influences the attitude. You have often heard the phrase, "in the world but not of it."[67] Brothers and sisters, this is each and every earth-person's situation. Many feel that they are wanderers from another planet. But we say to you that you are all natives of eternity. And you have all wandered to this place to be together and to help each other to see the Creator in the self, in others, and in each and every mote of manifestation.

The living flora of your planet sings the songs of its seasons in everlasting rhythms. As we speak, your great tree creatures lift their skeletal arms to the night sky about your dwelling. As the energies within them tuck themselves away for the winter's sleep, there is the evensong of praise and thanksgiving. It is possible to touch into this energy simply by remembering that all things are alive and aware and loved by the infinite One.

We would at this time hand the microphone to our dear brother Aaron. We leave this instrument in love and in light. We are those of Q'uo.

(Barbara channeling)

Aaron: My dear friend has made many important observations. I would especially emphasize the importance of the strong foundation before you build. He also spoke of living the simple life and not grasping at attainment, if one would live a life in spiritual consciousness. I want to expand a bit on this statement and also on Q'uo's statement that intimate contact with Deity can be fatal.

---

[67] "What I mean by living to one's self is living in the world, as in it, not of it...." William Hazlitt, "Table Talk," from *On Living to One's Self.* As quoted in *Bartlett's Familiar Quotations,* 14th ed., ed. John Bartlett (Boston: Little, Brown and Company, 1968), 539.

I would precede my remarks with this statement that on fundamental issues we speak from an identical voice. But of course we each do have our own bias. We are not afraid of that bias; we rejoice in our diversity. Where diversity exists in our biases, it does not lead us into irreconcilable differences, but rather, into expanding. Each of us is moving also to encompass each other's bias as understanding deepens. Finally, neither of us ever has a need to be right, because we know we are not speaking here of wrong or right but of interpretation of experience.

Q'uo says intimate contact with Deity can be fatal. Yes, it can. But I would expand this statement with the observation that intimate contact with Deity can be fatal if there is no foundation laid, because the high-frequency vibration resultant of that contact must have the foundation to support it. And, as Q'uo pointed out, that foundation is established by the daily workings of your life, which are the workings with the lower energy centers, with relationships, with the physical body, and so on.

Grasping at intimate contact with Deity or any grasping at spiritual enlightenment lays a fatal crack in the foundation when such grasping at contact or enlightenment comes from a place of fear rather than opening from a place of love. When the foundation is strong, when the homework has been attended, and the opening to the Deity is a natural opening of the loving heart from a place of no fear or no grasping, then it is never fatal, but expanding and wondrous. However, you are still in the incarnation. You cannot sustain the intensity of that contact. To seek to do so is to encourage another fatal crack. There must be a willingness to come back into the relative human.

I spoke some moments ago about a difference in bias. I speak from the bias of a being who has worked its way through the lower densities on the earth plane. I am quite in agreement with Q'uo that there is no rush. And I know that Q'uo is quite in agreement with me that each moment of incarnation is a precious gift and not to be wasted. And yet, from my human experience, I do feel an intensity that Q'uo does not feel. Neither of us is wrong or right. We merely each speak from our own perspective.

That intensity must be handled with caution. If it becomes the grasping of which Q'uo spoke, then you have the fatal crack. When the intensity derives from a loving heart that so deeply aspires to purify its energy and so deeply aspires to move itself into harmony, then that intensity becomes a powerful lifting device, moving the seeker forward on its path. When the intensity derives from the voice of fear that would fix that in itself that it sees as defective, then it is striving to build that third floor over the cracked foundation.

And so, there must be a deepening awareness of which voice is predominant. Usually both voices will blend. It is rare for the human to act solely on one voice or another. But that motivation comes both from the heart of love and from places of fear. You do not need to get rid of fear in order not to be reactive to fear. You do not need to get rid of fear to speak and move from a place of love. But you need to be honest about fear's presence and learn to make space for it so that it does not control you.

A wise man in your nation's history said, "We have nothing to fear except fear itself,"[68] referring to the potential to fear *fear* or to fear falling blindly into the grip of fear. But when we learn to relate lovingly even to our fear, then it no longer controls. It does not need to go away. Simply, it no longer controls. It no longer has the power to urge you to build that third story. It allows you to tend to the foundation.

Here I would pass the microphone to my dear brother/sister/ friend of Q'uo. That is all.

(Carla channeling)

Q'uo: We are again with this instrument.

We have spoken of several challenging concepts and would at this time pause to ask if there are questions concerning those things that the ones known as Aaron and we have offered. Is there a query at this

[68] Franklin D. Roosevelt, *First Inaugural Address,* March 4, 1933.

time that we or our brother Aaron might answer to make our concepts more lucid or more in focus?

R.: Are you saying that we should strive for the best effort but not for the best result?

Q'uo: My brother, we are saying that when one is striving to be one's best, there is skill in taking the self lightly. And when there is the lack of striving, then there is the opposite possibility that not enough effort is being made to live that moment to its utmost. The tendency is to strive for the visible or substantial goal and to gaze at the small, homely details of life as that which keeps one from the business of living spiritually, whereas it is precisely in those time-consuming, personal chores that the greatest opportunity for spiritual work comes. For each action, each relationship, and each detail of the day is ripe with the blossoms of love, beauty, and truth.

One who can see the holy in the homely has a greater life than one whose accomplishments are brilliant to the world but whose personal orientation toward large portions of the humble side of life is to get them done in order to get to the important things.

May we answer you further, my brother?

R.: I think I need to wait and look for the light side. Thank you.

Q'uo: We thank you, my brother. Is there a further query at this time?

I.: You mentioned high-frequency vibration with the spirit coming into contact with the mundane mind. I would like to understand that analogy better. Higher frequency in what respects?

Q'uo: My brother, are you familiar with the concept of octaves? The entire gamut of densities and subdensities is as the keys upon the piano, equally beautiful and worthy to be praised. But some notes are low and others are high. The various energy centers of the physical vehicle and its

attendant finer bodies are as the piano in that there are octaves of resonance between the so-called higher and so-called lower energies.

When the trine of lower energies is being attended to, then it is
simple and natural to move up to the next octave and the next and so
forth. When the lower energies are out of tune, however, it is as
though, when the musician takes the string to touch it at the half to
make the next octave higher, that octave also is out of tune with the
creation, having become distorted at the base. Thus, the entire spiritual
realm rings badly out of tune unless the foundation is first tuned.[69]

May we answer you further, my brother?

I.: The image I get is that we, in a way, are participating in the building
of a home for the spirit and that the building of the foundation firmly
allows that home to be well laid. There also seems, though, to be a
point of raising the point of habitation to a higher level of comfort.
The cracks that might appear with incorrect placement or perception
are really cracks of kindness as opposed to flaws. I'm sorry, Q'uo, I
can't formulate a further question. Thank you.

Q'uo: Perhaps it is a clearer analogy to compare the housekeeping of
the house that the vehicle of flesh inhabits. The upper rooms are
delightful. But there is no dining room or kitchen there, so that the
inhabitant of the house must first cleanse and make acceptable that
lower floor by stocking the refrigerator, having the appliances that create your cooked food in order, and tidying and sweeping and dusting
and making the windows shine. When that lower story is peaceful and
in order, then it is the time to ascend the staircase, to enjoy the den as
the room of rest, and to gaze with the higher and longer point of
view out the windows that give so much broader a perspective.

---

[69] It is a law of physics that if you halve the length of a string, such as a violin string or a
piano key's wire, you double the value of the tone. Thus, if you have a twelve-inch string
that sounds a certain tone when plucked, and you push down on the string so that it is now
only six inches long and pluck it again, it will sound the same tone, only one octave higher.

We mean simply to suggest that the humble and earthly things in your experience are precious and that this is far too often not realized. And in the lack of this concept, the unskillful soul can make itself rather uncomfortable. Then the self thinks, *How can I fix this? I shall meditate more. I shall contemplate more. I shall read improving works.* But instead, the actual point of departure often lies in going back to those simple things and giving them the honor and respect that you give to that which is obviously spirit.

There is a great shift of attitude that we are encouraging each to consider at this time. In the metaphysical world, thoughts are things. And this truth, being of the higher octave, overarches the smaller truth. You perhaps have heard the old maxim, "As above, so below."[70] The humble details of life are Deity, expressed many octaves lower. But in touching those lower notes, all the octaves resonate.

Is there another question for Aaron or ourselves at this time?

K.: Q'uo and Aaron, can you speak to the topic of the coming Earth harvest and any purpose we may have toward care in that future harvest? Or does this interfere with free will? And is there presently on the Earth or affecting the Earth a greater proportion of opposing force because of the harvest (or whatever that may be) interfering, or that may make it more difficult for us to be balanced and stay in tune?

(Barbara channeling)

Aaron: May I speak to your question, my sister? Yes, there is indeed a greater opposing force. This is not a problem. This is not bad or negative. When you lift weights, if you practice with increasingly heavier weights, you develop stronger muscles. When you practice returning love to increasingly heavy catalysts, you strengthen the ability to love.

---

[70] Three Initiates, *The Kybalion* (Chicago, IL: Yogi Publication Society, 1908).

494

And it is the strengthening of thaᵢᵢ ability to love that will offer the universe the ability to move into its potential of light.

The darkness is not your foe. It is your teacher. In the approaching harvest, the universe has the potential to arrive at a new balance. Please remember that not only positive polarity but also negative polarity is harvested. But please also remember that at a certain place within sixth density, negativity becomes a dead end.

The concern is that between third and sixth density, negativity can be a force for much suffering and harm. Therefore, your increasing ability to return love to negativity and not to heed it is one major force that will shift the balance. Negativity that cannot engender fear has no place left to go. This is your work. This truly is the core reason for this harvest: to bring all of the mature, loving, and wise energy into as strong a connection as possible in saying no to negativity, not with fear, but with love.

My friend of Q'uo would like to speak further to this question. I pause. This instrument returns to a deeper tuning. Please start the tape.

(Carla channeling)

Q'uo: We are with this instrument. We must pause, for this instrument needs to retune somewhat. We are Q'uo.

(Pause)

We would ask that you revibrate the query.

K.: I require deeper understanding of the urgency that I and my partner and many others around us are presently feeling with respect to our service and our purpose toward the coming harvest.

Q'uo: We thank you, my sister. The vibration allowed this instrument to come fully back into the tuning that it was seeking.

Perhaps you have heard the phrase, "The fields are white with harvest. But where are the laborers to make the harvest?"[71] The field of your planet has become ripe with harvest and the time of change has begun. It is a process that will take quite some of your years, perhaps as much as two centuries to fully express.

Those who have come here to aid in this harvest are activated if they are sensitive to the beating of their own heart. By this time there is often the sensation that there is some specific task to accomplish as a harvester. And sometimes there is. But the primary task of each who has come to serve is to be who you are. For this essence of being is your greatest gift to this planet at harvest. As more and more harvesters are activated, there is the acceleration of the cumulative effect so that it is as if one touches two, and two touch four, and four touch eight, and so forth.

By being yourself, by seeking to be more authentic and to be more fully that unique entity that you are, you are working in the field. For this harvest is a metaphysical one. And as the planetary vibration lightens, the strength of the positive orientation grows. The one known as M. who sits within this circle recently said to this instrument that after a long struggle to know what its service was, it finally realized that it was in the spiritual reserve and was content to wait until its activation notice.

May we answer you further, my sister?

K.: Thank you.

Q'uo: We thank you, my sister, most truly, and encourage you to wear that crown that lies heavy upon your head.

We would leave this instrument for this evening and transfer the microphone to the one known as Aaron, pausing only long enough to thank each for the beauty that you share, as you share your essence with us. We are overwhelmed!

---

[71] Matt. 9:37, Luke 10:2 AV.

For now, we are those of Q'uo. Adonai. We leave you in the love and in the light of the mystery that created all and is all.

(Barbara channeling)

Aaron: We pause while this instrument returns to a deeper tuning.

(Pause)

Aaron: I had earlier requested the opportunity to lead you in a meditation into the opening to the practice of forgiveness. I invite you here to join me. I know you are weary and I will be brief.

Please bring to your heart and mind the image or presence of one whom you love and who loves you. No matter how much love there may be between you, there are times when this one has hurt you and there are times when you have hurt this one.

We begin by asking forgiveness, speaking with open heart to this loved one. Can you offer the words, "I have hurt you, whether intentionally or unintentionally, through something I said or did or even thought. I have hurt you. I love you and do not wish to hurt you. It was my fear speaking. I am responsible for the manifesting of my fear and sorry that my reactivity to my fear led me to hurt you. I ask your forgiveness. Through the depth of your compassion and your kindness, can you forgive me?"

As much as is possible, relax and feel the forgiveness offered to you. Feel yourself allowed back into this one's heart. It may say to you, "Yes, for the ways you have hurt me or what you said or did or even thought. Yes, I forgive you and I welcome you back into my heart."

And he or she will ask you for the same opening. Think of the ways that this being has hurt you, intentionally or unintentionally. You might wish to tell him or her, "Love has been there between us, but also pain. Through something you said or did or even thought, you have hurt me. I forgive you. I understand the depth of your pain and I forgive you. I invite you back into my heart." Can you feel the wonder of the healing when that wall between you comes down? There is so much space in forgiveness.

We now turn to someone harder to forgive, which is the self. Please look at the self as you just looked at this loved one. What needs to be forgiven: the manifestations of fear as the need to control or as expressions of anger, greed, and pride? Observe the way the fearful self has moved on the basis of that fear and caused pain, not only to others but to the self. Observe the ways that self has hurt itself by not manifesting the fullness of self, but instead by hiding in a small place.

Here I would ask you to say your own name to the self and bring into the heart that which has been done that seemed difficult to forgive. *How have I abused myself? In what ways have I condemned myself or pushed myself so hard that I could not stably endure? These movements were prompted by fear's voice.*

Saying your own name to yourself, state, *I invite you in. You have been afraid and have acted on that fear. I love you. I hear you. I forgive you.* It is difficult to say those words to the self. *I love you. I forgive you.* Yet, these words become the basis for laying a firm foundation. They become the basis for the eventual dissolution of the myth of fear, like wading into that icy water on a warm day.

Enter this water of forgiveness and feel the peace in it. Speak your own name to yourself and say, *I love you. I embrace you. I forgive you. And I will explore the further depths of forgiveness so that I may open my heart ever deeper to myself and to all beings.*

My friends, your energy is low, so I will conclude. There is a third part in this process that I would ask you to experiment with on your own. As you become able to extend forgiveness to the loved one who has hurt you, to receive forgiveness from that loved one, and to extend forgiveness to the self for its seeming imperfections, can you then reach out even further into the icy water to one with whom there has been deep pain? Can you ask for forgiveness from this being? And then, if only for experiment's sake, can you breathe in and try the words, *I forgive you?*

Remember, it is a process. You are touching the possibility of for-giveness as you open your heart to the immensity of your pain and the infinite nature of your love.

May all beings everywhere love and be loved.

(Bell)

May all beings know the infinite spaciousness and joy of the forgiving heart.

(Bell)

May all beings follow this path of letting go into the deepest truth of their own being and therein find perfect peace.

(Bell)

I thank all of you for inviting us into your circle. I love you all and wish you a good night. That is all.

Session 30

Weekend 8, Part 4 of 4
(This session was preceded by a period of tuning and meditation.)

Group discussion: The group suggested a question-and-answer session with possibly more discussion regarding the forgiveness meditation.

(Carla channeling)

Q'uo: We are those of the principle known to you as Q'uo. With a light and merry heart we greet you in the love and in the light of the one infinite Creator. It has been such a blessing to spend these few hours with you in seeking together a more lucid distortion of the one great original Thought, which is love.

It has been such a pleasure to speak about living a life in faith and devotion. The one known as Aaron speaks for us when he says that he could discuss this subject at almost infinite length. For living devotionally is as much our hope as it is yours. And as the logicians have it, we keep getting halfway to the goal, then halfway to the goal, then halfway to the goal, and so on, closer and closer. Yet still the goal is before us, surrounded in sublime mystery.

There are relatively easy spiritual practices, such as meditation, prayer, contemplation, the reading of inspired works, the listening to inspired music, and the sharing of worship in groups such as this that light up your planet, especially on this Sabbath day.

And there are relatively difficult spiritual practices, such as standing in the checkout line at the grocer's and scrubbing the toilet bowl. The life of devotion is lived where you are or not at all. It is a common hope of those upon your earth plane someday to retire to a pleasant and secluded place where finally you can devote yourself to worship. But we suggest to you that the life of devotion is lived now, wherever you may be. It is the confidence and focus within that turns bare earth into holy ground, blazing with the incandescent light of love supernal, limitless, and whole.

It is your challenge to find ways of opening the heart to the present moment and to the love therein. You shall fail, according to your cruel judgment, again and again. We ask you to know deeply and surely that each error and each missed opportunity is a gift to the infinite One, just as much as each moment when you judge yourselves to be, as this instrument would say, on the beam or in the groove. Clumsy or graceful, awkward or flowing, your spirit is utterly beloved.

Begin to allow yourself to feel that you are never alone, never isolated, and never alienated in the world within that is as real to each of you as the world without. In that world you have many companions: those unseen that you call angels and those such as we who accompany those with the desire to ask for us as they sit in meditation or as they go about the small businesses of the everyday life.

May you encourage yourselves when you forget where your center is. May you rest in contentment and praise those sublime moments when you can feel the rhythm of creation and the rightness of all that there is.

You are the universe in little. And as a holograph, you are as whole and complete as the infinite illusion in which you and we dwell. Know that as you serve, either by disciplining and refining yourself or by being a part of the good in another's life, you serve the light.

Thank you for this great privilege. The one known as Aaron and we can never adequately express our love for your pilgrim souls. Blessings! Blessings! Blessings! How reluctantly we come to the end of our time on the soapbox.

Ah, the soapbox! The pedestal! We spout truth and then we come down and roll down the hill with you into the warmth of the water, splashing and playing in the sunlight. May you play together like otters. May you be merry with each other. May you share each other's burdens and joys. May you know that you are about the Creator's business.

We now open the working to your questions. As our beloved Aaron says, simply express which of us you wish to respond and we shall go from there. May we have the first query, please?

I.: I have one I would like to ask Aaron. This is a statement of my understanding of something he spoke about last evening. I will read it and ask for his enhancement to my understanding. "For the incarnate self, forgiveness is a process. But forgiveness radiates as an aspect of the whole self, so the process of forgiveness is part of the movement from a thought-point to a known space, a going nowhere." Could Aaron comment?

(Barbara channeling)

Aaron: Does the right hand need to forgive the left hand? If the baby, the fetus, is kicking in the night and wakes the mother, does the mother need to forgive the fetus? In the first example, the right and left hands are clearly a part of the same being. The mother and fetus still temporarily experience that state of nonseparation.

The angel aspect of yourself knows it is not separate from the small self nor from the Divine, and never has been separate. It knows the crystal clarity of its oneness, which could never become tarnished. To move into incarnation is to accept the illusion of separation and to agree to this veil of forgetting of your true being. Thus, you move into the illusion that there are spots on the wings, that the body and the mind are unclean in some way.

You have all heard me call you angels in earth-suits. I., from the human perspective, you practice forgiveness because there has been the experience of pain for the human, and the practice of forgiveness opens the heart. It is not just bringing you back to where you were. You are Love. And there is no limit to the amount of love that you can express. If there were a limit, there would be no reason to move into incarnation. As you are aware, the universe does not run on linear time. There is no rush, no schedule.

As Q'uo just expressed, that shining light is always ahead. One has never finished, even in sixth density. I am not finished. There is always more to learn about love. You have entered incarnation in faith that this is a tool that will help you to learn about love, not to a finished point but to continually enhance the process of loving.

We find that the wonder and beauty is that those who have graduated through the earth plane teach love and compassion to the rest of the universe. Truly, the masters of love in our universe are amongst those who have moved through Earth's catalyst. It is a very powerful teacher. Yes, I like your image. The spot expands.

There was never anything to forgive. But from the human perspective you have practiced forgiveness. That practice expands you out of the small ego-self and into the heart we all share. It expands you into that place where there is no individuated self taken as real, but only the illusion of individuated self, as you are learning, too. Thus, you practice forgiveness—not so much to forgive, although that is the idea within the relative mind, but to stretch the heart, and to move out of your illusions of separation.

You are unbalanced. I said to some of you this morning, you come into incarnation and you immediately pick up thick glasses that serve as a microscope. They allow you to tie and untie the knots, to see what you do. But they close you off to the vast perspective that you had before you came into incarnation.

If somebody lifts these microscope glasses for a moment, you look out and say, "Wow! There is all that space." Then the glasses slip back. How quickly you forget that space. When you regularly practice entering that space through any spiritual practice, you learn to rest very stably. But the knots still need to be tied and untied. If someone has stepped on you and asked your pardon, you still need to work with the pain and hurt and to come to the place where the human can offer forgiveness and can let go of its fear, anger, and separation.

The practice of forgiveness repeatedly leads you back to the angel. But the practice of forgiveness is also what allows the human to put its microscope glasses back on and to work with the knots of incarnation in a much more skillful and loving way.

Does this answer your question, I., or may I speak further to it? I pause.

I.: There are some new ideas. I have the feeling that I am substituting the idea of the angel state to erase the incarnate-self idea and I don't believe it's correct. Aaron is speaking about a partnership, a balance.

Barbara: A balance between the relative and ultimate self. Aaron says a partnership is a perfect word.

I.: I am currently walking between the two.

Barbara: Aaron says (I am paraphrasing Aaron), at first one tends to leap back and forth. He says to picture yourself alone on the seesaw, trying to get it to balance. First you run from one end to the other. And then you begin to understand how to keep your weight balanced equally on both ends. But you must not stand immovable in the center, but must move back and forth, present here, present there. He asks you also to remember his image of the box in the infinitely spacious room. The relative rests in the ultimate. You cannot leave the ultimate, but can only forget about it for awhile.

Aaron: Of course, for the angel there can be nothing to forgive. How could there be? Of course, for the human who is caught deeply in its own small ego-self, forgiveness is almost impossible. You are living in a balance, which is a partnership between the human and the angel, so that the human does not hear there is nothing to forgive because for the human there *is* something to forgive. But forgiveness is possible because you recognize that the angel exists and that you are both human and angel, with the balance of attention always changing slightly, depending on the needs and clarity of the moment. I pause.

I.: I like the idea of forgiveness as a spiritual practice.

Aaron: Only watch for pride and self-righteousness, which are apt to crop up when you become the one who is forgiving. And if they do

504

crop up, then shift the forgiveness practice to find forgiveness for the human who has found pride in its path. I pause.

May we hear your further questions? I pause.

K.: Please, Aaron and Q'uo, speak to us further and with more depth regarding pride. We are angels. When we discover this, how can we also not be clothed in pride?

Aaron: I hear your question, my sister. To be clothed in pride is just to be clothed in pride, just as to feel anger arise is just to feel anger arise, just as to step on a tack until the blood flows from your foot is just to step on a tack and have blood flow. Certain conditions give rise to certain inner circumstances. Yes, eventually you will reach a point where anger and pride do not arise, at least not nearly so often or forcefully. But this is not done through willpower.

There is a deep humility and understanding that you are human. And as you realize your angel, pride has arisen: *Here I am being the angel.* And suddenly, here is pride. So what else is new? You do not need to act upon that pride nor to get rid of it, but only to note, *Here is pride.*

Pride is part of the distortion of fear. It is part of that which wants to be somebody, to be safe and in control. How can the loving heart not open to the human who wants to feel safe and in control? When you embrace the fearful self that does not feel safe, the circumstances that gave rise to pride begin to diminish. And in that way, pride begins to dissolve. When there is nobody left who feels unsafe, then pride and anger and other such emotions will cease to arise. May I pass this further to Q'uo? I pause.

(Carla channeling)

Q'uo: My sister, perhaps you recall the parable of the teacher known to you as Jesus, concerning the Pharisee and the tax collector. The parable goes that there were two men in the temple. One was a Pharisee and the other a tax collector, which in those days was tantamount to the dishonest, greedy, and altogether undesirable. The Pharisee prayed thusly, "Lord, I thank thee that I am not as other men are: robbers, thieves, hypocrites. I fast two times a week. I tithe to the temple." The publican, on the other hand, was on his knees, praying, "Lord, have mercy on me, for I am a sinner."[72] Which of the two prayed well?

The issue of pride is going to be yours and every seeker's intimate companion for the foreseeable future. We ask you simply to view the self as if you were a rough, huge planetoid with deep ridges and valleys; that is, an elephantine chunk of jagged roundness, tiny in the infinite reaches of space. The influences and essences of the cosmos beam and radiate in a refining fire, lambently playing over those mountains of pride and all the associated errors of the soul in manifestation.

In the fullness of time, to use the least distorted word, those ridges shall be smooth. And through eons of lifetimes, with painstaking thoroughness, the path or orbit of your consciousness shall become smooth, and then smoother, until at last the mantle of rock that covers your surface, as flesh covers the living being within, shall finally be polished away. And the immense jewel that is your consciousness shall emerge and become as the sun. And this sun body, at last, will have no pride. For it shall simply be.

Do not hurry toward that destiny. Enjoy your crust of imperfections. They shall not harm your spirit, but only give it the catalyst that your consciousness seeks in order to buff and polish and slowly erode the parts of your self that are least true.

Know that all things are acceptable. Each entity sees its own shadows. And further, the more the spirit wishes and longs to be free of humanness, the more that humanness shall be unable to serve you and to teach you what you came to learn. We suggest you simply stop resisting these untoward and wayward tendencies. These are the shadows made dark because you are beginning to shine.

The taking of the spiritual temperature is judgment. And as you find yourself caught in pride and judgment, smile. Take those broken

---

[72] Luke 18:10–13 AV.

shards of your being and hand them on up to the infinite One. They shall be transformed in that mighty hand and return a hundred blessings as you yield them up with an honest and contrite heart. Meanwhile, this is the very creation and the exact moment into which you came to find your Creator. Drinking your coffee, you bring the world into balance.

May we answer you further, my sister?

K.: In this painstaking thoroughness we find ourselves entering into perfectionist behaviors, striving to reach what we already know we are. And knowing seems not to help very much. We become frustrated with this awful veil. We cannot be perfect and yet we know we are. What a struggle!

(Barbara channeling)

Aaron: I hear your pain. Yet, if you were already perfect in human terms, why would you have incarnated? The veil is not a burden to you; it is a gift that is not a very pleasant gift at times. But it is precisely the catalyst that you need.

Child, consider this yearning for perfection in you—this self striving to become what it already is, with the fears, the patterns of reactivity, and the pride. All of these are the yeast for your bread. In the astral plane and beyond, you will practice discarnate skills. You will practice your perfection. Why seek to practice that perfection within the incarnation? This does not mean that you do not aspire to perfection. But understand that the human is perfect in its imperfection.

I would speak also to the strength of your aspiring. There is such pain in many of your hearts because you see this brilliant light of the Divine and you see the shadow in the self and feel, *I can never be worthy of that.* You then wish so badly to be rid of the shadow. This is a piece of every seeker's path, that dark night of the soul. But when you pass through the dark night, you begin to see the truth of what Q'uo just said, which is that the shadows are seen only because of the inherent luminousness of your being. The brighter you shine, the starker are the shadows. Just let the light shine. Be the light and give kindness instead of contempt to this being who has agreed also to carry shadow. May I further answer your question or is this sufficient? I pause.

K.: Is loving more deeply one way to move out of perfectionism?

Aaron: It is the only way. I pause.

(Carla channeling)

Q'uo: My sister, you shall progress. You shall not know in this, your present illusion, how you shall progress or because of what stimuli. In fact, the whole point of this illusion is to so confuse and addle and aggravate the sentient self that eventually you stop attempting to make sense of it all and move from head to heart.

We ask that you employ that which you have in abundance: your sense of humor. Is your life not a marvelous situation comedy? In music you have many times experienced that when the conductor calls for the hush of singing quietly, the chorus begins to be heavy and instinctively begins singing more slowly and losing the pulse. The effort of creating the pleasant *piano* sound weighs down that sense of rhythm.

The answer to perceived error is not adding wisdom but rather lifting away into the rhythm. Lift when you experience this frustration and pain. Lift and laugh at the well-termed human comedy. There is great humor in the infinite Creator.

May we speak further, dear friend?

(Barbara channeling)

Aaron: I wish to inject something here. When I said love is the only way, I do not mean that you must find a love switch and flick it from off to on. The ability to love is a dimmer switch. You have found the switch. You keep nudging it up through many of the practices we have spoken of this weekend: through prayer and meditation, through the practice of generosity, through mindful awareness of how negative and harmful emotions arise, through reaching that hand up to Divinity and taking the help that is offered to lift you, and through cultivating faith and patience.

This is like the one who has walked a long path in the dark night without a clear sense of where she has walked. At dawn she finds herself higher in the mountain and, looking back, is able to say, *Ah! There's the ravine where I stumbled. There's the steep place. There's the place where there was mud. And I have come through them all.* And then you turn and look and notice that the mountain goes up and up and up. You are in process.

The love that is inherent to you cannot help but manifest itself if you give it the opportunity to do so. May we speak further or is this sufficient? I pause.

K.: I thank you both.

(Carla channeling)

Q'uo: We seem to linger on this issue with you, my sister. But we simply have such a love of talking!

We have one last suggestion in this regard, which is that you adopt for yourself the motto, "God bless this mess." We are those of Q'uo and are open to further queries at this time.

K.: I have a recurring dream of being in a situation where people are all standing around a huge trough of slop. And I find that it is mandatory that I dive into this trough. I have no choice. And as I go through this slop I feel no pain. And I suddenly arrive in an L-shaped, white room with those around me robed in white. I am feeling grateful, as these are my brothers and sisters or perhaps colleagues and teachers. Is this the school in which we learn while we're sleeping and not in the Earth?

(Barbara channeling)

Aaron: I hear your question, K. First, may I state that this dream is as perfect an illustration of the process of incarnation as I have ever heard: a pile of slop. Yes, as Q'uo said, "Bless this mess."

There are two different types of dreams: that which is symbolic and that which we call a teaching dream. This would seem to have a portion of both. The diving into the trough of slop is the symbolic part. The teaching is expressed by the awareness that only when you move through the messiness of incarnation, which is the messiness of a body and emotions, do you emerge as the angel that you are. It is like the chrysalis stage of the butterfly.

You stated that the people standing around seem to be teachers, but perhaps also colleagues. K., likely these are teachers. But teachers are also colleagues. One cannot teach without learning. It is a mutual participation.

The dream seems to represent not only a wish to arrive in this room, but also a statement of readiness. We on the upper planes use teaching dreams when the meditation practice is not sufficiently developed in order to allow you to hear us in a more conscious state. So we bypass that conscious state into the dream. It is a very effective way of reaching you. The only problem with it is that often there is not the practice to retain the dream afterward. So it is not as clearly integrated into the incarnate state as it would be in meditation. Those who have further developed the ability to hear their teachers while the body is in the state we call awake as opposed to asleep find that teaching dreams seem to slacken.

What I hear from you, K., is that there is a readiness to enter this realm. I would like to suggest that in the repeated dream or in meditation itself, you allow yourself to open to the experience of that room and then you make the very firm statement, "What do I need to learn? I am open. Please teach me," and just see what you hear. May I please pass this question, now, to Q'uo? I pause.

Session 30

(Carla channeling)

Q'uo: We have little to add to what our brother has said, except to say that the kindest thing that you can do, as the white-robed one who has taken on the mantle of Earth, is to trust in and cooperate with the rhythms of your unfolding destiny. Allow the falling away of things in their own time. Allow the contradictions, opposites, and riddles that characterize spiritual matters to tangle you up and to be untangled in the natural way.

We fear the hour grows late. We would ask for a final query at this time. We are those of Q'uo.

(There are no further queries.)

(Barbara channeling)

Aaron: In the process of moving through your incarnation, there are many times when there is simply pain in yourself and in others. And I am often asked, "What helps? What allows me to touch that pain with more kindness?"

There is a very powerful practice taken from Tibetan Buddhism. It is called tonglen, or "giving/receiving practice." I find it a very powerful tool to use in the case of suffering within the self or without. I would like to teach it to you.

I ask you to bring into your heart and mind the image of someone who is suffering. They do not have to be someone mired down by suffering, but someone who is experiencing pain. It could be someone in this room, someone in your family or your circle of friends, or even someone whose face you have seen on your television screen as a victim of a disaster of one sort or another. Normally before we do this practice, we ask the higher self of the person, "May I do this practice with you?" We do not impose our need to serve another on the person.

So, the first step is to invite this person into your heart and mind and ask, "May I do this practice with you?" Visualize or feel yourself

511

sitting within a cylinder of light. This is not something you need to imagine since you are already sitting in a cylinder of light. Simply open yourself in whatever way is appropriate to the experience of that light. If imagination is what works, that is fine. But remember, you are not creating by your imagination. You are merely allowing yourself into a different level of reality.

Breathing in, allow that light to come through the crown chakra and down to the heart center. Breathing out, feel it centered in the heart. Breathing in, form the intention to send it out to where there is suffering. And exhale, sending it out as a ray coming from the heart. You may also feel it as a ray coming through the third eye or even with the breath. Wherever it feels most natural to you, send it out. Breathing in, let light come into the heart center. Breathing out, let it stabilize. Breathing in, form the intention to release ... out, release ... in, light ... out, stabilize ... in, intention ... out, release ... in ... out ... in, release.

Now we are going to add the second part of the practice. With this next exhale, note the suffering as a heavy, black, tar-like mass. Breathe it in, taking it into the heart center. Notice any resistance to allowing that suffering into the self. Breathe out, feeling the heaviness of it. You do not need to carry this. You are merely the vehicle through whom it passes. Breathing in, intention to release ... breathing out, release it up through the upper chakras and crown chakra and back up to the Divine, letting it go.

Again from the beginning ... in, light ... out, feeling it fill the heart ... in, intention to release ... out, release ... in, the big, black mass ... out, feeling the weight of it ... in, intention to release ... out, release ...

You may do this practice at this speed, at double speed, or at half speed. In other words, in light and send it out ... in blackness and send it out. That is double speed. Or: breathing in light ... exhale ... breathing in, feeling that light filling, and then exhale ... in, noting the intention to release ... exhale ... in and then releasing it with the exhale ... in, drawing that heavy blackness into yourself ... exhale ... in, feeling the heaviness of it ... exhale ... in and out with the intention to release ... in, feeling it gathering from the heart center and rising ... and out, send it out.

I am going to be silent for several minutes. Please work at the speed that feels best to you. Please choose one and stay with it for the duration of these few minutes. Now, I will be silent.

(Pause)

(Bell)

May the love and light within this room shine itself out into the universe.

(Bell)

Everywhere in this universe, may all beings come to know their own infinite capacity as an instrument for light.

(Bell)

With the continued expansion of that capacity, may all beings find their way into the light and come to know their true being and thereby find perfect peace.

There are no words for my boundless love and appreciation of you. As you walk this path and sometimes feel alone, please remember how deeply you are cherished and be aware of all the hands that extend themselves in love to accompany you on the path. I pass this to Q'uo for the opportunity also to say farewell for a while, because, of course, there is never a good-bye when one soul speaks to another. That is all.

(Carla channeling)

Q'uo: We are those of the principle of Q'uo. Bon voyage. We are with you on the waves. We leave this instrument and you in the love and in the light of the one infinite Creator. We are known to you as Q'uo. Adonai. Adonai.

WEEKEND 9

We met one year after weekend 8. At the time we did not know that this was our last weekend together. But Carla's arthritic problems, which had gradually worsened over the years, became such that she could not physically tolerate the long sessions. And so an era of wonderful gatherings that brought together very special people to listen to Aaron and Q'uo converse came to an end.

Barbara and Carla have never lost their intense devotion to each other, and to the present day have kept their friendship fresh by getting together via relay telephone calls. This, then, was the last of the dialogues between Aaron and Q'uo.

Session 31

Weekend 9, Part 1 of 3
(This session was preceded by a period of tuning and meditation.)

Group question: Since we are all channels, how can we more purely bring our energy through? What would be the appropriate techniques to aid in becoming more clear?

(Barbara channeling)

Aaron: My greetings and love to you all. I cannot overly state the joy it gives to us on the spirit plane to gather together here, incarnate and disincarnate, to share together our energy, our thoughts, and our deepest seeking. I thank you.

I smile at the way Jim has written this question because it reflects a primary distortion. Your deep concern as humans is always, *How do I do it with more purity and with more clarity?* The question might be better phrased, *How do I do it with more love?* More love will probably bring that greater clarity and purity, but not necessarily. If there is fear that is creating distortion and you bring love to that fear, in the long run it will help to resolve the distortion. In the beginning it may not.

Bringing in love will not guarantee absolute purity but will enhance your compassion. My dear ones, if you plan to allow the universe to channel through you with absolute purity, then why are you in incarnation? It is very easy on my plane. Here is the greatest gift: to allow the expression of the universe filtered through the human! You are not here to learn perfection. You are here to learn faith and love. You are also here to learn compassion, although that is mostly the lesson of fourth density. But each of you is moving into that density.

The human is never going to be perfect. These fears that arise in you, and that create some sort of blockage to your work, are not problems. They are gifts. They are reminders to have compassion

516

for this human vehicle with all its complex mechanisms. This does not mean that you are not responsible for what comes through you. If it becomes increasingly distorted, you are responsible for recognizing that distortion and for doing the inner work to clarify the distortion to the point that it is again adequately clear. I stress *adequately*. I can channel the universe with absolute purity, but it lacks the gifts of human interpretation.

Can you see that it is only fear that drives the desire for perfection and not love? So may we rephrase the question as, *How do I learn to become a channel that offers what is most needed in the deepest spirit of love that is possible for me? And secondly, when I experience distortion, how do I greet that distortion with love?*

Whatever form your channeling takes, there is going to be distortion. And that very catalyst that creates distortion is the greatest gift because only through that distortion can you really practice compassion and kindness.

It was our idea that my dear brother/sister/friend of Q'uo would open this session. So with joy I hand the microphone to Q'uo. I pause.

(Carla channeling)

Q'uo: We greet you in the love and the light of the one infinite Creator. We wish to add our expression of gratitude for this gathering to that offered by the one known as Aaron, for each within this circle of seeking has sacrificed much to come to this circle. In our memory, we are aware of the seeming lack of time when in incarnation in your density.

The choice of where to place the attention is a choice full of weight within the incarnate scheme or nexus or arrangement of priorities. Scheduling of time simply to have come to this circle creates an opening of opportunity that cannot be purchased at any price. You have given yourself this chance and have given us an enormous gift. For in so doing you enable us to be of service. Sharing our thoughts with those who might find them interesting is our chosen form of service.

In giving us this opportunity, you enable us to progress in our own destiny. You could not give us a more precious present.

And we cherish this occasion, asking only, as always, that each seeker use her own powers of discrimination and retain only those truths that resound within as if she had already known those truths but had forgotten them.[73] Those are the truths that are personally yours. Allow us to share all our thoughts, but allow those thoughts that do not echo of recognition within to be gently left behind.

Let us, then, begin by gazing upon what this instrument would call the human condition. Each dwells in two distinct worlds, if we may oversimplify for the sake of discussion. There is the physical portion of existence, within which each has a physically typical type of second-density body, of the type this instrument would call the great-ape variety and what one of your philosophers has called the featherless chicken.[74]

This earthly, mortal, and limited vehicle contains brainpower specifically designed to solve problems and to make choices. This is practical and useful within the Earth world. We do not scorn the human brain. We simply note that it is either a servant or a master. Those who would spiritually advance are well advised, in our opinion, to reduce the dependency of the consciousness on the choices and intellectual structures that the human brain is so good at creating.

Within this earthly plane you are still completely a citizen of the universe. You are infinite, eternal, omnipotent, and omnipresent. You are what has been and what will be. You are a child of the Creator. And indeed, we all seek together for that place in space and time when we shall cease to be citizens of duality and move back into the heart

---

[73] The use of "her" and "she" does not indicate that only women were present at this gathering. Rather, it indicates the Q'uo group's indiscriminate use of male and female pronouns when speaking in general.

[74] Diogenes Laertius, third century AD, *Lives of the Philosophers*, Book 6. (The philosopher Diogenes used the term "featherless chicken" to refer to certain difficult aspects of second-density physical existence that accompany the human condition.)

of the one original Thought, which has created all that there is. That Thought is love and each of you is love.

Consider yourself within the earth plane as one who is upon a journey, sent forth from the beginning of time and space to gather experience; and always, always, returning and circling back to the Source, which is Love.

And at the same time that you are upon this plane, you are perfect, pure, unblemished, and without error. This identity remains absolute, no matter what your perception of yourself or your progression might be.

When you as a seeker, then, begin to desire to clear the channel for more pure channeling of the love and the light of the infinite One, there is the tendency to think in terms of working from the viewpoint of one who wishes to take from work in consciousness that which does not belong.

However, the concept that may in actual practice do the most to clear the channel is to go against logic and instead move back into those energies that, were the human structure as a house, would be in the basement. The clearing of channels continues in the progress made by joining the self as a whole with the lower energies in a loving and nonjudgmental way. Gaze with care upon the arrangement of what this instrument would call the dark side of personality, which is that side wherein those instincts for survival, sexuality, and human relationships with self and other selves reside.

The feeling is to get away from the body and its millions of complaints and needs. Yet in actuality you worked hard to deserve the opportunity to come into your physical body and into physical incarnation. It is continuingly important to attend to and embrace the nuts and bolts or the nitty-gritty of bodily awareness.

The confusion that swamps the entity because of the sensory input of the physical vehicle is a problem, for in confusion nothing can be known. The physical body is a blanket of confusion. And by dwelling within it you are removed from knowledge of the truth as to what your energies are actually doing. In the body you have no choice, if you are spiritually oriented, but to find faith and to use that faith in order to make your choices, beginning with how you relate to your self; to your intransigent need to continue to survive, to continue the species, and to attend to all of these things.

Do not brush these things aside, for the greatest of choices begins with these decisions. And as you embrace and involve yourself, so do you open the way to that center within called the heart chakra, or the green-ray energy center. The opening of the heart is possible only when the seeker gives up on the intellect and moves into unknowingness. The seeker lives in faith. What does this mean? As this instrument would say, "We'll talk!"

We turn over the microphone to our friend, our beloved brother Aaron, with great delight. We leave this instrument for the nonce. We are those known to you as the principle of Q'uo.

(Barbara channeling)

Aaron: As I begin to speak, I wish to echo Q'uo's thought. Please take what is useful of my words, as that which rings true to your own deepest truth, and allow it into your heart. As for the rest, discard it without a second thought.

Q'uo has spoken of the two aspects of your being. These are what I call the angel and the earth-suit. You are angels in earth-suits. If you wanted just to be angels and manifest perfect clarity, you would not have chosen to incarnate. Any being can manifest its energy with great love and clarity as an angel. Can you do it in the earth-suit? Even more important is what happens when you bring the balance of these two together. For you are not only the earth-suit. No! No! No! You are the angel *in* the earth-suit.

It is through this balance of taking the constant catalysts of the earth plane and drawing them into the heart of love that you not only learn for yourselves, but also manifest your energy into the world with increasing purity and love and thus offer that energy to all beings. Very often you become lost enough in the earth-suit catalyst that you lose view of what you are really doing. You are simply forging ahead blindly, and yet sometimes one has to do that.

Speaking of her drive to perfection, once, with this instrument, I asked her a question. I said to her, "Imagine that you are with a group of people on top of a mountain. You are walking, when suddenly the weather turns, clouds roll in, and it begins to snow. Where you had been hiking was very steep, with many precipices. You feel that you cannot walk because of the density of the weather, and yet you recognize that you must get off the mountain. What you really want is someone to come along from the group and say, 'I know this mountain so well. Follow me and I will lead you down.' But no one comes. Everyone sits down and shakes from fear and from cold. You are fully aware that in less than an hour of exposure to this treacherous wind and cold, people are going to enter into hypothermia and people are going to die. You do not know the path. You only had a glimpse of it as it lay ahead, just as the clouds rolled in. What are you going to do? Are you going to wait there for somebody else to say, 'I know the mountain. I will lead us,' or are you going to do it yourself? What if you are not perfectly prepared?"

When is it ego to say, "I will lead"? When is it love? More correctly phrased, when is it the voice of the small self who acts in service to that self, perhaps to enhance it or to self-inflate? When is it the voice of the large self that acts in service to all beings?

First you must allow that both voices are going to be present. You are this angel in an earth-suit. While the angel's voice may come through loud and clear, the human voice also must be present or else you are not having a human experience. Perhaps the angel's voice says, *I think I can do this. If I move very carefully, I think I can do this.* Then you hear the ego's voice saying, *Oh, won't everybody make a fuss over me when we get safely to the bottom.* Hearing that second thought, you may surmise, *This is not my deepest truth that says it can lead the descent. This is only ego.* If you strike out in anger against that ego's voice, then you cannot hear love's voice. You become so much at war with the small-self aspect of you that you shut out the existence of anything else.

On the other hand, you can hear that small self's voice and just say, *Aha! Here is the self that wants recognition. Here is the self that feels pain and wants to be a hero. Shhhh, I hear you. I hear how afraid you are and I hear the ego-self grasping at this opportunity for some notice.* When you treat the small self with kindness, its voice quiets. Then you have the opportunity to reopen once again to the voice of the greater self that is still insistently whispering, *We must get these people off the mountain or people are going to die. It will take courage from all of us, but it can be done.*

When you ask, "How can I become a purer channel?" that absolute purity is always accessible within you. Confusion and distortion are also always there. This shadow aspect of the self will exist. Do not fixate on it in any way and do not deny it. You do not need to be ruled by it and you do not need to fight against it. Your work is to draw it into the heart of love. When the conditions have ceased that gave rise to that particular wrinkle, it will go if you are not relating to it in a way that gives it further conditions from which to perpetuate itself! It will go. You do not need to push it away. To fret over it is a way of practicing it. Can you see that? When you are busy attacking the wrinkle, you are giving solidity to it. In karmic terms, your energy contracts around that particular wrinkle and it plants the seeds for the next moment.

I think it is very important to understand how that works. Let us use a hypothetical example, such as the thinking of the self as unworthy. This concept is the wrinkle. To strive to become a worthy person sets up a pattern of contractions every time there is an opportunity to be generous or kind. The generosity and kindness are gifts to another, of course. And yet, if there is a strong *somebody* being generous and kind, it sets up reverberations that solidify the self. That somebody who is struggling not to be unworthy is struggling to be worthy. In either case, it solidifies this self who must push away unworthiness and grasp at worthiness. It does not acknowledge the deeper truth that there is no such thing as unworthy or worthy. How could any human or any being on any plane be unworthy or worthy? One might be generous or perhaps wise/unwise, or skillful/unskillful—but worthy/unworthy?

Even such a movement as generous or greedy can set in motion this pattern of solidified self. You may see yourself as clinging or greedy and make the decision, *I'm going to defeat this wrinkle. I'm going to become generous each time fear arises.* And with this decision comes a clinging pattern. You castigate yourself and say, *Look how bad I am to have this fear energy. I'm going to be generous,* and you push yourself to give.

So long as you are fixated on being the generous one, you are going to continue karmically to enact situations in your life in which clinging or giving is primary. The mastering of this lesson does not involve only freely giving, even when there is fear. That giving will come naturally when there is no obstruction to it. The idea of the generous self, here, serves as an obstruction. The entire notion of the self as a giver or clinger or as a self that must be "fixed" must be released. Freedom from perpetuating this pattern comes when you can release fixation on the whole movement of clinging and giving.

Note the fear from which these patterns arise. Note that certain conditions give rise to that fear. Observe the self that is fearful with a great deal of kindness and compassion. Then this solid self is no longer the one who is giving or clinging. Then the heart knows what to do. There is no more giver and no more clinger. Giving happens. There is no subject and object. Nothing is given.

The fear does not automatically disappear any more than our would-be guide on the top of the mountain loses its fear when it says, "Follow me," and takes the first step. The fear may be immense. That is just it! If you were just spirit, Pure Spirit, giving or leading people down the mountain, there would be no fear and there would be no challenge. The challenge is not to be fearless. The challenge is to bring love where there is fear.

The work is to cease to fixate on getting rid of anything, such as fear, jealousy, greed, or anger, instead working to draw all of these emotions and the causes for them into the loving heart. Then you can watch these patterns come and go in yourself. A loving heart knows what to do. As Q'uo said, the brain stops directing the show and the heart becomes the ruler.

At this point I would like to pass the microphone back to my brother/sister/friend Q'uo. I pause.

(Carla channeling)

Q'uo: We are again with this instrument.

We can sense all of you experiencing these thoughts, feeding them back into your consciousness, and sorting through them as through items at a rummage sale. We appreciate the bewildering effect of so many old and new ideas intermingled.

But have faith! There is a part of yourself upon which you can rely that overarches and interpenetrates all of your self and experience. You already know that which is needful for you at this particular juncture. So relax the desire to comprehend while practicing the trust in your own deeper intuition that constitutes one way of expressing things.

We would like to describe for you an entry into that portion of self that has its selfhood in faith. It lies within the heart center. It is literally and figuratively at the heart and of the heart.

As the energy moves into the physical body through the feet and up into the root chakra or energy center at the joining of the legs, it encounters a beautiful crystalline structure. We give this instrument a picture of a geodesic dome, which is a structure in time and space that enables the ready energy of the Creator to express energy through that co-Creator's red-ray energy center. And as the energy gathers, that energy becomes more crystalline and transparent to that love and light that is expressing into manifestation from unmoved love, that love that is not reacting.

Moving upward, this energy encounters another beautiful crystalline structure that resides in the belly itself, which contracts against dangers of association with the self and with the complexity of dual and triple or completely unusual and conflicting needs of the self and one other self. As the seeker gathers experience, the choices made can more and more energize this nexus of energy.

And the energy allowed through moves up to that place where belly meets chest, that omphalos of power. This is the plane of your Earth. This is the social energy center where the self deals with society and its associations, whether the experience is as a member of a family, as a citizen of a country, or as a member of any group in which you are working with distortions of the yellow-ray energy center. And again, the choices that you make can, through the incarnate experience, help to crystallize and make transparent this center.

As one works with all of these energies to balance them, one is literally making more room for energy from the Creator to pour in its original strength into the heart center.

The problem with attempting to work in consciousness with ascended masters or entities such as we is that one is working from the top down, whereas the stable basis of energy shall always first depend upon the amount of energy that comes into the heart from the root chakra upward.

No matter how much energy is called into the system from the heart, it must move downward to the place where the energy from the Creator has originated its entrance into the mind and body complexes. Thusly, you see seekers who find themselves in desperate straits because they are attempting to open the heart by inspiration, and yet they have no home in which to place this inspiration. And so, like a bird, all that is felt from contact with that source flies away like lost hope and is gone when the eyes open and the entity is once again within the busyness of everyday life.

Come with us into the heart, just for a moment, where we feel that there is the need to experience love. We wish to tell you that you can do this at any time. But come with us now. Feel that energy coming through those distortions in each center, yet moving upward to the heart. See that energy coming from above that calls for inspiration and flows like liquid into the heart.

These two meet where lions guard the door. You bow to the lions and you do not say, "I deserve to be here." You say, "Have mercy on me, for I seek love." And the lions bow to you and the door opens and you walk into this room, this holy of holies. This is the open heart. Sit down. Take your shoes off. You are upon holy ground. Now you are with the Creator, who can give you rest. You are loved with a passion that creates and destroys worlds. Oh, how you are loved!

We turn the microphone back to our beloved friend Aaron.

(Barbara channeling)

Aaron: Where is that place of most brilliant light and love? Is it somewhere out there? Is it something you must attain through self-purification or other types of pursuit? No, it is within. It is that perfect sheet of paper that still exists, even though the wrinkles are also there. That Pure Heart-Mind is always available to you, my friends. It is not the existence of the wrinkles, of the shadow, that keeps you from that brilliant inner light. It is your relationship to those wrinkles and to that shadow.

I am back to the same point. The wrinkles will come and go. You are human. If you step on a tack, there is going to be pain and contraction of the physical and emotional bodies. If somebody screams at you insultingly, rudely, there is going to be a contraction of the emotional body. If you are very hungry and somebody takes away your meal, there is going to be fear. These movements do not prevent you from resting in that light, nor do they hinder you in manifesting from that brilliant and loving heart. They are simply fear, desire, anger, and confusion. They need no reaction from you.

You cannot get rid of these by forcing them out. By strong willpower you can rid your outer experience of them. But they still lie hidden in the ground, simply waiting for a break in your fierce suppression so that they can sneak through. But if you learn to allow these kinds of emotions and confusion, which are the human experience, to move through you while never losing that place of center, then you need fear them no more. You know you will never lose the awareness that you sit in the light. The Pure Heart is always accessible!

I would offer an example of what I have just said—and even more, of what Q'uo said preceding me. Returning to our guide on the mountain, you are this guide and you have said, "Stand up and walk with me. I will lead us to safety." For a while you follow the path. The snow has not yet obscured it. Then the snow drives harder and the wind is stronger. You become aware that you have lost the path. What are you going to do? You stop and acknowledge, *I've lost the path and don't know where I am.*

Fear may come up very strongly for those of you who aspire to live your lives with love. It might be a very fierce, self-critical fear that said, *You knew you couldn't do it. It was all ego that said, "I'm going to lead."* So what are you going to do, just tell everybody to sit down in the snow and die because you made a mistake?

What if it was fear that said, *I will lead?* Are you denying that there was also a deep wisdom that said, *We must make an attempt to get off the mountain?* It is certain death versus a possibility of survival. As soon as you open your heart to yourself and as soon as you hear your pain and fear, you reopen into the wisdom and the clear heart. And the clear heart says, *Okay, I made a mistake. I got lost.* That does not mean that negativity was leading, even if negativity was there. The loving heart was also there. Coming back to the loving heart, you simply pick yourself up, trail or no trail, and begin moving slowly down the mountain. On the trail it is easier. Off the trail it will be a little harder. The task is the same: You have got to get down from the mountain.

There is a teaching in both Buddhism and Christianity that I find useful here. This instrument has been reading a very clear book, written jointly by a Zen master, Robert Aitken Roshi, and a Jesuit priest, Brother David Steindl-Rast. It is called *The Ground We Share*.[75] The focus of the book is to explore the commonalities. Aitken Roshi speaks of a Buddhist teaching that is given the very technical name, *Three Kayas.* The word *kaya* means "body." It talks of the "truth body" or *dharmakaya,*

[75] Robert Aitken and David Steindl-Rast, *The Ground We Share* (Boston, MA: Shambhala Publications, 1996).

the ever-perfect. And at the other end is the "form body" or *nirmanakaya.*
This is not just the material body. By "form" I mean any kind of form.
A thought is also a form, as is an emotion. This is the outer-expression
body. There is a bridge that joins them, called the "wealth body" or
sambhogakaya. I call this the "transition body."

Think of the ever-perfect. Think also of the final expression. The
wealth or transition body is a bridge of intention, of karmic force,
and of other elements that serves as a vehicle for the ever-perfect to
express itself into the world.

A very simple example would offer the sun as a metaphor for the
ever-perfect. The expression of the sun on the earth plane might be
the heat that you feel on your back when you sit in the sun or it could
be a patch of sunlight on the grass. The atmosphere, the clouds, and
so on carry the particular qualities of the sun and permit them to be
expressed onto the physical plane. It is not a perfect metaphor, but
you can see the two ends and center of it clearly.

In Christian terms, within the Trinity we can substitute Father for
ever-perfect, Son for the form body, and Holy Spirit for the wealth
or transition body, which is the intention energy level. This is not a
perfect match but is quite adequate. You may think it is an uneven
match because the Son contains God and is a direct expression of
God. Yes! And the nirmanakaya contains the dharmakaya, too, and is
a direct expression of it! I find this a very valuable teaching for this
reason. No matter where one looks on your physical plane, you see
the self-display of the Divine.

In the teachings of both Buddhism and Christianity, the inner core
and outer expression are not separate. In Christianity, the Son is voice
of the Father, and the Son is the expression of God in the world. In
Buddhist teaching, everything on the form level or in outer manifestation is an expression of the ever-perfect. You cannot separate them.
This is vital.

In the transition body, we pick up the many energy streams that
may offer some distortion of the absolutely pure core. Please remember that within this core are the possibilities of distortion, or else dis-

tortion could not occur or would be dual with the core itself. The negativity in you is not in dualistic opposition to the Divine. It is simply a distortion of the Divine. Love is also a distortion of the Divine.

Some distortions, when you play them out in the world, may do harm. Then, clearly, you are responsible for that harm. You must clean up your spills. Some distortions may be of great service to others; nevertheless, they are distortions that carry adhering karma and must be attended. They are all a display of the Divine. My dear ones, you do not have to be afraid of what moves through you. There is nothing there but God. When you ask, then, *How can I manifest my energy more purely in the world?* remember that there is nothing there but God, sometimes being expressed with distortion or even great distortion. You have asked, *How can I come to a reduction of distortion?* You come to this state by offering forgiveness and kindness. *Hatred will never dissolve hatred and negativity. Only love will dissolve negativity.*[76] Only love will dissolve confusion and distortion. Whatever distortion expresses itself, you must bring it into the heart of love.

Ah, yes, the question is, *How do we do this?* Perhaps that is best left for tomorrow's discussion. I would leave you tonight with only this thought: *There is nothing that is not God.* Therefore, when you see in dualist terms, it is an invitation to remind yourself that what you are seeing is itself a distortion and is the voice of fear. Instead of trying to chase it away with a big stick, do as this instrument would do: Hold out a goody in your hand and invite it to come and take a taste of it. Offer it lovingkindness. Embrace your fear in that way. Do not hate it and order it away.

The distortion-free place is always accessible to you. When you are reacting from a place of fear, which is creating increasing distortion in the outpouring of the energy that flows through you, it is not a statement that absolute clarity and love are not available. It is only a statement that you are increasingly practicing the wrinkles. Then you

---

[76] These words are a paraphrasing of the opening lines of the famous Buddhist teaching, *Dhammapada.*

must come back to the ever-perfect. As I said, I would prefer to leave the *how* of how we do that to tomorrow so as not to overtax here with too many different thoughts.

At this point, and with great thanks for your willingness to hear me and open your hearts to these thoughts, I turn the microphone back to Q'uo. I pause.

(Carla channeling)

Q'uo: We would fairly briefly give you farewell.

We would make a request of you. Being aware of the questions within the group, we and Aaron naturally planned to open the dialogue to questions at our next session. It would be helpful, we feel, if the circle spoke together before the next session in order to work out what the group feels it wishes to offer as the next input to this dialogue. We would appreciate that effort. For the more total the group's comfort with each other and with the activity, the greater becomes our own ability to communicate with a corresponding focus.

We would leave you this evening with a brief return to the one known as Aaron's topic. We would take you into the office and place the paper with the wrinkle on the machine and make the copy. On the copy you may see every wrinkle. Turn the paper over. It is clean. This is actually more like what your situation is than the simple paper. For you, yourself, are as a shell of personality. As the mark of toner upon that paper describes those shadows of wrinkles, so the shell of personality that is living your incarnation and interacting with your human function is only as thick as a sheet of paper. All that you are resides in fullness. Each wrinkle and each shadow is sacramental. Each energy center is holy. The trick is to know each energy as a sacrament within.

Dear ones, we wish you deep sleep, joyous dreams, and a fresh day, beginning oh, so soon. For now, we leave this instrument in the love and the light of the one infinite Creator. We are known to you as those of Q'uo. Adonai. Adonai.

Session 32

Weekend 9, Part 2 of 3

(This session was preceded by a period of tuning and meditation.)

(On this occasion, Aaron and Barbara present practices.)

Barbara: I use this practice to remind myself that I have the ability to become a purer vessel and to remind myself to tend to all three areas of my extension into the world: body, speech, mind.

These are the positive precepts from traditional Buddhist teachings:

> With deeds of loving-kindness, I purify my body.
> With openhanded generosity, I purify my body.
> With stillness, simplicity, and contentment, I purify my body.
> With truthful communication, I purify my speech.
> With words kind and gracious, I purify my speech.
> With utterances helpful and harmonious, I purify my speech.
> Abandoning covetousness for tranquility, I purify my mind.
> Changing hatred into compassion, I purify my mind.
> Transforming ignorance into wisdom, I purify my mind.[77]

> If it were not possible, I would not ask you to do it.

> Abandon what is unskillful. One can abandon the unskillful. If it were not possible, I would not ask you to do it. If this abandoning of the unskillful would bring harm and suffering, I would not ask you to abandon it. But as it brings benefit and happiness, therefore, I say abandon what is unskillful.

> Cultivate the good. One can cultivate the good. If it were not possible, I would not ask you to do it. If this cultivation were

---

[77] From Friends of the Western Buddhist Order, *FWBO Puja Book* (Birmingham, UK: Windhorse Publications, 1971), 19.

to bring harm and suffering, I would not ask you to do it. But as this cultivation brings joy and happiness, I say cultivate the good. (The Buddha)[78]

Aaron will now lead us in guided meditation and prayer.

(Barbara channeling)

Aaron: To begin, draw in and exhale several deep breaths.

(Pause)

Relax the body, tension leaving with the exhalation, mind letting go, coming into *this* breath, *this* moment.

(Pause)

Make yourself at home in the universe, resting in that space that truly is yours.

(Pause)

Be present for this one eternal now.

(Pause)

Open totally.

(Pause)

If something hangs on or if there is aversion, it is okay. It will go on its own. Nothing to do but lightly touch all arising with choiceless awareness.

---

[78] *The Anguttara Nikaya: Book of Twos, #10.*

(Pause)

Opening into this precious moment, allow the awareness of your connection with all that is to arise in yourself—no longer your joy or your pain but *our* joy, *our* pain.

(Pause)

Seeing the joy and pain of all beings, allow to arise in you the aspiration to serve all beings; to move beyond your own small fears and troubles; and instead, to use energy, courage, and awareness to alleviate suffering throughout the world.

(Pause)

This statement of intention is important, bringing awareness from *my* suffering to *ours* and offering the self as instrument for the alleviation of suffering.

(Pause)

Rest in that intention for several minutes, allowing awareness to spread, moving beyond the small self.

(Pause)

As you expand outward and come to rest in the divine self, the eternal and Pure Awareness, feel the presence of the Divine in all its aspects.

(Pause)

Rest in the nature of Pure Awareness, Pure Mind.

(Pause)

Allow yourself to rest in that space, feeling the energy that surrounds you.

(Pause)

Now the second step: to ask for help from all that surrounds you. Open to the spirit plane and to the Divine in your own nature.

(Pause)

In your own words, ask for the ability to hear that wisdom and to share it for the alleviation of suffering of all beings.

(Pause)

Offer yourself as a receptive instrument, not for your own benefit only, but for all beings.

(Pause)

And rest in that space, open and attentive, heart unbounded, ready to listen with that loving heart.

(Pause)

Finally, offer thanks for whatever you will be given. Then sit for several minutes in silence.

(Longer pause)

I am Aaron. My love to you all.

Bring yourselves into your body. I request that you allow yourselves the experience of the inhale and the exhale and to come deeply into your body for this particular meditation. I would like you to feel that inhalation and exhalation in the belly. Breathe in … belly breath … feel the breath coming into the abdomen and then breathe out. Let the body be soft and open. Now, let attention move upward from the belly to the heart. This living heart is the core of your being. The brain is the servant. It is in the heart where the true Christ or Buddha self dwells.

The body may experience pain and react by distorting itself or contracting. The brain may experience fear or discomfort and turn to what it is good at, which is directing the show so as to protect the organism from that which it fears or finds discomforting. The heart can watch all of that movement and know that it is merely the superficial movement of waves on the surface and does not affect the true being.

It is in this heart that I invite you to rest. Whatever physical sensations may arise, you can skillfully attend to them, without fixation. Whatever thoughts or emotions may arise, you can skillfully attend to them, without fixation. From a loving heart, we offer the deepest affirmation of our being. Please join me silently in offering this affirmation if it feels appropriate to you:

> *Today may I offer my energy in lovingkindness to all beings, including myself. If judgment, fear, greed, anger, or any such contracted emotion arises within me today, may I greet it with love and invite it into the heart where kindness may soften and transform it.*
>
> *I fully offer myself as a servant of the light. To be a servant is not to be somebody but to be nobody. I simply offer my energy that the Divine may make use of it in ways that the Divine itself determines, not in the ways that I determine.*
>
> *As much as possible, I offer my energy in that spirit and my whole being in service of God, of love, and of light. I ask for whatever help may be offered to me by all loving beings on every plane to help me express and nurture this resolve.*

Through allowing myself to be an instrument of light, may I help to bring more light into the universe so that increasingly all beings everywhere may be free of suffering, may be happy, and may find perfect peace.

Barbara: The last writing on the page is also from a traditional Buddhist prayer. Please read it with me if you would like:

> By the power and truth of this practice, may all beings have happiness and the cause of happiness, which is lovingkindness.
>
> May all be free from sorrow and the causes of sorrow, which are fear, hatred, and delusion.
>
> May all never be separated from the sacred happiness, which is sorrowless.
>
> And may all live in equanimity, without too much attachment and too much aversion, and live believing in the equality of all that lives.[79]

It is traditional in these teachings to offer outward whatever merit comes from this work, not to take it for oneself, but to offer it back out to all beings. The offering reminds me of Jesus's words from the Bible, "Not my will, but thine...."[80]

> May whatever merit comes from this practice go to the enlightenment of all beings. May it become a drop in the ocean of activity of all of the Great Ones and their tireless work for the liberation of all beings.

---

[79] Sogyal Rinpoche, *The Tibetan Book of Living and Dying*, eds. Patrick D. Gaffney and Andrew Harvey (San Francisco, CA: HarperSanFrancisco, 1992).

[80] Luke 22:42 AV.

Group discussion: *(A question is formulated to address the concern that, while there may be no intention to harm, harm does sometimes occur: How do we work with this harm and with our own distortions so as more clearly to offer our energy with nonharm?)*

(Barbara channeling)

Aaron: My love to you all. We are talking of how we serve others and of purification of the self to be offered in that service. I would toss a question into your stew pot here. Some years ago C. and Barbara met with a man from their organization. He was very negative and expressed tremendous fear. He was violating the spirit of the gathering by bringing his fear in and publicizing it out to the meeting, vocally condemning and judging specific people within the group.

The three of them spent a number of hours talking together about what he called his righteous anger and need to denounce these others who had harmed him. The women were able to hear his pain. He was not really able to hear them and their suggestions that he bring love rather than hatred to these places of perceived harm.

One would have to say that this man was bringing in a very distorted channeling of his own negative bias. He was being a channel for fear and dissension. It caused much pain for many members of the church. Barbara and C. experienced his fear and negativity, not with pain or fear, but with a sense that they really could not speak to it. Yet this man opened so many doors for so many people through the catalyst he offered. Was what he offered of harm or of benefit or some of each? What does "good" mean? What does "bad" mean?

Clearly you do not intend to offer your energy with the intention of harm. And yet, even when there is no intention of harm, sometimes harm is what comes out. This man had no conscious intention of harm. He felt it a moral necessity to let people know that he felt they had harmed him. He felt it a moral necessity not to let them continue what he perceived as *their* distortion. That does not release him from responsibility for the great pain that he caused. But the negative bearing of his attack on others ultimately served as catalyst that brought much insight for many. So it needs to be understood that there are many factors that determine the labeling of "good" or "bad." That is all.

(Carla channeling)

Q'uo: We greet each of you in love and in light, those lasting and active principles of the one Creator.

We come to you as Brothers and Sisters of Sorrow, for we hear the call of your Earth. We hear and are pierced by your sorrow and distress. And we thank you always for this call and this willingness to work, not cynically but hopefully, with the catalyst that comes to you.

The deepest sorrow and the greatest pain are as fallow fields within which is sown the kingdom of love. There is the parable within the holy work known as the Bible, of the kingdom of love being one precious pearl buried in a field. The one who seeks the pearl sells all that he has and buys the field.[81]

We hope to help each of you relate to your humanity. But there are subtleties involved when the self-aware seeker turns within. The mind sees the self. It sees the self watching the self. It sees the self who is watching the self who is watching the self. When the self perceives negative emotion, it sees the self seeing negative emotion and the self seeing the self seeing negative emotion. This creates the crowded universe and does not enlarge mercy.

And so, we would suggest that as you watch yourself and as you perceive dealing with seemingly negative catalyst, you remain within that first self-awareness that observes, as would the observer in a courtroom, typing out what is said, responsible only for getting the words set down aright. There is no judgment involved in reporting what occurs.

Last evening the one known as Aaron and we worked with that crumpled piece of paper. And it is always helpful to remember that

---

[81] Matt. 13:44–46 AV.

no matter what you are perceiving, it is still no more than a temporary chimera that is as a shadow flashing upon a sheet of paper whose other side remains completely clean and untouched.

In working to become better, may we suggest that what each is actually responsible for is becoming more oneself. The urge to be better is answered within your Earth world by a list of preferred adjectives, including worthy, generous, and loving. You could think of desirable qualities for a good, long time and create wonderful, inspiring lists of good qualities. However, you are a unique being. You are like the snowflake: that crystal that is quite obviously snow, yet whose kaleidoscopic pattern is unique. Only you, in all of the created and uncreated universes, are you. Therefore, we ask that you encourage within yourself the perceptive ear that notes those moments when you can feel yourself being who you feel you are.

Each of you within this circle has, by seniority of vibration, earned the opportunity to incarnate at this time. Each of you has two main goals. You wished to move through the intense incarnate experience, repeating for yourself your lesson of loving, which you felt could use more polarity. And you also wished to lighten the planetary consciousness of this sphere you call Earth. For you, too, are Brothers and Sisters of Sorrow.

Your instrument is your self. Learning to play this instrument involves doing those practices or those scales, if you will, that enable you to develop a sweet melody as you live your life. If you can see the flute or recorder or any reed instrument, perhaps you can see your energy centers as those buttons that you press to make your melody. Thusly, you wish in each case to clarify the energy that is there, to make it more itself, and to make each energy true—not another's truth and not a teacher's truth, but your unique note of sound.

For example, let us take the note of any ray, say the yellow ray. Your hope is not to make that energy brighter or larger, but rather to find the truth, which is the balance that does exist. Once all the energies are played upon consciously, they begin to adjust and balance themselves.

We would at this time transfer the microphone to our beloved brother Aaron. We are those of Q'uo.

(Barbara channeling)

Aaron: Q'uo's example of the melody of the flute brings to mind another image, which is that of a pure spring giving rise to a series of streams running in different directions, eventually drawing together again as they enter the sea itself. The water that enters each stream from the pool around the spring is absolutely pure.

Think of yourself as this streambed. This pure water flows through you. Some streambeds have accumulated a good deal of debris. The purity of the original water never changes. If you add something into that pure water and then lift it out, the water is unchanged. If silt falls to the bottom of the clean, rocky streambed, it will affect the water until the streambed is cleaned again. Then the water will once again be pure. Even if you add a chemical pollutant into that water and then filter it out, the pure water remains. But for some periods of time it will be affected by the quality of the streambed or the additives.

As you experience that pure water moving through you, you bring different ingredients into it. Figuratively speaking, you bring chemical pollutants into the stream of Pure Awareness through fear, greed, and anger. If you do not attend to the pollutants and do not then filter them out, the person downstream who wishes a drink will receive water that is chemically impure. The pure water is there, but somebody has got to filter out the pollutants.

You have two areas of work, as I see it. One is consciously to deepen your intention to offer your energy with love. This means to pollute the water as little as possible or not at all. And second is to understand that because the human is what it is, it is going to pollute the water at times. Then you must be responsible for what you have created.

The problem is not that you occasionally pollute the water, but that when you do so, you then turn on yourself with shame and judgment instead of turning your energy to clarifying that which you have polluted. You let the pollution go past because you are so busy condemning yourself that the water became clouded in the first place.

My dear ones, if you were already perfect, if you did not occasionally offer your energy in distorted ways that give rise to cloudiness, you would not be here in incarnation. The more you can stay in each moment, noting the various contractions of mind and body that give rise to the distortion of fear, a distortion that tends to pour pollutants into the water, the less you actually have to pour those pollutants out into the stream of life.

By way of simple example, your intention is to offer your energy with kindness. Somebody who is feeling much fear and pain approaches you and belligerently attacks you with his words. When you notice your own defensiveness arising from discomfort and a desire to attack that which is the source of your discomfort, you find that the more present you are with that arising in yourself, the less you have to act it out. Noting how much discomfort there is in the self, you might also note the discomfort in your assailant. Allow your heart to open in compassion to that assailant. Then you respond from the heart, responding to his pain instead of reacting only to his words.

This response may be the statement, "No, you cannot attack me like that." The "no" is offered from a place of love, not from a place of need to defend and not from a place of fear. There is no ego involved in that "no." At that moment, it is the kindest thing you can say for yourself and for the assailant, who is creating a great deal of negative karma for himself: "No, you may not speak like that to me. And I will not stay here and hear it."

To be loving does not mean to be a doormat to negativity. It means to speak the truth from the heart. Step one, then, is to practice being present as much as is possible. Within that presence, you watch the conditioned arising of the body and mind and understand how you can move into negative mind states that wish to cling or defend, but that will, thereby, poison the situation.

A very useful practice is what I call "clear comprehension of purpose." This practice has several parts. Here I would speak only of the beginnings of the practice. First, is to understand your primary purpose. To defend yourself against that assailant is a purpose. It is not bad to wish to defend yourself. But there is a higher purpose, which is to create increasing harmony and understanding. Will you look at these two purposes and your choices of words or actions that lie before you? Which choices are most suitable to the attainment of the highest purpose?

In this practice of clear comprehension in a given situation, we note our highest purpose and we ask, *Is this proposed speech or action suitable to that highest purpose?* If it is not suitable, and yet the intensity of the catalyst is such that you enact that unsuitable movement and offer outwardly whatever reactivity may have been called forth by the catalyst, then you will have a new catalyst and may again examine the highest purpose. Is it to save face and lay blame elsewhere or to accept responsibility for what you have wrought?

Let us return to our metaphor. The water is polluted. Do you have the courage to be responsible for it? Your self-judgment and even your sense of shame are not ways of being responsible. They are deterrents to responsibility. What are you going to do, sit there and condemn yourself while others drink your poisoned water? Or are you going to go and clean it up?

You clean it up in very simple ways. You observe the source of the pollutant and close it off. If the source is great anger, you close off the anger by opening your heart to it, thereby making a bigger container for it within you so it does not need to pour out of you into the world.

Anger is not bad. Anger is just energy. When there is a lot of it, it needs a big space. If the source of the pollutant is seen as pride or jealousy or greed, you attend to each of those in the same way. There are many specific practices that are available to help you create this bigger container. One of my favorites comes from the teacher Thich Nhat Hanh.[82] It is very simple: "Breathing in, I am aware of my anger.

---

[82] Thich Nhat Hanh, *Peace Is Every Step: The Path of Mindfulness in Everyday Life*, ed. Arnold Kotler (New York, NY: Bantam Books, 1991), 57–58.

Breathing out, I smile to my anger," and again and again until you feel that space enlarging.

You must both acknowledge the heavy emotion and also offer a willingness to embrace it instead of attacking it, thereby to invite it into the ever-spacious heart. That is one way to become responsible for the pollutant that is already pouring out of you. The other is simply to ask for forgiveness. You cannot ask for forgiveness while distortion is still pouring out. You have got to attend to it first and then you mop up. Mop up by asking for forgiveness. If you are clinging to your shame and self-judgment, then those mind states are what need the bigger container. That is where the poison is coming from.

Remember that the pure spring is always there. Remember that in human form, you are never going to be a perfect channel for that pure spring. There is always going to be some distortion. Deep mindfulness will reduce that distortion. And a sense of loving responsibility will mop up and readjust the flow. It will clean up whatever distortion has been created.

Do you think you teach more when what flows through you is absolutely pure? Would it just be possible that you teach more when what flows through you does become distorted and you then very lovingly attend to that distortion, thus helping others also to learn that they do not need to be perfect; but rather, they need to be conscious, loving, and responsible?

Your distortion also offers a catalyst to others through which they are given the opportunity to practice with their own fears and distortions. This learning is, after all, the primary motivation for incarnate experience. This is not justification for poisoning the waters. But when the entire movement is deeply considered, it may be better understood that as long as you are human, there will be spills and they are all part of the learning process of the incarnate experience.

I would ask the same question also in a different way: In which way do you learn more? What would self-perfection teach you? This is the old story. One does not need pain to learn. But pain says, "Pay attention," and that attention allows learning. The pain of your mistakes does not teach you, but it does catch your attention.

Session 32

My friends, you do know all the levels on which you are working. You can never excuse great intentional harm to another by saying, *Well, it's their karma,* or *I'm working on a different level.* When you are working to the best of your intention by noting the arising of fear within you, attending to that fear with skill, and cleaning up after yourself for the bits of fear that have sent themselves out into the world, then you have got to have faith that, while some of this fear did escape and create pollution, that out of that situation can come some good because of the heart's great desire to offer its energy with love.

This highest intention to offer your energy for the good of all beings is of utmost importance. It is not up to you to determine how that good is going to come about, only to constantly ask yourself, *What is my highest purpose here?* and to work with clear comprehension of that purpose.

You know that the highest purpose is to offer the energy with love. Remember, you are in third density largely to learn faith and love. If you did not have this veil surrounding you so that you clearly understand exactly how different movements of energy through you become distorted, why they became distorted, and in what ways that distortion might actually be of service, you would be denied the opportunity to learn faith around these distortions. This is not to be taken as an instruction to consciously perpetuate the distortions. But if they occur, trust them and ask how you may purify them.

You wished for a clear-cut question and answer. There is no clear-cut answer, except for one: Pay attention and act with love. Be willing to be responsible and to learn. Do not be afraid. But if you are afraid, do not be afraid of your fear. Give that also a bigger container so it does not need to pollute the water. Where it has polluted the water, clean it up.

Whatever flows through you when your primary intention is to offer your whole being in loving service to all beings, the Divine will take and use for a holy purpose. It is that in which you need to have faith. Let the loving heart offer its intention for service. Act, speak, and think based on this intention and with awareness, and offer that which is prompted by fear and the notion of separate self to the Divine. Trust the divine plan, even when there is fear.

I will turn the microphone over to my brother/sister/friend of Q'uo. I pause.

(Carla channeling)

Q'uo: We are with this instrument.

The loving energy that is you is impossible to dissect. It has an integrity that is unique to your system. Often seekers target one or another aspect or energy center for renovation and feel that this energy needs to be improved, cleansed, or altered. This is a less skillful model than that approach to improving the instrument that sees as its first goal the balance of the instrument as a whole.

Some entities have little strength compared to others. Yet because they have somehow found the balance within and have harmonized that scale of being, that melody arrests the listening ear with delight. To have a more powerful indigo ray, for instance, has less virtue than to have an indigo ray that is euphonious and promotes travel between it and the other energy nexi.

In working with the self in this regard, we find it helpful to ask that which the one known as Ra first offered to this instrument: "Where is the love in this moment?"[83] By turning to this universal question through asking and desiring that quality or question, you open doors within your deeper self, that self that abides in the aware-

---

[83] Ra, An Humble Messenger of the Law of One, *The Law of One, Book One* (Louisville, KY: L/L Research, 1981). The quotation in its entirety, from Ra session 10, January 27, 1981, is "The moment contains love. That is the lesson/goal of this illusion or density. The exercise is to consciously see that love in awareness and understanding distortions. The first attempt is the cornerstone. Upon this choosing rests the remainder of the life-experience of an entity. The second seeking of love within the moment begins the addition. The third seeking empowers the second, the fourth powering or doubling the third. As with the previous type of empowerment, there will be some loss of power due to flaws within the seeking in the distortion of insincerity. However, the conscious statement of self to self of the desire to seek love is so central an act of will that, as before, the loss of power due to this friction is inconsequential."

ness to which you do not have access in your conscious mind. This deeper self knows where the love is. Therefore, by asking that question and then by abiding in faith with patience and an inner knowing, that which is sought shall come to you.

Thusly, the thousand and one specific details of everyday occurrences are taken from that world of manifestation and handed up as a noble and holy offering to the Creator: "Here is my confusion. Here is my pain. Here are all my emotions. Here is my mental anguish." And that great Being that lies within embraces the self, the concern, and the anguish of unknowing and responds in silence with love.

Within the moment of asking lies the perfect and balanced response. The skill of the seeker is to trust that process, to keep the mind upon the question, *Where is the love?* and to keep the mind upon the moment wherein the question is asked.

If you can come to the present moment and know it, you have entered eternity. If, when you come to that present moment, your question is, *Where is the love?*—in that moment you have entered love. The concern about articulating and beautifying or crystallizing the energies can then be set aside. For in the moment-by-moment-by-moment succession that the illusion of time offers, your instrument shall be aided.

And rehearsal always helps. Each moment is another rehearsal. The whole of your life removed from the illusion of space and time is a song. You can no more know the song than know your life. You are in the middle of creating a life that is a gift to the one infinite Creator.

The way the question is asked is far more important than what is asked. For the attitude that asks the question is that point of view that will limit the answer. Thusly, abide in love and look in all things for love, even when the experience is accompanied with rage, with fury, or with the strongest and heaviest of emotions. There is at the heart of that emotion a purity and an essence that is a color. And there is the same beauty in those dark colors of emotion as there is in those dark colors that create variety and depth in a tapestry. All things you experience are as these threads going into the tapestry of your life. To identify this or that thread, then, is to lose sight of the picture that is the whole of your tapestry.

At this time, we give our farewell to you for now, unless there are further queries after the one known as Aaron has completed the material that he wishes to share at this session. As always, we ask that you hear us with discrimination. Thank you beyond our ability to express through this instrument for this wonderful chance to share love with love. We leave you in that love that is all that there is and in that light that manifests in all this world of duality. We are those of Q'uo.

(Barbara channeling)

Aaron: I would like to share one thought with you and then ask for your specific questions. Last night we spoke of the wrinkled sheet of paper to illustrate the relative reality of the existing wrinkles and the ultimate reality of the ever-perfect sheet. We suggested that both realities are true and that it is useful to stay balanced between the two. When you are working with the wrinkles, with the so-called negative distortion of your being, are you any less perfect? Are you any less whole?

Most of you relate to yourselves as broken. When you ask, as Q'uo suggested, *Where is love to be found?* can you see that the love is to be found both in the idea of brokenness and in the idea of wholeness?

The love is always there in the wholeness. That is easy to see. The sense of brokenness is catalyst, which sets you looking for the love. Therefore, the love must also be in that sense of brokenness. The love is in the inspiration, which inspires you to seek the love, and that inspiration is often the negative and painful distortion. Nothing is dual here. Within the shadow is found the sunshine!

When you begin to experience with more clarity that love is in everything, not just in the ultimate perfection of you but in every expression of that perfection, then you do not need to worry so much over distortions nor to enhance judgment and shame about them, but simply to attend to them. Recognize, *This distortion does not separate me from wholeness, nor does it separate me from the Divine. It is simply a distorted expression of that wholeness.*

When you conscientiously work in this way, instead of each distorted expression becoming something that grabs at your energy so you must frantically go and fix it, each distorted expression just becomes a reminder to ask, as Q'uo suggested, *Where is the love? Where is God in this fear, in this anger, and in this judgment? Can I find God right here?* If you look, you will find you can.

When the expression is distorted and causes discomfort to self or to another self, it must be attended. But regardless of its effect, it is still an expression of the Divine. I would ask you to visualize a crystal. If you hold it up to the sun, the sun plays through the crystal and creates a rainbow of light. That rainbow is a direct expression of the sun. When you look at that rainbow of light, can you see that the sun is there? If the light is shining in somebody's eyes so that they are uncomfortable, then you must attend to the crystal. But there is no good or bad to it, just sun and its various expressions.

Using a different metaphor, when you sit in the sun and feel its heat on your back, that is a direct experience of the sun. It is of a different intensity than if you could fly up into the heart of that sun, but still it is the sun. Sometimes the heat on the back feels warm and gentle. Sometimes it may burn. We do not say that only the pleasant experience of the sun is the sun. Every experience of the sun is the sun.

When you ask, *Where is love to be found?* especially when involved in a painful experience, it is a way of reminding yourself, *Even right here is God.* With that reminder, your energy field opens. When you are closed and defended it is very difficult to learn. When you remind yourself, *This is okay. It's workable. And the Divine is present even in this,* you allow that opening of the self that is willing to be present with the experience with all its discomforts. Then love announces itself.

Here is where you become increasingly willing to offer that which has arisen, to let it be and allow the Divine to use it as it will. To offer it does not mean to get rid of it. It does not mean to say, "This one is bad, God, please take it." Rather, it is a statement, "I haven't the faintest idea what's going on here. But my deepest intention is to use all of this turmoil and confusion and everything that is coming through me as a way of offering service to all beings, for the good of all beings." You can say to yourself, *I don't know how to transform this mess. I don't know what to do with it. All I can do is offer love.* It is this way that you offer it.

There is a discarnate energy that is a guru to this instrument. He comes into her experience on occasion. During this summer she was on an extended meditation retreat and experienced the presence of this one. In offering her instruction, he offered the suggestion, "Let go of everything. Give everything away." At first she misunderstood, *Am I to give away my house, my car? What does he ask of me?*

Through the following months she moved to a deeper understanding of what "give it all away" means. Are you identified with your fear, with your unworthiness, with your shame, and with your judgments? Give away the identity with it. You may say you *want* to be rid of it, that it is very painful and unpleasant. This is fine. But nevertheless, you are invested in being that person who is fearful or is self-judgmental and who is going to be the one who improves. There is so much "somebody" in these notions. Be nobody. Give it all away.

Within this rising intention to allow whatever comes into your experience and to offer it to God, not holding on to any of it, lies the ultimate path to service, because with that offering "somebody" disappears and "nobody" remains. In more precise terms, that which is contracted can stay contracted or can open itself. This process does not mean making anything special happen, just allowing an open heart that watches it all moving through and continually offers whatever moves through with a trust that the Divine will make good use of it.

I would ask of you during your afternoon and evening to watch closely for something that arises in your experience. In very simple physical terms, if there is a loud noise, such as a shout, *"Hey!"* do you feel your body energy contract around that noise? Fear and the energy of fear contract. There is nothing bad or good about the contraction. It is simply a knee-jerk kind of reaction of the body. You may feel the reverberations of that contraction for a bit, and then eventually it will dissolve again. If, instead of a physical noise like a shout, what you experience is an energy catalyst such as somebody else's sorrow or anger, there will also be a response. You have emotional nerve endings as well as physical nerve endings. Your energy field will contract.

What if, instead of one shout, there was an ongoing unpleasant noise and a growing discomfort with that noise? The contraction changes from contraction as reaction to pure hearing, to a contraction around the feeling of strong aversion to what is being heard. That pure sense awareness of hearing is not the aversion to hearing. The relationship to the hearing is not the hearing itself. In hearing there is just hearing.

Each mind or body experience will have its own energy movements. Can you feel the difference as I demonstrate it here, how in that one shout, *"Hey!"* there is that momentary contraction, which then may continue with some reverberations and then release? It may have been unpleasant, but it is passed. There is nothing holding it. When it continues, fear may arise, as in, *How am I going to get rid of this?* Then there is a secondary contraction around the initial contraction. Or perhaps there is a contraction and then a judgment around the contraction, which is a different sort of secondary contraction.

What I would ask you to do is to deeply observe the movements. Note the physical or mental catalyst that accompanies the physical object contacting the physical sense or the thought touching the mind. Note that there is a contraction carried in the body when this occurs. The contraction in itself is just a contraction. There is no adhering karma in it. There is nothing that needs to be done with it other than to relax and observe it, just to know that it is present. Smile to it! If it is a difficult experience, do as Q'uo suggested and ask, *Where is the love?* with a truly open heart and mind.

If there is some relationship with the contact and the resultant contraction, note that as a new contact. For example, each reaction of judgment or aversion is a thought. They each touch the sense base of the mind. With that thought there will again be a first contraction, as just the wind rippling the water, so to speak. Again, note it as a contraction. Is there anything that follows?

It is not the experience of hearing, seeing, touching, knowing, and so forth that pulls you out of center and into a place of self where adhering karma is created, nor is it the contraction around that touch that pulls you out of center. It is your relationship to that contraction. It is this truth that I would ask you to observe for yourselves this afternoon and evening.

My deepest thanks to you for allowing me to share these thoughts with you and for your willingness to attend to your experience and do this deep work. That is all.

Questioner: Q'uo spoke about energy entering the being from below through the feet and from above, and that there was a meeting place for these energies that is somewhat dependent on the allowing of energy through the lower centers. Could Q'uo speak about what this meeting place is? And is this a place where energy entering into the illusion enters in a different way than the light issuing from the other energy centers?

(Carla channeling)

Q'uo: We believe we grasp your query.

The meeting place of the upward-spiraling light and the in-streaming inspiration has been known within your cultures as the kundalini. The ability of the self to become transparent to whatever distortions exist within the energy centers leads to an increased ability to experience a freely flowing upward motion, so that the kundalini, in your culture's terms, rises. This involves being friends with the various energies of the mind, body, and spirit, not for the perfecting of those energies but for the balancing of them in the acceptance of self as self without explanation or apology, as in that relaxed self-confidence that this instrument would say makes one comfortable within one's own skin.

Does this answer your query, my brother, or may we speak further upon it?

Questioner: So the distortions in the centers do not limit the rising of the upward-spiraling light, but rather the relationship, as you said earlier this morning, with regard to the relative harmony of the entity's acceptance of the aspects of self.

Q'uo: This is so, my brother.

Questioner: This sounds to me like what Aaron mentioned earlier when he asked us to consider the possibility that the distortions provide us with opportunities to learn and to enhance our abilities to offer learning experiences that help others, through our loving attendance to those distortions.

Q'uo: The entity who loves self, who loves self as it is in all its dirt, is an entity with mercy to offer to others in all their dirt.

To allow a knot to be a knot or a tangle to be a tangle is the beginning of the end of that tangle or knot. To ignore is not to allow. But to see, to love, to accept, to forgive, and to move on, knowing the whole—that is helpful.

Questioner: So, it is the distortions that allow one to increase polarity?

Q'uo: This is perceptive, my brother. Polarity is exquisitely central to your task here upon the third planet from your sun. You have one great choice to make: Shall you radiate or shall you contract and hold, giving it all away or grasping all for self? That polarity of radiance is the service-to-others path. It is what we came to share. And we say to you that it is your radiance within all the suffering of every day that expresses this polarity of love.

May we answer you further, my brother?

Questioner: No. Thank you.

Questioner: I don't understand the seeking polarity. Selfish or unselfish *what?*

Q'uo: To serve others is to serve the self. To serve the self is to serve all that there is. There is no answer to your question.

The attempt to separate selfishness from unselfishness works upon a false premise. The self is a whole, so polarity is expressed moment by moment, as you choose to forgive, accept, allow, and look for the ability to do this in difficult situations. And this continuing choice is that which will move you into a finer degree of awareness. Thusly, the very time of difficulty, where you see that the love energy is sacrificial and painful, is the time to rejoice. For in loving the unlovable, you are truly choosing to polarize in service to others.

We are those of Q'uo. And as the energy is moving away as we speak, we would close this meeting with the promise to ask for further queries at a future session. We leave you and yet leave you not. We leave you in all that there is. In the company of each other, see the face of the Creator. Adonai. Adonai, each light. We are those of Q'uo.

Session 33

(This session was preceded by a period of tuning and meditation.)

(Barbara channeling)

Aaron: My greetings and love to you all. My joyous welcome to this circle of seekers, and gratitude for the invitation to join you in your circle.

I want to return to this aspect of your experiences as a balance between the self that represents the ultimate essence of love that you are and the self that represents the human expression, with its physical body, which has aches and pains; its emotional body with its joys and sorrows; its mental body with its mix of clarity and confusion; and its spirit body.

You speak of taking incarnation and experiencing a veil of forgetting who you are, which pushes you deeper into the seeming confines of the human. This is just as it needs to be, because through this human comes the greatest expressions of compassion, generosity, and love.

I will give you a very simple example. If I had a vast apple orchard, with literally thousands of healthy, vibrant apple trees, what if a being knocked on my door and said, "Please, sir, would you give me an apple?" and then I gave him one? One might say that was an act of generosity. If I gave him a whole bag of apples, one might say that was an act of even greater generosity. Certainly it is. I have freely given something of mine to another. But while I am giving there is a clarity within me of the infinite abundance that lies behind me. There is no fear that prevents my giving or in some way influences my giving and makes me pause. Yes, it is still generosity if we define that word to mean freely giving from oneself. But what a difference if I have but one apple in my pocket and no access to more!

Consider that I know this single apple is my supper. I have walked for ten miles and just sat down under a tree in the shade, pulled out that apple, and polished it on my shirt. I am looking forward to its sweet juiciness to quench my thirst as well as my hunger. Then you approach me and ask, "Please, would you give me your apple?" Fear may now arise and say, *If I give, what will I eat? Will I be safe? Will my needs be met?* In order for the apple to be offered in that circumstance, the voice of love must speak through that fear with resounding clarity. It is the force of this voice of love that I define as true generosity.

You can offer that apple for many reasons. You may practice self-discipline by pushing the fear and annoyance away and giving the apple. Or the fear may remain silent beneath the surface and then the apple is given, but not with joy. To give the apple with real joy, you must have acknowledged and transformed your fear. Within fear is generosity. Fear transformed is generosity.

Here we have a different experience of giving. It is not just a joyful giving that comes out of the strength of knowing the infinite abundance of ten thousand apples. There is a deep joyfulness because you have moved through the fear with love. You have not allowed fear to control you, but have been able to give despite the fear and to transform the fear. It evokes faith that your needs will be met, although you still may not understand how, because that was the only apple.

There is a different possible scenario. If the other is grasping and punishing in order to shame you into giving the apple, there may be anger but also a fear that says, "I *must* give this apple in order to feel good, to feel generous." Here the primary fear is not whether one's needs will be met, but rather the desire to be "good" or to please another. One need not be a slave to that fear. "I *must* give" is a harsh judgment that considers the self to be less worthy to receive than is another. That is also a fear, which love can transform. Here the outcome is to say no to fear and to the asker, to keep and eat the apple or perhaps to share it. In this scenario one does not act to punish the other but to affirm that the self's needs are also to be honored. There is nothing wrong with this response. It is a different practice of generosity that responds lovingly to the fear with kindness to the self. The point is that when fear is not the master, the innate generous heart will know how to respond.

Fear is the catalyst offered to the human, which prompts it to learn how to transform that fear into lovingkindness or generosity. This is the love that the earth plane offers you the opportunity to manifest and to express in the world. I do not want to talk about degrees of love here, but love that is manifest in the face of fear is a far more transformative love. It is transformative because it touches that fear with kindness and teaches you the ultimate lesson that there is nothing to fear. Only through practice with fear do you learn that you do not have to be reactive to your fear but may relate to it from the ever-opening heart.

Your earth-plane experience constantly offers you such lessons because you live with this veil of forgetting. Of course, as you reach a point of deeper spiritual awareness, the veil has holes poked in it. It becomes translucent in parts so that the light shines through. It is even quite transparent on occasion. But as long as you are in human form it will never be continually transparent.

Your fear is not an obstacle. Your fear is wisdom itself when you abide with it, smile to it, and are not ruled by it. It is then that the heart develops. It is then that you truly begin to live in the heart and to express from that heart out into the universe.

You are in incarnation for a purpose. That purpose is not to have discarnate experience and not even continuous discarnate clarity, but to be incarnate and to work with the catalyst of your incarnation with love.

Here I would like to turn the microphone over to my beloved brother/sister/friend Q'uo. I pause.

(Carla channeling)

Q'uo: We are those of the principle known to you as Q'uo and we greet you in the love and light of the one infinite Creator. Let us give thanks to you one more time, each of you in the circle, for this opportunity to be a voice to you upon the path. We find your companionship heartening. We marvel at your courage, for you must express within this veil of unknowing.

There are two distinct ways to proceed upon a heartfelt path of learning and serving. And as we were saying to the one known as J. last evening, either technique of seeking is fruitful. However, seeking with mind and opinion is a search that takes place in the shadow world of night with just the dim moon to offer its mysterious light to the darkness. In this dimness it is very easy to misrepresent to the self that which is seen. Discernment is difficult. Upon the other path, which is the path of the open heart, the light of noon is offered to those who can surrender their small will and their hopes and expectations set upon defining that which is developed and manifest in the future.

Let us give a concrete example of the mix of these two ways. We describe now the way the one known as Jim came to the conclusion that he should join this instrument and the one known as Don. The one known as Jim had lived a simple and monastic life for some years before he encountered the ones known as Don and Carla.

He also was a good friend of another teacher who lived some two thousand miles from his home in rural Kentucky. He had decided that it was time to embark upon a path of service to others instead of remaining alone. His mind said to him, *I shall go two thousand miles and offer my service.* Thusly, this entity packed his worldly resources in the back of his truck and drove the two thousand miles.

When he arrived he found good work to do, but his heart kept knocking at the door of his awareness, saying, *Is this your place?* Finally, this entity honored that knocking on the door and determined to sit in silent meditation for the period of the weekend. He completed all his chores having to do with the service to the teacher and retreated for a long weekend alone. After all this preparation, he went into meditation and immediately knew he was to drive two thousand more miles back to Kentucky and join this instrument and the one known as Don.

Could the one known as Jim have come directly seventy miles down the road to L/L Research? We say to you, no. He could not. He was too sure that he knew his way. He had plans in hand and therefore had to work through these concepts and opinions. The miles were not at all wasted. There were no errors in this roundabout journey.

Now each of you seeks the most efficient way to serve. And whenever the grace comes upon you to stand in the noonday of that sun within, then we say, *Wonderful! Exquisite!* Yet it is not often the case that sufficient surrender to the spiritual forces molding your destiny is enough completed that the apparent shortcut can be taken. Most often there is the mixture of the self attempting to predict and control the flow of energy with that openhearted surrender.

What we wish to impress upon you is our honest belief that the longer and seemingly roundabout route is not merely acceptable as a substitute for the blazing purity of surrender, but offers a valuable catalyst that enables that sun within to begin to manifest within the inner consciousness. It is for this seemingly roundabout journey or this peering into the folds of velveteen night that you donned what the one known as Aaron has called the earth-suit.

We hope you may find it in your heart to embrace this walk in the shadows of mortality. We hope you may come to value and enjoy your swim through the seas of confusion, such that you may find play and sport in the swim and flow of inner tides.

You shall be tossed about in these currents of unknowing. And as you suffer, you may often doubt the efficacy of your own seeking. This is the very situation you came to Earth to experience. Within, at noon, you claim your wholeness easily. But you hoped to come into the shadow world and act as if you saw the noonday sun. Faith is that throwing of the self into the midair of complete surrender.

Against all logic, the time of blind choice comes in cycles. At those cusps there is the desire to do right. And the instincts of mortality are to hold, to control, to reach, and to pull. The muscular take of those who choose to develop these cusps is that brave decision to release and surrender, and also to claim the surety that all is well, that all will be well, and that for the moment it shall be given to you what to do.

We would at this time offer the floor to the one known as Aaron. We are those of Q'uo.

(Barbara channeling)

Aaron: Can you see that efficiency is often the voice of fear? There is that within the human that wishes to stay in control, not only for its own safety but also for the safety of those around it. It wishes to pattern the universe and make it predictable.

On the astral plane there is never a sense of being unsafe in the way that the human experiences such danger. It is clear on the astral plane that there is nothing that needs to be ordered or controlled, but that disorder has its own delicate and lovely order and you can just let it flow.

Who wants to be in control? Often your reasons may be the highest, as in wanting to offer one's energy in service to all beings and wanting to alleviate suffering. But my dear ones, life is chaos. Life is messy. Thoughts and emotions do not arise only when invited. And they do not act like good little children, reporting themselves and then stepping back into a line. Thoughts and emotions are a class of rowdy children raising their voices out of turn. This is human incarnation.

It is easy to keep your equanimity in heaven. You are incarnate here in order to learn this equanimity, regardless of the catalyst, and even regardless of your response to the catalyst. Then, while you are shrieking, *"Eeek!"* and running from the mouse, there will be that within that is centered, that is still, and that knows its safety.

In very practical terms, in fourth density you are going to move into telepathic energy groups. Every thought or emotion that arises in you will be telepathically received by your peers in the group. Every thought and emotion that arises in them will be heard by you. This is the nature of fourth-density experience. Thoughts and emotions are not going to cease to arise just because you are fourth density. If this circle were fully telepathic now, would that be okay with you? Is there something that has been said or thought that you would not wish to share with the whole group? Did you glance at someone across the room and think, *Her hair or clothing looks frazzled today,* or *Why did he frown at me?* Certainly each of you has had what we would call negative thoughts or emotions in the past three days. Would it be okay if everybody heard this thought, or would there be a sense of shame? What if you heard this from your neighbor? Would there be discomfort with that hearing?

You are not incarnate to stop thoughts and emotions from arising but to find equanimity with them so that when you enter fourth-density experience, everything within you can be shared, and everything from without can come freely to you. Judgment does not arise. Shame and embarrassment do not arise. Rather, there is complete equanimity with those thoughts and emotions so you can fully hear each other.

Now you are limited to learning from your own direct experience. What if you could totally empathize with another? Can you see that when there is total empathy, others' experiences also become very viable tools for your learning? The reason why compassion and wisdom are so deeply learned in a higher density is because so much more experience is directly accessible to you.

So, here you are in this third-density form, experiencing this wide array of thoughts and emotions of confusion, joy, and sorrow. Your first instinct is to wish to order this madness; to force it to stand in line and salute; and to force the array of thoughts and emotions to report, one at a time, and only that material that is pretty. But you cannot do it. That is not the nature of human experience. While it is often beautiful, the nature of human experience is also dirty, smelly, and chaotic. You are here to learn equanimity and to learn to open your heart to that chaos. The chaos is not your enemy. The chaos is your teacher.

You may ask, *How can I be a clearer channel in the way I wish to channel?* The fear of which Q'uo just spoke wants to order experience. It wants efficiency, as in, *Cut out that four thousand miles and go straight to Kentucky.* It does not leave room for the great journey in which you are immersed and that purifies and teaches you.

To desire order and efficiency is not bad. Of course some of that desire is from a place of love that wishes to release disorder to alleviate suffering. Only some is fear-based. Can you distinguish? If it is fear-based, can you observe that movement with kindness and without fixation on it? This instrument has a magnet in her office that says, "Bless this mess." It is precisely that attitude that you need to bring to your lives.

I would share a brief story about efficiency. Some years ago this instrument worked one day a week as a volunteer for a service organization known as Seva. She worked in the office, where her job was to receive the order forms for donations offered as a gift in another's name, such as to commemorate a birthday. She would send a "thank you" to the one who had paid for that particular donation and also send an announcement of the donation to the one in whose name it was made. These were all very loving donations in support of many beings. They were financial donations, such as merchandise ordered for self or other. They were also service donations, such as a cataract operation offered to a blind person in Nepal; or a goat offered to a woman in Guatemala, which would provide this woman with some means for a livelihood.

Barbara sat down one day with a great stack of these forms to be sent out. She saw how many thoughts she had, which slowed the process. She said, *This isn't efficient. What I'm going to do,* she thought to herself, *is to go through the whole list and write all the donor address envelopes, then choose the appropriate card that says, "Thank you for your donation," and slip it into the envelope. Then I'm going to go through the whole pile again and write recipient envelopes. I'll simply pull out the individual card: "A cataract operation in your name"; "Happy Birthday"; "Merry Christmas"; "A hundred dollars in your name"; "With blessings to you"* . . . So she started separating these gifts, creating an efficient order of replying. She spent a day on it. By the end of the afternoon she was weary and she had not really covered more ground. She took a walk and asked, *Where did I go wrong? Why didn't it go faster?*

Suddenly she realized the heart had not been present. Her previous process was slow because she would read the words and feel happy about how Mary Smith in Seattle offered this cataract operation with great joy to help another. And she thought about how much love Mary had for her mother to honor her and offer this gift in her name. When she wrote the cards, then her own joy at such generosity was a part of the writing. She was involved in the whole process and was honoring the process. The cards were done more slowly but with love.

My dear ones, it is so easy to fall into the trap of cutting out your heart in finding a mechanical path that does not have to feel the pain of the Earth. Mechanism insulates you against chaos, pain, and disorder. You are never going to create perfect order. You are not here to do that. You are here to find equanimity and love.

I am asked sometimes, "Aaron, if this disorder does in fact add to suffering, then why is it bad to attempt to order it?" To attempt to order it is not bad. Attachment to ordering it creates the suffering, not the disorder itself. When there is attachment, the motivation is largely fear-based. "I've got to fix this" is the stimulus. When there is no attachment, there is a willingness to go into things the way they are and to feel the wind blowing and pushing on you and the trees. There is a willingness to sway back and forth as you feel the currents of the river ebbing and flowing. There is a willingness to feel the whole movement of life.

When you feel in this way, in connection with all that is, then the loving heart can respond with an intuitive awareness, *If I offer love here, it will shift the current so that beings are not drowning in it. If I offer kindness there, it will gentle the push of the wind so that beings are not blown off their feet.* Then that movement comes from a place of deep love, which trusts the ways of the universe and which does not need to fight a war with the universe, but offers its deepest love as co-Creator of the universe. Offering that loving force, which the universe may draw into itself and use in the best ways, you are no longer saying, *This has got to be fixed.* You are saying, *Here is love, which can apply itself as it is needed.*

This is the greatest skill you can master. You master it first by observing how fear serves as a giant pusher and by observing how your energy field armors itself and wants to push back. As these pushes keep coming fiercely within this realm of chaos, you learn to dance with the energy. It pushes and you yield a bit and observe it. As the pushing stops, you let the energy flow back. There is no longer anyone who yields or pushes, only the play of the Unconditioned or the play of God. It is a dance of love, not fear. This is a skill that may be mastered. In order to learn it, you must first of all be present. You must observe the way that the physical world of material objects and thoughts pushes at you. You must observe the discomfort with that push and the small ego-self that wants to be safe and wants the others it holds dear to be safe. You observe the one who wants to fix the push or fight it.

As you observe the flow of these movements in yourself, increasingly you will see how much choice you have. The heart of love opens! You will cease to need to attack the voice of fear in yourself, but instead will offer compassion to it. This is the second phase after presence. It is characterized by a nurturing of the deepest truth and a resolve to live that truth until each moment of the mind and body cannot help but reflect truth. Thus, the lessons offered to you by that arising fear will be mastered, because fear will increasingly become a catalyst for compassion. And you will become a force in the world that is centered and offers love. No less important, you will ready yourself for fourth-density experience.

Each of you has some kind of mindfulness or meditation practice. It is very useful to use this time of practice, at least in part, as a way of observing your relationship to the aspects of life that push at you, and as a way of observing fear's reaction to fight back. To all of this you offer love, both to that which wants to fight back and to the catalyst itself. The more you practice this, the easier it becomes and the more freedom you have to live with great joy and peace within this chaos that we call third-density experience.

I would like to offer the microphone to Q'uo. Whenever Q'uo has made whatever statement it wishes to make, we will open the floor to your questions. I pause.

(Carla channeling)

Q'uo: Before we speak, we would suggest the time is right for the seventh-inning stretch. We shall be with you when you have stretched. We are those of Q'uo.

(Pause)

We are those of Q'uo and would offer to you last thoughts before the question period.

To know yourself as human, as the featherless biped, may seem a great restriction and a great inconvenience. But no! Know and trust that the moonlight is glamorous and deceiving and that your wandering steps are all perfectly as they need to be.

Take yourself lightly. Take love with profoundest dedication. Know that your greatest treasure, your central purpose, and your patience are all wrapped up in the everyday life devotionally lived. In the world of the Father, all things are featured. Persist in your attention to the daily. For each task, each tale, and each silly piece of paper in the paper mountain of your culture is full of learning for the one with ears to hear and a heart to understand. Know that as you touch others, you meet yourself.

The one known to you as Jesus offered two rules of life: to love the infinite Creator and to love the other self as the self. These suggestions encompass all you need for your journey.

This instrument sang this morning,

> To give and give and give again,
> What God hath given thee;
> To spend thyself nor count the cost;
> To serve right gloriously

The God who gave all the worlds that are
And all that are to be.[84]

May your worries be blessed with quietness. May your concerns be touched with grace. May your hearts open.

We would at this time open the meeting to queries of Aaron or ourselves or both. Please proceed with the question.

I.: Q'uo, I am interested that the path to equanimity seems to be anything *but*. It is not a process. How much of the instructions that we garner are just keeping us busy or stopping us in our tracks, and how much is a ladder to our goal?

Q'uo: My brother, all of the seemingly missed steps and mistakes are necessary. This instrument has a memory of the story from a friend whose cat, upon finding her mistress at the front door, would race around and around the living room, run between her legs, dash into the kitchen, jump up on the countertop, run around the counter, dash around the floor, jump at the refrigerator, and then walk to her bowl. The cat knew that only after she did these things would her mistress provide food.

The human mind says, *But it simply took that long for the woman to reach the storage place for the food. All the running was for nothing.* We say to you, did not the cat enjoy the exercise and otherwise enjoy the time between the coming of the mistress and the food?

You must do something between this moment and when you die from this planet. You can choose to rest and sit and wait, without motion. How this defeats the desire for which you entered this veil of illusion! The times of your life are instructional. They give you

---

[84] "Morning Song," words by Geoffrey A. Studdert-Kennedy, melody attributed to Elkanah Kelsay Dare, first published in *Wyeth's Repository of Sacred Music,* ed. John Wyeth (Harrisburg, PA: J. Wyeth, 1810).

exercise. They give your emotions opportunity to refine. That process creates the beauteous and clear emotion that integrates and harmonizes the mellow and harsh tones of the various positive and negative emotions.

It is the work of incarnation to begin to listen to and appreciate the dance of the emotions and mind and habit and encountered parts of the self, confusingly and seemingly wrongheaded as these things must be. For it is in the fires of these steps of learning that realization of wholeness is found.

So embrace the seeming trading of goals for mistakes and for seeming roads wrongly taken, and see that, truly, you cannot waste time as long as attention persists. Simply keep paying attention. Pay that treasure of time and talent. Pay it without concern for whether it seems worthwhile. Simply give of yourself as you see aright to do. And the moment of *samadhi* [85] shall take you in the midst of that sea of confusion and never leave for a moment.

May we answer further?

I.: No, thank you.

(Barbara channeling)

Aaron: I would like to add an illustration to the thought that Q'uo has just provided, taken from the experience of this instrument.

At one time she took a walk in the woods, in a lovely wooded park. Since her last visit, the trails had been changed. She knew from prior walks that there was a shortcut that led to the beach. She walked down a path that seemed to go in the right direction, but it became narrower and narrower. Then ahead she saw what seemed to be a dirt-covered clearing or patch of dirt, not quite as big as this room.

---

[85] Samadhi: "Concentration"; lit.: "the (mental) state of being firmly fixed." From Nyanatiloka Mahathera, *Buddhist Dictionary: Manual of Buddhist Terms and Doctrines*, 4th ed. (Kandy, Sri Lanka: Buddhist Publication Society, 1980), p. 191.

On the far side she saw the continuation of a trail. She stepped out into the bare patch and sunk literally up to her armpits in mud. She had the presence of mind to fling her arms out as far as she could. She was quite alone. Her feet were not touching the bottom, so there was nothing solid to push from. Slowly she grabbed the sticks and leaves that were within reach and built some kind of cushion for her body. Gradually she inched her way out of that mud, certainly not without fear. She crawled out to the other side, literally covered with black mud from head to toe.

She decided she needed to go back to the main trail and to stop looking for shortcuts, so she sought a way around this patch of mud. She tested with a stick and saw that the patch of mud was not an isolated one but was a strip of marsh that cut off the land nearer the beach from the land where she had at first been walking.

The undergrowth was very dense beside the trail that she followed. Thinking that eventually it would take her to a passage across this strip of marsh, she walked and walked for perhaps two hours. She found herself walking in circles and said, *But I was just here. Was I? Or was it just a look-alike?* She began to leave a small mark and proved that she was going in circles.

At first there was anger when she observed the circles. *I am wasting my time,* she thought. She was not concerned about getting into serious trouble. She knew she could push through the dense thorns to the beach and simply come out with some scratched skin. She knew if she did not return by nightfall, people would set out to look for her. By morning she would be found. But the night would be very cold and all she wore was a bathing suit.

All of these dark and dreary thoughts went through her head as she came to the same tree for the third time by a different route and said, *I'm still going in circles.* It was only after she had been around four times that she finally had the wisdom to simply sit down. She walked a bit until she came to a patch of sunshine where there was a clearing in the trees. She sat in the sun, which warmed her a bit, and began to meditate.

Session 33

When she opened her eyes, finally now at ground level, she saw before her a deer trail. She had only been walking on old human trails. Clearly, if anybody knew how to get through this muck, it was the deer. So she proceeded again, but this time crawling and following the deer trail, which took her across that strip of marsh by a very thin ridge of solid land and back to the main trail. She recognized the trail itself. The way back was but fifteen or twenty minutes.

Were those first few hours wasted? She could not have come to the readiness to crawl and thereby find her way out via deer trails until she had explored the human paths. I find this a perfect metaphor. Perhaps as you become more wise and experienced, you cease so strongly to be reactive to the voice of fear and begin to hear the voice of love earlier. Maybe then you only have to walk the unnecessary but once before wisdom steps in and says, *Settle down and listen.* Part of being human is not only learning how to listen, but how to listen *through* the voice of fear when it is going to set you walking in "meaningless" circles for awhile.

As Q'uo was talking just now, this instrument said to me, "The question is that I waste so much time walking these meaningless circles. I seem to learn so slowly." But, my dear ones, you learn as you learn. However many times it takes before you finally learn, it will take. Once you have learned it, that is it. Then the next division in the trail appears.

Again, you practice the same thing. It is very easy to hear love when fear is not shouting. When fear is shouting, you must quiet yourself enough to hear the whisper of love beyond the shout of fear. As Q'uo just said, no time has been wasted. You are learning to hear better.

May we speak to your further questions? I pause.

I.: Aaron just said that we come to the same lesson again and again. This is the lesson of love? And the teacher is always fear? A question: Is the teacher always fear?

Aaron: Fear is nothing but a distortion of love. Please do not think of the teacher as fear. Think of it as love in one of its many guises. I pause.

569

C.: Aaron has often said that whatever we choose to do is our own free will, but we will learn to make more skillful decisions. Q'uo said that there is no way to waste time. We learn from our mistakes.

I have a belief that we may ask for guidance from God or Spirit as to which path is the clearest or most skillful path at any moment. Could either Aaron or Q'uo speak to that? Is that correct?

Aaron: Both Q'uo and myself may wish to address this. I will speak first.

In accordance and full agreement with Q'uo, it is *impossible* to waste time. It is not wasted time. You are learning. And yet, when you do not pay attention because of the force of your fear, your learning takes longer. This is not to be viewed as wasted time. It is what you needed.

Yes, your learning can be less painful and more in accord with the paths of love. With that aspiration in mind, yes, you certainly may ask for help.

Your asking is a statement of your free will and a statement of your readiness to receive. In the story I just told, Barbara dashed in mad circles before she was finally ready to sit down and say, *I need help.* Fear was directing her, and it took her an hour and a half to settle her fear enough to simply realize that there had to be a better way, which was to sit down and meditate and ask Spirit, *How can I get out of this? Where is the path?* The time was not wasted precisely because the next time she came into a figuratively similar situation, she remembered the lessons of this situation and asked sooner.

What was driving her in the beginning? First there had been real terror in that pit. She screamed for help. There was nobody around. She realized that she literally could die in that mud hole, which was over her head, and that she had to get herself out. When she finally got herself out, then she allowed herself to give way to the terror she had felt and that she had pushed aside in order to escape.

If one were to find oneself in a similar situation, literally or figuratively, and remember how one had learned to bring kindness in and how to ask for help, then increasingly one would walk a harmonious, clearer path. Your primary question here is, *How can I become a clearer channel?* Everything you need for clarity is within you. Everything that prevents clarity is within you.

Clarity is only one goal. Learning, growth, and the expansion of the path of love are equal goals integrated into the whole tapestry. To grasp at clarity is to negate the other goals. I hesitate to use the word "goals." I think a better word would be fruits. Clarity is just one fruit. To grasp at clarity is to turn your back on the other fruits. At what cost, then, is that clarity attained?

You have stated your belief that we may ask God or Spirit for clarity as to the most skillful path. Yes, of course you may, but the most skillful path to what end? In the desire to avoid pain and confusion, do you wish clarity for comfort? Do you wish to cut out some of the loops because you are exhausted? Do you wish to cut them out to impress others or to feel like a "good" person? Do you wish to cut them out even because they seem unskillful in their impact on others? But perhaps those extra loops are precisely what is needed, as in the case of Jim's trip west before he knew where he must really go or this instrument's circles in the woods. The path is a treasure hunt. Clues are everywhere.

To ask is to acknowledge your confusion. It is to state your highest purpose, which is to enhance love and harmony. But what is the primary motivation for asking? Is there still a desire to control and fix? Asking cannot be fruitful if it comes from a place that merely seeks avoidance of pain.

To ask is not to request clarity about the path itself but to seek equanimity with the discomfort of the confusion. You open your heart to that discomfort. When the heart stays present, then as you just suggested, you open the heart and pray for guidance. It is not that the time would otherwise have been wasted. It is simply that you are now ready and expressing that readiness through your prayer. So the answer you requested becomes more available to you. Do you see how it works? I pause.

C.: There is an aspect of fear. Specifically, J. and I may work in Detroit in a hospice community. We have had one conversation with staff there. The opportunity came through a friend of mine. After one conversation we set a time for another. I know there is no necessity to do this work. It has come to us in a way. Part of what was discussed was teaching a class of staff members about how to meditate and how to work with their burnout. We are still looking at what will be taught and what is needed. Nothing is set. I see the fear rising in me saying, *I can't teach that kind of class.* Yet there are many things I know that can help those people.

My question is that I am aware of many places where our service would be appreciated and needed. I have been praying for guidance about this. When I hear Q'uo saying there is no way to waste time ...

I am not motivated by fear. My motivation is, *What is the wisest path? Is this the path to follow at this time?* Are there comments from Q'uo about making this choice wisely and not primarily out of fear?

Aaron: C.'s fear suggests that there is a certain goal, which is to offer the self in service and for others to benefit from that service. Fear suggests that anything that sidetracks from that is a waste of time and energy. To offer the self in service, for others to learn, and for others to have some of their suffering alleviated by that route is a fruit. For you to learn about the fear in yourself is another fruit.

The first time service is attempted, it may fall short of what you would desire in terms of the final offering. But if you thereby learn what you still need to practice and if you thereby learn to relax and allow your great wisdom to flow out of you, nothing has been lost. Such learning is a great fruit.

Can you see how you are clinging to what you believe must happen, in looking for a specific result? You are not being a co-Creator with the universe. You are trying to direct the entirety. Instead, you may offer your intention that you and all beings may benefit by this situation as much as is possible. You must acknowledge that there is also the motivation to be the "good servant," the fear that you will fall short, and even a motivation, if such exists, to be a helper to others or to win approval. Noting all the motivations and that love is primary, you may enter into the situation with an attitude of surrender of control, without expectation that something special is going to happen for you or anybody. You take these multiple motivations and with a loving and earnest heart offer the entire confusion to God while reaffirming the primary motivation. Then, whatever happens can be taken as learning. I pause.

C.: I have the same question. Is there guidance? I see that it is okay to go ahead with it. What I am asking is, are wisdom and guidance around in making such choices? No fear, just love. Is that available?

(Carla channeling)

Q'uo: We are with this instrument and, my sister, we believe we grasp your query.

Of a certainty, guidance is about you, and about all, at all times. The world of spirit greatly desires to support and strengthen each beloved spark of the infinite One. It is indeed a skillful and loving thing to ask for guidance. This instrument has a short phrase that it uses constantly within: "Lord, show me thy ways." It prays daily, "Lord, in all we do today, help us to serve you." This passionate embracing of guidance does not in any way fail. However, sometimes the answer from guidance is a silence and a lack of further information. Sometimes the answer is even "No."

One who passionately embraces equanimity is upheld from moment to moment. And of this you have been the witness many times. However, when the guidance is negative or simply silence, then the human must move forward without that feeling of being supported. The support is there. But at that crux, the guidance and support is opening by its silence the opportunity for moving in confusion.

One may move for months or years, sensing into and cooperating with the outpouring of one's destiny. But inevitably, for some entities, there comes the desert experience where the air may be full of night, the heart is blind, and the fear is joined by doubting.

At that time when the seeker feels most alone, when guidance seems gone, the act of love is simply to persist in faith, in that memory of how it is to live with guidance. In those times when spirit seems silent, we suggest persistent attention to the subjective coincidences and synchronicities of the moment-by-moment experience. For all creation is alive and is connected with you and your hopes and desires.

There is much time and skill behind your query. And we feel that you are aware of the guidance to a point that denies the possibility that there is none or that it is unwise to rely upon the support network of spirit.

Certainly, always open to the help available. But when that revolution of cycles comes and suddenly you find yourself riven, then you have the opportunity to walk by faith alone, untroubled by seeming flaws and disasters, large and small.

The human experience seems to be about doing things well. But you are not here to do things. Primarily you are here to develop an attitude or a core vibration of being, shall we say, that is as close as possible to the original vibration of love.

As you live through confusion, the way to maximize the proximity of your vibration to that of love itself is to surrender any holding on to the web of support, allowing it to seem to fail without becoming upset. You then have the chance to express a shining faith that says, *Whoops. I know nothing. I haven't a clue. But all is well and all will be well. And embracing that health that demands that I am whole, I have no clue at the moment. But I still know that I am precisely where I am and it is good.*

To view the mess that sometimes occurs and to dance in the tatters and in the cleaning up, and to joy in all of it—that is faith.

May we answer further, my sister?

C.: Thank you. No.

Q'uo: Is there a final query for Aaron or us?

J.: My observation is that as we experience this equanimity, we can have joy despite turmoil. Guides that work with us provide a shortcut, and part of their gift is quiet, letting us learn patience and love at a deep level. I really have no question, just my observation of what has been shared these past few days.

Q'uo: My brother, we could not say it better.

J.: Thank you for your gifts.

Q'uo: We truly thank you. We bless each. Enjoy your dance, my sisters and brothers, and know that no sorrow is wasted and no joy is unheard. We are those of the principle known to you as Q'uo and we leave this instrument and you in the love and in the light of the one infinite Creator. Adonai.

(Barbara channeling)

Aaron: I would also thank you for the great gifts that your seeking brings to all beings and for the gifts of your sincerity and loving hearts.

When there is confusion in your lives, can you remember to greet that confusion with love? The one known as C. said about this upcoming work, "I don't have a clue." That is a highly accurate statement for most of you at most times in your life. You often have no idea of what you are really doing while you are busy doing what you think you are doing. What can you do but smile and trust and take the next step? And when you do, you will find love there, I assure you. My blessings and love to each of you. That is all.

GLOSSARY OF TERMS

Note: Some terms are used by both Aaron and Q'uo but contain shades of difference in usage. In those cases, both meanings are included.

Adonai—In religious usage by Jews, it is a title of reverence for God, serving also as a substitute pronunciation of the tetragrammaton, JHVH. It is pronounced A-doh-NOY. As the Q'uo group uses the term, it is equivalent to *Adieu* or *Adiós*, meaning "Farewell" or "Go with God." The Confederation has suggested that the word is originally from Solex Mal, an extraterrestrial language. There is no earthly evidence to support this claim.

Adonai *vasu borragus*—The complete phrase can be translated, "Go with God, my brothers." Again, the Confederation suggests that this is originally from the Solex Mal language.

Akashic Records—According to Aaron, there are four worldly elements: earth, air, fire, and water. These four elements are the basic building blocks of the expressed world. These are expressed from a fifth substance called ether or akasha. Think here of a spring that forms into four streams, each distinct but containing water from the same spring. The uniqueness of each stream is shaped by the stream bed. The water is the same, yet the streams are quite different. Think also of genetic material that expresses outward, conveying information that informs the cells so they take a specific form or expression. Ether, also known as somniferous ether, carries information in this way.

Ether has two uses. The first is as this source of the elements. The second is as the storage space for all energy formations, which are imbedded into the ether much as one might imbed a recording into a musical disc. Akasha is another name for ether. Thus, the records of all thoughts and actions are called the Akashic Records. You may wish to think of the Akashic Records as a giant, universal library or filing cabinet where every human thought, word, and action is imprinted.

If you reflect deeply, you will see the connection between these two functions of ether or akasha.

As a supplement to Aaron's definition above, the following explanation from the Edgar Cayce Association for Research and Enlightenment may be of interest:

> The Akashic Records or "The Book of Life" can be equated to the universe's super computer system. It is this system that acts as the central storehouse of all information for every individual who has ever lived upon the earth. More than just a reservoir of events, the Akashic Records contain every deed, word, feeling, thought, and intent that has ever occurred at any time in the history of the world. Much more than simply a memory storehouse, however, these Akashic Records are interactive in that they have a tremendous influence upon our everyday lives, our relationships, our feelings, our belief systems, and the potential realities we draw toward us. (www.edgarcayce.org)

The Edgar Cayce readings contain many references to the Akashic Records, as in the following excerpt:

> As thoughts are deeds in the mental world, as are the activities of a physical being as related to the associations, the relations, the words, the activity in a material world, so do they leave their impressions and the titles and the activities of each entity are thus written upon the skein between time and space, that may be indeed a record ever for the entity to meet, to experience throughout its activity in whatever consciousness the entity may be. (Edgar Cayce reading 752-I, paragraph 4)

all-mind—*See* metamind

archetypes—An archetype is defined in two ways. Firstly, it is defined as "the original pattern or model from which all things of the same kind are copied or on which they are based; a model or first form; prototype." Secondly, it has a meaning within Jungian psychology, being defined as "a collectively inherited unconscious idea, pattern of thought, image, etc., universally present in individual psyches." The Confederation entity,

Ra, defines the archetypes in a session recorded on August 15, 1981, as "portions of the one infinite Creator or aspects of its face. It is, however, far better to realize that the archetypes, while constant in the complex of generative energies offered, do not give the same yield of these complexes to any two seekers. Each seeker will experience each archetype in the characteristics within the complex of the archetype that are most important to it."

astral body—The astral body is defined by www.dictionary.com as a Theosophical term meaning "a supersensible substance pervading all space and forming the substance of a second body, the astral body, belonging to each individual. It accompanies the individual through life, is able to leave the human body at will, and survives the individual after death." Ra, in a session recorded on April 18, 1981, defines it as "the green-ray body, which may be seen in séance when what you call ectoplasm is furnished. This is a lighter body, packed more densely with life. You may call this the astral body following some other teachings."

astral plane—The online Wikipedia entry on astral plane defines the term as "the first metaphysical plane beyond the physical. It is denser than the mental plane. The astral plane is also sometimes termed the world of emotion or world of illusion, and corresponds to Blavatsky's Karmic Plane." This term was made popular in the late nineteenth and early twentieth century by the Theosophical teachers, Annie Besant and C. W. Leadbeater. In a session recorded on February 3, 1981, the Ra group also described it as a metaphysical or "inner" plane and noted that it was inhabited by a variety of discarnate beings, from "thought-forms in the lower extremities to enlightened beings who become dedicated to teach/learning in the higher astral planes."

chakra—*chakras,* or rays of the energy body. The energy body interpenetrates the physical body during our lifetime. The Chinese call this body the electrical body. Acupuncture is based on working with this body. The chakras are centers of energy focus that run from the base of the spine to the top of the head. There are seven rays, the colors of the rainbow, red through violet. Red is the first ray and has to do with survival and sexuality.

Orange ray has to do with personal relationships. Yellow ray has to do with one's relationship to groups such as one's family and work environment. Green ray is the heart chakra and has to do with loving unconditionally. Blue ray is the chakra of communication and acceptance. Indigo ray is the chakra of work in consciousness. Violet ray is a report on the whole of the energy body, a kind of readout. *See also* chakra, first through seventh

chakra, first (base)—The red ray of the energy body, having to do with survival and sexuality.

chakra, second (spleen)—The orange ray of the energy body, having to do with personal relationships.

chakra, third (solar plexus)—The yellow ray of the energy body, having to do with one's relationship to groups such as one's family and work environment.

chakra, fourth (heart)—The green ray of the energy body, having to do with loving unconditionally.

chakra, fifth (throat)—The blue ray of the energy body, having to do with communication and compassionate acceptance.

chakra, sixth (brow)—The indigo ray of the energy body, having to do with work in consciousness.

chakra, seventh (crown)—The violet ray of the energy body that represents a constantly updated report on the whole of the energy body, a kind of readout.

channeling/channel—Channeling is defined by www.dictionary.com as "the practice of professedly entering a meditative or trance-like state in order to convey messages from a spiritual guide." A channel is a person who practices channeling.

Confederation of Angels and Planets—An alternate term for the Confederation of Planets in the Service of the One Creator.

Confederation of Planets in the Service of the One Creator—In a session recorded on January 24, 1981, the Ra group said, "I am one of the members of the Confederation of Planets in the Service of the Infinite Creator. There are approximately fifty-three civilizations, comprising approximately five hundred planetary consciousness complexes, in this Confederation. This Confederation contains those from your own planet who have attained dimensions beyond your third. It contains planetary entities within your solar system, and it contains planetary entities from other galaxies. It is a true Confederation in that its members are not alike, but allied in service according to the Law of One."

Cosmic Consciousness—This is a term originated by Richard Maurice Bucke in the late nineteenth century. In his book of the same name he spoke of three stages in the development of consciousness: the simple consciousness of animals; the self-consciousness of the mass of humanity; and Cosmic Consciousness, a faculty now beginning to emerge among spiritually mature humans. Bucke felt that it was the next stage of human development. Cosmic Consciousness is characterized by fearlessness, a sense of immortality, and a sense that all is one; that we live in a completely unified creation in which the worlds of nature, man, and the godhead principle are one.

density—The term "density" refers to the makeup of the light that forms the structure of the illusion within a quantum or level of experience. Sometimes the Confederation uses the term "dimension" interchangeably with the term "density," but when used as a synonym for density, it does not suggest an added dimension. Rather the term refers to the vibrations that are characteristic of each quantum level of experience within the creation. Each density has light vibrations that support the growth of its inhabitants and offer them the information needed to evolve.

In a session recorded on January 16, 1981, the Ra group said, "The term density is a mathematical one. The closest analogy is that of music, whereby after seven notes on your western type of scale, the eighth note begins a new octave. Within the great octave of existence that we share with you, there are seven densities. Within each density there are seven subdensities. Within each subdensity, are seven sub-subdensities. Within each sub-subdensity, seven sub-sub-subdensities, and so on infinitely."

In addition to these seven densities, there is an "octave" or eighth density that is also the first density of the next creation.

These densities also correspond to the colors of the rainbow. The first density corresponds to red and so forth up through the spectrum to the seventh density, which corresponds to violet. *See also* density, first through eighth

density, first—In a session dated January 29, 1981, the Ra group said,

> In a planetary environment all begins in what you would call chaos, energy undirected and random in its infinity. Slowly, in your terms of understanding, there forms a focus of self-awareness. Thus the Logos moves. Light comes to form the darkness, according to the co-Creator's patterns and vibratory rhythms, so constructing a certain type of experience. This begins with first density, which is the density of consciousness, the mineral and water life upon the planet learning the awareness of being from fire and wind. This is the first density.

It begins in the timelessness of the octave density and is the density of the elements and substances such as water, air, fire, and earth. It is the red-ray density.

density, second—In a session recorded on January 27, 1981, the Ra group described the second density as "the density of the higher plant life and animal life that exists without the upward drive toward the infinite." The second-density beings strive toward light and growth. Second-density entities have consciousness but do not have self-awareness. This is the orange-ray density.

density, third—The third density is the density of self-awareness. It is Planet Earth and its spiritual entities, otherwise known as people. It is sometimes called the density of choice. This is by far the shortest density, being only seventy-five thousand years long. Our purpose here in third density is to choose our polarity. If we choose to polarize toward service to others, we set ourselves on the path of positive polarity for the fourth and fifth densities also. If we choose to polarize toward service to self, we set ourselves on the path of negative polarity for the fourth and fifth densities. In a session recorded on January 29, 1981, the Ra group called third density "the first density of consciousness of spirit." It is the yellow-ray density.

density, fourth—Sometimes called the density of love or the density of understanding, this density is the next step up the spiritual evolutionary scale from our present third-density human condition. Here, spiritual entities refine their understanding of how to live in unconditional love. In a session recorded on January 16, 1981, the Ra group said of positive fourth density, "It is a plane of type of bipedal vehicle that is much denser and more full of life; it is a plane wherein one is aware of the thought of other selves; it is a plane wherein one is aware of vibrations of other selves; it is a plane of compassion and understanding of the sorrows of third density; it is a plane striving toward wisdom or light; it is a plane wherein individual differences are pronounced although automatically harmonized by group consensus."

Upon graduation from third density, there is a split into two paths, the positive path of service to others and the negative path of service to self. Thus, there is a fourth-density positive and a fourth-density negative. In negative fourth density, evolving entities learn the same lessons as in positive fourth density. However, the negatively oriented entities deny that they and their brothers are one. This negative path is often called "the path of that which is not" by the Confederation, since the negative path denies love in any aspect except self-love. This is the green-ray density.

density, fifth—Sometimes called the density of wisdom, this density offers lessons in refining the evolving spiritual entity once it has learned the lessons of unconditional love. In a session recorded on January 31, 1981, the Ra group noted, "The fifth-density harvest is of those whose vibratory distortions consciously accept the honor and duty of the Law of One. This responsibility and honor is the foundation of this vibration." For fifth-density positive, the entities tend toward working often in solitude to learn the ways of wisdom, while coming together for worship and socializing. In fifth-density negative, the entities are almost entirely solitary. This is the blue-ray density.

density, sixth—Sixth density is sometimes called the density of unity. The evolving spiritual entity works to unify the lessons of love and wisdom it has learned in the fourth and fifth densities. In a session recorded on February 19, 1982, the Ra group said, "In sixth density, the density of unity, the positive and negative paths must needs take in each other for all now must be seen as love/light and light/love. This is not difficult for the positive polarity that sends love and light to all other selves. It is difficult enough for service-to-self polarized entities that at some point the negative polarity is abandoned." It is the indigo-ray density.

density, seventh—In a session dated March 20, 1981, the Ra group characterized seventh density as "a density of completion and the turning toward timelessness or foreverness." It is sometimes called the density of foreverness. It is the violet-ray density.

density, eighth—Also called the octave density, this density holds the period of timelessness that separates one creation from the next. Its characteristic color is the blackness of the black hole. At the end of seventh density, the passage of time stops and timelessness reigns. When time begins again, the new creation has begun and its first density is ongoing. There are an infinite number of octaves of creation.

devachanic body—In Theosophical terms, the devachanic body is that body in which the spiritual entity lives between incarnations. In a session recorded on April 18, 1981, the Ra group said, "The light body or blue-ray body may be called the devachanic body. There are many other names for this body especially in your so-called Indian sutras or writings, for there are those among these peoples that have explored these regions and understand the various types of devachanic bodies."

dharma—In Buddhist terms, dharma has two meanings. Dharma with a capital D refers to the teachings of the Buddha, the essence of which is the impermanent and independent nature of all conditioned phenomena and the simultaneous existence of that which is beyond conditions, the Unconditioned. These teachings are presented in a large body of written material called sutras. Dharma is often spoken of as the deepest truth of things as they are. The word "Dharma" is derived from the root DHR—to hold—and its etymological meaning is "that which holds" the whole of creation. It is the eternal Divine Truth. Uncapitalized, the word "dharma" is simply a thing. An object is a dharma; a thought is a dharma. A famous Buddhist sutra, The Heart Sutra, says in part,

> … All dharmas are empty.
> They are not born nor annihilated.
> They are not defiled nor immaculate.
> They do not increase nor decrease.

This is a statement of Dharma.

Dharmakaya—"Truth Body": This is the highest, unconditioned, or divine aspect of being. In Buddhist terms it is the Unconditioned; in Judeo-Christian terms it conveys a meaning similar to God or Creator.

dimension—As used in *The Aaron/Q'uo Dialogues*, this term is a synonym for density. *See also* density

distortion—A distortion in the scientific sense is a representation of an observable physical phenomenon that does not faithfully reproduce that phenomenon. One can imagine this process as follows: There is an object that we observe, the process of observing conventionally being thought of as messages that the object sends to us. More accurately, however, in the process of observation we become entangled with the object being observed so that the message-passing mechanism changes both the object and us! This thing that we call observation, then, can never let us know the true unobserved state of the object because the very act of observation causes distortion!

Aaron adds that a definition in the scientific sense is one of many. It holds true only in a linear space/time. Out of that linear space/time, on an ultimate level of experience rather than relative reality, all distortions are only "apparent" and not actual. He further states, "A distortion is an apparent bend. It is neither good nor bad. Think of a ray of light hitting water, so that it appears to bend. It does not actually bend, but seems to because the water is of a different density than the air. I use distortion in this way."

As the Confederation uses the term, it has no pejorative connotation. To them, everything in the universe is a distortion of the infinite Creator's absolute unity. Thus, love and light are seen not only as the Logos of utter love and the building blocks of the creation, but also as distortions. Distortions are good things, deliberately set in place by the Creator so that it may know itself. *See also* distortion, first through third

distortion, first—In a session recorded January 21, 1981, the Ra group said, "There is a law that we believe to be one of the more significant primal distortions of the Law of One. That is the Law of Confusion. You have called this the Law of Free Will." In a session recorded on January 30, 1981, the Ra group was asked by Don Elkins, "In yesterday's material you mentioned that the first distortion was the distortion of free will. Is there a sequence, a first, second, and third distortion of the Law of One?"

The Ra group responded, "Only up to a very short point. After this point, the many distortions are equal, one to another. The first distortion, free will, finds focus. The second distortion is known to you as Logos, the Creative Principle or Love. This intelligent energy thus creates a distortion known as Light. From these three distortions come many, many hierarchies of distortions, each having its own paradoxes to be synthesized, no one being more important than another."

When Confederation entities like Q'uo use the term "distortion" it is not meant as an insult. It has no negative connotation. To their way of thinking, everything in creation is a distortion of the one infinite Creator.

Aaron uses the word "distortion" to describe a bend in direction. He uses the image of a beam of light as it hits the water and seems to bend because the water is of a different substance than the air. Again, the word has no negative connotation.

distortion, second—Love, the Logos, the creative principle or intelligent energy. *See also* distortion, first

distortion, third—Light. *See also* distortion, first

dzogchen—The Tibetan words *dzog chen* literally mean "not two." This is the practice of nondual Pure Awareness.

energy body—Also called the chakra body. Picture a pipe that runs along your spine from bottom to top. Along it lies a rainbow of energy centers or chakras. The incoming energy from the Creator enters the pipe at the lowest chakra or energy center, the red ray. It proceeds upward, if the pipe is not blocked, through orange, yellow, green, blue, indigo, and violet rays, exiting the body at the crown of the head and returning to the Creator from there. This energy body interpenetrates our physical body. We came into the physical body, as a spiritual entity, in this energy body, and we will take our energy bodies with us when we pass from this life.

energy centers—*See* chakra

energy rays—*See* chakra

form body—*See* nirmanakaya

four bodies—According to Aaron and to many other metaphysical teachings, we as humans utilize four bodies: the three heavier, which are physical, emotional, and mental; and the fourth, which is the spirit body. Each heavier body has four levels, which are form, energetic, etheric, and karmic levels. The first three are conditioned bodies, arising, changing, and passing away. The fourth, referred to as the Pure Spirit Body, is closest to what the Christian tradition calls "the soul."

free will—This is the first distortion of the Law of One. The Creator uses this first distortion to choose to know itself. The Creator then uses the second distortion of the Law of One, the Logos or love, to create the universe, using the third distortion of the Law of One, light or the photon, as building blocks. *See also* distortion

harvest of Earth—This concept of Judgment Day differs from the apocalyptic view of some Christians in that the one who judges us is not a God apart from us but the God within us. It also differs in that not all evolving spiritual entities shall be judged at once, but shall go through the harvesting process at various times.

As a result of this harvest, those who graduate will go on to positive or negative fourth densities, depending upon their polarity. Those who have not polarized sufficiently on either path will repeat the third density and work once again toward the making of the choice of polarity.

During this harvesting process, which the Confederation suggests will occur at each person's natural time of death, each spiritual entity will walk steps of light. Each step of light contains slightly denser light. Some of the steps are in third-density light and some are in fourth-density light. Each entity will stop along these steps at the place where it can tolerate the brightest light.

Those who have stopped while still in third-density light will repeat third density upon another planet. Those on the positive path of service to others who have stopped in fourth-density light will return to fourth-density Earth to continue their positive path of learning. Those on the negative path of service to self who have stopped in fourth-density light will go to a fourth-density negative planet to continue their negative path of learning.

The Earth itself, says the Confederation, will transit into fourth density in 2011 or 2012—both dates are suggested by them as the beginning of fourth density.

higher self—On March 10, 1981, the Ra group said,

> There is a dimension in which time does not have sway. In this dimension, the mind/body/spirit in its eternal dance of the present may be seen in totality, and before the mind/body/spirit complex that then becomes a part of the social memory complex is willingly absorbed into the allness of the one Creator, the entity knows itself in its totality. This mind/body/spirit complex totality functions as a resource for what you perhaps would call the Higher Self. The Higher Self, in turn, is a resource for examining the distillations of third-density experience and programming further experience.

Later in that session, Ra says, "The Oversoul, as you call it, or Higher Self, seems to exist simultaneously with the mind/body/spirit complex that it aids. This is not actually simultaneous, for the Higher Self is moving to the mind/body/spirit complex as needed from a position in development of the entity that would be considered in the future of this entity." Our higher selves function as our guidance systems, both during incarnations and between incarnations.

Aaron defines higher self a little differently, as the Pure Spirit Body and mental body, free of any influence of the physical and emotional bodies. He says our evolution is aimed in this direction, to resolve self-identification with the heavier bodies so we come to know ourselves as Pure Spirit and Awareness. The everyday self and higher self can commune, but some self-identity with the heavy bodies must be released to hear the higher self clearly.

inner planes—Within each density in the outer or physical plane lie seven inner or metaphysical planes: red, orange, yellow, green, blue, indigo, and violet. When the term is used here, it refers to the inner planes of third density, which are sometimes called the heaven world.
See also outer plane

The inhabitants of these inner planes of third density are those nonincarnate entities, energies, and essences, ranging from demons and monsters to angels and inner-planes masters, as well as those outer entities who come from elsewhere in thought-form bodies, such as the Confederation entities.

Between incarnations, we also inhabit the inner planes of third density. It is there that we consult with our higher selves and decide upon our next incarnation. It is in the inner planes that we walk the steps of light in the graduation process.

karma—The Wikipedia entry for karma states, "Karma is a concept in Hinduism which explains causality through a system where beneficial effects are derived from past beneficial actions and harmful effects from past harmful actions, creating a system of actions and reactions throughout a person's reincarnated lives." The Confederation suggests that the back-and-forth balancing of karma may be halted by the energy of forgiveness. On February 3, 1981, the Ra group stated, "In forgiveness lies the stoppage of the wheel of action, or what you call karma."

Karma is also a central teaching of Buddhism. Karma (Pali, *khamma*) literally means action or doing. Involuntary actions do not produce karma. Karma is a result of our free will to choose, with intention, to act in wholesome or unwholesome ways, to do good or harm. However we choose to act, we will reap the results of that action. A famous Buddhist sutra states it in this way:

> According to the seed that's sown,
> So is the fruit you reap there from,
> Doer of good will gather good,
> Doer of evil, evil reaps,
> Down is the seed and thou shalt taste
> The fruit thereof.
> (Samyutta Nikaya)

Karma arises from numerous causes. The main cause is the specific form of ignorance of not knowing things as they truly are. When we live in duality, karma arises out of the sense of a self and other, which duality produces craving and aversion states. The only other situation that is free of the production of wholesome and unwholesome karma is that there is no karma for the person resting in a state of complete nondual awareness.

For more detailed information about karma from a Buddhist perspective, the following website is recommended: www.buddhanet.net/e-learning/karma.htm.

kaya—Body; in Buddhist teachings there are three kayas: nirmanakaya or "form body," sambhogakaya or "transition body," and Dharmakaya or "Truth Body." They are not separate, but each connects to the others as a bridge connects two sides of a ravine. Thus, the three kayas are a statement of the nonduality of form and spirit. *See also* Dharmakaya, nirmanakaya, sambhogakaya

kundalini—This word means "coiled" in Sanskrit; it refers to the energy or life force coiled at the base of the spine, which may awaken with spiritual practice. The coil gives us the idea of untapped energy. Kundalini Yoga concentrates on the chakras of the body in order to generate a spiritual power, opening the kundalini energy.

Law of One—This law states that all is one. Everything and everyone in the creation is part of one interactive unity. The substance of that one thing is love or the Logos, sometimes called the one original Thought. Love uses light to manifest all of the things in creation, from the galaxies and stars to humans to the tiniest subatomic particle and everything in between. The Ra group describe themselves as humble messengers of the Law of One and state in a session recorded on January 15, 1981, "We are old upon your planet and have served with varying degrees of success in transmitting the Law of One, of Unity, of Singleness, to your peoples."

light—Sunlight is something we all experience, and light in this sense is close to the way the Confederation uses the term. However, light is also the third distortion of the Law of One. The first distortion is free will. The second distortion is the Logos (the Word, as John uses it in the first chapter of his Gospel) or love. The third distortion is light. Everything in the creation is made of photons of light. As light is split into the prism of rainbow colors, it shows the colors of the consecutive densities of the octave of creation. It also shows the consecutive chakras of the energy body. It is a very important concept to the Confederation. In a session dated January 15, 1981, the Ra group said, "You are every thing, every being, every emotion, every event, every situation. You are unity. You are infinity. You are love/light, light/love. You are. This is the Law of One."

Aaron also frequently refers to light; he says, "You are Love and Light, manifesting as form." *See also* distortion

light body—This is the Confederation term for what the Theosophists call the devachanic body. The Confederation also calls this body the blue-ray body. It is the type of body used by many inhabitants of the blue-ray portion of the inner planes of third density. It is also the type of physical body used by inhabitants of fourth density.

light plane—Aaron's shorthand for the inner planes.

Logos—This Greek term means "word." It is used by John in his Gospel, "In the beginning was the Word, and the Word was with God, and the Word was God. The same was in the beginning with God. All things were made by him; and without him was not anything made that was made. In him was life, and the life was the light of men" (John 1:1–4 AV). The Confederation usage of this word is close to this biblical quotation. The Logos, or original Thought, is further described by the Confederation as being a Thought of utter and unconditional love. The Logos, or love, is the second distortion of the Law of One, coming after free will. Love creates all that there is, using light in order to manifest both the physical and metaphysical creation. *See also* distortion

Love—The Logos, the creative principle, or intelligent energy, differentiated from lowercase *love*, which is the more human level. *See also* distortion, Logos

meridians, energy—There are numerous energy meridians that flow through the body. They connect the chakras, and may relate to specific organs.

metamind—The prefix "meta" is defined by www.dictionary.com to mean "a prefix appearing in loanwords from Greek, with the meanings 'after,' 'along with,' 'beyond,' 'among,' and 'behind.'" Metamind uses the term in its meaning of "beyond" and indicates the all-mind or the mind of the Creator.

metaprogram—The soul's highest understanding and intention when fully aligned with the Creator aspect of the self. The divine plan for the incarnation. A metaprogram on our computers is the program that controls all the other programs. The Confederation sees our brains as being computer-like. A metaprogram in the brain is the program by which a seeker can alter all of the programs of the brain that need alteration in order for the seeker to advance.

mind/body/spirit complex—This is the Confederation term for a human being. The term infers the makeup of human beings as including a mind, a body, and a spirit.

Glossary of Terms

mudra meditation—A form of meditation that works with energy.

mudras—Hand positions with spiritual significance.

nirmanakaya—"Form body"; nirmanakaya refers to both the physical and mental expressions. It is the outer body that is conditional and constantly changing.

old-mind—This term is used to describe the mind so deeply caught in old conditioning that it cannot see what is happening in this present moment.

outer plane—This term describes consensus reality as we know it on Planet Earth. Our physical world is the outer plane of third density. *See also* inner planes

oversoul—This is a Confederation synonym for the higher self. *See also* higher self

planetary energy web—If you think of Planet Earth as a living being, which the Confederation does, then it has an energy field or a planetary energy web. This web or field contains both the outer plane of third-density Earth and third-density Earth's inner planes. Spiritual entities such as you and I come into the planetary energy web when entering into incarnation.

The Ra group, in a session recorded on May 29, 1982, says, "As each entity enters the planetary energy web, each entity experiences two major planetary influxes, that of the conception, which has to do with the physical, yellow-ray manifestation of the incarnation, and that of the moment you call birth, when the breath is first drawn into the body complex of chemical yellow ray. Thus those who know the stars and their configurations and influences are able to see a rather broadly drawn map of the country through which an entity has traveled, is traveling, or may be expected to travel, be it upon the physical, the mental, or the spiritual level."

polarity—In science, a good example of polarity is the magnet, with its polarized positive and negative poles. Magnetized iron has the ability to magnetize other lumps of iron, or to act as a compass. That which is polarized can do work. In the Confederation philosophy, we choose the end of the metaphysical magnet toward which we wish to polarize. We have two choices, the positive and negative poles. The positive pole is called the service-to-others path. The negative pole is called the service-to-self path. Until we choose one polarity or another, we cannot do work in consciousness. Both Aaron and Q'uo are teachers of the service-to-others path of polarity.

polarity therapy—This is a health system that concerns itself with the flow and balance of energy in the human body. It does not relate to polarity in the above sense.

Pure Awareness—Pure Awareness is supramundane consciousness. Consciousness exists on a mundane and supramundane level. Mundane consciousness arises from the conditioned senses. For example, when the eye makes contact with an object, seeing consciousness arises. When the mind touches a thought, mind consciousness arises. When the mundane sense and the object cease to be in contact, mundane consciousness ceases.

Supramundane consciousness or Pure Awareness is not dependent on a conditioned sense but is awareness that arises from the core of being. It does not actually arise or cease; it is. Sentient beings come in or out of cognizance of the functioning of awareness.

Every consciousness needs an object. The object of conditioned consciousness is a conditioned object, an object that arises from conditions and will cease when the conditions cease. Pure Awareness takes the Unconditioned or Divine as object.

Pure Spirit Body—There are four bodies: physical, emotional, mental, and spirit. The Pure Spirit Body is the spirit body expressing with no influence from the heavier bodies.

rays—Red, orange, yellow, green, blue, indigo, and violet—*See* chakra, first through seventh

rigpa—The Tibetan word *rigpa* means the state of Awareness, untainted by everyday consciousness. This state of awareness is sometimes called the state of "luminous great perfection."

samadhi—Concentration; the mental state of being firmly fixed.

sambhogakaya—"Wealth body" or "transition body"; a bridge of intention, of karmic force, and of other elements that serves as a vehicle for the ever-perfect to express itself into the world; the intention energy level.

service to others/service to self—Every being moves at times in service to self. The question is not only whether a move is made in service to other or to self, but is about the nature of the primary intention, and the mode in which self/other is perceived. Aaron prefers to define positive and negative polarity by whether the choice is made from a state of contraction that narrows view into a separate self in opposition to others, or whether it is made from an uncontracted place that knows the nonduality of self and other.

Aaron said,

> When you understand the nonduality of self and other, every move in service to other is also in service to self, but not exclusively to the self. At this level there is no self or other. It is in this arena that positive polarity can most clearly express.
>
> When you do not understand the nondual nature of all things and experience a separation of self and other, only then is threat perceived, a seeming threat that leads to contraction and intentional action in service to the separate self and against the other. This misunderstanding and intention to self-service is a hallmark of negative polarity.

The service-to-others polarity may also be called the positive path of seeking, or the path of that which is. A person who is working toward polarizing in service to others makes choices that it feels will result in its being of service to other people, to the planetary population as a whole, or to the Creator. The Ra group suggests that a service-to-others polarity of 51 percent or more is required in order for a person to graduate from Planet Earth's present third density to fourth-density positive.

The service-to-self polarity may also be called the negative path of seeking, or the path of that which is not. A person who is working toward polarizing in service to self makes choices that it feels will result in its being of service to itself. Other people, the planetary population as a whole, and the Creator are not considered in making its choices unless they are relevant to its being of service to itself. The Ra group suggests that a service-to-self polarity of 95 percent or more is required in order for a person to graduate from Planet Earth's present third density to fourth-density negative.

Those who are purely altruistic—that is, those whose altruism is not calculated for self-gain—are service-to-others persons. Psychologists have names for service-to-self people: sociopaths and psychopaths.

social memory complex—In Confederation terms, we on Planet Earth are a social complex. In fourth, fifth, sixth, and seventh densities, because of there no longer being a veil between people, societies of spiritual entities form social memory complexes in which all the memories of all the entities are held in common. This is not the concept of "hive mind." Each entity is completely free to do what it wishes. However, it is also in harmony with all the other beings on its planet.

space/time—The space/time or outer-plane Earth world is that of our everyday consensus reality. It is our physical world. *See also* time/space

spirit plane or **spiritual plane**—The plane of nonphysical entities.

spiritual body—This is a Confederation term that is synonymous with the energy body or the chakra body. It is one of the three complexes of a mind/body/spirit complex or human being. In a session recorded on January 24, 1981, the Ra group said,

> The spiritual body energy field is a pathway, or channel. When body and mind are receptive and open, then the spirit can become a functioning shuttle or communicator from the entity's individual energy/will upwards, and from the streamings of the creative fire and wind downwards. (Session 6, Question 1, Don Elkins, Jim McCarty, and Carla Rueckert, *The Ra Material, Book I:* Atglen, PA: Schiffer Publishing Company, 1982)

tai chi—A Chinese martial art that works with chi energy and motion. It is practiced for health and balance of energy.

third eye—Relating to the brow chakra. This chakra is the focus of spiritual awareness. *See also* chakra, sixth

thought-form—This Confederation term has a meaning similar to Plato's plane of ideals. Thought-forms are templates of a certain kind of being. Our energy body holds the thought-form of our physical body. Other thought-forms with which we are familiar are ghosts. The Confederation moves in thought-form rather than in physical form from its native planets to our inner planes in order to respond to our call for spiritual help.

three kayas—*See* kaya

time/space—Just as space/time is our physical world, time/space is our inner world. Our thoughts arise in time/space. The inner planes of this planet are in time/space. *See also* space/time

tonglen—A giving/receiving meditation practice of Tibetan Buddhist origin, wherein one releases loving energy to others, and is willing to allow pain into the self.

transition body—*See* sambhogakaya

Truth Body—*See* Dharmakaya

wanderers—This is a Confederation term for spiritual entities of fourth, fifth, and sixth densities whose homes are other planets. They have chosen to incarnate upon Planet Earth to help with the harvest of Earth.

wealth body—*See* sambhogakaya

zazen—Zen meditation.

Zen—Zen is a school of Mahayana Buddhism. The other major Buddhist traditions are Theravada and Vajrayana. "Zen" is the Japanese pronunciation of a Chinese word *(Chan)*, which is a Chinese pronunciation of a Sanskrit word *(dhyan)*, meaning "meditation." "Zen" is the name most often used in the English-speaking world, but the tradition is known as *Chan* in China, *Seon* in Korea, *Thien* in Vietnam, and *dhyana* in India.

The establishment of Chan (Zen) is traditionally credited to Bodhidharma, an Indian prince turned monk who came to China to teach a special transmission outside the formal Buddhist scriptures.

The origins of Zen Buddhism are ascribed to the Flower Sermon. The Buddha gathered his disciples for a dharma talk. Instead of speaking, he sat in silence and held up a flower. One of the Buddha's disciples, Mahākaśyapa silently gazed at the flower and is said to have gained a special insight directly from the Buddha's mind, beyond words. The Buddha smiled at him, then acknowledged Mahākaśyapa's insight by saying the following:

> "I possess the true Dharma eye, the marvelous mind of Nirvana, the true form of the formless, the subtle dharma gate that does not rest on words or letters but is a special transmission outside of the scriptures. This I entrust to Mahākaśyapa." (Heinrich Dumoulin, *Zen Buddhism: A History, vol. 1: India and China*, Bloomington, IN: World Wisdom, 2005, 8–9, 68, 166–167, 169–172)

Thus, a path was furthered that concentrated on direct experience rather than on intellect or scriptures. Wisdom was passed, not through words, but through a lineage of one-to-one direct transmission of thought from teacher to student.

In Zen practice, meditation is used to achieve direct, experiential realization. The "Zen" of a thing, as used in this material, is the nonlinear, insight-driven feeling or immediate sense of that thing.

INDEX

415, 426, 443, 458, 461,
471–472, 477, 486, 489,
506, 518–519, 524–525,
559, 578, 580–583, 594
supramundane, 594
unconsciousness, 58, 98, 578
cooperation, 174, 244, 371, 392,
397, 511
Cosmic Awareness, 307
Cosmic Consciousness, 315, 581
Cosmic Healing, 22, 222
cosmology, 17, 198, 314
creation, 10, 25, 44, 94, 124–125,
185, 280–281, 301, 314, 377,
392, 398, 400, 414, 421, 445,
486, 493, 501, 507, 574, 581–
582, 584–586, 591–592
Creative Principle, 586
Creator, 1, 9, 29–30, 32, 42, 46–
48, 60, 62–63, 70–71, 74, 81–
82, 85–86, 90, 92, 94, 99–100,
107–108, 113, 124–126, 130,
132, 137, 141, 159, 174–175,
181, 184–186, 193–194, 196–
198, 204, 210, 212–213, 217–
218, 226–227, 229, 243,252–
253, 259–260, 271–272, 280,
283, 296, 301, 303, 305, 326,
334–336, 360, 362, 365, 372,
374, 376–377, 387–389, 392,
408–409, 411, 415, 417, 422,
433, 435, 446, 455, 465, 471–
472, 482, 486–487, 488–489,
500–501, 507–508, 514, 518,
524–526, 539, 547, 554, 557,

565, 575, 579–580, 585–588,
592, 595–596
crystal, 101, 502, 540, 549
crystalline, 260, 281, 524
crystallized, 434–435

Dalai Lama, 364
deafness, 11–12, 15–16, 21, 159,
346
death, 60–61, 164, 172, 245, 263,
281, 331, 334, 343, 357, 361,
401, 416, 527, 579, 588
Deity, 82, 486, 489–490, 494
density, 4– 6, 31, 44, 99, 136, 167,
258, 306, 312–314, 379, 384,
386, 393, 436, 486, 492, 581–
582, 585–586, 589
first, 5, 42, 313, 399, 582
second, 5–6, 42, 313, 371–
372, 384, 386, 518, 582
third, 4–9, 29–31, 42–43, 48–
49, 68, 79–80, 99, 123, 140,
157–158, 179, 181, 226,
231, 244, 254, 256–257,
275, 287, 297, 301–302,
306–307, 313, 340, 352,
361, 379, 384–386, 392–
394, 397, 399, 406, 409,
434, 436–439, 443, 456,
517, 545–546, 561, 564,
582, 588–589, 591, 593, 596
fourth, 6, 8–9, 140, 157–158,
162, 167, 255–256, 312–
313, 379, 384–385, 386,
392, 399, 409, 415, 444–

254–257, 263–264, 268,
277, 279–280, 282, 285–
288, 294–296, 298–299,
303–306, 310, 317–319,
321–322, 328–333, 343–
345, 350–351, 358, 362–
365, 369, 389–391, 397,
399–400, 406–407, 412,
414, 416–417, 424, 429–
430, 432, 435, 438, 444–
445, 452–453, 457, 462–
465, 468–470, 474–475,
478–485, 490–491, 495,
497–498, 503, 505, 507,
511, 516–517, 521, 523,
526–527, 529, 534, 536–
538, 541–542, 544–545,
549–551, 555–557, 560–
564, 568–570, 572–574, *See
also* emotions
nonfear, 191
fearlessness, 10, 45, 47, 65, 70, 485,
523, 581
feelings, 10, 13, 16, 36, 40, 53, 81,
89, 142, 184, 185, 203, 205,
218, 245, 260, 286, 365, 369,
407, 409, 461, 578
feminine/masculine
feminine, 45, 106, 196, 248,
296, 518
masculine, 45, 106, 196, 296,
518
fifty, 376, 386
fifty–three, 581

fight–or–flight, 148–149
finity/infinity
infinity, 85, 92, 145, 159, 271,
302, 311, 394, 582, 591
finity, 82
five hundred, 2, 581
Flower Sermon, 598
foreverness, density of. *See* density,
7th
forgiveness, 75, 86, 90, 105, 107,
132, 164, 229, 265–269, 331,
338, 345, 358, 405, 428, 457,
484–485, 497–500, 502–505,
529, 544, 589, *See also* blame and
acceptance/nonacceptance
four thousand, 561
free will, 6, 17, 51, 70, 83–84, 136,
157–158, 175, 185, 193, 217,
275, 312, 347, 376, 391, 443,
494, 570, 586–587, 590–592
frequency/vibration, 5–6, 8–10,
18–19, 23, 26, 32, 95, 113, 143,
230, 259, 281, 301, 314, 317,
319, 379, 399, 434, 436–437,
439, 490, 492, 495–496, 540,
574, 583
frightened, 63, 130, 135, 143, 152,
155, 201, 269
frightening, 12, 65, 235, 329, 388
Frost, Robert, 382
frustration, 37, 163, 175, 192, 260,
295, 384, 418, 507–508

Index

Index

Index

115–118, 218, 262–266,
345, 352, 364–370, 408,
414, 442, 470, 522, 550
worthy, 73, 114, 218, 264,
365, 367, 460, 492, 507,
522, 540, 556

yellow ray. *See* chakras, third

zazen, 410, 597
Zen, 72, 330, 527, 597

BARBARA BRODSKY is a nationally known dharma teacher in the Buddhist tradition and the founder of Deep Spring Center (www.deepspring.org), which offers non-denominational spiritual teachings and practice. She is also the channel for the spirit Aaron and with him offers both personal spiritual direction sessions and group workshops. In 1972 she became totally deaf; living with silence has greatly influenced her life and teaching. Brodsky has published a number of books of Aaron's teachings, including *Presence, Kindness, and Freedom,* and most recently is the author of *Cosmic Healing* published by North Atlantic Books. She lives in Ann Arbor, Michigan.

CARLA L. RUECKERT is best known for her channeling of the five volumes of *The Law of One,* also called *The Ra Material.* A Christian mystic and librarian by training, Rueckert is cofounder of and channel for L/L Research (www.llresearch.org), a nonprofit organization dedicated to discovering and sharing information for the spiritual advancement of all humankind. L/L Research holds workshops throughout the year along with weekly public meditations from September through May. Their community website, www.bring4th.org, serves the L/L readership with forums, blogs, and chat rooms. The author of several books including *A Wanderer's Handbook, A Book of Days: Channelings from the Holy Spirit,* and *Living the Law of One 101: The Choice,* Rueckert lives in Louisville, Kentucky, with her husband and research associate, Jim McCarty.